View of Birmingham from the far south-east edge
of the town, showing Bradford Street running
downhill and the main part of the built-up area
on the higher land in the distance. Reproduced
from Sir William Dugdale and others, *Warwickshire*
(1877).

STUDIES IN URBAN HISTORY 3

General Editor: H. J. Dyos
Professor of Urban History in the
University of Leicester

The Provincial Towns of Georgian England

A Study of the Building Process
1740-1820

C. W. Chalklin

EDWARD ARNOLD

© C. W. Chalklin 1974

First published 1974
by Edward Arnold (Publishers) Ltd.,
25 Hill Street, London W1X 8LL

ISBN: 0 7131 5761 5

Text set 11/12 pt. Monotype Ehrhardt, printed by letterpress, and bound in
Great Britain at The Pitman Press, Bath.

Foreword

Sixty years ago four-fifths of Britain's population could be classified officially as urban. It might be said of this country at least that the process of urbanisation had already come to an end since the proportion of the population living in towns and urban districts was to remain more or less constant down to the present time. It appears to us now, looking back, as something of a paradox that the study of the urban past, though never totally neglected in this country, should have been held in abeyance for so long after that phase of urbanization had closed. And if we widen the horizon to include, not merely growing numbers, but changing attitudes, movements, structure, images, the fact of the matter seems to be that an urban culture has arisen without an historical tradition that might explain it. Yet it was Britain which led the world, however unconsciously or even prodigally it may seem to have done so in human terms, in establishing a type of urban culture in the nineteenth century which has been transplanted or transformed over a much wider field in the twentieth. How surprising it therefore seems that it is only within the last generation, perhaps within little more than a decade, that urban history as such should have come to be recognized in this country as a proper and distinctive field of study and research.

So recent are these developments that their very limits and the techniques for discovering what they were about are still in a state of flux. So multifarious are the possibilities now opening up that most of the practitioners at work in this field are not yet rid of their initial sense of confusion. Nothing could, in fact, be less surprising. What they see before them is a field in which they must pay attention, not only to particular towns in all their peculiar detail—to urban societies fixed more or less in time and space—but a field in which they are being called upon to investigate historical processes and trends that completely transcend the life-cycle and range of experience of any single community when viewed in isolation. The global demographic

v

sweep of urbanization is already overturning our notions of what cities are or might soon come to be. Sociological concepts of urbanism are forcing us to look deeper for the generic differences between urban and agrarian life that common experience has led us so often to take for granted. The political realities of facing urban problems that have fewer national characteristics than fundamental human ones are suggesting inter-cultural comparisons of a type which historians grounded in empirical traditions have generally viewed with alarm. The interconnections between the growth of cities and the rise of industrialized societies have thrown into the study of their economic relations searching questions about the extent to which urbanization itself may be regarded as an initiator or a product of economic growth or decline.

The town, which was to historians for so long the unconsidered container of industry and trade and the anonymous masses, is therefore now assuming a new importance in its own right. Historians are addressing it *directly*, partly to understand urban changes better for their own sake but chiefly in order to relate them more coherently to economic, political, and cultural developments on an altogether wider plane. Purely 'biographical' studies of individual towns which leave no lasting impression when set in a void offer a basis for making their differences indelible when studied comparatively; investigations of urban life in microscopic detail are being matched by far-reaching research into the fundamental social processes leading towards the urbanization of the whole world. Historians are on common ground here with other disciplines, for towns have always embodied their own history with peculiar tenacity, and this is now causing scholars across a wide front to look at the urban past with growing curiosity. Among them are geographers, economists, sociologists, demographers, archaeologists, civic designers—each of them having distinctive approaches and techniques, all of them sharing the problem of inter-disciplinary communication. The present mood of urban history is therefore experimental and exploratory. The field is wide open and world-wide, as much concerned with concrete detail where it matters as with imaginative hypotheses wherever they lead, as readily approached by the geographer as by the sociologist or the historian. *Studies in Urban History* is a series designed in this mood. The volumes have a standard format but in all other respects remain completely un-stereotyped so as to give free rein to the most promising ideas, from whatever quarter or however remote their reference to time or place.

The present volume takes us back to a pre–urban state of society, to a time when less than a quarter of the population of Britain lived in towns of some size. It does so in order to explore an astonishingly obscure yet crucial element in the surging growth that was presently demanded of them. How were these towns made ready for the rapidly growing numbers of people required by the expansion of industry and trade to live and work in them? By what means, in what forms, and with what results were they all housed? What were the costs and the returns, the logistics, the business mechanisms of the operation? Just how was the land divided, the big and the little parcels distributed, access to the new social space meted out? In what ways did this complex business impinge on the larger processes of economic and social change then going on, and with what implications for the ever-multiplying urban populations of the two or three generations to follow?

For all the advance in urban history in recent years we still know precariously little about the material elements of our urban culture, and value its historical residues even less. With so many erasures now being made on the ground—and below it—it becomes not only more difficult to read the most tangible document to the urban past that we have but more difficult to visualize the historical importance of its physical and organic development. If we are to build an historical tradition that might explain our urban condition we must first explain how our towns were shaped, the slums and the suburbs formed, the artifact made. We must in the end make plain how the land was built on in the way that it was. And, in these respects at least, we need now to look away from London more. We have to realize that to ask how the means were found to enlarge the capacity of these towns is not only to ask questions about estate management, speculative building, the property market, the ebb and flow of investment, and the roles of landowners, developers, builders, building societies, banks, solicitors, and the rest. That should be less daunting than it is fundamental. Urban archives for such research are notoriously fissured, but in more places than might be imagined, even for the eighteenth century, the answers to many of these questions are obtainable by any one prepared to seek them—though seldom in suffocating detail. To ask about these things is also to take stock of cognate matters, like shifts in local employment, the varying eddies in migration between country and town, the inclination to marry, local patterns of fertility and mortality, the arbitrary interventions of war and the weather. There are, indeed, so many other things to measure that are less measurable but no less engaging—the whim of fashion, the imagination of architects, the aspirations of the middle classes, the very lie of the land—that the urban historian looking for the connections between the process of urban growth in this period and the shapes it produced on

vii

the ground might be forgiven for concentrating, as so many with less clearly-defined purposes have done, on some chosen spot. This is not such a book and it is all the better for it.

It is in fact the first full-scale study of the building process as it occurred in the urban history of this country to have been set within a satisfactorily comparative framework. It includes as exhaustive an account as it is possible to give of the developmental factors in the physical growth of some of the most important provincial towns of Georgian England. It offers this in both a regional setting, which includes some account of the influence of London, and a functional one, in which the interpenetration of national and local building fluctuations has been analysed in detail for the first time. Much of this, especially the slowly emerging picture of the interlocking functions of developers, building craftsmen, moneyed attorneys, and the like, has had to be developed in a solution of legal fact wrung drop by drop from vast deposits of title-deeds, Chancery proceedings, and manuscripts of various kinds. Printed sources, apart from newspaper advertisements and reports, directories, and maps, seem to have yielded virtually no evidence of value. In one sense Mr. Chalklin's remorseless ransacking of record offices and other repositories for comparative material over the last ten years has clearly been an act of necessity. The lack of material that might adequately portray certain aspects of the building process in one locality drove him time and again to seek them in another, so that his study offers a more synoptic view than he had originally expected. It has proved a disappointing as well as exhilarating quest, for he never found among the mountains of public and private papers that he moved a single cache of business archives ample enough to light up through its ledgers and letter-books the operations of one of his leading builders or developers in a completely revealing way. His picture is a mosaic, and he has had to build it up with great patience and scholarly forbearance. He has broken entirely new ground and given our understanding of the process of urban growth a new dimension. Here is a major work.

University of Leicester   H. J. DYOS
New Year's Eve, 1973

Preface

This book is about the building of towns. Despite the great advances made by urban history in the last ten years, this fundamental matter remains obscure. Houses erected in the eighteenth and nineteenth century have interested the social historian and the student of architecture, not the economic historian. So far as building has been his concern, the main theme has been the fluctuations over time of national building activity and its relation to the general growth of the economy. National aggregates are one thing; actual buildings, the men who erected them and the variations in practice from one place to another, are a different matter. Almost nothing is known about house construction at the level of the individual building speculator. This has not passed without comment. As Professor Hoskins has remarked recently: 'who built the needed houses, laid out the streets, financed the work, is still largely a mystery before the nineteenth century, above all in our provincial towns.'[1] It is with these problems that this book is principally concerned.

The book discusses building in the largest and most rapidly growing provincial towns of Georgian England. Apart from London there were fifteen centres with a population of over 25,000 in 1820. These were the industrial centres of Manchester, Birmingham, Leeds, Sheffield, Nottingham, Norwich, and Leicester, the dockyard towns of Portsmouth and Plymouth, the seaports of Liverpool, Bristol, Hull, Sunderland, and Newcastle, and the resort of Bath. Norwich had grown very slowly since 1700 and has been excluded; Brighton (24,429 in 1821) is discussed occasionally because of its rapid development as a resort from about the 1780s. Seven towns, Bath, Birmingham, Hull, Liverpool, Manchester, Nottingham, and Portsmouth, are selected for particular study. Several factors dictated their choice. Professor Beresford is studying building in Leeds since the eighteenth century, and Professor

---

[1] P. Clark and P. Slack (eds.), *Crisis and Order in English Towns 1500–1700* (1972), p. vii.

ix

Preface

Olsen is investigating the important Norfolk Estate in Sheffield. Dr. J. R. Ward has studied the great building boom in Bristol at the beginning of the 1790s. In the case of Newcastle and Plymouth the available material was disappointing. Because of their great importance Birmingham, Liverpool and Manchester chose themselves. Otherwise I wished to ensure that the four different types of town were all represented.

The first section provides a background to the major themes of the book. It assesses the extent of urban growth in the eighteenth and beginning of the nineteenth centuries, especially for the bigger provincial towns. The second part of the book deals with the work of the urban land promoter. Its theme concerns the methods by which land was prepared for building, the work of the original owner or land developer in surveying the site and roads and providing the basic amenities, whether the land was conveyed freehold or leasehold, and the extent to which control of builders was attempted by means of covenants. Financial factors such as the price of building land and the cost of preparing the sites, still more the potential financial returns from developing building land, are of basic importance. Several local studies have begun to open up this topic. In the case of London, Professor Olsen has studied residential estate management, especially the development of building land on two West-End estates in the eighteenth and nineteenth centuries.[2] Professor Dyos has discussed the effect of the pattern of landownership on housing development and the attempts to control building through the use of covenants in leases in relation to Victorian Camberwell.[3] Building land development in Glasgow has been handled by Dr. Kellett, and in Edinburgh by Professor Youngson, both in relation to the later eighteenth and early nineteenth centuries.[4] However, the major English provincial towns remain largely unexplored territory. This is partly a consequence of a lack of easily sifted sources. On a number of aspects of the theme printed material is virtually non-existent and accessible manuscript material is scanty, and I have tried to draw evidence from as many of the big provincial centres as possible, partly in the form of innumerable title deeds to houses.

The third major section of the book relates to the house builders. The study of residential construction has concentrated on the visual

[2] D. J. Olsen, *Town Planning in London: The Eighteenth and Nineteenth Centuries* (New Haven, 1964).
[3] H. J. Dyos, *Victorian Suburb: a Study of the Growth of Camberwell* (Leicester, 1961).
[4] J. R. Kellett, 'Property Speculators and the Building of Glasgow, 1780–1830', *Scottish Journal of Political Economy*, VIII, 1961; A. J. Youngson, *The Making of Classical Edinburgh, 1750–1840* (Edinburgh, 1966).

x

Preface

aspect. Works on domestic architecture, such as *Georgian London* by Sir John Summerson (1945) or *The Georgian Buildings of Bath* by W. W. Ison (1948) mention the business aspect of construction, but this remains subordinate to other topics. Little is known about the nature of investment in building in the eighteenth and nineteenth centuries, about the types of people who became speculative builders, the scale of their activity, the sources of their capital, and the profitability of their undertakings. Our existing knowledge relates principally to London. The nature of the financing of house-building in the Victorian capital has begun to be revealed in the recent work of Professor Dyos and Dr. Reeder, and for parts of these two centuries some evidence about the speculative builders of the West End and the scale of their operations can be found in the recent volumes of the *Survey of London*, such as vol. xxxvii on Northern Kensington. Apart from the intensive work by Professor Beresford on Leeds, house-building in the provincial towns remains almost an unknown subject.

The final part concerns the course of building activity over the eighteenth and beginning of the nineteenth centuries, on a local basis. National fluctuations in building have been examined carefully by Professor T. S. Ashton in his last book (*Economic Fluctuations in England 1700–1800* (1959)) and Professor J. Parry Lewis (in *Building Cycles and Britain's Growth* (1965)), principally by means of a number of statistical series of the output of building materials. This study tries to trace the extent to which local urban fluctuations moved in harmony with, or varied from, the national pattern, and in so doing to examine more closely the reasons for changes in the level of house construction at certain crucial dates.

Two important kinds of construction are not discussed. Public buildings, such as churches, town halls, schools, workhouses, and corn exchanges, need a book to themselves. Again, possibly just over half the dwellings erected in England and Wales between 1750 and 1820 were in the countryside, and these have also been excluded from the study.

By comparison with the historians of Victorian England, the student of house-building in the Georgian period has certain disadvantages. Sources are in general sparser, and on some crucial points virtually non-existent. Estate records are far less helpful than one might wish; there is little contemporary comment of the kind easily available to later scholars in *Parliamentary Papers* and journals such as *The Builder*. On the other hand, even the largest provincial towns of the eighteenth century have the great merit of being tiny (by later standards), and therefore manageable on a comparative basis. The basic aim of the book is to

xi

draw attention by the comparative method to a number of basic problems involved in the building growth of towns in this period. They are believed to be of basic importance both to the urban and the economic historian. It is not intended to provide a full answer to these issues, which will require many years of careful study of manuscript material by several scholars. The book will have served its purpose if the topics are regarded as worthy of attention by future regional historians, and if it suggests some of the types of evidence which may be used to handle them.

The study was begun during the tenure of a University of Wales Senior Fellowship at Aberystwyth between 1963 and 1965. It has been continued and finished at the University of Reading, in combination with the usual teaching duties. Both universities helped to pay my travelling expenses. I also received a grant for this purpose from the Twenty-Seven Foundation. Above all, the Social Science Research Council paid the salary of my Research Assistant, the late Miss B. M. Crook, between 1968 and 1970.

Miss Crook collected the material relating to Manchester and Nottingham, and part of that for Liverpool. I owe much to her painstaking work in libraries, records offices and deed rooms and her search for material in private hands. I was also helped in collecting material by Mr. Steven Blake, Mr. Peter Dewey and Miss Kathleen Youel. Among many archivists I owe much to the help of Mr. Andrews of the Birmingham Central Library, Mr. Willis-Fear of the Portsmouth Record Office, Miss Smith of the Liverpool Record Office, Mr. Bryant of the Bath Record Office, Mr. Cobb and Mr. Johnson of the House of Lords Record Office, Miss Meredith of the Sheffield City Library, Mr. Oxley of the Hull Record Office, Miss Williams and Mr. James of the Nottingham City Record Office, Mr. Dibben of the Coventry Record Office and the staff of the Newcastle Record Office. Mr. Wilkinson of the Town Clerk's Department of Manchester Corporation gave us every facility to consult the City's large deed collection. In Manchester we received much help from Mr. N. C. Wright, Messrs. Taylor, Kirkman and Mainprice, Mr. Corbett of the Co-operative Insurance Society, and many others. In London Mr. Sharp of the Treasury Solicitor's Office kindly allowed us to consult deeds in his custody, and we were similarly helped by the partners of Debenham and Co, solicitors. In Portsmouth the staff of the legal department of Messrs. Brickwoods gave us every facility in consulting their deeds. In Birmingham Mr. Derek Lea of Messrs. James and Lister Lea kindly arranged for me to see the Gooch MSS. in his custody. I also owe much to Messrs.

Burbridge, Brown and Norval of the Estate Surveyor's Department of the Midland Region of British Rail for helping me to consult the deed collections in their custody. I was also helped by the staff of the Town Clerk's Department of the City of Plymouth and by Mr. Severn of Nottingham Corporation Town Clerk's Department.

Dr. S. D. Chapman, Mr. D. R. Wilson, Dr. J. Tann, Mr. I. Mitchell, Dr. K. J. Allison, Dr. G. Jackson, Mr. P. Styles, Professor E. L. Jones, Miss E. M. West, Miss K. Youel, Miss J. Grubb and Dr. W. H. Chaloner gave me important references or drew my attention to useful material. In this respect I am particularly indebted to Dr. J. R. Ward, who allowed me to see his notes on suits in the Public Record Office series Exchequer Bills and Answers and Chancery Proceedings, and encouraged me to study the former series (which otherwise I should have overlooked).

Professor W. G. Hoskins gave me much early encouragement. At Aberystwyth I benefited from discussions with Professor E. B. Fryde, Professor S. H. F. Johnston, Professor H. Carter, Dr. M. I. Williams, Professor D. Williams and Professor Roberts. At Reading I have discussed various themes of the book with Mr. E. A. Smith, Dr. M. G. Woodhouse, Dr. J. R. Wordie, Miss B. Dodwell, Mr. T. A. B. Corley, Dr. E. J. T. Collins, and Mr. M. S. Utton. Professor J. C. Holt advised on the appointment of a research assistant. Other scholars who have made valuable suggestions or given general advice include Dr. Chapman, Professor M. W. Beresford, Dr. D. A. Reeder, Professor S. Pollard, Mr. H. J. Habakkuk, Mr. B. Eccleston, Dr. J. R. Kellett, Professor E. H. Robinson, Professor Glanmor Williams, Professor W. E. Minchinton, Dr. J. D. Marshall, Dr. K. J. Allison, Professor G. E. Mingay, Dr. J. R. Ward, Professor R. S. Neale, Mr. P. Laxton, Dr. F. H. W. Sheppard, Dr. R. A. Houlbrooke, Dr. A. Rogers, and Professor D. J. Olsen. Professor Dyos read the MS three times and I owe much to his perceptive comments. Professor Neale, Mr. Eccleston and Dr. P. L. Cottrell read the last section, and Miss P. J. Corfield read the first part.

Abbreviations

B.P.P.	British Parliamentary Papers
B.R.L.	Birmingham Reference Library
B.M.	British Museum
Econ. H.R.	*Economic History Review*
H.L.R.O.	House of Lords Record Office
Hull R.O.	Hull Record Office
Liverpool R.O.	Liverpool Record Office
Nottingham Archives	Nottingham Central Library: Archives Department
Sheffield Archives	Sheffield Central Library: Archives Department
Portsmouth R.O.	Portsmouth Record Office
P.R.O.	Public Record Office

Contents

Contents

Appendices

Plate Acknowledgements

Plate 1 is taken from S. and N. Buck *Buck's Perspective Views of Cities and Chief Towns in England and Wales*, II (1774); Plates 2–5 were kindly supplied by Mrs. E. L. Green Armytage, Plates 6 and 7 by Mr. W. G. Belsher; Plate 8 is reproduced by courtesy of the Local Studies Department, Birmingham Reference Library; Plate 9 is reproduced from the *Transactions of the Birmingham Archaeological Society*, LVI (1932); Plate 10 is reproduced from the *City of Liverpool 1911 Health Report*; Plate 11 is reproduced by permission of the Liverpool Corporation, City Engineers Department; Plates 15 and 16 by permission of Manchester Public Libraries; Plates 18–21 by permission of Nottingham Public Libraries; Plates 22, 24 and 25 by permission of the City Architect, Portsmouth; Plate 23 by permission of the City Librarian, Portsmouth; Plates 26 and 27 by permission of Hull Local History Library; Plates 28 and 29 by permission of the Hull Daily Mail; Plates 12–14, 30 and 31 were supplied by the author.

Illustrations

Tables and Figures

Maps and Plans

To
Andrew, Heather and Rebecca

Part I
The Growth of Urban Society
1700–1820

I

The Town in a Rural Community

England was not an urban nation in 1700. Over three-quarters of the population of between five and six million lived in the countryside. Many of the towndwellers lived in London, which, with half a million inhabitants by 1700, was the second city in Europe. Its dramatic growth had been the result of the economic, social and political changes of the previous two centuries.[1] However, London was unique as far as England was concerned. No provincial town rivalled it even remotely in size. The two next largest towns, Norwich and Bristol, had about 30,000 and 20,000 inhabitants respectively, and most had less than 1,200 or 1,500 people. The total number of people living in towns with over, say, 2,000 inhabitants was less than the population of London.

By the standard of the middle or the latter half of the nineteenth century the change towards an urban-dominated society during the period covered by this book was small. It was still significant. There was a broadening in the type of town existing in the national community. There was, of course, nothing new about the existence of industrial centres in the later eighteenth century. Tiverton, Colchester, Canterbury, and particularly Norwich, were important instances in 1700. Even the dockyard towns of eighteenth-century Portsmouth and Plymouth

[1] The size of London was based partly on its leading role in foreign trade, and its function as a distributive centre in coastal and inland commerce. These had led to the creation of processing industries such as sugar-refining or corn-milling, and to the development of ancillary trades such as shipbuilding and repairing. Further, Westminster was the seat of the court and government and the meeting-place of parliament, and the law courts and inns of court were also in London, attracting litigants and students of the law in hundreds. Finally, because of these functions as a capital city, London was also a great social centre for the aristocracy and wealthier gentry, who either had their own town houses or occupied lodgings in the season. Not only did this multitude of officials, members of parliament, lawyers and litigants and wealthy visitors provide employment for many thousands of servants, they also encouraged the growth of a wide range of luxury industries such as silk in Spitalfields, watch-making in Clerkenwell, furniture manufacture, coachmaking and dressmaking.

3

had their precursors in the Thames estuary from Tudor times. On the other hand the eighteenth and early nineteenth centuries may be said to have created the English *residential* inland watering-place. People had been visiting inland spas since the time of Elizabeth I, but there were few or no leisured residents before the eighteenth century. First and pre-eminently Bath, and then in the early nineteenth century Tunbridge Wells, Cheltenham and Leamington, had a rapidly growing number of inhabitants of independent means. Further, it was the early eighteenth century that saw the beginning of the addiction for sea-bathing, and the reputation and rapid building development of Brighton, Weymouth, Margate and Scarborough began in the following decades.

More significant than these things in the history of English urbaniza-tion was the rapid growth of a few provincial towns. In 1820 between three-fifths and two-thirds of the population were still country-dwellers. Many market towns had grown no faster than the total population of their districts over the previous 120 years. On the other hand the indus-trial changes, and to a lesser extent the growth of trade and the rising popularity of resorts and the needs of naval warfare, brought into prominence fourteen or fifteen centres which have dominated the urban map of provincial England ever since. These were the ports of Liverpool, Bristol, Hull, Newcastle, and Sunderland; the manufacturing centres of Manchester, Birmingham, Leeds, Sheffield, Nottingham, and Leicester; the dockyard towns of Portsmouth and Plymouth; and the resorts of Bath and Brighton. In 1700 there was only one provincial town (Norwich) with more than 25,000 inhabitants; by 1820 there were fifteen. By then the population of Sheffield, Leeds, Hull, Nottingham, Bath, Portsmouth, and Plymouth had increased at least five times since 1700, while the total population of England and Wales little more than doubled. Above all, Liverpool, Manchester, and Birmingham together had fewer than 20,000 people in 1700; by 1820 their total was about 400,000. Numerous smaller towns also grew very rapidly in the later part of the period, particularly in the industrial districts, such as Bury, Bolton and Preston in Lancashire, and Huddersfield, Halifax and Bradford in the West Riding, but it is with the emergence of the larger provincial towns that this book is principally concerned.

I THE URBAN MAP OF ENGLAND AT THE BEGINNING OF THE EIGHTEENTH CENTURY

In relation to the size of the country and the number of its inhabitants, England was well endowed with towns in 1700, but they were nearly all tiny. There were as many as 500 market centres with mainly local spheres of influence having populations of between 400 and 500 and 1,500 or 1,800.[2] On the other hand there were only forty or fifty towns with a population of between 2,000 and 5,000, depending on a local industry or more often acting as regional centres with a hinterland far larger than that of the average market town. Only about twenty-four towns had a population of between 5,000 and 10,000, and six or seven had more than 10,000 people; most of these were exceptional regional centres, nearly all of them helped by a strategic position on a waterway or by an industry.

The several hundred small towns were nearly all market centres with a hinterland of between 3 to 6 miles in radius. These acted primarily as centres for trade between local producers and consumers, whether farmers or craftsmen, and were collecting or distributing points for a wider regional trade. Although these towns were in the country they were not wholly part of it. A difference between their activities and those of their hinterlands was visible already. Most of the occupations of the tradesmen and craftsmen, such as tailors, shoemakers, millers and blacksmiths, were also to be found in the countryside, but the majority of townsmen did not work the land directly. Many of them, such as

---

[2] The total number of towns is subject to the particular definition of a town that one chooses to adopt. In *Index Villaris or an Alphabetical List of all Cities, Market Towns, Parishes, Villages and Private Seats in England and Wales* (1680), John Adams implied the existence of 788 market 'towns', but some of the listed markets were decayed or discontinued, and the contemporary hearth-tax assessments reveal that many of these settlements had only a few dozen inhabitants. Following A. F. Weber (*The Growth of Cities*, New York, 1963, p. 10), it has been assumed that towns should have an agglomerated population as well as a nonagrarian function. It seems reasonable to think in terms of a minimum population for a town at this date of 400 or 500 people (or about 100 households): the papers of the contemporary demographer Gregory King suggest that he thought predominantly on these lines, though he is not fully consistent in this respect (D. V. Glass 'Two Papers on Gregory King', in D. V. Glass and D. E. C. Eversley (eds.), *Population in History*, 1965, p. 178.) The following urban population figures are mainly derived from the hearth-tax assessments of the 1660s and 1670s, the Compton Census of 1676 in the William Salt Library, Stafford, and various local censuses taken in the 1690s. Only the last provide a reasonably exact guide to population. The hearth-taxes list householders and the Compton Census usually the number of inhabitants over 16. Total population can only be estimated approximately. For the hearth-taxes the total number of listed people is usually multiplied by a figure between 4 and 5; some more recent estimates for the largest towns have also made an additional allowance for servants (W. G. Hoskins, *Industry, Trade and People in Exeter, 1688–1800* (Manchester, 1935), p. 114; L. M. Marshall 'The Rural Population of Bedfordshire', *Publications of the Bedfordshire Historical Record Society*, XVI (1934), p. 10; R. Howell, *Newcastle upon Tyne and the Puritan Revolution* (Oxford, 1967), p. 8; *V.C.H. Yorkshire: The City of York*, 1961, pp. 163–4). In the case of the Census one may assume a proportion of about 40 children to 60 adults (W. G. Hoskins, *Local History in England*, 2nd edn., 1972, p. 173; C. W. Chalklin, 'The Compton Census of 1676: The Dioceses of Canterbury and Rochester', *A Seventeenth Century Miscellany*, Kent Records XVII, 1960, p. 157). A difficulty with the hearth-taxes is that some are a more complete list of householders than others, and I have tried to use the most complete assessment; a problem with the Census is that a few of the figures for populous parishes are clearly just rough estimates in round figures. In the case of the smaller towns—a large part—account has been taken of the rural population of their parishes. Some towns do not have a satisfactory hearth-tax assessment or Census figure; others have one or the other. In any case population estimates derived from these sources must be treated as very appropriate.

millers and maltsters and tanners, processed agricultural products; others were concerned with agricultural tools and equipment such as scythe-makers, wheelwrights and blacksmiths, but relatively few farmed land. In Petworth, Sussex, in the seventeenth and early eighteenth centuries many of the tradesmen of the surrounding hamlets were smallholders, while in the town 'apart from the butchers and maltsters only three men out of ninety-two [for whom evidence survives in probate inventories] . . . had a significant stake in the land'.[3]

Some specialization of trades might exist, but not always, especially in the smaller towns. The town of Tonbridge in the Kentish Weald, with about 600 or 700 people in the 1660s, had only the common craftsmen concerned with food and drink, clothing, building, agricultural trades and general services.[4] On the other hand such small centres often had a handful of professional men, since apart from the ubiquitous clergy these people tended to live where their services were most accessible to the population of the area. Thus, besides clergy and schoolmasters Tonbridge had a lawyer and a scrivener and two or three doctors and surgeons.

Some of the larger towns in this category had sources of employment in addition to their basic local trading function. A few had well-known markets which drew on the produce of a wide area. Farnham in Surrey, which seemed at the time 'a large populous market-town', though it only had about 1,400 people in 1664 and 1,716 in 1741, funnelled the surplus corn grown in part of west Surrey and northeast Hampshire to the London market: according to Defoe it was 'the greatest corn-market in England, London excepted . . ., particularly for wheat, of which so vast a quantity is brought every market-day to this market, that a gentleman told me, he once counted on a market-day 1,100 teams of horse, all drawing waggons, or carts, loaden with wheat'.[5] Burford in Oxfordshire was a posting station and because of this was full of inns; it was also known for its harness-making.[6] Shipbuilding in tiny private yards and fishing were omnipresent in the small coastal towns. On the Sussex coast Defoe found Shoreham to be 'a sea-faring town, and

---

[3] G. H. Kenyon, 'Petworth Town and Trades', *Sussex Archaeological Collections*, XCVI, p. 86.

[4] C. W. Chalklin, 'A Seventeenth-Century Market Town: Tonbridge', *Archaeologia Cantiana*, LXXVI (1961), pp. 158–60; Kent Hearth Tax, 1664, listing 141 households in Tonbridge town: Kent Archives Office Q/RTh.

[5] C. A. F. Meekings (ed.), *Surrey Hearth Tax 1664*, Surrey Record Series, 1940, p. cxxx (229 households in Farnham town); W. Wales, *An Inquiry into the Present State of Population in England and Wales*, (1781), p. 67; Daniel Defoe, *A Tour through the Whole Island of Great Britain*, (1928), I, p. 142.

[6] R. H. Gretton, *The Burford Records* (Oxford, 1920), pp. 209, 219–20.

chiefly inhabited by ship-carpenters, ship-chandlers, and all the several trades depending upon the building and fitting up of ships'.[7]

In the industrial areas such as the textile regions of the West Riding or of south Lancashire, or in the Black Country, most towns were still service centres for a hinterland. There were differences from the primarily agricultural market town. The townsmen worked up or distributed raw materials such as wool, yarn and bar iron, and stored and dispatched the finished product outside the region. As the population of the area was often denser than in agricultural districts and a large part was engaged in manufacturing, the town distributed corn and other foodstuffs imported from outside the region. Since in general the areas were far less self-sufficient than some agricultural regions, the towns were primarily the link between the area and much of the rest of the country. Most were old market centres in which local industry was the main stimulus to growth. Miss M. Gray has analysed the trades of Bury in Lancashire between 1701 and 1773: the size of the food and drink trades, building and clothing crafts reflected the importance of Bury as a service centre; industrial workers comprising weavers, clothiers and chapmen and one or two cloth-finishers such as fullers and dyers were just as numerous.[8]

Some of the forty or fifty towns with a population of between 1,800 and 5,000 were partly dependent on local industry for a livelihood.[9] Usually the manufacturing towns were as much service centres for a partially industrial hinterland as sites of industry themselves. At Walsall in the Black Country the manufacture of metal wares such as saddlers' ironmongery took place as much in the surrounding countryside as in the borough itself.[10] Another small group were basically distributive centres, ports which handled coastal and perhaps river trade with other parts of England and sometimes overseas commerce,

---

[7] Defoe, *Tour*, I, p. 130; Shoreham had about 800 or 850 inhabitants in 1676 (MS. Compton Census, p. 114: 500 adults over sixteen).

[8] M. Gray, 'The History of Bury Lancashire from 1660 to 1876', Oxford B.Litt. thesis (1964), pp. 65–6; exceptionally in this period before the coming of the industrial revolution, the growth of an industry in a district centring originally on a village brought into being a new town for which market rights were acquired; this was the case at Wednesbury in Staffordshire, which obtained a market charter in 1709; here industry overshadowed the service function in the occupations of the inhabitants by the end of the seventeenth century, despite the growth of the general trades; thus between 1678 and 1699 the parish registers refer to seventy-three colliers, eighty-three nailers, twelve bucklemakers, two ironmongers, two iron fitters, four locksmiths, two edgetool makers, eight potters, and only sixty-one other tradesmen, craftsmen and labourers (J. F. Ede, *History of Wednesbury* (Wednesbury, 1962), pp. 99, 133, 147).

[9] E.g., Sandwich: Chalklin, *Seventeenth-Century Kent* (1965), pp. 30, 124.

[10] E. J. Homeshaw, *The Corporation of the Borough and Foreign of Walsall* (Walsall, 1960), pp. 4–5: part of the population of 5,816 in 1699 lived in the 'foreign', i.e. outside the town.

such as Boston, Southampton and Whitehaven. For example, South-ampton, with 2,939 inhabitants in 1696–7, had an important trade with other south-coast ports, London and the Channel Islands in goods such as timber, salt and wine.[11]

The majority of the towns of this size, though often with minor industries, were basically regional commercial centres, whose hinter-lands often included several smaller market towns. The market might be well-known outside the area for the sale of one or more of the special products of the region, besides handling larger quantities of goods than the average market town. Many of them probably contained whole-salers who served the little grocers and mercers of the smaller urban centres and villages; typically, they included a range of more specialized retailers not found in most of the lesser towns. Many were county towns which attracted the gentry and their families to the assizes and quarter sessions, or the sees of a diocese with well-to-do families of cathedral clergy in the close which became social centres with residents of in-dependent means, though most towns had a few leisured people to whom the name 'pseudo-gentry' has been given.[12]

Some of these regional centres lay on navigable rivers or were also seaports. Bedford, with about 3,130 inhabitants at the beginning of the eighteenth century, was an inland port on the River Ouse, a county town, and according to Defoe 'the best market for all sorts of provisions, that is to be seen at any country town in all these parts of England'.[13] Others had to use just the roads. Among them was Lichfield, with 3,038 inhabitants in 1695, an important diocesan and commercial centre in a prosperous farming region in east Staffordshire, with a flourishing agricultural processing industry (brewing and malting), some minor industries such as linen manufacture, silk-weaving and tobacco pipe-making, and a group of resident gentry. No doubt because of its gentry, its cathedral clergy and other professional men, Defoe was to describe it as 'a place of good conversation and good company'. As an example of the specialized trades of the regional centre, Samuel Johnson's father, a native of the town, was a bookseller and stationer and manufactured

[11] A. T. Patterson, *A History of Southampton, 1700–1914*, Vol. I (Southampton, 1966), p. 6; T. S. Willan, *English Coasting Trade, 1600–1750* (Manchester, 1938), pp. 152–3.

[12] In a sense these regional centres had two hinterlands: the first was the typical local market area for which they supplied the usual basic services; the other was the bigger district for which they provided certain more specialized commercial and administrative and social services; for the pseudo-gentry see A. Everitt, 'Social Mobility in Early Modern England', *Past and Present*, no. 33 (1966), p. 71.

[13] T. S. Willan, *River Navigation in England 1600–1750* (1936), p. 128; Defoe, *Tour*, II, p. 113; C. M. Law, 'Some Notes on the Urban Population in the Eighteenth Century', *The Local Historian*, X, No. 1 (1972), p. 22.

parchment, selling in neighbouring towns such as Birmingham, and as far away as Gloucestershire.[14]

About twenty-five large towns had a population of between 5,000 and 10,000. Many of them relied on several functions. About half were regional centres similar to those just described, but only two, Bury St. Edmunds and Chester, relied mainly on this role. Bury, with about 5,500 to 6,100 people in 1675, was important both as a regional and social centre. Richard Blome remarked that its market had 'extraordinary quantities of corn brought to it, for which tis usually the standard of the country', and Celia Fiennes found 'a great deale of gentry which lives in the town .[15] Seven other regional centres of an agricultural district were supported by industry either within the town or in the hinterland. These were Canterbury, Ipswich with its shipbuilding and fishing, Leicester, Nottingham, Salisbury, Worcester and Shrewsbury. For instance, Salisbury, with a population of 6,976 in 1695, was the see of a diocese with a group of cathedral clergy who helped to make it an important social centre, it shared the role of county town of Wiltshire with Devizes, and was a general market centre. Further work came from the making of white broadcloths and flannels: in Defoe's words, 'Salisbury, and all the county of Wilts, . . . are full of a great variety of manufactures. . . . Salisbury has two remarkable manufactures . . . namely, fine flanels, and long cloths for the Turkey trade, call'd Salisbury whites.'[16] Even the important regional centres of Oxford and Cambridge

[14] H. Thorpe, 'Lichfield: a Study of its Growth and Function', *Staffordshire Historical Collections* (1950–51), pp. 183–90; Warwick, with about 3,300 inhabitants in 1676, a county town and important market centre in a fertile agricultural region, was similar in its social structure and economy to Lichfield; it had its resident gentry and a few specialized craftsmen, such as a watchmaker, bookseller and goldsmith in 1694, not often found in the smaller market towns: Warwickshire County Record Office: Warwick Fire Records, vol. inscribed '(167)'; for population see Compton Census (1,992 adults over sixteen), quoted with comment in *V. C. H. Warwickshire* VIII: *The City of Coventry and Borough of Warwick* (1969), p. 418.

[15] R. Blome, *Britannia* (1673), p. 210; Defoe, *Tour*, I, p. 52; for population MS. Compton Census, p. 186 (3,703 adults over sixteen) suggesting about 6,100–6,200 inhabitants; the hearth-tax of 1674 gives a figure of at least about 5,500 (1,224 households listed); *Suffolk in 1674: The Hearth Tax*, Suffolk Green Books No. xi, Vol. 13 (1905), p. xxix; C. Morris (ed.), *The Journeys of Celia Fiennes* (1947), p. 152; Chester had 1,618 households in 1664 and about 10,000 inhabitants in 1720: it was a county town and cathedral city, had a large coastal trade and dominated commercially the neighbouring counties in Wales: E. J. D. Morrison, 'The Hearth Tax in Chester', *Journal of the Chester and North Wales Architectural Archaeological and Historical Society*, n.s., XXXVI (1946), p. 31; Willan, *Coasting Trade*, pp. 181–2; J. Ogilby, *Britannia* (1675), p. 46; information from Mr. Ian Mitchell.

[16] *V.C.H. Wiltshire*, VI, pp. 72, 129; Defoe, *Tour*, I, pp. 188–9; Ogilby, *Britannia*, p. 51; Canterbury, with about 7,500 people in 1676 (Chalklin, 'Compton Census', p. 160: 4,482 adults over sixteen), relied on silk manufacture and the 'new draperies'; it was also a diocesan see and the chief market town of east Kent. Ipswich (1,631 households in 1674) was also the regional centre of east Suffolk: *Suffolk in 1674*, p. xxix; Willan, *Coasting Trade*, pp. 133–5; Defoe, *Tour*, I pp. 40–47. Worcester, with 8,000 or 9,000 people (but figure uncertain), was a county town, cathedral city, a big agricultural market, port on the Severn and another

MAP 1. *The larger towns of England and Wales in 1700*

centre of the cloth industry: Defoe, *Tour*, II, p. 46; Ogilby, *Britannia*, p. 4. Shrewsbury, also on the Severn, was the commercial and social capital not only of its own county but of the adjoining part of Wales: its Drapers Company still dominated the marketing and finishing of the woollens of north Wales: Defoe, *Tour*, II, p. 75; A. H. Dodd, *The Industrial Revolution in North Wales* (Cardiff, 1951), pp. 12–13; the hearth-tax of 1672 lists 1,544 households in the town and liberties, but some of the liberties may have been rural: W. Watkins-Pitchford (ed.), *The Shropshire Hearth-Tax Roll of 1672*, Shropshire Archaeological and Parish Register Society (1949).

relied partly on services for the University. At Oxford in 1667 just over 2,000 of its 9,000 people were members of the University and their dependents and servants.[17]

In fact there seems to have been a limit to the size of towns that were just regional centres.[18] Because much agricultural production was sold locally, the basic urban services were done by the small market towns with hinterlands of between 3 and 6 miles. While the regional towns were usually administrative centres, held bigger or more specialized markets, offered a wider range of services in their shops and tended to attract a small leisured population, the total demographic effect was limited unless other work was available.

Eight of the towns in this group relied almost solely on industry. The economy of four or five was based on their own manufacture and on the services provided for a primarily manufacturing hinterland. These were Birmingham, Coventry, Leeds, Manchester and probably Tiverton in Devon.[19] For example, the economy of Coventry, with 6,710 people in 1694, was in these years based largely on worsteds, such as tammies, manufactured both within the town and in its neighbourhood.[20] Further, Chatham and Portsmouth depended on naval shipbuilding; Plymouth was primarily a naval station and a royal dockyard was founded in 1689.[21]

Apart from the special case of these three southern towns which all depended on the needs of the Navy, there were several reasons for the importance of industry in so many of the towns with a population of between 5,000 and 10,000. This was in spite of the fact that many manufacturing processes were done on an outwork basis in rural cottages

[17] As well as being a university town, Oxford was an important road and Thames-side communication centre and market town, a see of a diocese and county town: H. E. Salter (ed.), *Surveys and Tokens*, Oxford Historical Society, Vol. 75 (1920), pp. 215–16; Ogilby, *Britannia*, p. 157. In the case of Cambridge, out of a population of 7,778 in 1728, 1,499 people were members of the University and another one hundred their servants: *V.C.H. Cambridgeshire* III (1959), p. 97.
[18] As further instances, both Lincoln and Winchester held the sees of important dioceses and were county towns, but the population of Winchester was about 3,600 in 1676 (MS. Compton Census, p. 64: 2,181 adults over sixteen), and that of Lincoln about 4,400 in 1721 (981 families): F. Hill, *Georgian Lincoln* (Cambridge, 1966), p. 146.
[19] For Birmingham, Manchester and Leeds, see below, pp. XX; Tiverton, with 8,000 or 9,000 people in 1705, probably falls into this group, though part of its population would have been dispersed over its huge parish of 17,650 acres; it shared the dominance of the Devonshire serge industry with Exeter, controlling the manufacturing branch of the trade while Exeter handled the finishing: W. G. Hoskins, *Industry, Trade and People in Exeter, 1688–1800* (Manchester, 1935), pp. 11–19, 114.
[20] *The History and Antiquities of the City of Coventry* (Coventry, 1810), p. 86; R. Prosser, 'Coventry, a Study in Urban Continuity', Birmingham M.A. thesis (1955), p. 38.
[21] For Chatham and Portsmouth, see below, pp. XX; Plymouth also had a coastal trade and some private shipbuilding: R. N. Worth, *History of Plymouth* (Plymouth, 1890), p. 363; Willan, *Coasting Trade*, p. 163; Deptford and Greenwich are not included in this survey because their economy was closely linked to that of London.

and workshops, often combined with the cultivation of a smallholding. This was true of the basic spinning and weaving processes in most textile industries, and in nailmaking in the Black Country. The needs of water power in copper and iron smelting and in brass-making, and of charcoal fuel in addition in the case of the iron industry, scattered these metal manufactures over the countryside in small works of no more than a few score men. Coal, lead and copper mines were also to be found where the mineral was most accessible and marketable, though occasionally, as at Neath in south Wales, they were sited on the edge of the town.

The number and populations of towns dependent on industry were swelled in at least three basic ways. Firstly, they were distributing and collecting centres for the industry of the hinterland. The linen drapers of Manchester were 'buying and selling, putting out linen yarn [and] cotton wool to the spinning, winding, warping, weaving', as a contemporary put it, these being done by manufacturers or dependent spinners and weavers in the adjoining parts of south-east Lancashire.[22] Secondly, because of the increased population supported by industrial areas outside the town itself, there was more work for urban shopkeepers and general craftsmen. Defoe wrote of the worsted area of Norfolk as 'very populous and throng'd with great and spacious market-towns, more and larger than any other part of England so far from London, except Devonshire, and the West-riding of Yorkshire'.[23] Thirdly, manufacturing processes were done in most of these towns: while it was in part the same basic processes of spinning and weaving, or the nail, tool or cutlery manufacture which also thrived in the hinterland, much consisted of finishing trades relating to products whose manufacture was largely completed. In Birmingham the gunmakers assembled the parts manufactured elsewhere in the Black Country.[24] Certain of the smaller textile industries such as silk-weaving were more exclusively urban, and some of the worsteds such as the tammies of Coventry had the basic processes, especially weaving, located as much in town as in country. Sometimes a more skilled range of tasks was done in the towns. In the Black Country Wolverhampton made buckles and locks, Walsall concentrated on saddlers' ironmongery, and Birmingham made buckles and toys, needing more skill than the nail-making done in many of the villages.[25]

[22] A. P. Wadsworth and J. de L. Mann, *The Cotton Trade and Industrial Lancashire 1600–1780* (Manchester, 1931), pp. 78–80; the same practice was followed by the linen drapers of Bolton (*ibid.*, pp. 82–3).
[23] Defoe, *Tour* I,, p. 61.
[24] M. J. Wise, 'Birmingham and its Trade Relations in the Early Eighteenth Century', *University of Birmingham Historical Journal*, II (1949–50), p. 59.
[25] Wise, 'Birmingham', and 'Some Factors Influencing the Growth of Birmingham', *Geography*, XXXIII (1948), p. 184.

Finally, the towns with a population of between 5,000 and 10,000 included three seaports. These were Liverpool, Hull and Sunderland, all with about 5,000 or 6,000 people in 1700.[26] They may perhaps be described as national distribution centres, at a time when bulky goods were normally moved by water, but none of them was a fully regional centre. They were not county towns or diocesan sees. It is true that in the absence of an established town of any size in the neighbourhood, the rising port of Liverpool had probably created its own hinterland by 1700; on the other hand Sunderland's immediate commercial hinterland was probably restricted by that of Durham, and Hull's by Beverley.[27] The chief role of all three lay in the almost countrywide waterborne distribution of a range of important products.[28] Hull lay near the mouth of the River Humber, thus dominating the coastal and overseas trade flowing to and from the industrial areas of the West Riding and the east Midlands along the Rivers Ouse, Aire, Don and Trent, and their tributaries.[29]

In addition, there were six or seven towns with a population of over 10,000 people whose functions need to be discussed in more detail. York, with about 10,000 or 10,500 inhabitants in 1672, was the only one to lack an industry and to rely principally on its role as a regional administrative, commercial and social centre. This it owed to its strategic position in the Vale of York, with easy communications with the partly industrial West Riding and the agricultural East Riding, and from the see of the Archdiocese of York. Defoe commented on the 'abundance of good company' and that 'abundance of good families live here'. Because of its position near the West Riding and on a navigable river linking it to the Humber, it may also have been a distribution centre, though not of

---

[26] According to one authority, Liverpool had 5,714 people in 1700: Wales, *An Inquiry into the Present State of Population in England and Wales*, p. 67; Sunderland was said to have about 6,000 people in 1719: W. Hutchinson, *The History and Antiquities of the County Palatine of Durham*, II (1787), p. 524; Hull had about 6,000 or 7,000 people between 1700 and 1740: G. Jackson, *Hull in the Eighteenth Century* (1972), p. 2. Lynn in Norfolk had about 4,600 people in 1676 (MS. Compton Census, p. 177: 2,774 adults over sixteen) and may possibly have passed 5,000 by 1700; Hereford had 5,592 in 1757 (M. D. Lobel, 'Hereford', ed. Lobel, *Historic Towns: Maps and Plans*, Vol. I, 1969, p. 10) and Northampton 5,136 in 1746 (R. Price, *Observation on Reversionary Payments*, Vol. I 1792, p. 8): both may have had more than 5,000 in 1700.

[27] Significantly, both Durham and Beverley were county towns, and Durham the see of a diocese.

[28] Among the three ports Sunderland was exceptional in that it relied mainly on the distribution of one product, coal. It owed its prosperity to the fact that the coal from the mines north-east of Durham was more easily transported down the Wear to Sunderland than overland to Newcastle on the Tyne.

[29] Jackson, *Hull in the Eighteenth Century*, p. 2 and chs. 2–4.

the importance of the seaports just mentioned.[30] In contrast, the other town of approximately the same size, Colchester, relied on industry. Though an important agricultural trading centre in north-east Essex, it was not the county town, and the manufacture of bays explains its large size. In Defoe's words 'the town may be said chiefly to subsist by the trade of making bays, ... tho' indeed all the towns round carry on the same trade ... and the whole county, large as it is, may be said to be employ'd, and in part maintain'd, by the spinning of wool, for the bay trade of Colchester and its adjacent towns.'[31]

Exeter and Newcastle were roughly the same size. Newcastle had between about 12,000 and 13,500 inhabitants in 1665 (2,513 households) and Exeter about 500 or 1,000 fewer in 1671–2 (2,365 households, without the suburban parish of St. Thomas). Because of their prosperity, both may have had 1,000 or even 2,000 more inhabitants by 1700. Yarmouth may also have had over 10,000 people. All three were seaports, and acted as national distribution centres. At Newcastle Celia Fiennes found 'the harbour is full of shipps ... its a town of greate trade'; the great Durham and Northumberland coalfield made it the leading coal-exporting town in the country, dispatching coal all down the east coast, to London and abroad.[32] Yarmouth handled an important coastal and foreign trade in fish, coal, corn, Baltic timber and naval stores, and especially the textile products of Norwich and its neighbourhood.[33] Exeter had the most important role in foreign trade of the three ports.[34] However, none of them relied exclusively on waterborne commerce. Newcastle was the natural regional centre of Northumberland, and it early developed small industries based on coal as fuel, such

[30] *V.C.H. Yorkshire: the City of York*, pp. 163, 219: the population figure in the *V.C.H.* is based on 2,124 households and allows for servants; Defoe, *Tour*, II, pp. 230–31; Willan, *Coasting Trade*, pp. 84, 119.

[31] A. F. J. Brown, 'Colchester in the Eighteenth Century', ed. L. M. Munby, *East Anglian Studies* (Cambridge, 1968), p. 146; Defoe, *Tour*, I, p. 17; Morris (ed.), *Journeys of Celia Fiennes*, p. 142; A. F. J. Brown, *Essex at Work, 1700–1815* (Chelmsford, 1969), pp. 93, 98–9; Colchester had *c.* 2,100 households in 1670, from which Dr. Brown suggests a population of 9,500; this makes no allowance for servants and may be a little low even without this; in any case, in view of the industrial prosperity of Colchester towards the end of the seventeenth century, it is probable that the population had grown by at least several hundred by 1700.

[32] Morris (ed.), *Journeys of Celia Fiennes*, pp. 209–10; Willan, *Coasting Trade*, pp. 114–6; R. Howell, *Newcastle upon Tyne and the Puritan Revolution* (Oxford, 1967), pp. 2–3, 8, 20 (for population).

[33] MS. Compton Census, p. 166 (for population of Yarmouth): the Census numbers 7,561 adults over sixteen, suggesting a population of 12,600, nevertheless the Compton Census figure cannot be confirmed by the existence of any other source; according to the number of hearths taxed in 1662, Yarmouth ranked seventh among the provincial towns, *after* Ipswich: Hoskins, *Local History in England*, p. 177, but this is not an exact guide to the relative size of a town; Willan, *Coasting Trade*, pp. 129–31.

[34] Hoskins, *Exeter*, p. 114 gives a population of 11,500 in 1671–2 (not allowing, as Howell does for Newcastle, for servants) without the suburb of St. Thomas, with about 2,000 people.

as glass-making and saltworks.[35] Yarmouth was the largest English fishing centre, particularly for herrings. Exeter was the regional capital of Devon and Cornwall, and it was also the base of the Devonshire serge industry, now at the peak of its prosperity, supplying the wool, and handling the dyeing, finishing and marketing of the cloth of which Tiverton was the manufacturing centre. According to Celia Fiennes its trade in serges was vast: 'the whole town and country is employ'd for at least 20 mile round in spinning, weaveing, dressing and scouring, fulling and drying of the serges.'[36]

Fiennes described Bristol, with 19,403 people in 1695, as 'a very great tradeing citty as most in England'. It was the most important of the provincial distributive centres. This was partly because it was the largest centre for foreign trade outside London, benefiting by its situation in the West Country from the growing North American and West Indian commerce. Because it lay at the focal point of two systems of water communications, that of the Bristol Channel and the River Severn, it was able not only to distribute widely tropical products such as sugar and tobacco, but to handle such wares as Black Country metal goods, West Country cloth, Welsh coal and wool, and Cornish tin. Small industries such as sugar-refining, glass- and copper- and brass-making added to the employment of the town.[37]

Norwich, England's leading provincial city, had a population of a little under 30,000 in the 1690s. Its position as the hub of the road system of Norfolk and its role as a county town and see of the diocese made it the leading regional centre in Norfolk. Its function in this respect has been described recently by Miss Corfield. Because of its strategic position it was a major market for the dispatch of livestock and grain outside the county, and the centre for the distribution over Norfolk of groceries, coal and other goods imported into the county. It also provided a winter season for the Norfolk gentry, and meetings of assizes and quarter sessions drew them to town in the summer. Its theatres, balls and assemblies, its wide range of professional services, including architects, publishers, lawyers, musicians, and its role as an informal money market are all indications of the town's importance as a regional capital.[38] Yet its exceptional size among provincial towns was the result of its

[35] Willan, *Coasting Trade*, p. 115.
[36] Morris (ed.), *Journeys of Celia Fiennes*, p. 245; Hoskins, *Exeter*, pp. 28–44.
[37] Morris (ed.), *Journeys of Celia Fiennes*, p. 237; D. V. Glass, 'Two Papers on Gregory King', p. 192, n. 27; W. E. Minchinton, 'Bristol—Metropolis of the West in the Eighteenth Century', *Transactions of the Royal Historical Society*, 5th ser., IV (1954), pp. 70–78.
[38] P. Corfield, 'A Provincial Capital in the Late Seventeenth Century: the Case of Norwich', in Clark and Slack (eds.), *Crisis and Order in English Towns 1500–1700*, pp. 290–94.

position at the heart of the East Anglian worsted industry, now near the peak of its expansion. Apart from the finishing and marketing of cloth manufactured in the surrounding countryside, much of the population was engaged directly in weaving. According to Defoe, 'if a stranger was only to ride thro' . . . Norwich for a day, he would have much more reason to think there was a town without inhabitants, than there is really to say so of Ipswich . . . but the case is this; the inhabitants being all busy at their manufactures, dwell in their garrets at their looms, and in their combing shops, so they call them, twisting-mills, and other work-houses.'[39] A comparison with York is particularly apposite: as a regional capital York may have been the more important; however, without an industry its population was only about 40 per cent of that of Norwich.

Although it is impossible to estimate the proportions exactly, only about 22 or 23 per cent of the population of England and Wales were towndwellers in 1700.[40] Of these between one-third and one-half lived in the capital. Basically, the fact that most Englishmen lived in the country reflected the nature of the contemporary economy and social structure. By modern standards agricultural productivity was low; though farming rotations and the range of crops grown were slowly improving, machinery and artificial fertilizers were still far in the future. The majority of farms were small and because of low yields their tenants were only marginal producers for the market. The wages of labourers were mainly absorbed in the purchase of basic foodstuffs and the payment of cottage rents. Thus the demand for the services of shop-keepers by these two numerically important rural groups was limited, though it nevertheless existed. Even clothing was made at home in many parts of England. Most crafts and manufactures using simple hand tools on domestic premises could be as well done in the hamlet or the village as the town. Most food was sold and eaten in the area in which it was produced. Thus towns were small and widely distributed.

The existence of administrative centres, and more important, the need of the growing middle class and leisured people for the services of specialized shops, professional services, entertainment and suitable residences, and the need for big markets where the surplus produce of

---

[39] Defoe, *Tour*, I, p. 63.
[40] On the basis of King's figures of 105,000 houses in London and 195,000 in other towns, and of his estimates of the ratio of persons per house in London, other towns, and rural areas respectively, about 25 per cent of the population lived in urban settlements. But the figure of 195,000 houses is based on his estimate of 794 as the total number of towns and his erroneous belief that they all had at least 150 houses each; for King's evidence, see Glass, 'Two Papers', and my comment on King's evidence, p. 5, note 2.

the region could be collected or sold for dispatch to other districts had brought into being over the previous centuries regional centres which were larger than the typical market town. Because waterborne transport of bulky goods was reasonably cheap, the previous two centuries had seen the development of interregional trade in products such as coal, corn, salt, dairy produce, groceries which some or all regions had to import: this had led to the fairly rapid growth of the provincial distributive centres such as Bristol, Newcastle, and Liverpool. Undoubtedly the concentration of most overseas trade in the port of London had helped to prevent the more rapid foreign commercial expansion of ports such as Yarmouth, Lynn and Hull; on the other hand, London's colossal demand as a consumer had helped to develop interregional trade and in this sense had increased the coastal trade of ports such as Newcastle (for coal) and Lynn (for corn). Finally, the increasing tendency for industrial specialization to take place regionally naturally encouraged the growth of towns both as locations and as service centres for manufacture. By 1700 industry was already making a major contribution to the economy of most of the centres with a population of more than 5,000.

2 URBAN EXPANSION, 1670–1750

Between the middle of the seventeenth and the middle of the eighteenth centuries the population of England and Wales grew only slowly. Numbers may have risen by about a million, from five to six million, though all firm estimates are questionable. Over the whole century between 1650 and 1750 the proportion of town-dwellers is unlikely to have risen more than 5 or 6 per cent, from, say, about one-fifth to a quarter. As 200,000 or 300,000 people were added to the population of London during the period, the capital alone may have contributed at least half the total urban increase.

The hierarchy of provincial towns just described was still not static. Many of them were growing slowly, and a few were developing rapidly. Table 1 suggests that the population of many of the largely non-industrial regional centres was growing, though not dramatically. At least a few were not expanding at all. Hypothetically one would expect to find widespread signs of general urban growth. Nearly the whole century appears to have been a period of commercial development. The trade in agricultural and manufactured products and colonial imports was increasing. Town and village retail shops were spreading. Merchants, wholesalers and other middlemen 'increased in numbers,

TABLE I. *The estimated population of some regional centres, c. 1670–1750*[41]

York	1670: *c.* 10,000–10,500[42]	*c.* 1730: 10,800[43]
Chester	1664: *c.* 7,500[44]	1720: *c.* 10,000[45]
Cambridge	1674: *c.* 9,000–9,500[46]	1728: 7,728[47]
Bury St Edmunds	*c.* 1675: *c.* 5,500–6,100[48]	1757: 5,819[49]
Gloucester	1695: 4,756[50]	1743: 5,291[51]
Northampton	1676: *c.* 4,500[52]	1746: 5,136[53]
Lincoln	1676: *c.* 4,100[54]	1721 *c.* 4,400[55]
Warwick	1676: *c.* 3,300[56]	1730: *c.* 4,000–4,500[57]
Southampton	1697: 2,939[58]	1757: 3,300[59]
Chichester	1676: *c.* 2,400[60]	1739: 4,030
		1740: 3,712
		1762: 3,610[61]
Bedford	1671: *c.* 2,200[62]	1706–21: 3,130[63]
Faversham	1676: *c.* 2,000[64]	1753: 2,145[65]
Stratford-upon-Avon	1670: *c.* 1,950[66]	1765: 2,287[67]
Guildford	1676: *c.* 1,800–1,900[68]	1739: 2,574[69]
Hertford	1676: 1,670[70]	1753: 2,145[71]

[41] There is a dearth of reliable evidence relating to the population of towns of this type in the mid-eighteenth century; the towns in this table are those for which material has been found. Market towns are excluded because I have only traced evidence for two or three of them.

[42] See above, p. 13.

[43] C. Creighton, *A History of Epidemics in Britain* (Cambridge, 1894), II, p. 64.

[44] See above, p. 9 note 15.

[45] See above, p. 9 note 15.

[46] There were 1,674 households in the borough and 1,352 members of the University: *V.C.H. Cambs.*, III, pp. 501–4.

[48] See above, p. 11 note 17.

[47] See above, p. 9 note 15.

[49] Law, 'Notes', p. 25.

[50] M. D. Lobel and J. Tann, 'Gloucester', in Lobel (ed.), *Historic Towns: Maps and Plans*, I (1969), p. 14.

[51] *Ibid.*

[52] MS. Compton Census, p. 329: an approximate estimate allowing for the fact that the figure for the smallest of Northampton's four parishes is missing.

[53] See above, p. 13 note 26.

[54] J. W. F. Hill *Tudor and Stuart Lincoln* (Cambridge, 1956), p. 210: 2,461 adults over sixteen.

[55] See above, p. 11 note 18.

[56] See above, p. 9 note 14.

[57] *V.C.H. Warks.*, VIII, p. 418: *c.* 916 'houses'.

[58] See above, p. 8.

[59] Patterson, *Southampton*, p. 40.

[60] MS. Compton Census; pp. 118–19: an approximate estimate allowing for the fact that the figure for one small parish is missing.

[61] A. Hay *The History of Chichester* (Chichester 1804), p. 573.

[62] *Publications of the Bedfordshire Historical Record Society*, XVI, pp. 144–8; 501 households.

[63] See above, p. 8 note 13.

[64] Chalklin, 'Compton Census', p. 167: 1,200 adults over sixteen.

[65] Law, 'Notes', p. 24.

[66] *V.C.H. Warks*, III, p. 223.

[67] L. Fox, *Stratford-upon-Avon* (Stratford, 1953), p. 48.

[68] MS. Compton Census, p. 75: 1,100 adults over sixteen.

[69] E. R. Chamberlin, *Guildford: a Biography* (1970), p. 9.

[70] L. Munby, *Hertfordshire Population Statistics 1563–1801*, Herts. Local History Council (Hitchin, 1964), p. 34, from Compton Census.

[71] Law, 'Notes', p. 24.

efficiency, and degree of specialization'.[72] Greater agricultural output increased the need for people to process it, such as millers, maltsters, brewers and tanners, the makers and menders of agricultural equipment, dealers and carriers. Many, though not all, of these people lived in the towns. Finally, the increased wealth of the middle classes helped the development of a small leisured class, which tended to congregate in regional centres. Altogether the possible contributions to growing urban commercial prosperity were numerous.

In fact, as we have seen, a number of factors, such as the competition of the market towns, the role of the regional towns as administrative centres (which did not expand), and the small size of the leisured class, helped to limit the size of the regional centres. A further reason for their slow growth lies in the almost stable population of the countryside they served, particularly in the early eighteenth century. The increasing demand for urban services derived basically from rising real incomes, not more people.

The most rapidly growing towns were to be found among the ports with a great coastwise and overseas trade, and especially among the manufacturing centres. The general expansion of trade just described was reflected in the faster development of some of the major seaports. With the further expansion of its overseas, coastal and inland commerce, 5,000 to 10,000 people were added to the population of Bristol in the first half of the eighteenth century.[73] The biggest growth, however, took place in the two ports on the Irish Sea. Whitehaven was developed in the 1670s and 1680s by the Cumberland landowner, Sir John Lowther, for the export of coal mined on his estates. The port grew quickly in the early eighteenth century: its population was 2,222 in 1693, 4,000 in 1713, 6,000 in 1730, and 9,063 in 1762. To the export of Cumberland coal, especially to Ireland, was added the coastal distribution of colonial wares such as tobacco and sugar, and in 1745 it was 'deem'd the 3rd if not the 2nd port in the Kingdom on the Tob.° way'. It was probably at the height of its prosperity in the middle of the eighteenth century.[74]

More important was the development of Liverpool. At least by the beginning of the seventeenth century its ships were visiting Irish, French and Spanish ports, but the growth of trade had been interrupted in the 1640s and 1650s. It was not until the later decades of the century

[72] R. B. Westerfield, *The Middleman in English Business, 1660–1760* (New Haven, 1915), p. 127.
[73] A suggested figure based on the considerable building expansion of Bristol.
[74] J. E. Williams, 'Whitehaven in the Eighteenth Century', *Econ. H.R.*, 2nd ser., VIII (1956), pp. 393–402; D. Hay, 'Whitehaven in the Eighteenth Century', *Whitehaven News* (29 December 1938).

that the rapid expansion of the commerce of the town began, with the growth of the American trade through the import of tobacco and sugar, the increase in its coastal commerce in such products as salt, and above all in its trade with Ireland. From a population of about 1,500 in 1673, the town had over 5,000 inhabitants in 1700 and about 22,000 in 1750, or an increase of about four times in fifty years. Its shipping rose from seventy vessels employing 800 men in 1700 to 220 with 3,319 men in 1750, based on the further expansion of the coastwise, Irish and American commerce in sugar, tobacco, salt, coal, textiles and hardware and many other goods. The comparative security of the sea lanes of the Irish Sea during the war in the 1740s enabled traders to capture commerce which had previously been based on London.[75]

The ports on the north-west seaboard developed faster than those on the east coast, partly on account of the development of trade with the colonies and Ireland. All the large coastal distribution centres benefited from the general expansion of overseas and interregional trade and the consequent need for entrepots to assemble or break up large cargoes in important products such as coal, salt, hardware, sugar and tobacco. For many of these ports it was the rising populations of the industrial districts in their hinterlands, both as producers of manufactured goods and consumers of raw materials and imported foodstuffs, which was the biggest dynamic factor in their development.

The expansion of manufacture made the greatest contribution to rapid urban development. Industry did not prosper uniformly in the early eighteenth century. In some cases stagnation of a textile manufacture led to some population decline in the early eighteenth century. Exeter and Tiverton suffered from the difficulties in the marketing of serges after the Treaty of Utrecht, and the population of both centres probably fell over the whole period 1700 to 1750.[76] The vicissitudes of the Essex bay industry led to a slight demographic decline in Colchester: in the 1740s Morant spoke of houses demolished and empty, and the population was probably a little less than it had been in 1670.[77]

On the other hand, the expansion of the textile industries of the Midlands and the North naturally led to the rapid growth of several centres. Coventry's population grew from 6,710 in 1694 to 12,117 in 1748,

[75] F. E. Hyde, *Liverpool and the Mersey: An Economic History of a Port 1700–1970* (Newton Abbot, 1971), pp. 2–4; *V.C.H. Lancs.* IV, pp. 23, 30; C. N. Parkinson, *The Rise of the Port of Liverpool* (Liverpool, 1952), chs. 7, 8; C. Wilson, *England's Apprenticeship 1603–1763* (1965), p. 275.

[76] Wilson, *England's Apprenticeship*, p. 290; R. Pickard, *The Population and Epidemics of Exeter in Pre-Census Times* (Exeter, 1947), p. 20; for Tiverton, see below, p. XX.

[77] Brown, *Essex at Work*, p. 99.

partly as a result of the introduction of the silk-ribbon weaving industry, reflecting the growth of English silk manufacture in the early eighteenth century.[78] Both Nottingham and Leicester were increasingly important as centres of the framework knitting industry. They were county towns and the leading market centres of their counties; Nottingham in particular was an important social capital, and significant signs of its role as a regional service centre were the establishment of two printing presses about 1710 and the early emergence of a bank.[79] Their growth in the eighteenth century owed far more to the hosiery manufacture of the east Midlands. In the early eighteenth century the industry benefited from the increasing demand for plain (cheaper) stockings and the failure of the Framework Knitters Company in London to regulate the Midland producers. Nottingham had about 5,500 inhabitants in 1676, about 7,000 in 1700 and 12,000 in 1750.[80] Leicester was a little smaller, with an increase of population of not less than 30 per cent between 1670 and 1712, to about 6,000 people; by 1730 there were about 8,000 inhabitants.[81]

According to Celia Fiennes, in the 1690s Leeds in the industrial West Riding was 'esteemed the wealthyest town of its bigness in the Country, its manufacture is the woollen cloth the Yorkshire Cloth in which they are all employ'd'.[82] By the end of the seventeenth century it had eclipsed its former rival, Wakefield, in the competition for the economic dominance of the region. It was basically a manufacturing, finishing and trading centre for the cheaper, rough woollens known as 'Northern Dozens' and kerseys, but in the early eighteenth century it began to trade in the rapidly growing products of the worsted industry primarily made around Bradford and Halifax. It had about 5,000 or 6,000 people in 1700 and about 10,000 by the 1740s.[83]

---

[78] Out of a total of 488 freemen resident in Coventry who were sworn in April 1734, there were seventy-three silk-weavers, though the number of other weavers (186), presumably in worsteds and to a lesser extent in woollens, suggests that other textiles remained an important basis of the town's livelihood; Prosser, 'Coventry', pp. 41–2, 69; Coventry Record Office A14f: Council minutes 1722–38, pp. 252–69.

[79] J. D. Chambers, 'Population Change in a Provincial Town: Nottingham 1700–1800', in L. S. Pressnell (ed.), *Studies in the Industrial Revolution* (1960), pp. 103, 122; D. Gray, *Nottingham: Settlement to City* (Nottingham, 1953), pp. 42–3; *V.C.H. Leics.*, IV, p 191.

[80] *V.C.H. Leics.*, IV, pp. 191–2; R. A. Church, *Economic and Social Change in a Midland Town: Victorian Nottingham 1815–1900* (1966), p. 3; Chambers, 'Nottingham', p. 122; for the population of Nottingham in 1676, E. L. Guilford, 'Nottinghamshire in 1676', *Transactions of the Thoroton Society*, XXVIII (1924), pp. 107–8: 3,328 adults over sixteen, from ecclesiastical census in Bodleian Library (Tanner MS. 150 f. 129).

[81] *V.C.H. Leics.*, IV, pp. 191–2.

[82] Morris (ed.), *Journeys of Celia Fiennes*, p. 219.

[83] Wilson, *England's Apprenticeship*, pp. 192, 294–6; W. G. Rimmer, 'Working Men's Cottages in Leeds, 1770–1840', *Publications of the Thoresby Society*, XLVI, Miscellany 13, part 2 (1960), p. 169.

Across the Pennines Manchester's population roughly quadrupled between about 1660 and 1760. With about 5,000 people in 1660, Manchester and Salford had between 10,000 and 12,000 inhabitants by 1717 and 19,839 in 1758. On account of its strategic position in south-east Lancashire and southern Rossendale, Manchester had long been the heart of the textile region. In the later seventeenth century small wares such as tapes, ribbons and garters were made in the town itself, while its inhabitants were also merchants and employers and finishers for the more widely spread linen manufacture. During the early eighteenth century the prosperity of Manchester increased further with the spread in the range of the types and patterns of its cotton-linen textiles, such as cotton velvets in the 1740s.[84]

The rapid development of Manchester and Leeds in the century after 1660 was more than matched by that of the two great hardware-producing centres, Birmingham and Sheffield. In the Black Country the population of Birmingham rose from about 4,400 in 1676 to between 5,000 and 7,000 in 1700; in the next fifty years it at least trebled and possibly quadrupled, rising to 23,688 in 1750.[85] As one contemporary claimed in 1750, 'this place has been for a long series of years increasing in its buildings and is superior to most towns in ye kingdom for [the] number and wealth of the inhabitants; its prosperity is owing greatly to ye industry of ye people who have for many years carried on an extensive trade in iron and other wares . . . .' Birmingham had long led the towns of the Black Country, far outstripping in size Wolverhampton (7,454 inhabitants in 1750) and Walsall (with only 5,177 people in the Borough as late as 1801). Its rise to pre-eminence may probably be explained by its strategic position on the south-east edge of the Black Country, on the main route out of that region to London and other markets in the south and east. In 1726 it was said that there were daily in the town 'a great number of carriages, constantly passing, laden with iron and iron wares from Wolverhampton and thereabouts to Birmingham and from thence to London'. It had many of the ironmongers who supplied the region with imported bar iron and distributed its output. Its own manufacturers relying on more skilled labour concentrated on the specialized and hence more expensive metal wares such as guns, buttons, light steel toys and brassware. The early existence of theatres and publishers, and of a local newspaper from 1743, are signs of the

---

[84] Wadsworth and Mann, *Cotton Trade*, chs. IV, V, pp. 173–4, 509–10.
[85] S. Bradford, *A Plan of Birmingham* (1750); the figure of 15,000 often quoted as the population of Birmingham in 1700 is wrong, and my approximate estimate is based on the parish registers of St. Martin; there were about 11,400 people about 1720: *V.C.H. Warks.* VII, p. 7; MS. Compton Census, p. 276: 2,623 adults over sixteen.

general services provided for the population of its industrial hinterland as well as its own inhabitants.[86]

The economy of Sheffield, like that of Birmingham, was based on the industry of the town and the neighbouring villages; in contrast to Birmingham its hinterland was small and much of it thinly populated, and it was thus much less important as the regional centre for a manufacturing district. In view of the geographical isolation of Sheffield and the consequent cost of road transport out of the district, the rapid growth of the town may seem something of a mystery. Presumably it may be explained partly by its natural advantages for the manufacture of metal goods—the existence of numerous rapids and waterfalls and access to ironstone, timber and millstone grit, the early establishment of the reputation of the neighbourhood in this field and the presence of a nucleus of skilled workmen which could be expanded, and the fact that the high value of the finished goods—cutlery, scythes, files, saws and edged tools—in relation to their weight minimized the cost of their carriage to the main markets. With the expansion of domestic and overseas demand in the early eighteenth century output increased enormously, and it is not surprising that in the 1740s it was a local craftsman who discovered an improved method of making steel which was to be the standard technique for more than a hundred years. The town of Sheffield had less than 3,500 inhabitants in 1700; by 1736 there were 9,695 people and in 1757 12,001.[87]

Of a special type were the towns dependent on shipbuilding. This is an assembly industry in which the work is concentrated in the town itself. Private boat construction was not on a large enough scale to expand work massively in any town, but naval needs in the wars of the later seventeenth and early eighteenth centuries led to a great influx of shipyard workers, first into Chatham and later into the Portsmouth suburb of Portsea and the Plymouth suburb of Dock. Chatham had grown rapidly in the wars of the later seventeenth century, and had at least 5,000 people by 1700.[88] After the beginning of the eighteenth century its development slowed. With France and, to a lesser extent, Spain now the national enemies instead of the Dutch, the dockyards at Portsmouth and Plymouth in the Channel naturally received most of the Admiralty expenditure on new dock facilities. Dock, founded after 1689, had 3,361 inhabitants in 1733; Plymouth town had 8,400 people

---

[86] Wise, 'Birmingham and its Trade Relations', pp. 58–62, 71, 73–5; Bradford, *Plan*.
[87] G. P. Jones 'Industrial Evolution' and S. Pollard and A. J. Hunt 'The Growth of Population, in D. L. Linton (ed.), *Sheffield and its Region* (Sheffield, 1956), pp. 155, 172; information from Miss K. Youel.
[88] Chalklin, *Kent*, p. 31.

in 1740, and after the further expansion of the war in the 1740s the total in the two settlements is likely to have been 13,000 or 14,000, representing a doubling of the population at least since 1700.[89]

At Portsmouth the expansion of the dockyard during the Dutch and French wars of the later seventeenth century raised the population from about 3,500 in 1664 and 4,300 in 1676 to well over 5,000 by 1700.[90] The suburb of Portsea which originated in the opening years of the War of the Spanish Succession, had several thousand inhabitants by 1750. According to Defoe in the early 1720s: 'since the encrease of business at this place by the long continuance of the war, the confluence of people has been so great, that the town not admitting any enlargement for buildings, that a kind of a suburb, or rather a new town has been built on the heathy ground adjoining to the town, which is so well built, and seems to encrease so fast, that in time it threatens to outdo, for numbers of inhabitants, and beauty of buildings, even the town it self.'[91] By the end of the War in the 1740s, the combined population of Portsmouth and Portsea was probably at least 10,000,[92] compared with about 3,500 in the 1660s.

The other major contributor to urban growth in modern times, that of the demand for special resorts for summer visitors and well-to-do leisured residents, exercised little influence on the development of larger towns before the nineteenth century. A case on its own was Bath, the major inland resort throughout the eighteenth century. In 1660 Bath had a population of about 1,100, but by 1742 there were 1,362 houses, suggesting between 6,000 and 6,500 inhabitants. Reflecting the growing popularity of the spa both for summer visitors and permanent residents, the building of the town suggests that most of the increase came after 1700.[93] As Bishop Pococke commented in 1750, 'great additions have been made without the walls of late years, as of all Queen's square to the north-west, mostly inhabited by persons who live constantly at Bath . . . and since that a great pile of buildings . . . called the North and South Parade'.[94] Otherwise the influence of the growing popularity of resorts on urban growth was insignificant. In 1750 Buxton and Tunbridge Wells had only a few hundred inhabitants each, and the

[89] Information from Miss E. M. West.
[90] 770 households in 1664: P.R.O. E179/176/565; MS. Compton Census, p. 59: 2,560 adults over sixteen.
[91] Defoe, *Tour*, I, p. 139
[92] It is impossible to give even an approximate figure for the population of Portsea, and this suggestion is based on my knowledge of its building history.
[93] Bath Reference Library: C. P. Russell, 'Maps and Plans of the City of Bath', p. 3.
[94] J. J. Cartwright (ed.), *The Travels of Dr Richard Pococke*, Camden Society (1888), I, p. 154.

economy of several small coastal towns had only just begun to be affected by the new fashion of sea-bathing. Pococke described Margate as 'a fishing town, and of late much resorted to by company to drink the sea water, as well as to bathe', and Brighton as 'a long fishing town . . . greatly improved of late by the concourse of people who come to it to bathe and drink the sea waters'; but the effect on the size of either town was as yet insignificant.[95]

Urban growth in provincial England was not new in the later seventeenth century. A few towns had expanded rapidly in the general demographic and economic growth of the sixteenth and early seventeenth centuries. Norwich, Colchester and Exeter had grown because of their textile industries, Newcastle on account of its coal trade. The population of Norwich grew from 12,000 or 13,000 to 20,000 in the early decades of the seventeenth century.[96] Nevertheless, the rate of growth of the majority of the bigger towns was faster after 1670. This is particularly true after 1700: at this date there were six or seven towns (apart from London) with a population of over 10,000. By 1750 there were at least fourteen to fifteen. Further, although Norwich and Bristol were still the largest provincial towns, the next biggest were now Birmingham, Manchester and Liverpool. Towns such as Nottingham, Sheffield and Leeds were also among those which were to see the largest expansion during the next two centuries. Colchester, Exeter, Yarmouth and York had passed the peak of their *relative* prosperity. England was to remain for several more decades a predominantly rural nation, but it was between 1670 and 1750, and on a tiny scale, that the pattern of modern urban England began to take shape.

3 COUNTRY TOWNS AFTER 1750

In the second half of the eighteenth century the population of England and Wales rose from between about 5,500,000 and 6,000,000 to just over 9,000,000. Twenty years later the figure had reached twelve million. The proportion of townsmen increased: by 1800 between about 28 and 33 per cent of the population were town-dwellers. By 1820 the proportion of urban inhabitants had probably grown by another 4 or 5 per cent.[97] Thus between about one-third and two-fifths of the nation lived in towns in 1820, compared with less than one-quarter in 1700.

[95] *Ibid.* (1889), II, pp. 86, 104.
[96] Corfield, 'Norwich', pp. 263–5; the population rose again in the 1670s and 1680s.
[97] Because of the problem of defining urban boundaries, it is impossible to be more exact without exhaustive research. An attempt was once made by T. A. Welton to estimate the percentage of urban inhabitants in 1801, but as it failed to solve the boundary problem it cannot be accepted as it stands: see Appendix I.

MAP 2. *The larger towns of England and Wales in 1820*

However, most urban demographic growth in excess of the general population expansion was concentrated in the industrial centres and the ports dependent on them, and to a lesser extent in a few resorts. In the agricultural counties many of the market towns and regional centres grew no more quickly than the population of the countryside around them and none of them developed at the pace of the most rapidly growing industrial towns.

26

It is a little surprising that the populations of the market towns and regional centres in the later eighteenth century did not rise much faster than that of the countryside because of the rapid growth of inland trade. As in earlier periods it is impossible to measure the expansion of domestic commerce, though there are numerous indications of its development. Apart from the canals made in the agricultural regions, their trade benefited from the gradual improvement in the surfacing of some sections of the main roads, and from the development of more and faster transport services by stage coach, mail coach (after 1784) and wagon. Improved road transport by carrier helped the dispatch of heavy goods, while faster coaches speeded the movement of salesmen and their samples, of banknotes, commercial paper and coin, and light valuable wares such as silks and millinery. Other signs of commercial expansion are the emergence of a multitude of country banks as separate institutions (though banking facilities had been available before 1750), often with accounts with London bankers, and the growing use of banknotes, bills of exchange and promissory notes as a supplement to coin, the rise of provincial newspapers with their trade advertisements, and, towards the end of the century, of urban directories listing the principal tradesmen and craftsmen. With the spread of enclosure of the open fields and wastes and of improved techniques, agricultural production rose—though, at least in the case of corn, the increase was not as fast as population growth—and this led to the expansion of marketing and processing such as milling, malting and tanning. Falling prices of some manufactured articles, particularly cotton goods, metal wares and pottery, swelled their consumption in the agricultural areas and increased the need for the services of wholesale and retail shopkeepers. Probably some of the great increase in imports of tea, coffee, wines, sugar, and tobacco found their way into these regions and had a similar effect. As in earlier decades, inter-regional trade was developed by the growing concentration of industry in the Midlands and the north, and the greater dependence of these areas on foodstuffs produced outside the district, acting in conjunction with the improvements in transport.[98]

---

[98] While the growth of trade led to an increase in the demand for urban services, and most likely to some growth in employment, its precise effect on population expansion would be impossible to estimate even if the amount of commercial development was known. An additional labour input might have derived from an increase in the workload per person, perhaps through a reduction in under-employment or extension of working hours, without the need for extra manpower. Again, the increased demand pressures on shopkeepers, innkeepers, carriers or processors of agricultural products might have led to a more efficient use of their services: the higher incomes that presumably resulted would have had some multiplier effect through an increase of spending power, but there seems no reason why this should have had a demographic effect comparable to the expansion of trade.

On the other hand, a consideration of the likely pattern of consumption in the largely agrarian counties and the south of England in general suggests factors which may have retarded urban development. The growth of the national income in relation to total population suggests that there was an increase in average consumption per head in England in the later eighteenth century and beginning of the nineteenth century, though the extent of the change is not clear. According to one estimate real consumption per head rose very slowly between 1751 and 1781, but jumped in the prosperous 1780s. From 1801 the figures relate to Great Britain, but if one assumes that the figure for Scotland was lower than for England and Wales, then any decline in English consumption per head in the 1790s had been made good by 1811, and there was a sharp rise in the following decade:

TABLE 2. *Private consumption per head at constant prices, 1751–1821*[99]

Area	£ (at 1791 prices)
England and Wales:	
1751	10·1
1761	8·3
1771	10·5
1781	10·4
1791	12·0
Great Britain:	
1801	8·7
1811	11·8
1821	14·2

However the increase in consumption was not evenly distributed, either between the industrial and the agricultural areas or between social classes. One would expect that the population of the manufacturing regions received a higher than average proportion of the increase, partly because the rapid economic expansion increased the number and wealth of the middle classes, and partly because real wages were rising, at least until the 1790s. Outside the industrial districts it is true that rising agricultural prices brought higher incomes to landlords and farmers, resulting not only in an increasing demand for the general services of shopkeepers and craftsmen such as tailors, shoemakers,

[99] J. E. Williams, 'The British Standard of Living, 1750–1850', *Econ. H.R.*, 2nd ser., XIX (1966), p. 596; comment by B. R. Mitchell, 'Periodical Literature, 1966 (iii) 1700–1800', *Econ. H.R.*, 2nd ser., XX (1967), p. 574.

bricklayers, carpenters, smiths and wheelwrights, but also for the more specialized services of attorneys, apothecaries, milliners, stationers, and bankers. Thus the number of country banks rose from about a dozen before 1750 to 291 in the 1790s and about 650–750 between 1810 and 1815.[100] It was a sign of the rising prosperity of the attorneys during this period that 'ideas about professional conduct and professional solidarity began to be common and important, calling for societies [to] implement them.'[101]

On the other hand, wages in these parts of England were lower in real terms after the 1760s than they had been earlier in the eighteenth century. Wages of agricultural workers lagged behind rising corn prices in the period before the 1790s, and in some areas during the war years when corn prices were particularly high.[102] This was also true of some craftsmen. In the case of one group of wage-earners in southern England, the building craftsmen, an index has been prepared which expresses wage rates in terms of a composite unit of consumables: real wages were lower in each decade between 1760 and 1790 than they had been in the two decades before 1760, fell again in the 1790s and further in the 1800s.[103] It is likely that the decline in the purchasing power per head of part of the population helped to check the demand for some urban services, such as semi-luxury goods stocked by the general shopkeepers. In some rural areas the enclosures of open fields, and especially of commons and wastes, provided additional employment for a rising population, and, in districts close to the manufacturing centres and to London, emigration helped to reduce the surplus agricultural labour force. Elsewhere the absence of long-distance migration and a consequent over-abundance of agricultural labour kept wages down and threw more and more families on the poor rates. It is possible that a vicious circle developed: the relative poverty of the mass of the population in the countryside held down the demand for urban services, while the consequent slow growth of the market towns cut off a potential outlet for the surplus rural labour force.

The extent of population growth in market towns and regional centres

[100] L. S. Pressnell, *Country Banking in the Industrial Revolution* (Oxford, 1956), pp. 10–11.
[101] R. Robson, *The Attorney in Eighteenth-Century England* (Cambridge, 1959), p. 36.
[102] M. W. Flinn, *Origins of the Industrial Revolution* (1966), p. 63; J. D. Chambers and G. E. Mingay, *The Agricultural Revolution, 1750–1880* (1966), p. 119; A. H. John, 'Agriculture during the Napoleonic Wars', in E. L. Jones and G. E. Mingay (eds.), *Land, Labour and Population in the Industrial Revolution* (1967), pp. 32, 34.
[103] E. H. Phelps Brown and S. V. Hopkins, 'Seven Centuries of the Price of Consumables, compared with Builders' Wage-Rates', in E. M. Carus-Wilson (ed.), *Essays in Economic History*, II (1962), pp. 195–6.

compared with the total increase in the counties in which they lay may be illustrated by the pattern revealed in four counties for which suitable evidence survives.[104] While it is true that the majority of towns grew faster than the total populations of their respective counties, there were still many that grew at a slower pace; only a small number more than doubled their population. The possible significance of the extent of trade expansion in the small amount of urban growth in the agricultural areas in the later eighteenth century is suggested by one or two examples. The growth of Hereford, with 5,592 inhabitants in 1757 and 6,828 in 1801, was retarded by poor communications, and by its competitors as a market centre, hops being drawn to Worcester, wool to Ross, and all products to the general market at Leominster.[105] Again, the population of Tenby rose from about 800 in 1670 to only 984 in 1801, probably on account of its isolated position on the Pembrokeshire coast.[106]

By contrast, some towns grew disproportionately on account of their strategic advantages. In 1782 Dunstable in Bedfordshire, which almost doubled its population between 1760 and 1801, was said to be chiefly supported by 'the great passage of travellers'.[107] In Essex, Maldon's population grew from about 1,250 in 1700 to 2,679 in 1801 on account of the expansion of its maritime trade, and that of Chelmsford rose from about 1,900 in 1723 to 3,755 in 1801, because of its important market and situation as a road junction. In some areas there was a tendency for the bigger market towns or regional centres to increase in importance at the expense of the smaller towns as better communications rendered the greater trading facilities of the larger centres more attractive: thus in Essex, Rochford, Rayleigh and Chipping Ongar had a declining trade;[108] in Lincolnshire, while all the parishes containing market towns grew in population between 1705 and 1801, the bigger towns of Boston, Spalding, Stamford and notably Lincoln itself, produced some of the largest rates of increase. In the case of Lincoln, its expansion depended partly on waterborne trade. According to Sir Francis Hill, writing of the waterways which served Lincoln, 'the Fossdyke gross receipts, which a little exceeded £500 in 1750, had reached £2,000 just before the outbreak of war with France in 1793; in 1763-4 the tolls on the Witham at Lincoln and Boston brought in

---

[104] See Appendix II.
[105] Lobel, 'Hereford', *Historic Towns: Maps and Plans*, ed. Lobel, I (1969) p. 10.
[106] 'Pembrokeshire Hearths in 1670', *West Wales Historical Records*, XI, 1926: 175 households.
[107] *Bedfordshire Historical Record Society*, XVI, p. 20.
[108] Brown, *Essex at Work*, pp. 97, 115, 120.

£263; by 1771 £316; by 1782 they had risen to £498; and by 1790 to £898'.[109]

The result of the relatively slow growth of most market towns and regional centres in agricultural areas during the course of the eighteenth and in the beginning of the nineteenth centuries was that their average size remained small as late as 1821 both in comparison with the bigger industrial centres and major seaports, and in comparison with the towns of the later nineteenth century. Most market towns were under 3,000 or 4,000 in size, and there were very many with only between 1,000 and 2,000 inhabitants, if account is taken of the rural population in towns lying in large parishes. Most of the regional centres in agricultural areas were far from being outstanding in terms of number of inhabitants: after York and Chester, Reading was among the largest, with 12,867 in 1821, having developed particularly rapidly on account of its exceptional strategic position at the junction of two major inland waterways, the Thames and the Kennet, its place on the main road from London to Bath and Bristol, its milling, malting and brewing, and minor industries.[110] More common was the regional centre with 5,000 or 10,000 inhabitants, such as Chichester (7,362) and Lewes (7,083) in Sussex, Warwick (8,235) and Lichfield (6,075) in the west Midlands, or even Lincoln, with still only 10,367 inhabitants. Thus even in 1821 one must look outside the basic agricultural-servicing functions to manufacturing and the increasing popularity of the resorts in seeking to explain the most rapid urban development of the period.

[109] Hill, *Georgian Lincoln*, p. 134.

[110] Maidstone had 12,508. York was the largest of the older non-industrial regional centres, with 21,711, but the fact that its population had only roughly doubled since 1670 is also a reflection of the general pattern of slow urban growth outside the industrial and resort centres. Similarly, Chester had 19,949 inhabitants, representing an increase of only about two-and-a-half times since the 1660s.

2

The Origins of an Urban Nation, c. 1750-1820

The most important influence in English provincial urban growth between 1750 and 1820 was the development of industry. Its earlier expansion had already led to the rapid growth of several towns in the first half of the eighteenth century. During the next seventy years, as the pace of industrialization became more rapid, its effect was magnified. It increased the size of towns in areas in the Midlands and the north where manufacture was already established, by expanding the distribution of raw materials, the marketing of finished goods and the other specialized services provided by urban centres, and by increasing the number and to some extent the size of industrial units within towns. It was also the major influence in the growth of several northern seaports which handled the raw materials and finished goods.

In East Anglia, in southern England and in the West Country, stagnating or declining textile manufacture retarded the expansion of the towns which served it. The largest was Norwich. Its place as the second city of England at the beginning of the eighteenth century had originated largely from its role as a centre of the worsted industry, and throughout the eighteenth century the West Riding was the faster-growing producer. From being negligible around 1700, the output of the West Riding had become equal to that of Norfolk by about 1770, and by the 1780s the East Anglian industry was suffering from the competition of both West Riding worsteds and Lancashire cottons. However, textile output as a whole was maintained for the rest of the period, partly through diversification into cotton and silk manufacture: in 1814 Norwich was producing 'crapes, bombazines, camblets, damasks, satines and alopeens in great abundance, together with linen, cotton,

32

woollen and gauze manufactories in a very extensive degree', and as late as 1818–19 the industry enjoyed a period of great prosperity, when 'everyone was anxious to become a weaver and to have their children taught.'[1]

Various reasons have been suggested for the decline of the East Anglian industry relative to that of Lancashire and particularly of the West Riding. They include the greater vulnerability of the industry in the domestic and export market on account of the concentration on better-quality cloths. Manufacturers in the West Riding specialized in cheaper products, its merchants pushed sales, and life in an industrializing area accustomed them generally to change. Since Norwich's role as the regional capital of East Anglia remained unchallenged, the stagnation of its major industry was the principal reason for the absence of population growth in the later eighteenth century. The population of Norwich had been 36,196 in 1752; in 1786 it was 40,051, and in 1801 only 36,832, though it was noted that 'those serving in the Navy, Army and Militia, are not included'. By 1821 the figure was 50,288. The census return of that year attributed the increased population in several parishes to the prosperity of silk and worsted manufacture in the preceding years. This ultimate demographic expansion may also have been the result of the growth of the service trades in Norwich which probably accompanied the population increase in Norfolk as a whole at the beginning of the nineteenth century.[2]

Some of the older textile centres were less fortunate than Norwich. In Devon the decline of serge manufacture during the eighteenth century depressed the economy of the two urban centres of the industry. Tiverton, the manufacturing centre, was said to have had about 2,000 fewer people in 1770 than it had had forty years before; later some new work was found in the making of other textiles, but the parish had only 8,631 inhabitants in 1821, compared with 8,000 or 9,000 in 1705. In the case of Exeter, the impoverishment caused by the gradual loss of its staple industry was reduced by its role as the economic and social capital of the far south-west, and its growth as a resort for leisured people.[3] Even so, the population only doubled in the 150 years after

[1] R. G. Wilson, *Gentlemen Merchants: The Merchant Community in Leeds 1700–1830* (Manchester, 1971), p. 7; M. F. Lloyd Pritchard, 'The Decline of Norwich', *Econ. H.R.*, 2nd ser., III (1950–51), p. 373; J. K. Edwards, 'The Development of Norwich, 1750–1850, with special reference to the worsted industry', (Leeds Ph.D thesis, 1963), pp. 300, 309 and *passim*.

[2] See footnote 1; T. Peck, *The Norwich Directory* (Norwich, *c.* 1803); in 1801 the population of Norfolk was 273,371, in 1821 344, 368; R. G. Wilson, 'The Supremacy of the Yorkshire Cloth Industry in the Eighteenth Century', in N. B. Harte and K. G. Ponting (eds.) *Textile History and Economic History* (Manchester, 1973), p. 245.

[3] J. Dugdale, *The British Traveller*, II (1819), p. 184; Hoskins, *Exeter*, pp. 127, 149–50.

1670, with 23,479 inhabitants in 1821. The pattern in the other traditional textile centres is revealed in the available population figures. Coventry's relatively small expansion in the later eighteenth century

TABLE 3. *Population change in textile towns of East Anglia, southern England and the West Country*[4]

Colchester	1670: *c.* 9,500	1801 : 11,520	1821 : 14,016
Canterbury	1676: *c.* 7,500	1801 : 9,071	1821 : 12,745
Salisbury	1695 : 6,976	1801 : 7,668	1821 : 8,763
Worcester	1700: *c.* 8,000–9,000	1801 : 11,352	1821 : 17,023
Shrewsbury	1750: 13,328	1801 : 14,739	1821 : 19,602
Coventry	1694: 6,714	1801 : 16,049	1821 : 21,242
	1748: 12,117		

is associated with the relatively slow growth of the English silk industry; elsewhere the stagnation or decline of manufacturing employment was compensated for partly by continuing importance of regional service centres. The expansion of several of these towns, such as Canterbury and Worcester, was recovering by the beginning of the nineteenth century.

In the most prosperous textile-producing areas the later eighteenth century was a period of rapid urban growth. This was most marked in Lancashire. The phenomenal expansion of the cotton industry is well-known: retained imports of raw cotton rose from an annual average of 2·81 millions pounds between 1750 and 1759 to 42·92 million pounds between 1795 and 1804; in the 1760s a contemporary estimated the value of annual sales of cotton goods at only £600,000; by 1802 they made up 4 or 5 per cent of the national income, and by 1812 between 7 and 8 per cent.[5] With the expansion of spinning based on waterpower before the 1790s and of 'putting-out' weaving using handlooms, part of the growing industry was located in the countryside, and population thickened in the villages and hamlets. However, the population of most

[4] The bay industry of east Essex was almost extinct by 1800, which was only partly compensated for Colchester by the growth of commercial services for an expanding agricultural district; for Worcester it was said in 1782 that 'the clothing trade is totally gone', though other industries such as the making of gloves and carpets took its place to some extent; Shrewsbury lost part of its trade in Welsh woollens, though it expanded as a social centre and hub of the main-road communications in the north-west Midlands and north Wales.

[5] P. Deane and W. A. Cole, *British Economic Growth, 1688–1959* (Cambridge, 1964), p. 51; P. Deane, *The First Industrial Revolution* (Cambridge, 1965), pp. 85, 88.

of the cotton towns grew much faster than that of the county as a whole. According to one estimate the population of Lancashire was about 318,000 in 1751; by 1801 it had reached 694,202 and by 1821 one million.[6] By comparison the number of inhabitants of some of the cotton centres increased several times before 1800, and rose further in the following decades. In 1773 the town of Bury had 2,090 inhabitants, their number having no more than doubled since the 1660s, but by 1801 the figure was 7,072. Bolton town in about 1750 was said to have been no more than a single street; in 1773 it had 4,568 inhabitants and in 1801 its population was 12,549.[7] All the cotton towns grew rapidly between 1801 and 1821.

TABLE 4. *Population growth of the cotton towns, 1801–21*

Town	Population in 1801	Population in 1821
Wigan	10,989	17,716
Bury	7,072	10,583
Oldham	12,024	21,662
Blackburn	11,980	21,940
Bolton	12,549	22,037
Preston	11,887	24,575
Stockport, Cheshire	14,850	21,726

While some aspects of cotton marketing and the provision of certain specialized services concentrated increasingly on Manchester, these centres all contained dealers in cotton, wool and yarn, serving the spinners and weavers of their respective districts. The manufacturers in weaving who put out work to domestic handloom weavers tended to congregate in towns such as Blackburn and Bury, where many had warehouses from which sales might be made. The towns also provided a convenient location for the manufacturing processes for the spinning and weaving, printing and finishing of the cotton cloths. In 1795 Aikin mentioned the many factories along the rivers and brooks of the parish of Bury.[8] Further, the rapid growth of the manufacturing population in the town and the neighbourhood expanded the demand for the services of the general tradesmen and craftsmen.

[6] Deane and Cole, *British Economic Growth*, p. 103.
[7] J. Aikin, *A Description of the Country from thirty to forty Miles round Manchester* (1795), pp. 261, 266; P. Mantoux, *The Industrial Revolution in the Eighteenth Century*, (1964 edn.), p. 359; Gray, 'Bury', p. 1.
[8] M. M. Edwards, *The Growth of the British Cotton Trade 1780–1815* (Manchester, 1967), pp. 113, 120, 133, 164; D. Bythell, *The Handloom Weavers* (Cambridge, 1969), p. 29; Aikin, *Description*, p. 267.

In a much larger way, all these factors were important to the growth of Manchester. Its population (including that of Salford) rose from under 20,000 in the 1750s to 27,246 in 1773–4, at least 50,000 in 1788, and 84,020 in 1801; if the suburbs of Chorlton, Ardwick and Hulme are included in 1821 (as they should be), the population had risen to 149,756 (the corresponding figure for the same area in 1801 having been 88,134).

With the rapid growth of the cotton industry, it was natural that much of the cotton merchanting in the hands of the larger dealers of the area should concentrate in one centre: in view of its nodal position in south Lancashire and its historical development as the regional capital, it was understandable that the centre should be Manchester. It appears to have been a cumulative process which widened Manchester's sphere of influence, with country spinners and manufacturers selling in Manchester coming from much further afield by the 1820s than they had done in the 1760s. For the convenience of outside buyers, it was advantageous that there should be a main meeting-place for cloth sales. Increasingly cloths were marketed in Manchester warehouses: in 1760 'the merchants of Bolton used warehouses of their own', but only ten years later 'they had chiefly transferred all to the Manchester market, to meet the demands of their London friends'.[9] That Manchester had established its reputation as the chief cloth market in which a substantial south Lancashire cloth merchant had to have a base almost as a matter of course is suggested by the presence of agents of foreign firms in the town by the 1790s. In 1795 Aikin was able to write: 'Manchester, being the first repository of manufacturers, is daily frequented by foreigners and town and country buyers.' Again, Manchester dealers were increasingly supplying cotton wool not only to the spinners of the town and its immediate hinterland, but also to the smaller dealers and bigger spinners of the smaller towns; by the 1790s Manchester was also dominating the yarn market in the same way. To sum up in the words of *The Commercial Directory* (1818): 'the manufacturers from all the neighbouring towns resort here to sell their goods, and purchase fresh supplies of cotton or other materials; so that very few cotton goods are disposed of, without having, in one stage or another, increased the wealth of the inhabitants of Manchester'.[10]

Further, because Manchester controlled the market of cloth it played a major role in cloth bleaching and printing: 'most finishing was done

[9] Edwards, *Cotton Trade*, pp. 172–3; W. H. Chaloner, 'Manchester in the Latter Half of the Eighteenth Century', *Bulletin of the John Rylands Library*, XLVI (1959–60), pp. 48–50.
[10] Edwards, *Cotton Trade*, p. 129; J. Pigot and R. and W. Dean, *The Commercial Directory* (Manchester, 1818), p. 296.

on commission and the location of merchanting functions governed the location of the finishing industries, since the latter depended for their existence upon easy contacts with the grey and finished cloth market in Manchester.' The basic processes of spinning and weaving were also conducted in the town: on the spinning side the first cotton mill, that of Arkwright, was erected in 1783, and by 1800 there were dozens in the town or the immediate neighbourhood, an expansion made possible by the increasing use of steam power in place of water power in the 1790s. In the first quarter of the nineteenth century it has been estimated that 'roughly one quarter of the total spindles engaged in cotton spinning in the whole of the United Kingdom were at work within the town'. Presumably the proximity to sources of raw materials and to markets offset the rather bigger costs involved in the higher rents paid for an urban compared with a rural site. In Arkwright's time, Manchester offered the advantage of an ample supply of female and child labour; later, with the spread of mule spinning, the availability of skilled mule spinners may also have been important.[11]

Because of its crucial importance as a cotton trading and manufacturing centre, Manchester also became the main supplier of certain specialized services to the industry. Aikin in the 1790s commented on the existence of firms making steam engines, and, according to the *New Manchester Guide* in 1815:

> 'The great extent of the several branches of the Manchester manufactures, has likewise greatly encreased the business of different trades and manufactures connected with, or dependent on them. Paper of all sorts is made here in great perfection; and there are no fewer than twelve capital iron founderies. Tin-plate workers, braziers, clockmakers, and harness-makers, have all found additional employment in preparing and fitting-up the various engines of recent invention, for manufacturing cotton, etc.'[12]

Finally, Manchester's importance lay in the general services it provided as the regional capital of south-east Lancashire. One example of this was in the supply of foodstuffs to the markets of the smaller towns: Aikin records that the two weekly markets of Rochdale were supplied with meal, fruit, vegetables and roots of all kinds from Manchester, and that Bolton received its oatmeal from Manchester and

[11] R. Smith, 'Manchester as a Centre for the Manufacture and Merchanting of Cotton Goods, 1820–30', *University of Birmingham Historical Journal*, IV (1953-4), pp. 48, 61, 62; Chaloner, 'Manchester', pp. 48-9.
[12] *New Manchester Guide* (Manchester, 1815), p. 61.

Preston, and its fruit and vegetables from Manchester markets, or the Warrington district. Another aspect of this role was the development of specialist and other luxury trades and crafts for the use of the whole region. In 1818 Manchester had its specialist silversmiths and jewellers, coachmakers, wine and spirit merchants, barometer and looking-glass-makers; none is mentioned in the corresponding directories for Bolton and Bury.[13]

In the other developing textile areas, urban growth was also impressive. In the West Riding textile region the expansion of the woollen and worsted manufactures was the basic cause of the growth of the main centres. Production of narrow woollen cloths more than doubled between about 1740 and 1820, and that of broad woollen cloths grew about seven times.[14] Among the four towns of Bradford, Halifax, Huddersfield and Wakefield, the last had the most diversified base to its prosperity. Before 1700 it had lost its long battle with Leeds for the role of the leading cloth market of the area, but on account of its position on the Aire and Calder Navigation at the eastern edge of the industrial region, it 'became a funnel through which passed much of the raw material and food produced in eastern England for consumption in the expanding industrial areas of south Lancashire and the West Riding, especially the populous Calder valley'. Grain warehouses and a corn exchange were built in the eighteenth century; though it remained a cloth marketing and finishing centre, its major industrial importance lay in its great wool market. It was also 'the seat of local government for the unincorporated parts of the West Riding'.[15] On the other hand, Aikin could write of Huddersfield that it was 'peculiarly the creation of the woollen manufactory, whereby it has been raised from an inconsiderable place, to a great degree of prosperity and population', specializing particularly in the finer cloths. Halifax and Bradford handled the marketing of worsteds; after 1800 Bradford grew the faster, with the early establishment of spinning mills in the town: in 1810 it had five, and in 1820 twenty mills.[16] But in general, urban growth was slowed because mechanization and factory organization was more gradually adopted in Yorkshire than in Lancashire: in 1813 only one-sixteenth of the Riding's cloth output came from factories, and the basic processes of spinning

[13] Pigot and Dean, *Commercial Directory*, pp. 79–86, 95–99, 298–333; Aikin, *Description* pp. 248, 261.
[14] B. R. Mitchell and P. Deane, *Abstract of British Historical Statistics* (Cambridge, 1962), p. 189.
[15] W. G. Rimmer, 'The Evolution of Leeds to 1700', *Publications of the Thoresby Society*, L. Miscellany 14, part 2 (1967), pp. 126–8.
[16] Aikin, *Description*, p. 552; J. James, *Continuation and Additions to the History of Bradford* (1866), pp. 220–23.

and weaving were still primarily carried out in the village and the hamlet instead of in the town.

TABLE 5. *Urban population growth in the West Riding, 1801–21*

Town	Population in 1801	Population in 1821
Halifax[17]	8,886	12,628
Wakefield	8,131	10,764
Huddersfield	7,268	13,284
Bradford	6,393	13,064

In the words of Aikin, 'though the woollen trade in Yorkshire has properly no one common centre, yet the town of Leeds has latterly been always reckoned, in opulence and population, the principal place of the West-Riding.' Its population grew about five times during the eighteenth century: in 1775 there were 17,121 inhabitants, in 1801 30,669 and in 1821 48,603.[18] Yet its dominance of its hinterland was not as complete as that of Manchester in south-east Lancashire. Wakefield rivalled it as an importer of food and raw materials into the region; much of the trade in worsteds passed through the piece halls of Halifax and Bradford; further, except for a handful of cotton, flax, worsted and woollen factories from the 1790s, partly because of the lack of interest on the part of the long-established merchants of Leeds, large-scale manufacturing failed to take a hold in the vicinity of Leeds as it did at Huddersfield, Bradford and Halifax, at the end of the eighteenth and the beginning of the nineteenth centuries. There was a secular decline in the proportion of the inhabitants engaged in textile production.[19]

It is still not difficult to explain why its population was as large as those of the other four towns combined by 1801. The creation of the Aire and Calder Navigation under the act of 1699 had placed Leeds at its western extremity, 'an inland port serving the industrially expanding West Riding hinterland'; the turnpike network developed in the 1740s and 1750s had strengthened its links with the other centres. Already at the beginning of the eighteenth century Leeds was the main cloth market of the region, and the transport developments allowed it to maintain its leadership in this respect during the course of the rapid

[17] In 1766 Halifax town had 1,272 families, or about 6,000 people: Aikin, *Description*, p. 566.
[18] Aikin, *Description*, p. 570; Wilson, *Gentlemen Merchants*, p. 202.
[19] E. M. Sigsworth, 'The Industrial Revolution' in M. W. Beresford and G. R. J. Jones (eds.), *Leeds and its Region* (Leeds, 1967), pp. 147–9; W. G. Rimmer, 'The Industrial Profile of Leeds, 1740–1840', *Thoresby Society*, L, Miscellany 14, part 2, pp. 135–6, 153; Wilson, *Gentlemen Merchants*, pp. 106–8.

growth of textile manufacturing. Apart from the cloths marketed at Leeds, those sold in the other cloth halls often passed through Leeds for shipment overseas. Both practices encouraged the dyeing and finishing of cloths in the vicinity. Nearly all advertisements in the *Leeds Mercury* in the later eighteenth century which concern premises suitable for merchants also made reference 'to dressing shops, dye-houses and tenters'. Again, because of its strategic position at the entry of the West Riding and its proximity to agricultural areas to the north and east, Leeds became an inlet through which passed the foodstuffs and raw materials needed by the growing population of the industrial area; according to Aikin 'the whole country westward into Lancashire does not produce grain or feed sufficient to supply one fifth of the inhabitants'. Grains, wool, dye-stuffs, oil, and flax passed through Leeds into the West Riding. Further, because it was the most important centre of the textile region, Leeds attracted a range of crafts intended for the service of the whole area: 'Leeds was a centre for entertainment and wholesale distribution, for books and newspapers, wallpapers, chinaware, bricks, tailoring, and the best wigs, medical treatment and furniture'.[20]

The other major textile centres which grew at a rapid rate in the later eighteenth and beginning of the nineteenth centuries were Nottingham and Leicester. The population of Nottingham began to grow more quickly from the later 1740s; by 1779 it had reached 17,771 and by 1801 28,861; in 1821 the town held 40,415 people, but if account is also taken of the suburbs beyond the common fields, the figure would be several thousand higher.[21] The population of Leicester rose from about 8,000 in 1750 to 16,933 in 1801 and 30,877 in 1821, or a growth of nearly 80 per cent in twenty years. Both were county towns and therefore social centres, and their market function was important. Leicester had its assembly rooms and its Race Week, 'the social and recreational zenith of the year, when most of the rank and fashion of Leicestershire flocked into the county centre'; 'its Saturday market for provisions, corn and cattle was claimed to be one of the greatest in England. Nottingham, like Newark and Mansfield and other places in the county, was an important malting centre.[22] However, the rapid expansion of Nottingham and Leicester was principally the result of the growing prosperity of the hosiery industry. Manufacturing was undertaken over part of

---

[20] Sigsworth, 'Industrial Revolution', pp. 148–9; Rimmer, 'Industrial Profile', pp. 135–6; Wilson, *Gentlemen Merchants*, p. 72.
[21] Part of the population of Radford (2,269 in 1801, 4,806 in 1821) and Sneinton (588 in 1801, 1,212 in 1821) should be included with that of Nottingham.
[22] A. T. Patterson, *Radical Leicester* (Leicester, 1954), pp. 14, 4; R. Lowe, *General View of the Agriculture of the County of Nottingham* (1813), p. 138.

both counties, and several smaller market towns such as Hinckley and Mansfield contributed to textile output, but Nottingham and Leicester were generally acknowledged to be the two centres of the industry. By the end of the eighteenth century Leicester specialized more in worsted and Nottingham in cotton hosiery. In Nottingham the number of hosiers, the merchant employers in the industry, rose from seventy in 1771 to 199 in about 1800, taking advantage of the adaptation of the stocking frame to new meshes and garments such as underwear and handkerchiefs; some of the framework knitters worked in neighbouring villages, while an increasing number occupied back-to-back tenements in the town which could hold two or three frames. Small cotton mills appeared after that worked by Arkwright in 1769, during the following decades, and from about 1784 the lace industry, technically an offshoot of the hosiery trade, expanded rapidly, attracting some of the best workers on the hosiery side. Nottingham's role as the service centre for an industrial district which covered half the county may be seen in the specialist crafts related to the hosiery trade: in 1807 there were forty-seven master framesmiths in Nottingham.[23]

In Leicester the period between the later 1780s and about 1810 was afterwards regarded as having been the golden age of framework knitting. It had seen (according to Temple Patterson) 'the repeated introduction of new types of goods, following each other in increasingly rapid succession . . . . Each new line, requiring novel techniques or more than average skill, gave rise to an increased demand for labour. The resultant high wages paid in that particular branch attracted many new workers, former agricultural labourers and others, from outside the hosiery industry'. The first decade of the nineteenth century, when the population rose from 16,933 to 23,146, was long remembered (according to an old hosier thirty years later) as 'the most flourishing period of the trade', when it was 'impossible to execute all the orders received' for hosiery, and an 'immense number' of new frames were constructed. As at Nottingham, while part of the knitting work was put out to neighbouring villages, the number of knitters using small workshops or house rooms within the town rose with the general growth of the industry. The expansion of the industry, and of the general trade of the town, was aided by the system of canal navigation being created from the 1790s, replacing (in the case of many goods) slower and more expensive carriage by road.[24]

[23] S. D. Chapman, *The Early Factory Masters* (Newton Abbot, 1967), chs. 1 and 2, and 'The Transition to the Factory System in the Midlands Cotton-Spinning Industry', *Econ. H.R.*, 2nd ser., XVIII (1965), p. 536.
[24] Patterson, *Leicester*, pp. 38–9, 48–54.

2 OTHER INDUSTRIAL CENTRES

The production of metal wares was also an important stimulus to urban development. In the Black Country Birmingham consolidated its metropolitan role in the later eighteenth century. The villages and hamlets continued to produce increasing quantities of basic metal wares such as edge tools, locks, and especially nails, and Birmingham benefited as the main service centre of the region: in 1776 Arthur Young found between Birmingham and West Bromwich 'for 5 or 6 miles . . . one continued village of nailers', many being served by nail ironmongers in Birmingham who acted as merchant employers, supplying iron rod to the nailers and marketing their produce.[25] Its vital function in the distribution of the output of the Black Country is indicated by its place as the hub of a network of canals by the early 1790s. They linked it with other Black Country towns such as Dudley, Wolverhampton and Walsall and with distant centres such as Nottingham, Coventry, Oxford and Liverpool. The existence of four banks by the 1790s, the great increase in the number of retail shops and wholesale warehouses for general goods, its newspapers, and the development of specialized trades and crafts such as those of opticians, picture-frame makers, miniature painters, perfumers, the numerous printers and booksellers and the men involved in the allied paper trades, all reflect its predominant commercial status in the Black Country. Even in the sale of fat cattle Birmingham could be called 'the grand mart' of the west Midlands.[26]

In the town there was a multiplication of small workshops producing guns, buttons, metal toys and jewellery. Several factors encouraged the urban concentration of these manufactures, such as the availability of cheap coal after the opening of the Birmingham canal in 1770, the general industrial reputation of the town among retailers outside the region, the existence of marketing services and an Assay Office. The most important were probably the plentiful supply of skilled labour for increasingly specialized products, and the separation of processes, such as casting, stamping and plating, between workshops. The increasingly complex division of labour between workshops, and the importance of rapid communication between them is illustrated by the development of a gun quarter in the later eighteenth century: 'the guns in course of manufacture, that is to say assembly, passed from shop to shop . . . within the gun quarter around Steelhouse Lane and St. Mary's Church. . . .

[25] W. H. B. Court, *The Rise of the Midland Industries, 1600–1838* (1938), pp. 195, 199.
[26] P. Barfoot and J. Wilkes, *Universal British Directory*, II (1790), pp. 206–42; W. Marshall, *The Rural Econony of the Midland Counties*, I (1790), p. 371.

Small boys acted as the conveyor belts between the shops.'[27] In 1781 the population reached 50,000; by 1801 there were 69,384 and by 1821 106,722 inhabitants (including the small suburb of Edgbaston). Most of the increase came in the 1770s (after the opening of the first canal, which halved the cost of coal in the town, and encouraged by the expansion of the domestic market for metal wares), in the great national economic boom of the later 1780s and beginning of the 1790s, and between 1800 and 1820.

The other towns of the Black Country were now completely overshadowed by Birmingham, though all were local marketing centres as well as sites for metal workshops, Wolverhampton, with the largest agricultural market in Staffordshire, and a centre of the production of locks as well as other hardware such as buckles, watch chains and tools, was the biggest of these towns, with 11,368 inhabitants in 1788, 12,565 in 1801, and 18,380 in 1821.[28]

In the metalware-producing district of the West Riding, the population of Sheffield almost trebled in the later eighteenth century, with 12,983 inhabitants in 1755, 26,538 in 1788 and 35,344 (including the suburb of Brightside Bierlow) in 1801; by 1821 the figure had reached 48,772. Sheffield differed from Birmingham in that its hinterland was small and it remained relatively isolated geographically: though the Don was made navigable to Tinsley 3 miles away in 1751 and turnpikes improved the going overland, no canal reached Sheffield until 1819. The prosperity of the town rested almost entirely on the growth of industry in the locality. A directory of 1787 shows the cutlery trades and toolmakers, which continued on a small-scale domestic basis, scattered throughout the town, particularly on the western side. Again, the skilled and specialized nature of the crafts, and the proximity of waterpower, help to explain the urban concentration, though similar manufacturing also existed in hamlets and villages in the area.[29] Among those not concerned directly in manufacturing were merchants and factors getting a living from the distribution of raw materials or the sale of finished goods, or, more commonly, supplying the general crafts and services needed by the manufacturing population.

The organization of the shipbuilding industry, with the various trades concentrated in the yards, gave a special economic structure to the

[27] B. M. D. Smith, 'The Galtons of Birmingham: Quaker Gun Merchants and Bankers, 1702–1831', *Business History*, 9 (1967), p. 137.
[28] W. Pitt, *General View of the Agriculture of the County of Stafford* (1813), pp. 230, 233; Wolverhampton Reference Library, 'A Plan of the Township of Wolverhampton' (1788).
[29] Aikin, *Description*, p. 550; A. J. Hunt, 'The Morphology and Growth of Sheffield' in Linton (ed.), *Sheffield and its Region*, pp. 232–5; information from Miss K. Youel.

dockyard towns. The service trades and general crafts relied on the townsmen for their livelihood, and minimally on the population outside the town. As earlier in the century, the Channel dockyard towns of Plymouth and Portsmouth grew fastest. With the continued expansion by the Admiralty of the facilities of the dockyard, particularly during the War of American Independence and the later part of the Napoleonic wars, the population of Dock had risen from about 4,000 in 1750 to 23,747 in 1801 and 33,578 in 1821; with the town of Plymouth and the other settlement of East Stonehouse, the total figure was 43,194 in 1801 and 61,121 in 1821. Portsea also grew rapidly during the same war periods: the combined population of Portsea and Portsmouth was 33,226 in 1801 and 45,648 in 1821. The long peace after 1815 brought the period of rapid but intermittent expansion, which had characterized the whole of the eighteenth century in Portsmouth and Plymouth, to an end.

Apart from the smaller dockyard centre of Chatham, the only town of more than 10,000 people in 1821 which depended on manufacturing industry or mining concentrated entirely in the immediate locality was Merthyr Tydfil. Merthyr was an isolated village in the mountains of Glamorgan, until ironworks were established from 1757. Ironstone, water-power, timber and coal were all on hand, though growth did not become rapid until the 1780s. Cort's puddling and rolling process, perfected in 1784, helped the massive local expansion of the industry from the later 1780s by allowing all the stages in ironmaking to be concentrated in one spot: of the four big ironworks established in the vicinity, each with workmen's cottages adjoining, the largest, Cyfarthfa, was claimed in 1803 to employ 2,000 men. By 1801 Merthyr was by far the largest town in Wales with 7,705 inhabitants, and by 1821 the figure had reached 17,404.[30]

Elsewhere industrial development was not large enough to produce towns of more than a few thousand people at the most. Before 1800 the settlement of Amlwch in Anglesey, based on the mining and smelting of the ore of the Parys Mountain after 1770, appeared to be growing almost as quickly as Merthyr: by 1801 the 900 inhabitants of the parish in 1768 had become 4,977. In the first two decades of the nineteenth century, the contrasting fortunes of Merthyr and Amlwch revealed the effect of sole dependence on a single industry. While Merthyr prospered during the war years, there was a decline in employment in the copper

[30] C. Davies, 'Evolution of Industries and Settlements between Merthyr Tydfil and Abergavenny from 1740 to 1840' (Wales, M.A. thesis, 1949), pp. 23–7; T. S. Ashton, *Iron and Steel in the Industrial Revolution* (Manchester, 1924), pp. 95–97.

industry of Amlwch and the population fell by more than one-sixth to 4,210 in 1811; although the industry was more prosperous by 1821, the population at 5,292 was only 300 more than in 1801.[31]

The other manufacturing or mining settlements based on one or more firms were all tiny in this period. For example, the largest copper-smelting settlement in south Wales was Morriston, with 619 inhabitants in 1796, and about 1,100 in 1815, most of its services being supplied by the neighbouring port of Swansea.[32]. The rapid expansion of the potteries led to the emergence of possibly two towns with more than 5,000 people, Burslem and Hanley, by 1821, acting as service centres both for the pottery works within the town and in the neighbouring villages.[33]

In general, the larger of the rapidly growing industrial towns were restricted to four main areas, south-east Lancashire, the West Riding, the Black Country and the east Midland counties of Nottinghamshire and Leicestershire. Even in these regions there were only six centres with more than 25,000 inhabitants in 1821, and only thirteen with more than 15,000. In these instances what was new was the rate of urban growth, as a result of the expansion of manufacture, not the creation of new towns or even the transformation of primarily agricultural marketing centres. The increasing tendency for the textile industries which were expanding to concentrate in the east Midlands and the north slowed the growth of the older manufacturing towns of the south and east and encouraged exceptionally rapid urban expansion in three out of four of these regions. To a lesser extent, proximity to iron and coal was the basis of the development of those towns which served the metal industries. However, in these four areas almost all the towns had existed in 1700—though some had been tiny—and had been industrial centres. Merthyr was perhaps the biggest exception to the general tendency for the industrial towns to grow out of long-established roots.

In the case of the few big towns dependent on large-scale production, particularly the dockyard towns, the reasons for growth are clear. It is less easy to generalize about the majority of the industrial towns, and especially about those which assumed semi-metropolitan functions. In detail at least, their economic structure varied considerably. In

[31] J. Rowlands, 'Social and Economic Changes in the Town and Parish of Amlwch, 1750–1850' (Wales, M.A. thesis, 1960), pp. 64, 90–105.
[32] J. Fox, *General View of the Agriculture of the County of Glamorgan* (1796), p. 43; W. Davies, *Grneral View of the Agriculture and Domestic Economy of South Wales*, I (1815), pp. 134–5.
[33] *V.C.H. Staffs.*, VIII (1963), pp. 80–173; J. Ward, *The Borough of Stoke-upon-Trent* (1843), p. 43; the census returns based on an area bigger than that of the towns make it impossible to give an exact figure for either town.

Manchester, factories for cotton spinning were important in the economy
by the beginning of the nineteenth century; in Birmingham and Sheffield, production was largely based on the workshop, and in Nottingham
the framework-knitters used the attic stories of their own homes. The
nature of the production also differed: in Birmingham the making of
metal wares was highly skilled and based on considerable division of
labour; the Nottingham framework-knitters were working on relatively
simple basic processes; the dyeing and finishing of both cottons and
woollens and the printing of cotton cloths in Manchester and Leeds were
other specialized functions relying on a considerable throughput.
Again, the extent of the metropolitan role differed among these towns.
The dependent area of Sheffield was small both in terms of acreage and
of population compared with that of Birmingham or Manchester.
Certain of the service functions of the textile regions of the West
Riding were shared by Leeds with Wakefield.

Yet certain general factors do much to explain the rapid growth of
the largest centres, assuming the general development of the industry
of the region. Several types of manufacture tend to be usually, though
not exclusively, urban in location. Certain trades, particularly those
involved in the making of metal wares, but also those in the potteries, or
in watchmaking, were highly specialized operations requiring a highly
skilled labour force and relying on considerable division of labour
between workshops. The need for an available pool of skilled artisans
and the advantages in the geographical concentration of these workshops
appear to have been important factors in urban location where these
trades were concerned. Again, finishing trades (pre-eminently in
textiles) were largely urban because the volume of goods being handled
encouraged the trades involved to group themselves around the places
of transfer—markets, inns and warehouses. Possibly, too, the specialized
nature of some of these trades encouraged them to set up where trained
artisans were most likely to exist.

Again, production in miniature factories was mainly urban even in
the eighteenth century: in Ashton's words:

'When, about 1717, Sir Thomas Lombe set up his mill for throwing
silk he found his site in the town of Derby; and when in the
'forties and 'fifties the silk industry spread, it took over and adapted
corn mills or fulling mills in urban centres such as Manchester,
Stockport, and Macclesfield. . . . When, in the last quarter of the
century, water-power was applied to the spinning of cotton, some
of the new factories were built in the country, in hamlets like

46

Cromford, Mellor, and Styal. But others were set in or near urban communities, as at Chorley, Bury, and Holywell; and when steam-power was harnessed to cotton spinning, nearly all the new mills were in towns.'[34]

The location of so many cotton mills in the 1780s and 1790s on the edge of Manchester and the other Lancashire towns, and the siting of the few textile mills of Leeds and Nottingham in the towns in the 1790s, is best explained on the basis of access to a sufficient labour force, even though it was to some extent composed of women and children; in the countryside labour was scanty and the male adults prejudiced against factory work.[35] Presumably this factor much outweighed the slightly higher capital costs involved in the purchase of an urban or semi-urban site as against a rural building plot. Again, a rural location sometimes necessitated, in the later eighteenth century, the special construction of workers' dwellings because of the absence of a potential workforce living in the locality.

Finally, as we have seen, townsmen in all the centres of the four main industrial regions provided the general services for the manufacturing and agricultural inhabitants of the hinterland. This was naturally important in the growth of the largest towns. In addition, because of their strategic position (and, at least by the middle of the eighteenth century, their existing size) they tended to attract specialized trades, crafts and markets intended for the service of the whole region. Lines of communication tended to be adapted to centre on these towns. Thus the further concentration of the basic industries in the locality was encouraged: big manufacturers and small independent artisans alike had an incentive to migrate to metropolitan centres such as Birmingham and Manchester.

3 THE SEAPORTS

In a different category were the major provincial seaports, the natural trans-shipment centres, nearly all of which were developed in the later eighteenth century with the great expansion of inter-regional and overseas trade.

The majority had manufactures, but they tended to be small and to give comparatively little employment. More important, the extent of each town's growth depended on the presence (or absence in the case of Lynn and Southampton) of an industrial hinterland and the rate at

[34] T. S. Ashton, *An Economic History of England: the Eighteenth Century* (1955), p. 96.
[35] A. Redford, *Labour Migration in England, 1800–1850* (Manchester, 1926), ch. II.

which its output was expanding. Liverpool, Bristol, Newcastle, Sunderland and Hull grew faster among the big ports; Whitehaven, Lynn, Yarmouth, Southampton and Exeter all developed slowly. In the later eighteenth century the prosperity of Whitehaven was stagnating, with 9,063 inhabitants in 1762 and only 10,628 in 1801. Its basic role, that of the export of coal from its hinterland, weakened as its coal exports began to fall after about 1789, when rival ports on the Cumberland coast captured some of the trade; its other function as a distributive centre for colonial products was declining, basically because of its remoteness from the big centres of consumption and the superior strategic position of Liverpool in this respect.[36] Whitehaven was probably only slightly smaller than Sunderland in 1760, but the latter had about 24,500 inhabitants by 1801 (that is, including the suburbs of Bishopwearmouth and Monkwearmouth) and 30,887 in 1821. Because of the semi-metropolitan role of Newcastle in the far north-east, Sunderland's role as a regional centre was limited like that of Whitehaven. On the other hand, its coal exports more than doubled between 1750 and 1820, A rapidly increasing tonnage of locally owned colliers encouraged the growth of shipbuilding and ancillary trades for shipyards. There were minor industries depending on coal such as glassware, copper and pottery. But the differing fortunes of the two towns as coal-exporting ports is the basic reason for their contrasting development.[37]

The population of Newcastle roughly doubled during the eighteenth century. By 1801 it had 28,294 inhabitants and its suburb of Gateshead, according to a contemporary 'generally considered as forming a part of Newcastle', had 8,597 people. By 1821 the corresponding figures were 35,181 and 11,767. It grew more slowly than Sunderland in the eighteenth century. This may have been because of its role as the regional capital of a big agricultural hinterland as well as of a mining district. Like Sunderland, Newcastle's coal exports more than doubled between 1750 and 1820, and thus remained considerably larger throughout the period. Other industries developed in the wake of the coal trade. In 1790 and 1791 Newcastle built the largest shipping tonnage of any port after London, and over three times the amount of Sunderland or Whitehaven. Glasshouses, ironworks and lime kilns lined the banks of the Tyne.[38]

[36] Williams, 'Whitehaven', pp. 399–404; the figure of 10,628 includes outlying rows of houses often omitted from the population figure.
[37] I owe this information on Sunderland to a former pupil, Mr. Butchart; Mitchell and Deane, *Historical Statistics*, pp. 109–11.
[38] Mitchell and Deane, *Historical Statistics*, pp. 109–11; D. Akenhead, *The Picture of Newcastle upon Tyne* (Newcastle, c. 1820), p. 7; R. Davis, *The Rise of the English Shipping Industry in the Seventeenth and Eighteenth Centuries*, (1962), p. 70n.

The commercial basis of the economies of Bristol, Liverpool and Hull was more diverse. All depended on an important overseas as well as coastal trade. While they had an immediate geographical hinterland, each relied to a greater extent on more distant industrial hinterlands to which they were linked by water communications. The growth of Bristol was the slowest in the later eighteenth century, its population (including that of the suburbs) being about 64,000 in 1801. Its importance as the metropolis of the west was declining. The canal system took an increasing proportion of the product of the west Midlands to Liverpool. A rising amount of the industrial output of south Wales was handled by its own ports, particularly Swansea, thus displacing Bristol as an entrepôt. Bristol's involvement in the slave trade and West Indian commerce was surpassed by that of Liverpool, and its American trade did not recover after the Revolution. However, its commercial decline as a whole was in relative not absolute terms. The development of Clifton as a fashionable resort provided a little addition to the livelihood.[39]

The growth in size of Liverpool, Bristol's great competitor for the Atlantic trade, was comparable in size to that of Birmingham and Manchester. In 1773 its population was 34,407, in 1786 it was 41,600 and in 1790 it was 55,832. In the years of exceptional prosperity between 1786 and 1793 it outstripped Bristol in numbers and by 1801 it had become the second largest town in England (if the seamen in port and the inhabitants of the suburbs of West Derby and Toxteth Park are included). Its population was then 88,358;[40] by 1821 it was 150,486.[41] The rapid rise in the importance of the port is perhaps best indicated by the increase of its shipping tonnage, which was 19,175 in 1751, 72,730 in 1787 and 129,470 in 1801. The growth of the slave trade and industries such as sugar and salt refining and shipbuilding contributed to the prosperity of the community. Its basic role continued to lie in its overseas, coastal and inland trade. Sugar and tobacco remained staple imports for distribution in Lancashire, Yorkshire and the west Midlands, with sugar showing the faster increase: 'between 1704 and 1711, the imports of tobacco increased from approximately 600 tons to just short of 1,600 tons . . .[and] . . . the import of raw sugar rose from 760 tons

---

[39] Minchinton, 'Bristol', p. 88; no exact estimate of the population of Bristol is possible from the 1801 census.

[40] The figure for 1790 presumable excludes the suburbs; in 1801 there were 77,653 in Liverpool, plus 6,000 seamen, and 4,705 in the suburbs.

[41] On the basis of maps and other data, I have included the suburbs of Toxteth Park (12,828), West Derby (6,304), Everton (2,109) and Kirkdale (1,273) in this figure, but Walton, Wavertree and Bootle have been excluded; 9,000 seamen are included.

to 1,120 tons' ... 'Between 1785 and 1810, annual imports of sugar rose from 16,600 to 46,000 tons, and those of tobacco from 2,500 tons to 8,400 tons.' The service of the Lancashire cotton region became of crucial importance by the 1790s: raw cotton passing through the port rose from just under 2,000 tons in 1785 to 40,000 tons in 1810. With the help of the growing canal system, Liverpool participated in the shipping of growing quantities of west Midland metal wares and pottery, of Lancashire cottons, and especially of Cheshire salt and Lancashire coal to coastal ports and overseas.

> 'By 1796, 100,000 tons of salt were being unloaded in Liverpool and 186,000 tons by 1820. In this year, 58,500 tons of rock salt were exported from Liverpool to markets overseas.'

It is the continued expansion of these basic trades that best explains the great expansion of the town from the mid-1780s.[42]

Hull's prosperity, like that of Liverpool, had grown with the rise of inland industrial areas on the expanding canal network as well as through the expansion of its overseas and coastal trade. Its biggest business was for the West Riding woollen industry. In 1789 it was said that wool destined for the region came along the coast to Hull and there transhipped into smaller boats. Hull also handled the dispatch of rapidly increasing quantities of dozens, bays, shalloons and stuffs. More and more Lancashire fustians were also passing through Hull on their way to Europe from the 1770s. In 1795 Manchester men referred to it as 'the key through which our manufactures can alone find a passage[to] ... Germany, Switzerland, and Italy'. For the Sheffield cutlery industry Hull was the chief exporting port, as well as the source of Swedish and Russian bar iron. Derbyshire lead, Nottinghamshire hosiery and Birmingham hardware were other products to pass through Hull. Apart from raw materials such as wool and iron, Hull handled increasing amounts of luxury goods from London 'ranging from wigs to paper dress patterns, from books to harpsichords, from fire engines to furniture, from wallpaper to brass fenders' (in the words of Dr. Jackson), and deals, fir, flax, hemp, pitch and tar from the Baltic, all largely destined for the inland manufacturing centres.

Again, Hull developed industries linked to its function as a port. At the end of the eighteenth century it was one of the most important provincial shipbuilding towns; it had sugar refineries and firms involved in the extraction of oil from the growing amounts of linseed imported

---

[42] *V.C.H. Lancs.*, IV, p. 32; Edwards, *Cotton Trade*, pp. 110, 176; Hyde, *Liverpool and the Mersey*, ch. 3.

from the Baltic. From the mid-1780s whaling was important, the blubber being processed in 'Greenlandhouses' on the edge of the town; the linseed oil was used in making soap and paint, the whale oil for soap and candles. However, its trade was the most important factor in the expansion of Hull, whose population had reached 27,609 by 1801, and grew by another 40 per cent, to 39,040 by 1821. Thus Liverpool and Hull grew faster than other major provincial ports, basically (though not solely) because of the growth of their enormous industrial hinterlands. The greater expansion of Liverpool reflects the more rapid development of the American trade by comparison with that of northern Europe.[43]

The importance of one or more growing industrial hinterlands in the expansion of these ports may be illustrated further by comparing the fortunes of Great Yarmouth and King's Lynn. In 1801 Yarmouth had 14,845 people and Lynn 10,096. In 1819 it could still be said that 'Yarmouth stands unrivalled in the Herring Fishery'. As a port its dependence on agricultural exports and on a textile industry whose relative importance was declining provided a brake to its growth.[44] Lynn, which continued to act as the main port serving a huge agricultural inland area of the south-east Midlands, barely doubled its population between the later seventeenth century and 1801: in 1700 it was about the same size as Hull; by 1801 it had little more than one-third of the population of the northern port.

4 THE RESORTS

A smaller contribution to urban development between 1750 and 1820 was made by the growth of the resorts. Basically, the expansion of the inland spas, especially Bath, and the emergence of seaside resorts was the result of the growing wealth and numbers of the middle and upper classes. With a rising total population, and a bigger proportion of the growing national income passing to these social groups, the number of people able to make a summer visit or to live permanently at a resort was increasing fast. For some seasonal visitors, the opportunity to drink or bathe in the medicinal waters for health reasons was the chief attraction. For most this was a pretext cloaking the real motive, the lure of the entertainments provided by parades, assembly rooms and card rooms, and theatres. For residents, the spas offered plenty of company, amusements throughout the year, and a reasonably cheap mode of living.

[43] Jackson, *Hull*, chs. II–VIII, *passim*.
[44] Dugdale, *Traveller*, III, p. 612.

Among the inland spas, Bath remained the undisputed leader. Its residential population continued to grow. By 1801 it had 34,160 inhabitants. There was a further large influx of people in the second decade of the nineteenth century, when the population rose by 21 per cent to reach 46,588 in 1821.[45] Possibly because the size of Bath deterred some potential residents, it now had an inland competitor in Cheltenham, of which the population rose from 3,076 to 13,396 between 1801 and 1821[46]. On the other hand, in 1821 Tunbridge Wells had 2,000 or 3,000 people at the most. The emergence of Leamington Spa (2,183) had hardly begun.

By the second half of the eighteenth century some seaside towns were competing with the inland resorts for summer visitors, and later leisured residents. Before the eighteenth century the sea had been feared as the source of shipwrecks, pirates and intermittent foreign attack: as late as 1690 Teignmouth was sacked by the French. After the Restoration, bathing in rivers and streams was apparently becoming more common, and doctors began to advocate cold bathing for health purposes.[47] Then in the early eighteenth century opinion regarding sea-bathing began to change. The influence of Scarborough may have been important: the fact that the waters were drunk at the foot of a cliff by the seashore may have encouraged the idea of sea-bathing. Certainly bathing began very early here, about 1730. For centuries bathing in the sea had been prescribed by doctors, but for only two reasons, as a cure for melancholia and as a precaution against hydrophobia. Now they recommended bathing as a more general remedy. Dr. Richard Russell wrote *A Dissertation on the Use of Sea-Water in the Diseases of the Glands* in 1749, stating the conditions for an ideal bathing resort. In 1754 he built a house at Brighton to give personal supervision to the bathing treatment of his patients. But the doctors probably only succeeded in popularizing a habit which had been growing since the 1730s and 1740s. That the Reverend William Clarke visited Brighton for bathing in 1736, and Weymouth Corporation leased the site for two bathing houses in 1748, suggests that the habit was well established in the town. Much is made of the royal patronage of some resorts in the last decades of the century, particularly the visits of the Prince of Wales to Brighton from 1783 and of the King to Weymouth after 1789. Yet the visits were more of an

---

[45] To arrive at this figure, the following parishes have been treated as urban: St Peter and St Paul, St James, St Michael, Walcot, Bathwick, Lyncombe and Widcombe.

[46] This suggestion has been made to me by Professor R. S. Neale.

[47] R. Lennard, 'The Watering-Places' in Lennard (ed.), *Englishmen at Rest and Play* (Oxford, 1931), pp. 74–7.

indication of the fashion of seavisiting than a cause of the growth of these resorts.[48]

A seaside resort needed certain natural features, emphasized by Dr. Russell and other writers, such as a sandy and flat seashore for bathing, and if possible cliffs for riding, fresh air, and good views. It also needed lodgings and rudimentary trading facilities which an existing fishing village or minor seaport could provide. For this reason most seaside centres represented the expansion of existing towns or villages. Once the reputation of the resort was established, people were willing to build lodging houses, shops and other amenities to cater for the visitors. Brighton was the biggest resort in 1801. Its population was about 2,000 in 1761, about 3,500 in 1783, 5,669 in 1794 and 7,339 in 1801, thus showing a particularly rapid increase in the 1780s and 1790s: in 1760 there were only 400 visitors, but in 1794 there were over 4,300.[49] Among the other larger resorts, Weymouth had grown from about 1,500–2,000 to 3,617, Margate 4,766, Ramsgate 3,110, and Scarborough 6,409.

By 1821 Brighton's population (24,429) had more than trebled since 1801, and doubled since 1811. The other sea resorts were still under 10,000 in population, but had shown rapid rates of increase. Hastings had 3,848 inhabitants in 1811 and 6,085 in 1821. Among all the resorts expansion was particularly great in the decade 1810–20, possibly connected with the return of peace and the settlement of retired army and naval officers with their families. However, the livelihood of the inhabitants did not solely depend on their visitors and leisured residents, although the importance of the latter was growing; Scarborough had limited trade and shipping, and Margate dispatched corn grown in east Kent for the London market.[50] There were numerous other settlements on the east and south coasts which attracted the leisured classes by the 1790s, such as Eastbourne, Seaford, Worthing, and Littlehampton in Sussex. Their population was generally tiny, and they could not yet be regarded as towns. Except for Bath and Brighton, the contribution made by the resorts to the growth of towns was still small.

New building in most eighteenth-century provincial towns was piecemeal and spasmodic, simply because their growth was slow. In

[48] E. W. Gilbert, 'The Growth of Inland and Seaside Health Resorts in England' *Scottish Geographical Magazine*, LV (1939), pp. 21–7; H. C. Brookfield, 'A Regional Study of Urban Development in Coastal Sussex since the Eighteenth Century' (London Ph.D. thesis, 1954), pp. 97–9; information from Mr S. Blake.
[49] A. Dale, *The History and Architecture of Brighton* (Brighton, 1950), pp. 59, 61; E. W. Gilbert, *Brighton: Old Ocean's Bauble* (1954), p. 92.
[50] T. Hinderwell, *The History and Antiquities of Scarborough and its Vicinity* (York, 1811), pp. 238–9.

both Reading and Maidstone, two of the bigger regional centres in southern England, about 1,000 houses or less were built over the whole period 1700–1800, an average of about ten a year. In both towns the majority were erected in the last three or four decades. Even so, no more than thirty or forty a year were built in each centre in the 1780s and 1790s. Even between 1801 and 1821, less than 1,000 dwellings were erected in each town. Much of the new building in the market towns and regional centres was sited in courts and gardens behind older houses in the main streets. Most of the rest were scattered along the main roads out of the town. With population growing so slowly, the supply of new housing was unlikely to have been a major problem. The demand for additional housing was much greater in the relatively few towns which grew rapidly as a result of commercial development, popularity as a resort, and especially industrial expansion. The biggest of these towns were often attracting immigrants at the rate of between 500 and 1,000 a year (and occasionally much more) from the 1780s. Birmingham added about 20,000 people between 1780 and 1790, Hull about 12,000 between 1800 and 1820. Building plots and streets had to be laid out, numerous carpenters, bricklayers and other building tradesmen employed. Many thousands of pounds of local capital had to be found and spent in any year on construction. It is to these towns and the building problems with which they were faced that the rest of this book must be chiefly given.

Part II
The Building Land Promoter

3
Landowners, Developers and the Supply of Building Land

Most of the cost of erecting a house came from the price of building materials and the wages paid to the craftsmen. The share of land was relatively small. If the site was bought, between about 5 and 25 per cent of a builder's outlay might be on the purchase of the land; 10 or 15 per cent was perhaps most usual. If the land was rented, the initial outlay was tiny or nil.[1] Yet a study of land development must be a crucial part of any account of urban house building in modern British history. Before builders could start work the streets and building plots had to be planned and staked out on the ground. The levelling, paving and draining of the roads became increasingly common in the later eighteenth and beginning of the nineteenth centuries. Each individual plot had to be sold or leased to a builder by a formal conveyance, either before or after the dwellings were erected. If the conveyance was made after construction, building was preceded by a contract known as a building agreement to convey the land once the houses had been erected. When better-class streets or squares were intended, land promoters tried to control the appearance and structure of the houses by covenants in the conveyance or in the building agreement. Numerous original owners of land, from dukes to local tradespeople and developers who bought or leased estates for conveying to builders in small lots, were attracted by the high potential rewards and undaunted by the risks.

Generally, the original owner of the land was not the builder. Sometimes, when cottages were erected in the gardens and yards behind older houses, the original owner was responsible. But in the large, rapidly-growing provincial towns, most houses were erected on new land,

[1] Sometimes ground landlords did not demand a rent during the period of house construction.

57

particularly from the 1780s, and this involved at least one property conveyance of the site, either before construction began or after it was finished. Sometimes the existing landowner, or his agent, was the building land promoter. In this case plots comprising between a few hundred and as much as 1,500 square yards, suitable for the erection of one or a small group of houses, passed direct to the individual builders. The landowner had the ground surveyed and levelled, the roads and plots marked out, the roads made, and he sometimes provided other amenities such as paving and sewers, or credit to the builders. His profit came from the rise in the value of the land following its conversion to building use.

Alternatively, the landowner conveyed the whole or large parcels of the potential building land—varying in size from half an acre to as much as 40 or 50 acres in a few cases—to middlemen, subsequently referred to in these chapters as *developers*. They acted as land promoters, instead of the original owners. Sometimes the latter were still responsible for the ground plan of the promotion, and occasionally for the amenities. More often this work was done by the developers. Often they also built several houses or lent money to builders to help the project along. Their profit was part of the increment derived from the conversion of the land from agricultural to building use.

A wide variety of owners, corporate and individual, held the potential building land. Chief among the corporations were the municipal authorities. Much of the ground at Bath, Leicester, Liverpool and Newcastle was owned by their respective corporations, and those at Bristol, Hull, Nottingham and Portsmouth had smaller holdings. More numerous, but generally small, were the charity, hospital and school building estates, and the properties of ecclesiastical owners. Private owners included peers such as the Duke of Norfolk at Sheffield or the Earl of Sefton at Liverpool. Well-established families of gentry who supplied building land included the St. Aubyn family at Dock, the Mosleys in Manchester, and the Gooch family at Birmingham. In most of the towns local families whose living or recent members had been successful traders or professional men in the town were prominent among the landowners who converted land to building use. For example, the vendors of land at Nottingham between the 1780s and the 1800s included a local barrister, a pot-maker, the trustee of a hosier, and a local banker's widow.[2]

Developers came from many occupations among the more substantial townsmen. Some craftsmen-builders, bricklayers, carpenters, joiners

[2] Nottingham Archives: deeds M.18063, 21956-9, 23102-3, 23121, 23141-2.

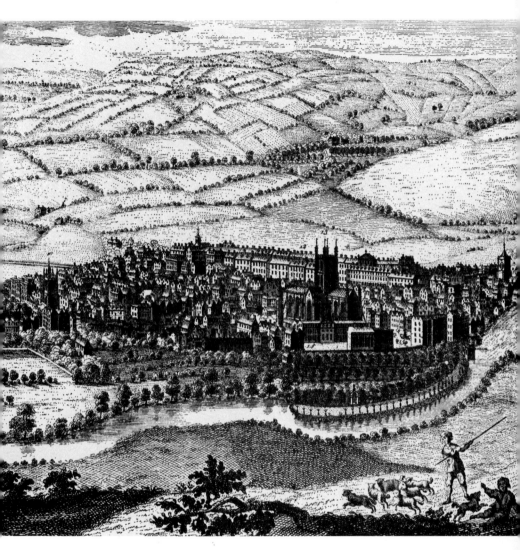

1 The south-east prospect of Bath, 1731. Up to this time Bath lay mostly within the line of its medieval walls, as did towns such as Canterbury, Exeter and Chichester.

I THE LEASEHOLD TOWNS

2, 3 Houses in Westgate Buildings, Bath (*left*) erected by William Selden in 1765–6. The developers required that the facade be constructed in a manner 'agreeable to a design or plan drawn of the elevation of the whole pile of the building'. Houses in Bennett Street (*below*): a small development on Corporation land by a Bradford-on-Avon clothier, Richard Atwood. No. 3 was erected by James Margerum, plasterer and tyler, and sold in 1778 for £1100.

4, 5 South Parade, Bath (*above*). The Parades were a development by the elder John Wood. The corner house was erected by Samuel Emes, mason, in 1743 with the help of a £400 loan from a physician. It was sold in 1750 for £1025, when its rent was £70, yielding a gross return of just under 7 per cent. The adjoining house was probably built by Emes in 1749–50, with the help of a £450 mortgage from a clergyman. Norfolk Crescent (*below*) was the centrepiece of the development by Richard Bowsher and two craftsmen, begun in 1792. The project was hit by a financial crisis in 1793 and the ensuing building depression. Bowsher was still trying to complete it in 1810.

6, 7 A court in Bromsgrove Street, Birmingham (*left*). The view from the rear of a court surviving in 1973, looking towards the street seen through the passage under the front house. The two-roomed tenement on the left was erected on a site leased by Sir Thomas Gooch to William Thompson in 1791. Two other tenements at the back of the court were demolished about forty years ago. Houses (*below*) in Hurst and Inge Streets, Birmingham, built on a site leased by Sir Thomas to John Willmore, builder, in 1789. In 1888 the houses in Inge Street were back-to-backs and were probably built as such, since this followed a typical pattern in Birmingham at the end of the eighteenth century.

8, 9 (*above*) Small Birmingham houses. Erected in the early 1780s these were two-storey tenements with one, or possibly two, small rooms per floor. A house (*right*) on the Colmore Estate, Birmingham, of typical double-fronted design. Erected by John Hadley and occupied by him until its sale to Thomas Aris, stationer and printer of the *Gazette*, in 1760.

12, 13 (*above*) Rodney Street, Liverpool. (*left*) The corner house was erected by John Gladstone, merchant, on a site leased from the Corporation in 1799 and sold in 1801 for £1365. Houses in Seel Street (*right*) were erected by William Harvey, builder and bricklayer, on a site leased from the Corporation in 1791. Both were sold in 1800 for £650 and £800 respectively.

10, 11 (*opposite*) Liverpool courts built in the early nineteenth century. The top court, *c.* 1820, is of unusual triangular shape and adjoined Back Chester Street on the edge of the former Toxteth Park Estate. The irregular shape of the building site gave its residents the use of substantially more space than the typical rectangular court, seen below.

14 (*below*) Williamson Square, Liverpool. The square and adjoining streets was one of the leading developments on Corporation land in Liverpool by the well-to-do Williamson family. Begun in the 1740s houses were still being built in the square in the later 1770s.

15, 16 St James Square, Manchester, originally developed *c.* 1740 (*above*). Although largely altered, the square itself survives to illustrate the small size of many squares in the major provincial towns. It was 'intended when built . . . for the residence of persons of a respectable situation in life'. Shepley Street, Manchester (*below*) showing houses built in the great boom of the 1780s and '90s. Edward Shepley, brickmaker, was active both as developer and builder in this part of Manchester. These houses had three storeys, with cellar, two rooms per floor, and originally most had individual or shared yards at the rear.

and the like, were land promoters everywhere, because of their special skills and experience. Since so many were speculative builders, understandably a few of the more successful and ambitious moved into the potentially profitable if risky field of land promotion. In doing so, most combined erection of a few houses on the land with the disposal of sites to other builders.

Another group among the promoters were men who handled land in the course of their main profession or occupation. Surveyors, who gained a specialized knowledge of land values and the needs and wishes of builders, and could use their own professional skill in handling building land projects, sometimes acted as developers. More important were attorneys. Because of their intimate knowledge of the local property market, their access to credit and their ability to handle conveyancing, land promotion was for them the ideal business enterprise. Their role was particularly important in Liverpool at the beginning of the nineteenth century, but dealings in building plots by attorneys are traceable almost everywhere at the end of the eighteenth and beginning of the nineteenth centuries.

Merchants, well-to-do tradespeople, professional men or manufacturers were to be found in land development throughout the eighteenth century. This type of developer appeared in every town. In Manchester and Hull, merchants and people in other important trades, such as brewing, dyeing or shipbuilding, dominated the supply of building land. The role of such people reflects a tendency for the land developers, particularly those handling larger projects, to be men of greater substance and possibly higher social standing than the majority of men who were principally builders. Even the craftsmen who moved into land development had often handled successively several small building projects. They were thus well-known in the community, had possibly amassed some savings and were thought creditworthy. The distinction is particularly noticeable among those outside the building trade. While merchants and men in similar leading commercial or industrial occupations were important as land promoters, investment in building houses tended to be left not only to craftsmen but to victuallers, grocers, tailors, to small manufacturers in the industrial centres, and mariners and shipwrights in the ports.

Men with considerable capital or access to credit were attracted into land development because of its potentially high profitability.[3] On the other hand, the bigger financial outlay and often greater risks in land promotion compared with the typical small-scale building project tended

[3] On the profitability of land development, see below, ch. 6.

to direct those of less substantial means into investment in houses. One indication of the greater financial burden involved in land promotion is the tendency for developers to work in partnership, while builders nearly always acted singly. Sometimes the syndicate represented a pooling of financial resources; alternatively one or two of the partners provided the technical skill and experience needed for planning and surveying the ground or conveying the plots, others the initial finance. Partnerships involving one or two craftsmen, an architect or surveyor and one or two men outside the building trade, such as an attorney or merchant, were common.

Loan capital for land development was obtained in the town itself, in the surrounding countryside or in a neighbouring town. The sources were well-to-do tradespeople, attorneys, the occasional manufacturer or professional man, and leisured men and women. Exceptionally, original owners made credit available to developers on their estates. Borrowing outside the region was not unknown in the later part of the period, particularly when several thousand pounds or more was needed. During the outflow of capital from London into the provinces at the beginning of the 1790s, one of the biggest builder-developers in Manchester, Joshua Reyner, obtained credit from several sources in London and the Home Counties.[4] A leading attorney-developer in Liverpool in the 1800s, Robert Kirkpatrick, raised credit both in Lancashire and London.[5] But despite the growing emergence of a national capital market, such loans were unusual even in the beginning of the nineteenth century.

There were several ways in which original landlords or developers might dispose of sites to builders. The simplest form of site conveyance was to sell the freehold outright. Perhaps about half of all building land in the leading provincial towns was conveyed in this way. In six of the leading provincial towns—Nottingham, Hull, Portsmouth, Leeds, Leicester and Brighton—most land was conveyed freehold for a down payment. The sale of building plots in perpetuity for an annual rent, sometimes called a 'fee-farm rent', was common in Manchester, Bath and Bristol. Long building leases for at least several hundred years (such as 999 years) were the other main tenure in Manchester and were also used in Sheffield. All these tenures gave the builder and his assigns the indefinite use of the land, provided the rent was paid.

There were two other types of building lease. One involved the use of lives as the basis of the length of the lease. At Plymouth leases were granted to builders for three lives, that is, the lease lasted until all three

---

[4] P.R.O. E112/1530/232: I owe this reference to Dr J. R. Ward; P.R.O. B1/110, p. 182.
[5] P.R.O. PL.6/103 f.17.

people named in the lease had died; in Liverpool sites were conveyed for three lives and a further twenty-one years. The annual rents were small, but a cash payment or 'fine' was made both initially, for a new lease, or to replace one or two of the lives. Plots were also leased for between forty and 120 years (and particularly ninety-nine years), in which case the land and its buildings were surrendered to the ground landlord at the end of the term. He could then let the houses if they were in reasonable condition. In addition to the outstanding instance of London, leases for ninety-nine or 120 years were normal in Birmingham, and were used in Bath and Sheffield. Similar leases for a fixed number of years were used by some estates in most of the other leading provincial towns.

Landlords and developers had varying opportunities to influence the character of their building estates and the nature of the houses erected by the builders. Development projects might be purely for occupation by the most numerous group of the urban population, the craftsmen. petty tradesmen, artisans and unskilled labourers, or schemes in which most of the social strata of the town were to be represented, including at least a few of the more substantial merchants or manufacturers or professional men, or developments in which well-to-do residents were to be numerically strong. If land was intended mainly for artisan housing, it was tempting for the promoter to make a street plan which allowed the maximum number of plots. A project mainly for the well-to-do needed not only large houses (and hence big plots) but wide streets, and perhaps squares, crescents and pleasure grounds. This was partly because open spaces were believed to be healthy, being 'airy' or providing 'ventilation'. Residence in squares was fashionable throughout the period, and crescents were widely popular from the 1780s.

In fact the promoter was influenced in his choice by the income and social status of the people from whom the demand for houses would come. In the few towns with a big wealthy class, such as London, Edinburgh, Bath and Bristol—and Brighton and Cheltenham at the end of the period, land promoters had the opportunity to create estates for well-to-do residents. Surviving buildings in all these towns are physical evidence that many promoters made this choice.

Elsewhere they were more restricted. In most provincial towns the independent, professional and prosperous trading and manufacturing groups were a minority. Some of them preferred an important main street site for their dwelling, which might be combined with warehouses and workshops. They would not expect to live in a select residential area. Consequently the occasional square or select thoroughfare tended to be an island in a sea of small artisan housing. An example was the tiny St. James's Square in Manchester, laid out about 1739. According to a statement in 1820, it was 'intended when built and has been ever since used for the residence of persons of a respectable situation in life', in contrast to property to the south 'being narrow streets and formed altogether or chiefly of houses of an inferior description inhabited by a numerous population composed of persons of the lowest classes of life'.[6] Any scheme involving a small group of select streets typically took decades to be fully built. Towards the end of the period, at the beginning of the 1790s and after 1800, they became more numerous. This reflected the growth of the well-to-do trading and manufacturing class, and the emerging tendency among some of the richest inhabitants, such as the merchants in the ports, to separate residence from place of work. Even so, the acquisition of sites by builders was very slow.

There were both advantages and disadvantages in the development of building land for better-class housing.[7] If the sites were let on 'short' leases of forty, sixty, eighty, ninety-nine or 120 years, the estate would benefit from the higher reversionary value of larger houses. On the whole this type of property was more soundly built than artisan housing. There was a greater possibility of the houses being handed over in a suitable condition for renting by the landlord when the ground leases expired. But the main financial attraction was the higher ground rent or sale prices obtainable, because of location in a wide road, square or crescent, amenities such as good-quality paving or drainage, and the reputation for respectability created by the control of building by covenant, and exclusion of nuisances. In Birmingham sites forming a crescent on the north-west edge of the town in the 1790s were advertised

[6] P.R.O. PL.6/111 ff. 93-7.
[7] The two following paragraphs examine developments for well-to-do residents from the financial aspect. Occasionally English building land promoters were motivated to some extent by other influences: according to Professor Olsen, some of the landowners in the West End of London felt that artisan housing was not regarded as desirable, whereas high-quality dwellings redounded to the credit of the landowner: 'the ideal estate would serve both to ornament the metropolis and to remind its inhabitants of the splendour of the House of Russell or Grosvenor': D. J. Olsen, *Town Planning in London: The Eighteenth and Nineteenth Centuries* (New Haven, 1964), p. 16; again it is believed that at Bath the elder John Wood, who was primarily a developer, aimed to re-endow Bath with Roman monuments as well as to make money; but it would be right to assume that the main (and in most cases the sole) motive of most provincial promoters was financial.

MAP 3. (*opposite*) *The growth of Manchester, 1750–1820* (references on the map are to landowners, except for the districts of Hulme, Charlton Row and Ardwick, and street names etc.)

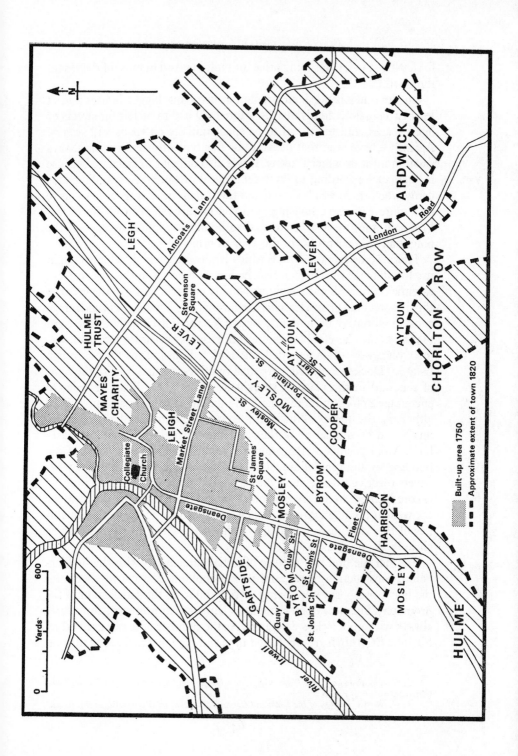

ARDWICK

LEGH

Ancoats Lane

LEVER

London Road

HULME TRUST

Stevenson Square

MAYES CHARITY

AYTOUN

CHORLTON ROW

LEIGH

Portland St.

Hart St.

AYTOUN

Market Street Lane

Mosley St.

MOSLEY

COOPER

Collegiate Church

St James' Square

BYROM

Deansgate

MOSLEY

HARRISON

GARTSIDE

Quay St.

BYROM

St John's St.

Fleet St.

St John's Ch

Deansgate

MOSLEY

River Irwell

HULME

Yards

600

0

Built-up area 1750

Approximate extent of town 1820

for letting at twice the going price for building land in most of the rest of the town.[8]

On the other hand, land promotion involving bigger houses had at least two possible disadvantages. More land had to be left for streets or open spaces, and more had to be spent initially on roads and sewers. Again, we have seen that demand for this type of property was always small in most provincial towns. It was also difficult to estimate because it fluctuated according to the level of local prosperity, expanding suddenly when trade was booming and the beneficiaries were able to move into more expensive housing, and contracting when times were bad. Probably, too, the market tended to be over-supplied because of the potentially higher profits of this type of project.

There were several methods which landowners and developers might use to influence the character of the houses erected on their estates. An essential requirement in avoiding shoddy construction was the grant of the sites freehold or on a leasehold tenure of sufficient length to encourage substantial outlay by builders. Leases for three lives without the right to renew (and therefore for an uncertain time-span) or for less than, say, forty years were often regarded as too brief. Thus in 1791 the St. Aubyn Estate at Dock introduced 'perpetual right' leases (that is, with the right of renewal) in the place of straight leases for three lives 'in order to encourage a more endurable mode of building than at present prevails'.[9] Otherwise the quality of the houses erected seems to have been generally unaffected by the nature of the site tenure, whether freehold or leasehold. More positively, the promoter could influence the nature of the building by the type of amenities which he provided. Wide and well-paved roads, gardens, good drainage, and possibly a church were an encouragement to the erection of larger and more substantial houses for the well-to-do. High ground rents which normally accompanied amenities of this kind discouraged artisan housing, which had to be built as cheaply as possible.

Another method was the use of initial agreements with the builders before construction began, and the withholding of a conveyance until the house or houses were partly or fully built, to the satisfaction of the promoter. This was done sometimes with artisan property, and nearly always with upper-class dwellings. As the number of leases granted by Sir John St. Aubyn grew between 1755 and 1772, it was decided to grant

---

[8] C. Norton, *Proposals, with Plan and Specification, for building the Crescent in Birmingham* (Birmingham, 1795), p. 8.
[9] R. N. Worth, *History of the Town and Borough of Devonport* (Plymouth, 1870), p. 49.

builders their leases after instead of before construction to try to ensure that the dwellings were built more uniformly.[10]

Covenants in the lease or sale, or the initial building agreement, were a general means of influencing the work of builders. These regulations varied from town to town, and sometimes from estate to estate. In leasehold promotions it was common to require the builder to erect within a fixed period, such as two or three years, of the date of the lease or the agreement. This was usually accompanied by a clause concerning the minimum sum to be spent on the house or houses, the figure being usually more than £100, and sometimes rising to several thousand pounds when a row of substantial houses was envisaged by the landlord. Together these two clauses were intended to secure the ground rent by ensuring that building took place within a reasonable time.

Clauses concerning the structure of the buildings to be erected varied greatly in detail. Attention was often paid to the front of the houses merely in general terms, to ensure that they were properly aligned with adjoining dwellings, and were of similar height. Where stricter uniformity was desired, as in the case of larger housing, the builder would be asked to follow an elevation attached to the lease, or to construct the front according to strict specifications regarding materials to be used. Covenants concerning the construction and materials (apart from the facade, and general requirements regarding the use of the best brick and timber) were inserted much less frequently, and were often absent even in cases in which the housing was clearly intended to be of high quality. Such clauses might stipulate the thickness of the outer walls and the dimensions of the summers, joists, wall plates and rafters. The prohibition of trades which would be likely to cause a nuisance to neighbouring households was frequent.

On the whole the tendency to try to control building by means of covenants was growing. They were becoming more detailed in relation to the development of land for more substantial housing, and their use was spreading in promotions planned for more modest terrace property. In part this probably reflects an improvement in the quality of estate administration, with the increasing use of trained surveyors and efficiency and the professional training of agents.[11] In the case of estates leasing building land over most of the period, such as the Corporations of Liverpool and Nottingham, it is possible that earlier mistakes were being learned, though of this there is no explicit evidence.

[10] H.L.R.O. Main Papers 1774, 15 April: the date of the change is not stated.
[11] C. W. Chalklin, 'Urban Housing Estates in the Eighteenth Century', *Urban Studies*, V (1968), p. 81.

It may also have been the result of a desire among a growing number of townsmen for higher standards in the urban environment, which appeared in many ways. One major indication was the spate of local acts setting up improvement commissions, with powers controlling such matters as lighting, watching, nuisance removal, street widening and paving. Some covenants, such as those for building within a stated period, were intended to ensure the payment of rents, while others, such as those controlling nuisances, reflect in part the expected wishes of most of the new residents. The same may be true of covenants concerning the erection of facades uniform with those of adjoining houses, and perhaps according to a prepared elevation. They reflect thoroughness on the part of the estate officials, but they may also have been intended to satisfy the wishes of a growing number of house owners and occupiers. Among the well-to-do, accommodation in substantial houses in terraces built according to a uniform elevation was increasingly fashionable because of the prevailing architectural conventions. It is understandable that intending residents of smaller houses in turn should want such standards to be applied to their own homes. The land promoters may have been expressing rather than shaping the evolving needs and demand of the urban community.

2 THE LOCATION OF BUILDING LAND

As far as is known, builders in the major provincial towns were never hindered by a lack of plots on which to work. This was in spite of the fact that the population of nearly all these towns grew several times between the 1740s and 1820, and there were periods such as the 1770s, about 1785–93, and after 1800, when the number of inhabitants in some centres increased by as much as 40 or 50 per cent in a decade or less. In several towns building in some locations was impossible as a result of physical barriers or legal constraints, but elsewhere in the town there was normally a choice of districts in which to build.

Throughout the period, land suitable for building existed in nearly every town both within and beyond the limits of the built-up area. Inside the town, innumerable gardens and yards were used for additional housing; more rarely within the built-up area, closes of between half an acre and several acres in size were available for building. In the larger towns of medieval origin and the fewer which had expanded in the Tudor and Stuart eras, the land plots behind houses in the central thoroughfares which had existed for centuries, disappeared piecemeal now as the population grew. Leeds, Hull and Nottingham were all medieval towns which provided these innumerable tiny building sites during the later eighteenth century. The towns which had grown partic- ularly rapidly in the early eighteenth century, such as Birmingham and Portsea, show a similar pattern. As they continued to expand and the value of the more central plots grew, so gardens attached to houses erected in earlier decades in what had been the outskirts were converted for building as occasion offered.

This type of development was universal. Sometimes the business use of part of the front premises led to the erection of workshops or a warehouse on the land in the rear. More often it became sites for cottage tenements. Many gardens had survived the initial period of develop- ment in the street for the convenience or pleasure of the occupants of the front house, or simply on account of lack of demand for back cottages on the outskirts of the town. But a change in the personal circumstances of the owner or the arrival of a new one led eventually to the land being used for building. If the builder was the occupier as well as the owner of the front house, then there was the benefit of tenanted house property within immediate reach; more generally there was the advantage of the existence of basic amenities such as water pumps.

On a bigger scale, land sufficient for one or more streets of houses was occasionally made available by the demolition of old buildings with large gardens. Closes comprising up to several acres within the built-up area became available for building sites from time to time. Some had been used for grazing livestock or market gardening; more rarely they had been orchards, bowling greens, or industrial enclosures of various kinds. These needed the planning of new streets and staking out of plots. The survival of several closes well within the built-up area was particularly common among some medieval towns, such as Nottingham and Leicester and, to a lesser extent, Hull. Presumably expansion since the Middle Ages had not been rapid enough in these towns for all or most of such land to be used by the eighteenth century, and much sur- vived until the 1780s or later.

In towns which had been tiny centres or mere villages in the Middle Ages, the occasional parcel of land which was by-passed as the town spread outwards in the early or mid-eighteenth century eventually became available to builders. However, it was comparatively rare for substantial plots of land to be by-passed in this way, unless some legal obstacle prevented it or the owner had purely personal reasons for keeping it open. Normally land came on the market while it still lay on the outskirts of the town because of the financial attraction of its sale or leasing for building.

When builders were active there was always a keen demand for land at the centre. Prices for plots were often at least two or three times those for sites of the same size on the urban perimeter. Because of their proximity to the central business area they were valuable for commercial premises more often than not combined with residences, such as shops, merchants' counting houses, and warehouses where goods might be inspected. Professional men, particularly attorneys, but also sometimes surgeons and teachers had a preference for such locations. In Hull a new street, Parliament Street, was developed within the line of the medieval walls in the later 1790s: in 1822 its occupants were chiefly solicitors and merchants.[12]

The majority of the faster-growing towns, such as Liverpool, Manchester, Birmingham, Sheffield, Sunderland, Bath, Bristol and the dockyard towns, housed most of their population by building outward from the early eighteenth century. In Hull and Leeds and probably in Newcastle and Leicester, most houses erected before about 1780 were placed within the old physical boundaries. In the greater expansion thereafter most building land was found outside the town. Places of work in the middle of the town were still within easy reach. Even after 1800 the outskirts of most towns were generally under a mile from the centre. They were within easy walking distance of the docks or quays in the case of seaports, or the market places and main business streets in the inland towns.

Although dwellings in central locations were still desirable for some occupations, accommodation on the outskirts was for many people an advantage. As towns grew, so did their trade, manufactures and communications. Innumerable small workshops or factories or canal wharves were sited in the outskirts, providing increasing employment. Promotions which were predominantly for the well-to-do tended to be sited on or beyond the edge of the town, partly on account of the space required, but also because of the attractiveness of a house apart from the bustle of central areas and the liking for a high site with views of the country or the sea. This was particularly important at Brighton, Bath and Bristol. It also influenced the location of the occasional land promotions in towns such as Liverpool and Birmingham by the 1790s.

[12] *V.C.H. Yorks.: East Riding*, I, p. 448; R. G. Battle, *New Directory for Kingston-upon-Hull* (Hull, 1822).

MAP 4. (*opposite*) *The growth of Hull, c. 1780–1820*

(Names refer to landowners)

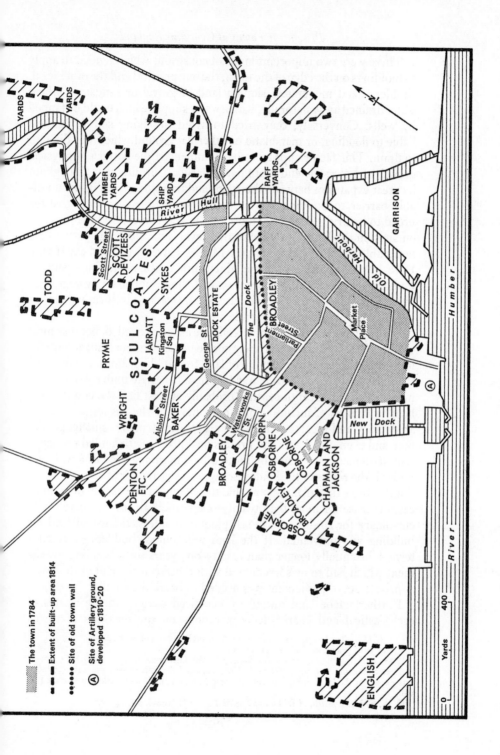

YARDS

YARDS

TIMBER
YARDS

SHIP
YARD

RAFF
YARDS

River Hull

GARRISON

Scott Street

SCOTT
DEVIZES

TODD

SYKES

Old Harbour

PRYME

S C U L C O A T E S

JARRATT

Kingston
Sq

DOCK ESTATE

The Dock

BROADLEY

Parliament
Street

Market
Place

Humber

WRIGHT

Albion Street

BAKER

George St

(A)

DENTON
ETC.

BROADLEY

Waterworks
St

CORPN.

OSBORNE

New Dock

OSBORNE

BROADLEY

OSBORNE

CHAPMAN AND
JACKSON

River

ENGLISH

Yards

0   400

The town in 1784

Extent of built-up area 1814

Site of old town wall

(A) Site of Artillery ground,
     developed c1810–20

There were two important kinds of constraint which tended to apply to buildings on the edge of the town, the one physical and the other legal. Builders liked moderately sloping land of gravel or sandstone where water drained away naturally, with a water supply which could be tapped by wells. Conversely, they tried to avoid low-lying soil which was liable to flooding, or marshland or other flat ground which was difficult to drain. This factor appears to have influenced the pattern of physical growth at Leicester, and more particularly at Birmingham throughout its great expansion between the 1700s and the 1780s.[13] An insurmountable barrier to building was naturally posed by rivers that were too broad to be bridged, or even more by the sea. It increased the pressure on sites on the landward edge of the town. The effect was particularly noticeable at Liverpool, where the Mersey barred westward expansion. Here by the beginning of the nineteenth century the fines paid by builders for leasehold land were several times higher on average than the sums paid even for the purchase of *freehold* land in Birmingham, an inland town of almost comparable size.[14]

Building land usually became available as it was needed, because most of it was held by individuals or corporate bodies with no insurmountable legal restrictions on the disposal of land for building. For the individual the most likely legal obstacle was tenure of his estate under strict settlement. In the eighteenth century probably at least half the country was held in this way, including not only most of the big estates of the aristocracy and greater gentry, but also those of many smaller gentlemen and even merchants and professional people with landed property. The settlement was generally created by a marriage deed or a will, and under it the rights of the landowner were restricted for at least a generation.[15] In particular he was unable to sell any of the estate, or in most cases to lease for more than twenty-one years.[16] In towns where it was customary for landowners to sell plots to builders, the use of land for building was prevented. If the land was rented, builders expected a term substantially longer than twenty-one years for a building investment which had to be surrendered with the site at the end of the lease. A private act of parliament was needed to break the entail.

Further, glebe land owned by beneficed clergy and the estates of ecclesiastical and charitable corporations on the outskirts of towns

---

[13] *V.C.H. Leics.*, IV, pp. 155, 195–6; on Birmingham see below, pp. 81–9.
[14] For land prices, see below, pp. 140–6.
[15] G. E. Mingay, *English Landed Society in the Eighteenth Century* (1963), pp. 33–4; A. E. B. Simpson, *An Introduction to the History of the Land Law* (1961), pp. 220–23; estate acts passed in the later eighteenth century reveal many examples of settlements created by will.
[16] W. S. Holdsworth, *A History of English Law*, VII (1925), pp. 241–2.

could only be let for up to forty years, under acts of 1571 and 1572, and archbishops and bishops were restricted to twenty-one years or three lives.[17] In London some corporations, such as St. Bartholomew's and St. Thomas's Hospitals, ignored the statutes and let land for longer terms, but in the provincial towns corporate bodies and clergy normally secured private acts to allow them to let on building leases.

Before the inflation of the 1790s, a private act for this purpose cost an individual or a corporation between about £150 and £300.[18] In the case of a large development of 10 or 20 acres this was a relatively minor charge, which with the other costs involved in land promotion was amply recovered in the long run from the increase in the value of the land. The spate of estate bills passed through parliament for lay, ecclesiastical or charitable property from the 1760s suggests that numerous owners were not deterred by the cost from submitting a bill.

In the case of small properties of up to 3 or 4 acres, the cost of a bill was sometimes a deterrent. For example, the agent of Earl Fitzwilliam was doubtful in 1790 whether it would be more profitable to let about 5 acres on the edge of Sheffield for building rather than for use as allotments, because the former would need an act costing £300.[19] To take a hypothetical case in which a bill cost, say, £200 and the remaining charges on the promotion (for such items as roadmaking) were £100 or £150 an acre: on a 2-acre scheme the charges relating to the act would double or almost double the total cost; on a 10-acre project they would be one-fifth or less of the outlay.[20] In fact no common pattern is visible concerning little parcels of development land, and acts were obtained for closes much smaller than that with which Fitzwilliam's agent had to deal.[21] This was because other costs varied sharply, and the rents or sale prices received for the land differed according to its location. But these occasional parcels were far too small to have much effect on the total supply of building land available on the edge of the town.

---

[17] 13 Eliz. c.10 and 14 Eliz. c.11, c.14: provided the amount let did not exceed ten acres, that the accustomed rent was reserved, and the property not let in reversion: R. Burn, *Ecclesiastical Law*, I (1763), pp. 649, 651–2; B. A. S. Swann, 'A Study of Some London Estates in the Eighteenth Century' (London, Ph.D. thesis, 1964), p. 13.

[18] E.g., H.L.R.O. draft acts 1764, 1766, 1786; Sheffield Archives: Fitzwilliam MSS., letter from Bowns to Fitzwilliam, 1790: I owe this reference to Miss K. Youel.

[19] Fitzwilliam MS., 1790.

[20] For examples of outlay on building projects, see below, pp. 146–54; no accounts or estimates covering the cost of a bill and the other charges of development survive for a small project, to allow me to quote an actual case.

[21] Four years before the proposed Fitzwilliam development was discussed, an act was obtained to enable the Vicar of Sheffield to let about two acres for building: H.L.R.O. Committee book 30, pp. 37–9; in 1774 the Vicar of St Nicholas Newcastle was given the power to let less than three-quarters of an acre on a 999-year lease: J. Brand, *The History and Antiquities of the Town and County of the Town of Newcastle upon Tyne I*, (1789), p. 595.

Occasionally the conversion of agricultural land to other profitable uses (though still less remunerative than for building) delayed the availability of other small amounts of land. Garden plots were in demand from townsmen by the later eighteenth century, and their leases generally fetched high prices. Ropewalks occupied parcels contiguous to housing in the ports and their shape facilitated building development. There were often personal motives delaying the conversion of land for building use. But while such factors may have delayed the release of some land for one or two decades, the continued pressure of applications from developers or builders or simply the change of ownership through death or sale of the whole estate was sufficient to bring the land on the market eventually. Meanwhile the profitability of land development ensured that land was obtainable from other owners. Where much of the land on the perimeter of a town was held by one owner, as at Liverpool (the Corporation), Sheffield between the 1770s and 1800 (the family of the Dukes of Norfolk), and at Dock (the St. Aubyn family), land appears to have been let for building by the estate as it was needed.

Common land or ground where grazing rights were exercised for part of the year by freemen or inhabitants of the town was sometimes more difficult to release for building. This was because of the rights of a large number of people in the property. The Nottingham case is well-known. The town was surrounded on three side by fields subject to common rights which hindered the natural outward expansion of the town. But there was much potential building land within the ring of common fields for most of the eighteenth century, and land beyond the fields, still within easy walking distance of the market place, became available after 1796.[22]

In contrast to Nottingham, most centres had no commons in the neighbourhood, or they lay beyond the expanding limits of the town (as at Manchester, Birmingham, Liverpool, Newcastle and Brighton). At Leicester the South Field with its common grazing rights was enclosed in 1804, well in advance of large-scale expansion in a southerly direction,[23] In two instances, at Bath and Sunderland, the physical direction of building expansion was marginally affected by the presence of a common on the edge of the town, but ample alternative building land was available.[24] Generally speaking, in the large towns commons and common rights did not create a problem for builders in our period.

[22] See below, pp. 113–22.
[23] *V.C.H. Leics.*, IV, p. 197.
[24] At Sunderland the Town Moor barred expansion southwards from the middle of the eighteenth century, but builders worked westwards instead along Sunderland High Street to Bishopwearmouth, a very natural tendency in view of the proximity of the River Wear to this development.

4

The Greater Urban Estates: Bath, Birmingham, Manchester and Liverpool

The next two chapters discuss some of the principal features of land promotion in each of the seven provincial towns. Two themes in particular are discussed. One is the extent to which the physical pattern of ownership of the potential building land affected the way the landlord or developer laid out the streets and building plots. On the edge of each of the four towns discussed in this chapter there were numerous little properties consisting of no more than one or two closes. There were also estates including large singly-owned blocks of land of between 30 or 40 and 80 or a 100 acres. These offered the possibility of large-scale urban planning. Some owners did not take this opportunity, allowing developers to promote independently one section after another of their property.

A second theme is that of the people in each town involved in the supply of building land and the functions they performed. To what extent were original owners active in initiating land promotion, in laying out streets and plots, providing the basic amenities and possibly trying to control the nature of the buildings erected through the use of covenants? Or how far was their role passive—were they content merely to sell or lease their land to developers? In this case, what range of functions did the developers perform? It is the differing roles of original owners, the presence or absence of developers, and the tasks assumed by one or other, or both of them, that provides much of the variety and interest in a detailed study of building land promotion.

In none of these four towns was there much freehold land promotion. Sites were conveyed either on short building lease (predominantly in Birmingham and Liverpool, and in parts of Bath), long building lease

73

or in perpetuity for an annual rent (in the case of Manchester and parts of Bath). Liverpool leases were distinctive in that their grant was accompanied by the payment of a fine, and the rents were small. The role of custom was clearly important in Liverpool, Manchester and Birmingham. In both Liverpool and Birmingham one big estate set the pattern for leasehold development which others followed. In Manchester leases in perpetuity or for more than several hundred years reflected the general practice in south-east Lancashire.

I BATH

As late as 1700 Bath lay almost entirely within its medieval walls, enclosing an area of about 40 acres. There was also some small ribbon development along the four main roads out of the town. In these ways the city was typical of many English walled towns of medieval origin, such as Canterbury, Exeter or Chichester. In the first two decades of the eighteenth century several small new streets were laid out on the edge of the town. But the history of Georgian Bath, with its squares, crescents and terraces of substantial stone houses for its well-to-do seasonal visitors and leisured residents, spreading far beyond the limits of the old town, begins in the later 1720s.

The first two major promotions, which helped to set the pattern for later developments, were begun in 1727 and 1728. A development on lands called King's Mead, belonging to a local charity, St. John's Hospital, between the west walls of the city and the River Avon, involved two squares and three streets.[1] The other was the famous promotion of Queen Square to the north-west of the city by the elder John Wood.

Land promotion and building was more subdude between about 1735 and 1755. There was a surge of activity between about 1755 and the early 1770s, which abated for only three or four years at the end of the 1750s and beginning of the 1760s. Architecturally, the highlights of these years were the Woods' promotion of the King's Circus and the adjoining streets, and in the later 1760s the designing of the Royal Crescent by the younger Wood. They were accompanied by at least a dozen smaller promotions, each involving one, two or three terraces. Whereas earlier building had been on flat or gently rising land to the west or on the south-east of the city, developers were now using the sharply changing

[1] Ison, *Bath*, p. 33.

MAP 5. (*opposite*) The growth of Bath, *1725–1820*

74

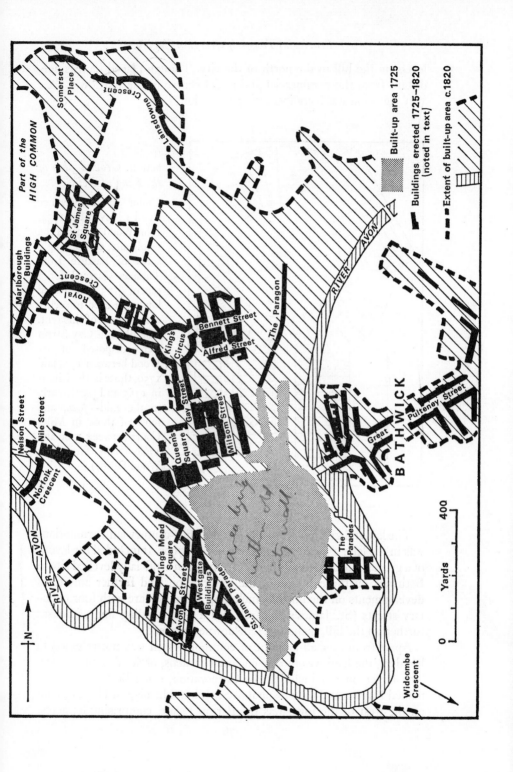

Part of the
HIGH COMMON

Somerset Place

Lansdowne Crescent

St James
Square

Marlborough
Buildings

Royal Crescent

King's
Circus

Bennett Street

Alfred Street

The Paragon

RIVER AVON

Nelson Street

Nile Street

Norfolk
Crescent

Queen's
Square

Gay Street

Milsom Street

Great Pulteney Street

B A T H W I C K

RIVER AVON

King's Mead
Square

Avon Street

Westgate
Buildings

St James Parade

The Parades

Widcombe Crescent

0   400
Yards

N

Built-up area 1725

Buildings erected 1725–1820
(noted in text)

Extent of built-up area c.1820

levels on the hill to the north of the city. Though placed increasingly distant from the commercial and social centre in the old town, their very elevation was a compensating attraction.

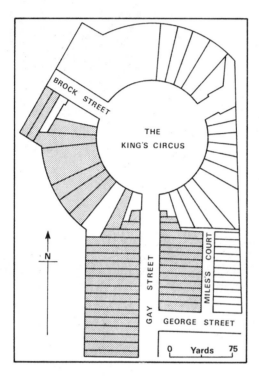

MAP 6. *Ground plan of the King's Circus*

Under a conveyance dated 1 November 1754, John Wood acquired the whole site, comprising 9 acres of pasture from Thomas Garrard for a rent of £163. The shaded lots were used to secure the payment of this rent. The plots in Gay Street were disposed of by Wood between 1755 and 1759, those in the Circus in 1755 and particularly in the mid-1760s, and most of those in Miles Court between 1766 and 1768 (Bath Guildhall: Wood Deeds)

The last and greatest wave of the eighteenth-century land promotions was in the later 1780s and beginning of the 1790s. It included the layout of a great suburb by the Pulteney family on an artificially levelled site in Bathwick on the east side of the River Avon, and further ambitious developments on the hillside, including a large square with four tributary streets (St. James's Square), and a long winding line of houses further up the hill, including Lansdowne Crescent.

Apart from a small amount of common which was not released to builders, the land was mostly enclosed gardens, orchards and pasture. The larger owners included the Corporation, some Berkshire gentry named Haynes and the Hospital of St. John. The biggest block of land on the west of the town was the Barton Estate, comprising 85 acres, belonging to a family whose representative in the 1720s was Robert Gay, a London barber surgeon, and in 1790 Sir Peter Rivers Gay of Winchester. An even larger singly-owned tract lay on the east side of the Avon, the property of the wealthy Pulteney family, represented by the statesman the Earl of Bath until 1764, and then in succession by his brother, his cousin by marriage, and the latter's daughter, Henrietta Laura. But the key figures in land promotion in Bath were the developers. Many of them were local building craftsmen or architects, tending to be those whose earlier success in the construction of individual houses gave them the capital, or the access to credit, to launch into the more ambitious field of land promotion. Often they worked in partnership. One of the large terraces built on Lansdowne Hill at the end of the 1780s, Marlborough Buildings, was promoted by a tyler and plasterer named Fielder, a carpenter called Broom, and a statuary mason named Thomas King, on several acres obtained in 1787, and the three of them were joined by another craftsman, Richard Hewlett, in the development of the nearby St. James Square at the beginning of the 1790s.[2] We have seen that craftsmen acted as land promoters in all the major provincial towns; their special role at Bath probably reflects their key significance in terms of wealth and standing in a community whose livelihood came from the accommodation as well as the entertainment of leisured residents and visitors. Attorneys and well-to-do tradesmen in Bath or the neighbouring towns such as Bristol or Bradford-on-Avon were also developers.

Occasionally the original owners leased or conveyed in perpetuity for an annual rent direct to builders. Usually these were small promotions involving single rows of houses.[3] The major exception was the Pulteney Estate, planned by the architect Thomas Baldwin for the family, and part of which was leased in small parcels direct to builders by Miss Pulteney.[4] Normally one or more developers intervened. It is true that landowners sometimes approved (and occasionally may have decided) the general plan and elevations of the houses or stipulated the minimum amount to be spent by the developer and his builders. For example, when Gay leased the site of St. James' Square in 1790 to the four craftsmen, they were required to spend at least £10,000 'in erecting buildings and finishing stone messuages', but they themselves employed an architect, John Palmer, to design the layout and elevations for the

[2] Bath Guildhall: deeds re. 1 Marlborough Buildings; Philip George MSS. bdl. 28.
[3] Bath Guildhall: leases re. Bladud Buildings, 1755; deeds re. New Bond St.
[4] Ison, *Bath*, p. 38; P.R.O. E112/1938/633; Bath City Library: deed re. Laura Place; Somerset Record Office DD/X/SAL C/1537: deed re. 12 Great Pulteney St.

Square.[5] Generally, the tasks of disposing of the sites, preparing the ground for building, supervising and sometimes financing the builders were done by the developers.

Everything as regards land promotion on the typical estates of eighteenth-century Bath was bigger and more costly than in the average developments in the other provincial towns. Much land was dedicated for open space, for squares and gardens. Building plots had a frontage of 20, 22 or 24 feet to accommodate the substantial stone terraced houses which, at prices of between £500 and £1,500, each cost several times more than the typical front house in an industrial town. Rents per plot were high: on one street in Corporation property, Milsom Street, developed in 1763 on ninety-nine-year leases, rents were between 4d. and 5d. a square yard, compared with a price of 1½d. in main streets on the edge of Birmingham in the 1760s.[6]

Because of the expense of amenities and levelling on the hillsides, and sometimes the provision of credit to builders, development costs were particularly high at Bath. One minimum indication of the outlay of developers on some of the bigger promotions is obtainable from the size of loans they raised. In October 1771, the younger Wood owed £8,000 to a Bath man and a Bristol man secured on the ground rents of his developments since his father's death in 1754.[7] The developer of Lansdowne Crescent, a coachbuilder named Charles Spackman, borrowed a total of £14,317 from a Bath banker in 1790 and 1792, the loan being secured on the ground rents.[8]

An important visible legacy of the work of developers is the detailed uniformity of the facades of houses in terraces and crescents. It was founded on the careful regulation of the builders through the covenants inserted in the conveyances of the plots by the developers. This may be seen in a typical terrace development in the mid-1760s called Westgate Buildings ⟨*see* plate 2⟩. The developers, a tailor and the widow of a hosier, both of Bath, not only expected the builders to erect 'with all convenient speed' a substantial stone and timber house 22 feet wide in a line with the rest of the houses in the block, but to erect the whole front and particularly the windows and doors 'of such height and with such ornaments and in such manner agreeable to a design and plan drawn of the elevation of the whole pile of building' which both the developers and builders had signed to show that they were in full agreement.[9]

[5] Ison, *Bath*, p. 171.
[6] Bath Guildhall; Milsom St. leases.
[7] Bath Guildhall: Wood deeds 11 October 1771.
[8] P.R.O. C12/202/30; I owe this reference to Dr Ward.
[9] Bath Guildhall: deeds re. 11 Westgate Buildings.

Nothing is known about the degree of supervision of the builders, but the numerous surviving terraces of Bath, with their elegant proportions, their carefully-designed cornices, architraves and other features, assuredly confirm the success of the developers in this respect.

Two instances may help to illustrate the role of Bath developers. The first relates to the development of Bennett Street on the Corporation Estate in the mid-1770s. In 1763 the Corporation granted a lease for three lives or ninety-nine years of a garden of about 2 acres adjoining the Lansdowne Road on the north side of Bath to a local victualler. Later it was acquired by a Bradford-upon-Avon clothier, Richard Atwood, who was granted a building lease for 102 years on 30 August 1774. The lease was 'to the intent and purpose that he the said Richard Atwood shall and will with all convenient speed lett out the same premises to be built thereon agreeable in all respects to the plan already agreed to by the said Mayor ... and the said Richard Atwood'. The Corporation and Atwood were to join in granting building leases of the plots, the Corporation receiving one-third of the ground rents. Atwood was to be 'at all expences for plans, writings, and preparing the ground for building'. Plots were laid out on each side of the new street with a frontage of 22 or 25 feet. In the leases builders were required to erect a stone or timber messuage before June 1775, according to an agreed plan 'under the direction and to receive the approbation' of Atwood. All offensive trades (some of which were named) were banned, as was usual in residential property of this type. The houses were duly erected within one or two years ⟨*see* plate 3⟩.[10]

On the far west of the town near the river, an attorney, Richard Bowsher, working with two craftsmen-builders, began a large development involving leases in perpetuity early in 1792, near the end of the great boom in land promotion and building. This centred on Norfolk Crescent ⟨*see* plate 5⟩. In the words of one of the builders, a statuary mason named William Lancashire speaking fifteen years later, Bowsher 'having taken a large piece of ground ... on a building lease at a large ground rent ... in the same year published ... certain proposals for building streets on the said piece of ground ... and invited your orator, your orator's said father Francis Lancashire and several other persons builders to meet him at a tavern dinner to take into consideration the said proposals'. Again, according to Lancashire, at the meeting 'in order to engage the several parties present in the said undertaking he promised to find them money as it should be wanted from time to time

---

[10] Bath Guildhall: deeds re. Bennett St. especially No. 1.

to cover in the houses to be erected on the same ground in a certain pile of buildings to be called Norfolk Place and that when the said houses were covered in he would advance or procure to be advanced for the purpose of finishing the said houses the sum of eight hundred pounds on each house'. Bowsher denied this, but confirmed that when building was in progress he advanced money to one of his fellow-developers who was watching construction 'to be lent by him to such builders as he in his discretion should think fit and where the repayment thereof would be safe', Lancashire receiving £462 9s. 6d. Lancashire and his father each leased a site for one house, and other builders did the same. After the financial crash of March 1793 many of the builders 'by reason of the pressure of the time became embarrassed' and stopped construction. The scheme was renewed by Bowsher over a decade later with the layout of two new streets, Nelson Place and Nile Street, another road in the original plan having been abandoned. Norfolk Crescent was still only half complete in 1810, when Bowsher tried a tontine subscription to carry on the work. It was eventually finished some years later, the houses being erected 'agreeable to the elevation plans and designs' of Bowsher.[11]

Georgian Bath is a unity, but it is a unity created by its building material, stone, and the classical uniformity of its architecture, not by its general planning. The division of the building land among a number of owners on the north and west of the city prevented the working out of any homogeneous plan. Furthermore, growth was slow: only about 5,000 houses were erected between the 1720s and 1800, or an average of about seventy a year, and one would not expect contemporaries at any time to plan on a big scale for a future demand which they are unlikely to have foreseen. Developers handled several acres at a time, and prepared schemes which were complete in themselves but often unrelated to neighbouring projects. Although on the large Barton Estate Queen Square, the Circus and the Royal Crescent were all planned separately, the Woods linked the Circus with Queen Square, and it was the younger Wood who linked the Crescent to the Circus. On the other hand, St. James' Square, planned in 1790 on the same estate by different developers, bears no relation to the Wood developments. It is significant that the one large area to be subject to a single plan, the Bathwich district, was promoted by a single owner and planned at a time when demand for housing in eighteenth-century Bath was reaching its peak, in the later 1780s.

---

[11] P.R.O. E112/1949/1032, 1015; Bath Guildhall: deeds re. Norfolk Crescent; Bowsher lent money to at least one builder in Nelson Place.

2 BIRMINGHAM

According to a writer in 1755, Birmingham 'stands upon the side of a hill forming nearly a half-moon, the lower part is filled with the workshops and warehouses of the manufacturers, and consist chiefly of old buildings, the upper part of the town . . . contains a number of new regular streets and a handsome Square'.[12] The comment reflects the nature of the physical growth of the town during the last half century. South-eastwards from the original settlement round the old market place, the Bull Ring, expansion had been discouraged by the floodplain of the River Rea; building moved north-westwards and northwards up the hillside on the more suitable sandstone, which was both well-drained and had plentiful supplies of well water. It was drawn particularly to the main lines of road communication with other parts of the Black Country, of which Birmingham was increasingly the metropolis.

The opening of the Birmingham Canal on the western edge of the town in 1770 stimulated further building on the west and north-west of the town during the great expansion of the 1770s. The significance of the proximity of a canal for house builders is illustrated by evidence given to the House of Lords in February 1771, when it was considering a bill for extending the Canal into the building estate of the Colmore family. Charles Colmore believed that this would increase the demand for building sites on his land, and his agent said that many people would take his land on building leases, but were waiting to see which way the canal was continued.[13] The bill was successful and the Colmore Estate was one of the principal suppliers of building land in the 1770s.[14]

There was persistent reluctance to build on the south-east side of the town, on the lowlying alluvial land which was subject to occasional flooding. To start development in 1767, one owner, Henry Bradford, advertised land free: four years later he was offering to let land for $\frac{3}{4}$d. a square yard, while sites on the north-west of the town fetched $1\frac{1}{2}$d. a yard at the same date.[15] It was not until the 1780s, when there was a further great population expansion and a canal was dug into the district, that there was a massive occupation of the land by builders.

Even in the boom of the 1780s and that of c. 1808–16, the majority of

---

[12] Quoted by M. J. Wise and B. C. L. Johnson, 'The Changing Regional Pattern during the 18th Century', *Birmingham and its Regional Setting* (Birmingham, 1950), p. 177; there were of course many 'workshops and warehouses of the manufacturers' in the newer part of the town.
[13] H.L.R.O. Committee book 19 (1770–72), p. 15.
[14] T. Hanson, *Plan of Birmingham* (1778).
[15] J. A. Langford, *A Century of Birmingham Life* (1870), I, pp. 107, 111, 305; B. R. L. Colmore and Gooch MSS.

sites were leased on the undulating higher land on the north-west, north and north-east of the town. Some of the high situations were attractive for their views of the country, but for most promotions in this area proximity to the main road and canal communications with the rest of the Black Country were more important. One large development in the later 1780s and beginning of the 1790s on high ground beyond the north-east of the town, the Ashted promotion, was advertised as being particularly healthy, 'not likely to be surrounded by buildings', and containing lots 'very inviting to ladies and gentlemen wanting a pleasing retirement'; it was also advertised as including 'many advantageous situations for manufactures or other business', and having a canal running through the estate.[16]

Until the mid-1740s, building land was supplied by at least a dozen owners, each scheme involving just a few acres. Freehold promotion was more common than leasehold. From the 1740s to 1780, during which period the town doubled in size, about half the building was located on two big properties.

One was owned by the Colmore family. An ancestor had been a mercer in the town in the early sixteenth century, and another had erected New-Hall, a large house about half a mile from the Bull Ring at the beginning of the seventeenth century.[17] The family had long left Birmingham and entered the ranks of the gentry. The other property, consisting of the demesnes of the manor of Birmingham, belonged to the Bishop of London, Thomas Sherlock, in the middle of the eighteenth century. His nephew, a Suffolk landowner named Sir Thomas Gooch, succeeded to it in 1764.

The Colmore Estate became available to builders under a private act of 1746. It set aside restrictions in family settlements by making binding on all heirs leases granted for up to 120 years.[18] It consisted of a large, roughly rectangular block of land on the north-west of the town, extending to about 100 acres, and at least three smaller parcels on the north and west of the urban perimeter. The manorial estate was leased to builders under the provisions of an estate act passed in 1766.[19] It comprised at least 150 acres in several large blocks on the west, south

---

[16] R. K. Dent, *Old and New Birmingham* (Birmingham, 1880), p. 208, and *The Making of Birmingham* (Birmingham, 1894), p. 227.
[17] W. Hutton, *A History of Birmingham*, 3rd edn. (Birmingham, 1806), p. 32.
[18] 20 Geo. 2 c. 16.
[19] 6 Geo. 3 c. 61.

MAP 7. (*opposite*) *The growth of Birmingham, 1750–1820* (names refer to landowners)

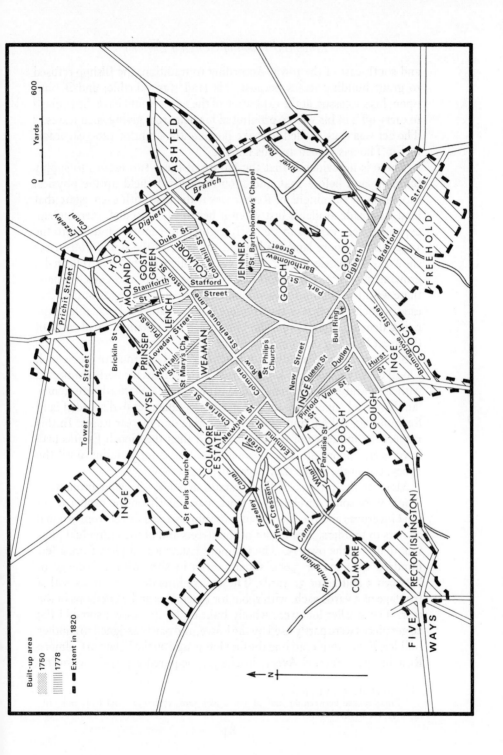

Built-up area

1750

1778

Extent in 1820

and south-east of the town. According to tradition, the Bishop refused to grant building leases because 'his land was valuable, and if built upon, his successor, at the expiration of the term, would have the rubbish to carry off'; in his will he prohibited his heir from giving such leases.[20] The act was thus needed to make possible the grant of 120-year leases by Sir Thomas Gooch and his heirs.

There is no evidence that the failure of these two estates to supply building land before 1746 and 1766 respectively held up the physical expansion of Birmingham. Rather was it the case with each estate that land was made available just when it began to be needed. Birmingham expanded very rapidly in the early eighteenth century, and before the 1740s the Colmore land lay beyond the edge of the town. Plot prices show no sharp rise during these years, which might have reflected a growing shortage of building sites[21]. In the case of the Gooch Estate, there was little building in Birmingham for most of the 1750s, and several estates, including that of the Colmore family, made land available in the rising demand after 1759. The Gooch act was obtained in advance of the great building development of the 1770s.

Smaller owners of building land included the Governors of the School, a local charity named the Lench Trust, two families formerly connected with local industry, Jennens and Weaman, and a Staffordshire gentry family named Inge. Only the last needed an estate act to dispose of land for building. All let land under ninety-nine or 120-year leases. In this respect the influence of the Colmore and then the Gooch Estates may have been important. The Weamans sold land for building until the 1760s, but in the 1770s they began making leases.

Most of the owners of these estates acted as the land promoters. There were some developers at work, particularly on the properties of the Governors and the Trust, but most plots passed direct from original owners to builders. The layout of the streets and of the individual plots was done by the owners. The Colmore Estate leased plots from a few hundred to 2,000 or 3,000 square yards in size, with a frontage of between 5 and 20 or 30 yards. These were intended for houses with a frontage of 5 yards each, with room for tenements and workshops in the rear. The smaller lots were wholly built on by the lessee; some of the larger pieces were partly used by the lessee, and partly assigned to another builder. For example, among the first lots leased on the Estate in Colmore Row in 1747, Samuel Avery, bricklayer, acquired a parcel measuring

[20] *V.C.H. Warks.*, VII, p. 8.
[21] Prices ranged between 6d. and 9d. per square yard, 1700–1720, and 6½d. and 11d., 1730–45, for freehold land.

20 by 50 yards: he erected four houses on half the land and conveyed the rest to a carpenter and joiner.[22] On the Gooch and Weaman properties the plots were on an average smaller.

For the two big estates this meant the disposal of many hundreds of plots over several decades. Between 1747 and 1794 there was only one year (1755) in which the Colmore Estate leased no sites; in other years the number of conveyances varied between one or two and sixteen or seventeen. The last of the building land was leased in the beginning of the nineteenth century. A small part of the estate nearest to the centre of the town was developed by the early 1750s, using existing lanes and two new streets aligned roughly parallel with one of them. Almost the whole estate is shown as planned with a pattern of streets on a map of Birmingham in 1778; probably the scheme had been designed in the early 1770s. This part followed a more regular gridiron pattern than the earlier section used for building; it included a church in a square and several streets about 20 yards wide.[23]

The slow disposal to builders of the Colmore Estate is partly explained by its size; it was also the result of its oblong shape, lying roughly at right angles to the north-west edge of the built-up area of Birmingham. The block of about 40 acres owned by Sir Thomas Gooch on the west of the town, which included the main wharf, was used more quickly. Again, a rough gridiron pattern was devised for the ten streets, based on two main streets lying at right angles. 139 plots were leased between 1766 and 1780, and of the remaining seventy plots, sixty-two were conveyed in the next decade.[24]

Three estates, those of the Jennens, Colmore and Weaman families, provided sites and money for a church on their land. The Gooch family considered doing the same. Charles Colmore provided 3 acres for a church and a cemetery, and £1,000 towards the building costs. Though piety may have been important, the proprietors were aware of the higher rents obtainable from sites near a church. When in 1772 the Weaman Estate gave a site for a church, the neighbouring Lench Trust agreed to an exchange of adjoining lands and to open a new street 'being desirous to assist in promoting so pious a design and apprehending that the building of a church upon the land of the said Dorothy Weaman and

[22] B.R.L. MS. 409278 and West Hagley MS. 85.
[23] B. R. L. Colmore MSS., including plan of the Colmore Estate numbering the building plots [undated: 19th century].
[24] Messrs. James and Lister Lea, Newhall St., Birmingham: Gooch MSS., including vols. entitled 'Survey of Birmingham Estates' [undated] and 'Sir Thomas Gooch Bart. Birmingham Rental' (1800).

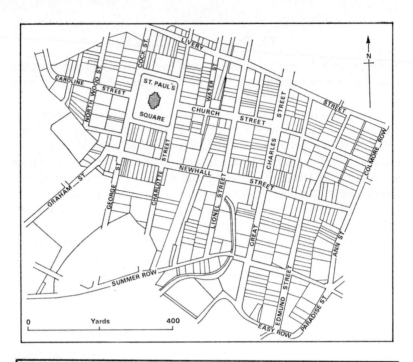

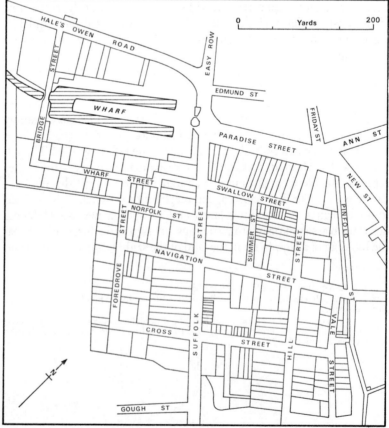

Mary Weaman will increase the value of such of their lands as lye adjacent to the said intended church . . .'.[25]

The great building and land promotion boom of the later 1780s and beginning of the 1790s involved new landowners as suppliers of land in addition to those estates which had been active in the 1770s. They included the Rector of Birmingham (who obtained the right to grant leases for up to 120 years under an act of 1773[26]), and several minor landowning families resident in Warwickshire or Staffordshire. Apart from the Colmore and Gooch properties, the largest source was the estate of the Holte family, who had been owners of Aston Hall in the adjoining parish of Aston since the early seventeenth century. At least 100 acres of the estate on the north-east of the town was used or partly used by builders between 1788 and 1820.[27] By the end of the 1780s it had passed to a son of the Earl of Dartmouth, Heneage Legge. The estates with previous experience of leasing direct to builders, those of the Gooch, Colmore and Inge families, continued to do so in the main, and the practice was followed by one or two of the estates disposing of building land for the first time.[28] However, the boom of the later 1780s and beginning of the 1790s, and to a lesser extent that of *c*. 1808–16, encouraged the demand for land for development as well as building purposes, for parcels of 2 or 3 acres (and sometimes more) which could be used for profitable subletting in small plots to other builders and

[25] B.R.L. MS. 324373.
[26] 13 Geo.3 c.6.
[27] 57 Geo.3 c.38.
[28] E.g. Prinsep Estate: B.R.L. Lee, Crowder MS. 1276.

MAP 8. (*above opposite*) *Plan of the Colmore Estate*
The first sites were leased in 1747. By 1750 most of Colmore Row and Ann Street had been lined with houses. By the end of the boom in the 1770s houses stretched as far as Lionel Street, the Church had been built, and the rest of the land surveyed for building.

MAP 9. (*below opposite*) *Plan of the Gooch Estate, 1796*
Part of the Gooch Estate, promoted from 1766, showing the building plots. One hundred-and-thirty-nine lots were leased between 1766 and 1780 to 128 different building tenants, and 62 out of the remaining 70 lots were disposed of in the 1780s.

perhaps some small-scale building by the developer. The attraction of this type of speculation during a time of rising demand for land is made clear by an advertisement in August 1792, relating to the Ashted development:

> 'The takers of land are sure to be recompensed either from a certainty of tenants, in case they are inclined to employ their money in building, or from the annual increase in the value of the land, if taken upon speculation, as is proved by those who have taken lots more than sufficient for their own purpose, having, in the short space of three years, gained, by letting to under tenants, at the rate of from ten to twenty pounds an acre per annum, over and above the rent they pay.'[29]

The leasing of land in larger parcels was found particularly on the newer building estates, which lacked the tradition of leasing in small lots direct to builders.

The biggest developer in Birmingham in this period was an attorney named John Brooke who was responsible for the Ashted promotion. In November 1787 he paid £4,200 for the assignment of building leases to about 41 acres on the Holte Estate. He 'laid open and converted the greatest part of the . . . land into streets for building houses to constitute the hamlet of Ashted', converted an existing country house into a chapel, and he and his sub-developers were soon leasing plots and building. To finance the scheme he borrowed extensively outside Birmingham. He obtained £3,000 from a resident of King's Bromley in Staffordshire, Samuel Barnett Esq., in May 1789, and further sums in 1790 and 1792: Barnett also lent £4,500 to one of the leading sub-developers, William Windsor, builder, in March 1791. Brooke also borrowed by notes and bonds from a fellow attorney in Stratford-upon-Avon who was also a banker, C. H. Hunt. The latter claimed that the debts amounted to £3,181 11s. 7d. in August 1793. Brooke's grandiose scheme was not typical of land promotion by developers in eighteenth-century Birmingham.[30] On the other hand, ambitious land development projects of this kind occurred in other towns in these years of rising optimism in the building and land development market.

Because of the exaggerated optimism induced by several years of construction at a high level, much of the land already surveyed and

[29] Dent, *Making of Birmingham*, p. 227.
[30] B.R.L. MS. 371948; Coventry R.O. Town Clerk's Deeds: 1960 Nov. box 4; P.R.O. B1/87, pp. 163, 198.

staked out, or lying perhaps in streets in which a few plots had been leased, remained unused. On the Colmore Estate, land in several streets marked out for building plots by 1750 remained unused until the 1760s, and the same happened after the great building expansion of the mid-1770s.[31] This characteristic was most marked in the last eighteenth-century boom. On the Gooch Estate, more than a dozen streets were laid out from the mid-1780s on a block of closes near the River Rea on the south-east of the town, and sites in the middle of the area surrounded by semi- or fully-developed streets were still being leased forty years later.[32] Presumably on account of the heavy debts which he had incurred, Brooke went bankrupt following the financial crisis early in 1793: much of his land remained unleased, and parts were still being conveyed after 1816.[33]

Little attempt was made to control the nature of the buildings erected by the use of covenants on the big estates before the 1780s. For example, in most of its leases the Colmore Estate merely specified the minimum sum to be spent and that the buildings were to be in a straight line or of three stories.[34] Neither the Colmore nor the Gooch Estate made much attempt to control builders for the rest of the period. Several of the landowners leasing building land for the first time from the 1780s were more thorough. In the case of some plots leased in 1790, Legge expected builders to follow detailed specifications regarding the dimensions of the timbers used in the interiors; the facade was to have a stone cornice and there were to be stone sills to the windows.[35] The use of detailed restrictive covenants was thus becoming more common in the later part of the period.

3 MANCHESTER

Most of the dwellings of seventeenth-century Manchester had been clustered in short winding streets near the Collegiate Church overlooking the River Irwell, and along two main roads leading out of the town, Deansgate and Market Street Lane. Between about 1700 and 1820, while the number of houses grew about twenty times, the town spread southwards and eastwards over a largely flat ground for about three-quarters of a mile in both directions. Suburbs were springing up beyond the main built-up area from the 1790s in the townships of Hulme, Chorlton Row

[31] S. Bradford, *Plan of Birmingham* (1750); Hanson, *Plan.*
[32] B.R.L. Gooch MSS. e.g. Coventry St. leases dated 1788 (4), 1789, 1808, 1813, 1826.
[33] B.R.L. Lee, Crowder MS. 481.
[34] B.R.L. Colmore MSS.
[35] B.R.L. Town Clerk's Collection 458-9.

and Ardwick. These were based on the presence of a canal or industry. At least one, that of Ardwick, attracted well-to-do manufacturers or merchants; in 1795 Aikin spoke of it as 'particularly distinguished by the neatness and elegance of its buildings' and as 'principally inhabited by the more opulent classes'.[36]

During the early and middle eighteenth century, building mostly took place on some fifteen or twenty closes, mostly in separate ownership. Promotions were consequently on a modest scale. During the great building expansion of the 1770s and the later 1780s and early 1790s, land promoters made particular use of five larger properties. Almost all of these were laid out in a gridiron pattern of roads still identifiable in the street plan of modern Manchester.

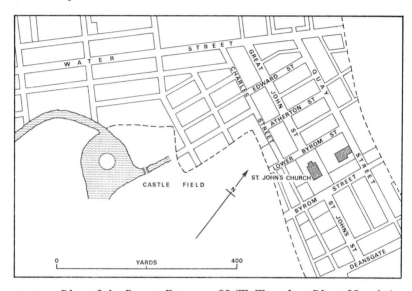

MAP 10. *Plan of the Byrom Estate, 1788* (T. Townley, *Plan of Lands in Manchester the Property of Henry Atherton Esq. and Miss Byrom*)

Probably the earliest to be taken up belonged originally to Edward Byrom, a partner in Manchester's first bank, who had inherited his estate. After his death in 1773, his two daughters and son-in-law continued the promotion of the estate for building. Their large block of land consisted of 80 or a 100 acres between Deansgate and the River Irwell on the south of the town. A single road, Quay Street, was laid across the property after 1735 to link Deansgate with a new quay on the

[36] Aikin, *Description*, p. 205.

Irwell. A member of the family erected a large house in the street by 1741, but building development was restricted until the 1770s. In 1768 Byrom founded St. John's Church, and by the early 1770s building had begun in four streets between the church and Deansgate. The presence of a church and the existence of a street 20 yards wide (St John Street) linking its square to Deansgate, several other neighbouring wide streets, and some much narrower thoroughfares, suggest the intention of a mixed promotion to include some larger houses. Development proved very slow, with plots being used faster in streets intended for artisan housing than on the grander roads. The whole block of land had been laid out for building by 1788, but about half was still unused in 1820.[37]

The promotion of 7 or 8 acres on the other side of Deansgate which was also owned by the family had a similar lengthy history. Byrom sold at least one plot as early as 1759, while others, each containing a few hundred yards, were sold from the 1770s, yet the family were still disposing of lots in the 1820s. Several acres were acquired from the Estate in 1795 by a merchant named George Phillips and an architect called McNiven, 'with the intention to dispose of for building': several lots were conveyed by them to builders in 1804 and spasmodically in the following years, but others were still on their hands in 1818.[38]

The exceptionally slow disposal of its building land by the Byrom Estate is partly explained by the fact that after the middle of the eighteenth century Manchester expanded eastwards more intensively than southwards. The other principal building estates lay across the main path of the growth of the town to the north-east, east and south-east. Another large piece of land on the edge of the town was the Chorlton Hall Estate, which stretched south-eastwards into the township of Chorlton Row. It had been owned by the Mynshull family at least since the 1720s. In 1769 a Scots army officer, Roger Aytoun, married Barbara, widow of Thomas Mynshull, who was said to have been 'greatly his senior'. It was he who began the development of the estate for building in the early 1770s. Simultaneously the estate became encumbered with mortgages, totalling £10,000 by 1775, when a receiver of rents was appointed to pay the interest. Their size in relation to the acreage being

[37] W. H. Thomson, *The Byroms of Manchester* (Manchester, 1968), III, p. 20; L. H. Grindon *Manchester Banks and Bankers*, (Manchester, 1877), pp. 24–6; W. Axon, *The Annals of Manchester* (Manchester, 1886), pp. 98–9; R. Tinker, *Plan of Manchester and Salford* (1772); T. Townley, *Plan of Lands in Manchester the Property of Henry Atherton Esq. and Miss Byrom* (1788); J. Pigot, *A New Plan of Manchester and Salford* (1819).
[38] British Rail: Hunts Bank Deed Room, Manchester, deeds of Manchester Central Station, 9, 67, 71, 90, 112, 129, 190, 194.

developed makes it unlikely that they represented entirely the costs of land promotion. It is tempting to regard them as at least partly the debts of a young spendthrift husband, and the disposal of building land as intended to meet the interest charges, but of this there appears to be no proof.[39]

In December 1772 Aytoun was advertising 'to be sold upon a chief rent' 'any part of a large quantity of building land between Garret Lane and Didsbury Lane', on which there were 'several remarkably fine

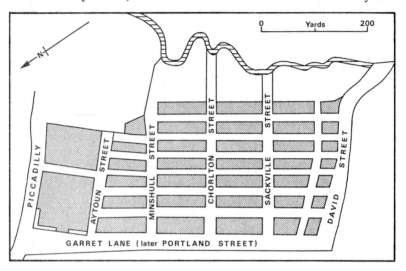

MAP 11. *Manchester land development in the 1770s: the early promotion of the Aytoun Estate, showing the typical street pattern in 1776* (plan by H. Oldham, see footnote 40)

situations for building upon'. This section of the property was laid out in a gridiron pattern of streets of various sizes. By 1776 about 15 acres had been taken up by developers and builders. The sale of lots continued in the 1780s, and in 1792 Aytoun, now resident again in Scotland, sold the rest of the estate to a syndicate of four men which included two merchants and an attorney. They paid £42,914 for about 70 or 80 acres, the Hall, three cottages and some barns. According to Robert Owen, then resident in Manchester, the purchase was made 'with the view of building a new town upon it', to include cotton mills as well as houses. Much, perhaps most of the land was still unsold when they split the property amongst themselves in 1808, and plots were being sold in the

[39] Axon, *Annals*, p. 98; Manchester Town Hall: deed bdl. 8/708.

later 1810s.[40] In 1816 the attorney-developer was advertising building land on a large board, saying that 'money will be advanced to any persons inclined to build'.[41]

A third large property lay to the north and east of the Aytoun land, belonging to Sir Ashton Lever of Alkrington, one of a family of minor Lancashire gentry who had owned the Manchester land since 1612. He began conveying land about 1770; according to his biographer, the aim was to help defray the expenses of a growing natural history museum which he had formed at Alkrington.[42] On the other hand, the land was well placed for building at the top of Market Street Lane, and in the expansion of the 1770s the disposal of lots would have been a natural action without pressing financial need. Through the 1770s Lever was selling small lots along the main road, but most of the property was conveyed in a few large parcels to developers. One close of several acres was sold before 1771 to a local merchant named Marsden Kenyon; this took nearly twenty years to be used by builders, the developers including Kenyon, his son and a soapboiler and drysalter who obtained 8,920½ square yards in 1785.[43]

A far bigger parcel comprising about 25 acres was sold by Lever in December 1780 to a minor local landowner, William Stevenson of Urmston. It was laid out in a gridiron pattern with streets of various sizes and a square, Stevenson Square, at the centre. The street pattern left small rectangular blocks of building land of between about 1,700 square yards and an acre. Once again, development was long drawn out. Despite the great building boom in the later 1780s and early 1790s, much of the land was still unused in 1794, and plots round the square were being sold by Stevenson's son in the next period of high activity in 1804.[44] Lever disposed of the rest of his Manchester land with other property to a merchant named Richard Powell in 1787 for £9,197 18s. 0d., which Lever used to pay off a debt of £11,000. Nearly all was soon in the hands of sub-developers in parcels of several acres each. They included

[40] *Manchester Mercury* 1 Dec. 1972; 'a plan of land near the Infirmary, the property of Roger Aytoun, Esq., by H. Oldham, 1776', *Manchester Notes and Queries*, VII (1888), p. 192; Town Hall Deeds T22; W. H. Chaloner, 'Robert Owen, Peter Drinkwater and the Early Factory System in Manchester, 1788–1800', *Bulletin of the John Rylands Library*, XXXVII (1954), p. 98.
[41] P.R.O. E112/1548/831.
[42] W. J. Smith, 'Sir Ashton Lever of Alkrington and his Museum, 1729–1788', *Transactions of the Lancashire and Cheshire Antiquarian Society*, LXXII (1962), pp. 61–82.
[43] British Rail: Mornington Crescent Deed Room: Piccadilly Station deeds 10, 10a, 10b, 13, 63 etc.
[44] H. Oldham, *A Plan of Lands ... the Property of William Stevenson Esq.* (1780); Manchester Town Hall deeds box 39C 2.

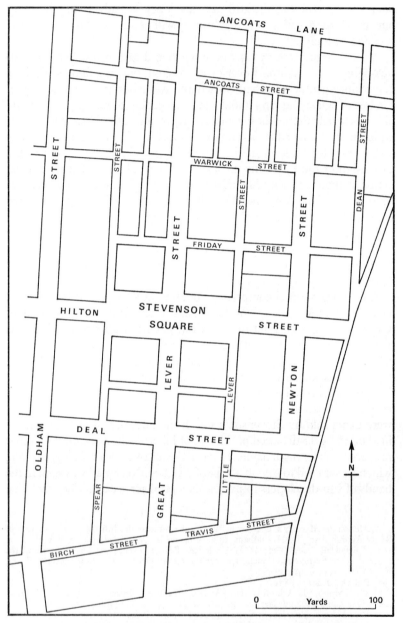

MAP 12. *The Stevenson development, Manchester: layout of streets in December, 1780, centring on Stevenson Square* (plan by H. Oldham, see footnote 44).

two brickmakers, a merchant and two dyers: again, their disposal of
the individual building lots was continued into the 1800s.[45]

The other larger landowners involved in building promotion were the
Legh family, who were Cheshire gentry, and the lords of the manor of
Manchester, the Mosleys, who had been landowners in the town before
1600. The Legh land, some 50 acres on the east of the town, was partly
laid out by the later 1770s, and was far from fully built on by 1820.
The Mosleys owned land in various parts of the town, but their principal
promotion was on 30 acres adjoining the Aytoun land. It had been laid
out by 1783 in the typical gridiron pattern of main thoroughfares and
back streets. Much of the land had been used by 1794, including plots
in the two main streets, Mosley and Portland Streets, which developed
a reputation as fashionable streets occupied by the well-to-do.[46]
Neither of the two estates was based on a square, as in the case of the
Stevenson scheme.

Much more than at Birmingham, Manchester witnessed an investment
in potential building land far in advance of construction. This was because of the important role of developers in land promotion. Landowners
occasionally sold small parcels direct to builders, particularly along the
main streets, but nearly all building lots had passed through the hands
of one, two, or even three or four middlemen. Typically, each paid a
rent to the landlord or another developer and hoped to make a profit
either by leasing it in sections to other developers or in small lots to
builders in order to receive a total rent much higher than the rent they
were paying. For example, a brickmaker, Edward Shepley, leased about
3 acres of the former Lever property from Richard Powell for 999 years
in March 1788, paying £59 8s. 5½d. a year, or about £20 an acre. Part
was subleased in 1790 and 1791: he contracted to lease 990 square yards
at £20 12s. 1d. in 1790, the equivalent of about five times the amount he
was paying Powell. Much of the land remained in his hands for between
fifteen and twenty years; in 1804 and 1805 Shepley was subleasing
parcels at rents which were the equivalent of about six times his own
ground rent.[47]

Developers who timed their promotions correctly found exceptional
opportunities for profit in the great boom at the end of the 1780s and
beginning of the 1790s. In December 1787, two dyers leased 18,407
square yards, again from Powell, at a rent of about £36. A few days later

[45] British Rail Mornington Crescent Deed Room: Piccadilly Station deeds.
[46] Manchester Town Hall Deeds bdls. 33 and 34, T.10, box 30A pcl. 7; T. Sharp,
A Plan of Lands . . . the Property of Sir John Parker Mosley Bart (1783); J. Croston,
County Families of Lancashire and Cheshire (Manchester, 1887), pp. 346–52.
[47] Piccadilly Station Deeds 39, 40, 45 etc.

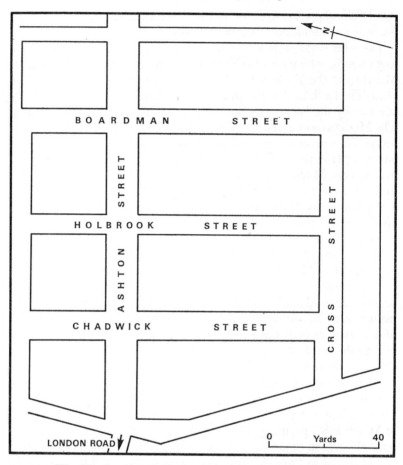

MAP 13. *The Shepley Development, Manchester*
Three acres leased by Edward Shelpley, brickmaker in December 1788. Part
was sub-leased as late as 1805 (Picadilly Station Deeds).

they subleased the whole for £34 10s. 0d. and a down payment of £50
to three grocers. At the end of 1789 two merchants subleased 16,295
square yards for £84 17s. 4¾d. a year. A month later a builder-developer,
Joshua Reyner, was assigned the whole 16,295 square yards, paying
their ground rent, and £59 8s. 2½d. a year to each of them.[48]

Others were less fortunate. Many of those who had acquired development land in this boom were left with it on their hands in the later

[48] Piccadilly Station Deeds 8.

1790s and were unable to find any builders to take it. For example, in December 1793 three cotton merchants and a Bury man acquired about 20 acres in Chorlton Row for building at a rent of £548 18s. 4d. Even in the building boom of the mid-1800s little or none of the land was sold, and in 1808 three of them assigned the whole estate to the fourth without payment since they had decided that the premises were not of any value (i.e. presumably over and above the fee-farm rent being paid).[49]

The contribution of landowners and developers to the preparation of land for building varied from estate to estate. Most of the biggest owners, Byrom, Legh, Mosley and Aytoun (before 1792), surveyed and staked out the roads and building plots in their property. At least two went further. One of the smaller owners disposing of land in the 1780s, William Cooper, not only planned but levelled the roads, while the work of paving, flagging and making drains was done by the developers on the property.[50] Adjoining him, the Mosley Estate had its streets paved and drained, charging each developer or builder for his share.[51] Some of the largest developers undertook the whole work of land promotion. In 1796, 1799 and 1803, James Mallalieu, merchant, and Benjamin Outram, engineer, acquired lands on which the total rent amounted to nearly £700; several plots were sold, but in 1806 a surveyor estimated that the developers would need to spend between £2,700 and £3,000 on levelling and making the streets and the common sewers and sluices on the remaining 10½ acres.[52]

There is no evidence that the precise arrangements made by landlords or developers for the provision of amenities made any difference to the speed with which building land was sold or leased, or the size of the rents. On the other hand, the choice of the conveyancing term certainly was important by the 1780s and 1790s. Most land was disposed of for a fee-farm rent or on a 999-year or similar long lease. Estates confined legally to leasing for a shorter term were at a disadvantage by 1790. In 1793 the Greene family applied to parliament for a private act to allow it to let property near Manchester for building for any number of years or in perpetuity. A power to lease for up to ninety-nine years under a family settlement of 1782 was claimed to be insufficient because 'in the neighbourhood of Manchester there are few persons, if any, who would

---

[49] Wilsons Brewery Deeds 11.
[50] Manchester Town Hall Deeds S.125, R.17.
[51] Wilberforce House, Hull: J. R. Pease MS. 123: Pease was a building owner in Mosley St., and in 1784 his agent paid Mosley £4 3s. 9d. for 'soughing' and £29 10s. 5d. as his share 'for the paving of the streets'.
[52] H.L.R.O. Main Papers 28 April 1806: Outram estate bill, and Committee book (1806), pp. 274-5.

97

be willing to treat for building leases for a less term than 999 years. And that the rents which can be procured upon grants in fee-farm are much more considerable than upon leases for any term of years, and upon leases for (999) years than upon leases for any shorter term.'[53] As a witness for another Manchester estate remarked to the House of Lords Committee in 1793, 'I would rather give three pence a yard for lands holden for a term of nine hundred and ninety-nine years, than one penny a yard for lands holden only for a term of ninety-nine years', because 'the prejudice of the people in that part of country are such, that they would not build upon so short a term.'[54]

For the same reason, the trustees of a corporate estate, the William Hulme Trust, applied to parliament for a private act in 1795.[55] It was reported to the House of Lords that much of the property was unbuilt, and a map of 1794 shows two closes belonging to the Trust well situated for building within the built-up area of the town; the delay in their use may have been the result of this legal difficulty.[56] The Trust had secured an act to lease for ninety-nine years in 1770, and it is likely that builders' preference for longer leases or grants in perpetuity had been hardening during the 1770s and 1780s, and the practice was more general than at an earlier date.[57]

An important contrast between Birmingham and Manchester is the greater role played by developers in Manchester as middlemen between the original owners and the builders. Estate layout in Manchester was generally done by the owners, or in two or three cases by developers such as Stevenson who acquired very large parcels. Thus much of Manchester, like Birmingham, was developed in large land blocks consisting of a gridiron pattern with an occasional square or church at its centre.

4 LIVERPOOL

By the early eighteenth century Liverpool land promoters and builders were working far beyond the streets of the mid-seventeenth century town. As late as about 1660 it had consisted of seven streets (with a few side lanes and alleys) in the shape of a double cross, above the River

---

[53] H.L.R.O. Main Papers 1793: Greene estate bill.
[54] H.L.R.O. Committee book 37, 1792–3, p. 111.
[55] H.L.R.O. Main Papers 30 March 1795: Hulme estate bill.
[56] Green, *Map of Manchester* (1794).
[57] H.L.R.O. Main Papers 5 March 1770: Hulme estate bill.

MAP 14. (*opposite*) *The growth of Liverpool, 1725–1820* (names refer to landowners).

EVERTON

Built-up area 1725

Extent of built-up area c 1820

0   Yards   600

E · V · E · R · T · O · N

(TOXTETH PARK)

C · O · R · P · O · R · A · T · I · O · N

River — Mersey

King's Dock

Old Dock

Frederick St

Sparling St

Park Lane

Cleveland Sq

St. James's Street

Great George Street

Great George Sq

Kent Sq

Harrington St

Upper

Rodney Street

Mount Pleasant

Brownlow Street

Clarence St

Seel Street

Duke Street

Cropper St

Bold Street

Cable St

Drury Lane

DERBY

CROSS

St. CROSS

Preston St

Clayton Square

Williamson Square

Lime Street

Gloucester Street

Russell Street

Seymour St

Hill

London Road

St. Anne Street

Byrom Street

Soho Street

Chatham Street

Abercrombie Square

Mosslake Fields

CROSS

PLUMBE

St Pauls Square

Rigby St

EARLE

TYRER

Edmund St

Mersey. All the roads had existed in the fourteenth century. Houses extended a mere 300 yards from north to south, and a shorter distance eastwards from the waterfront. By the 1720s a new network of streets had appeared between the southern edge of the original settlement and the town's first dock, built between 1709 and 1715. Houses were already appearing to the south of the dock, and for 200 or 300 yards on the rising ground to its east.[58]

During the next hundred years the urban area grew some ten or fifteen times. It spread southwards beside the Mersey for a further 1,200 yards, and eastwards up steadily rising ground for about the same distance. Northwards the expansion was slower.[59] Over half the building was located on the Corporation Estate. In 1672 the Corporation leased about 1,000 acres for the same number of years from a local landowner, Lord Molyneux. During the next century it was gradually converted into closes following successive leases of numerous parcels for three lives and twenty-one years. Part of it was used for building. In 1776 the descendant of Lord Molyneux, the Earl of Sefton, granted it outright to the Corporation for only £2,250. Thus, as a supplier of building land in this period, the family was restricted to the Toxteth Park Estate lying beyond the southern limits of the Corporation land. By its long lease and later purchase, the Corporation became by far the largest corporate promoter of building land in England during this period. On the north side of Liverpool, land was supplied by a number of smaller properties belonging to the Earls of Derby, minor Lancashire gentry and Liverpool merchants.[60]

On two or three of these estates, landlords dealt directly with the builders. On the Corporation Estate, it had become the established practice by the 1730s and 1740s to work through developers, and the Sefton Estate followed suit in the 1770s when the Toxteth Park property was made available for building. Developers thus played a key role in land promotion in Liverpool. For most of the eighteenth century they comprised the usual range of local notables, including many merchants, professional men including attorneys, and the occasional craftsman. By the beginning of the nineteenth century attorneys were becoming more

[58] J. Touzeau, *The Rise and Progress of Liverpool* (Liverpool, 1910), p. 283; *V.C.H. Lancs.* IV, pp. 1, 30; *Plan of Liverpool* (1725).
[59] This was probably the result of the fact that in the eighteenth century the docks stretched further southwards than northwards, not of different landownership.
[60] H. T. Hough, 'The Liverpool Corporation Estate', *Town Planning Review*, XXI (1950), p. 242; Aikin, *Description*, p. 374; J. A. Picton, *Liverpool Municipal Records (1700–1835)* (Liverpool, 1907), p. 137; British Rail: Hunts Bank, Manchester Deed Room: Lancs. and Yorks. Railway deeds 2891, 2925, 2941, 2950, 2987; Liverpool R.O. Council Minutes XI: 21 April 1760.

and more important in building development, working closely with craftsmen-builders to whom they supplied credit. For example, in August 1813 a joiner named Simnor mortgaged two houses in the London Road to two solicitors who were the developers, Statham and Hughes, 'because the said Robert Simnor is indebted unto the said William Statham and Thomas Hughes for the purchase of the said land and for advances made to the said Robert Simnor and other persons at his request to enable him to erect and build the messuages . . . and for advances made to the said Robert Simnor on other accounts and the interest thereon,' the debt totalling £1,223.[61] Sometimes an attorney was in partnership with a surveyor, architect or craftsman, the one providing the money and handling the conveyancing, the other the practical work of laying out the ground and possibly supervising the paving and making of the sewers.

The nineteenth-century historian of the building of Liverpool, J. A. Picton, condemned the lack of proper estate planning on Corporation property in the eighteenth century. Speaking of its building land promotion on the south-east of the town between 1725 and 1769, he bemoaned 'its zigzag winding streets, the land laid out too deep in some cases, too shallow in others, with angles of every imaginable form'. From the 1770s he noted that the opportunity had been lost to lay out the rest of the Corporation Estate like contemporary Edinburgh.[62] If Picton had in mind an estate similar to that of Edinburgh New Town, predominantly for well-to-do residents, based on wide streets and squares, his point was hardly justified, since middle-class demand for such a development was not great enough in Liverpool. Some *sections* of the Estate were formally planned. It is true that the Corporation never prepared a general plan for the future layout of its whole property. Some of the major roads just followed the line of the existing lanes between the closes into which the waste had been converted. Other roads varied in width, reflecting the fact that the land alongside had been planned for building at different times. For example, in the words of a contemporary guide book, Duke Street, one of the most fashionable streets at the end of the century, 'increases in width as it ascends'.[63] This was because the upper parts of the street had been laid out more recently. The initiative for building land development tended to come from the lessees of the individual closes. They were thus responsible for its timing. While the proposed street layout was subject to revision by a

[61] Liverpool R.O.: deeds 698D.
[62] J. A. Picton, *The Architectural History of Liverpool* (Liverpool, 1858), pp. 31, 37.
[63] W. Moss, *The Liverpool Guide* (Liverpool, 1797), p. 20.

Corporation committee and officials, minor roads were often planned without reference to neighbouring promotions.

One reason for the absence of unified building development was that the method of leasing the closes when in agricultural use placed difficulties in its way. Leases were for three lives and twenty-one years subject to an initial fine and small annual rent, and with the right to replace lives, or renew the full lease, on payment of another fine. Consequently the financial interest of existing tenants was far greater than holders of land under an agricultural lease for seven, fourteen or twenty-one years who paid a rack rent but no fine. The problems involved are illustrated by the largest scheme planned by the Corporation, concerning about 60 or 70 acres known as the Mosslake Fields. After a gridiron street pattern centring on a square was devised by the Corporation surveyor in May 1800, the consent of the lessees had to be obtained, arbitrators had to be appointed to value land needed to be exchanged or surrendered so that the regular layout could be effected, and an exchange and purchase of land for a boundary road had to be made.[64] Individual cases of land exchange or surrenders involving compensation for road widening or access had been handled by the Corporation for many decades, but the scale on which they would have been needed would have been some deterrent to the making of a unified scheme of this size at an earlier date.

It would be wrong to assume that the Corporation generally took little interest in the building development of its estate. As early as the 1740s, a Committee of Views considered each application for a grant of land and made a report to the Council; the Council minutes contain numerous references to piecemeal road widening by negotiation with existing lessees, and to new roads being planned on the Corporation initiative. Among the business dealt with by the Council in 1777, for example, was an order on 2 April to the Committee of Views to note and report any new streets being laid out for building by lessees which were narrower than the Council had agreed, and to buy land from several owners in a street called Park Lane to widen it; on 5 November the Council agreed to spend £164 on buying out the interest of a lessee in some land, because it was 'greatly for the interest of the town to have a road thro' it'.[65] From the 1780s and 1790s the Corporation began evolving schemes for the layout of two or three parts of its estate, on the south-east edge of the built-up area. Each involved about 20 or 30

[64] P. Mathias, 'The Liverpool Corporate Estate: A Study of the Development of Housing in the Moss Lake Fields of Liverpool 1800–1875' (Liverpool M.A. thesis School of Architecture, 1957), pp. 178–83.
[65] Liverpool R.O. Council minutes X (1738–55), XI (1756–76), and XII (1776–90).

MAP 15. *The layout of the Liverpool Corporation Estate*

Part of Liverpool in 1821, showing the extent of street planning by the Corporation. The unbuilt Mosslake project is shown on the southeast edge of the town. Smaller unified schemes centring on Rodney Street and Great George Square, respectively, are also seen. Less control is visible on the land east of the Hay Market, where the smaller streets were laid out without reference to those on neighbouring developments (from Sherwood's *Map*, 1821).

acres, and the property of several lessees. One concerned the Rodney Street district: on 4 February 1801 the Council allowed a tenant in Hope Street (parallel with Rodney Street) to change three lives in his lease, on the understanding that a new street was to be opened on the south side of the land 'as in the general plan for the neighbourhood'.[66]

From the 1780s the Corporation was taking an increasing interest in the buildings erected and the nature of the amenities provided. When it

---

[66] Liverpool R.O.: Council minutes XIII; it is likely that an area of about twenty-five acres centred on Great George Square, once held by three lessees, was also developed subject to a Corporation plan: this is suggested both by the regular layout of the district with the Square as its nucleus, and a Corporation minute (4 May 1803) for special covenants in leases in the district regarding nuisances and the enclosure of areas by iron palisades.

appointed a General Surveyor, Charles Eyes, in 1786, he was expected to 'set out the buildings according to the exact dimensions expressed in the lease. That where any elevations of buildings, or streets, are to be executed to a regular design, the Surveyor shall inspect the design and attend the course of the buildings that the same may be properly executed agreeable to it.' Further, he was to make plans of all new roads and lay them out, see that the streets were properly levelled and that the drains and sewers had least falls.[67] In the same year it decided that all future leases should contain a clause declaring them void if the tenants let the cellars of buildings as separate dwellings.[68] The surveyor was equipped with a growing salaried staff. On 7 September 1803, the Council decided that as its surveyor, John Foster, was handling a growing amount of business he needed more assistance; Foster was to have another clerk as a draughtsman and another to superintend outdoor business. Foster had been obliged to hire a draughtsman himself for the last two years and the Council agreed to repay the salary he had been given of sixty guineas a year.[69]

Some of the Corporation's covenants were difficult to enforce. As an ultimate weapon it refused to grant a lease or add a new life if its requirements were not obeyed. For example, on 4 March 1801 it refused to sign a lease of a new house in Lime Street for which permission had been given the previous August until a butcher's shambles had been demolished. On 7 October it decided that building leases should be withheld if previously agreed paving instructions had not been carried out. Later it began requiring bonds from its lessees to ensure compliance. On 13 August 1810 an attorney, John Leigh, was required to enter into a bond for £300 to ensure he did the paving in some streets on land he was leasing, when asked to do so by the surveyor.[70]

The efforts of the Corporation to enforce covenants is illustrated in the case of a substantial land promotion involving about 14 acres on the eastern edge of the estate begun in 1799. Among other covenants, the developer, James Gill, was to pave to the satisfaction of the Committee for Pavements, and to make sewers if the Committee should think them necessary. Gill proceeded to dispose of plots to builders. In 1805 he was instructed by letter to do his paving, but seven years later he admitted

---

[67] Mathias, 'Liverpool Corporate Estate', p. 116; subsequent grants to developers noted in the minutes suggest that the original proposals for plans often still came from the developers, though the surveyor could revise them, e.g. Council minutes, XII (7 Oct. 1789), XIII (12 Sept. 1797).
[68] Liverpool R.O. Council minutes, XII (1 Feb. 1786).
[69] *Ibid.*, XIII.
[70] *Ibid.*, XIII and XIV.

that part was still not done. When a sub-developer applied to the Corporation for a lease of about half an acre of the land, he was refused because Gill had not complied with the covenants about paving and sewers, and had allowed cellars to be separately let. As regards sewers, Gill claimed that he had had no instructions before 1812, but he admitted that he had been at fault over the paving and that some of the builders had allowed separate occupiers to live in the cellars. He tried to defend himself by saying that 'he believed that there was scarcely a

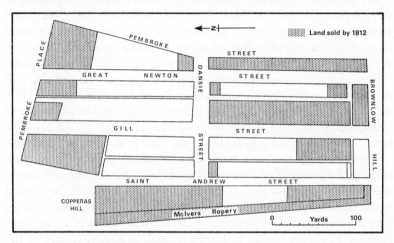

MAP 16. *The development of James Gill from 1799, showing land sold by 1812* (P.R.O. C13/723/11)

lease under the Corporation of Liverpool in which all the covenants had been complied with'.[71] Other evidence suggests that paving and the making of sewers generally was done with more speed than by Gill, though the cellar covenant was widely ignored. On the other hand, the case reveals the difficulties which the Corporation had to face from time to time in handling recalcitrant developers.

The Corporation also played a part itself in the provision of amenities. At the beginning of the nineteenth century part of the work of levelling and paving the new streets and making sewers was done by the Corporation, part by the developers. In both cases they recovered the cost from those to whom they assigned their land. For example, in the case of the Mosslake scheme the Select Improvement Committee

[71] P.R.O. C13/723/11.

decided in March 1815 that the sewers should be made by the Corporation at the expense of the principal lessees, and that the latter should see to the levelling, paving and flagging.[72] In the later eighteenth century, the Corporation handled some of the paving work in new streets, but the role of developers, and the extent to which the Corporation tried to recover the cost from developers or builders, is not clear. In the middle of the century there may have been no uniform policy in these respects.[73]

Throughout the period, intending developers began by applying to the Corporation for a building lease for three lives and twenty-one years. Normally they had either possessed an existing lease for some time or just acquired it from a lessee with the specific intention of developing the land for building. The amount of the fine paid to the Corporation for a building lease depended not only on the size and situation of the land but also on the number of lives in being (if any) on the lease to be surrendered. Fines were nominal if all the lives were in being, but substantial if two or three had dropped. In the case of a recent purchase of an existing lease, payment to the former lessee was much more substantial unless the lease had nearly expired. The layout of the land was agreed with a committee or the surveyor. The developers made their profit through charging fines for the plots which they passed to the builders. The Corporation granted the builders individual leases for three lives and twenty-one years, in return for a rent of 1s. per yard frontage when the houses had been erected. A special feature of the building lease to the developer was an undertaking by the Corporation that it would grant such leases to the builders without a fine, provided application was made within six months of the assignment of the plot by the developer.

Some developers undertook several projects in the course of their career, and a few occasionally had two or three promotions in hand at one time. As elsewhere, capital might be locked up in a project for many years because all the plots took time to be sold. Naturally the biggest developments involved the greater outlay and often took two or three decades to complete. Gill paid the former lessee of his land £5,670 in 1799. Although many plots were conveyed to builders during the next few years, he was still disposing of some of them in the later 1820s.[74] In April 1813 an architect, Edward Eyes, agreed to pay another

[72] Mathias, 'Liverpool Corporate Estate', pp. 184–5; Liverpool R.O. Treasurer's accounts (1804–14) *passim*; P.R.O. C13/652/32 and 723/11; Liverpool R.O. deeds 865A etc.
[73] Liverpool R.O. Corporation Ledger 1789–98, Council minutes X (7 Nov. and 5 Dec. 1750, 5 Mar. 1755), XII (11 May 1790 etc.).
[74] Liverpool R.O. deeds 407B.

developer holding a Corporation lease £11,000 for a close of 6 or 7 acres on Mount Pleasant; in addition he had to open, level and pave the streets at his own expense to the satisfaction of the Corporation's surveyor.[75]

But the majority of developments were on a more modest scale. Some promoters formed syndicates and moved from one scheme to the next. Their method of working may be seen by a study of two small projects. Between 1795 and 1803 Charles Eyes, surveyor, and John Foster, architect, 'dealt together in the buying and selling of lands, tenements etc.' This had involved agreements to buy for building from existing lessees a field on Brownlow Hill for £2,400 in 1795, and another parcel for £900 in 1798. Foster claimed that in fact Eyes had made no financial contribution to either purchase. In 1802 they decided to buy a field near Brownlow Hill; presumably because all the lives on the existing lease were in being, the fine of £3 3s. to the Corporation for a building lease was nominal, whereas the former lessee was paid £2,800. The lease was granted subject to a plan regarding street layout and paving already agreed with a Corporation committee. The lease was made out in the name of Foster, but Eyes offered to take a half share, to pay half 'of all expences whatsoever in laying out, levelling and paving the streets', to superintend this work and handle the sale of the plots. According to Foster, Eyes paid no money nor did any work; consequently he himself was 'obliged at a great loss and inconvenience to employ his principal clerk . . . to superintend such works and paid the whole expense thereof'. Eyes' only contribution had been to dispose of three small lots for £377 14s. 6d. and to help the clerk mark them out on the ground.[76]

The other case concerned a Warrington attorney, John Fitchett, a local attorney named Robert Kirkpatrick, and a surveyor, Edward Eyes. Kirkpatrick was well known in Liverpool for his land promotions in the 1800s. He drew heavily on sources of credit outside Liverpool. Before 1807 he was helped by a London merchant firm; then between March 1807 and 1810 Kirkpatrick was accommodated by a Lancaster cotton manufacturer, Adam Unsworth, who claimed to be owed at least £3,742 by the end of 1809; then up to August 1810 Unsworth persuaded another London firm to accept bills which he procured for Kirkpatrick. Kirkpatrick also borrowed on mortgage in Warrington through a fellow-attorney.[77] Eyes was involved as a sub-developer in the Gill project and may have been the man described as an architect who agreed to pay £11,000 for the land on Mount Pleasant in 1813. Fitchett was a

[75] P.R.O. C13/2887.

[76] P.R.O. C13/652/32; Liverpool R.O. Council minutes XIII (14 April 1802).

[77] P.R.O. PL6/103 f.17 and E112/1545/710. In 1808 Fitchett was trying to borrow locally for their schemes.

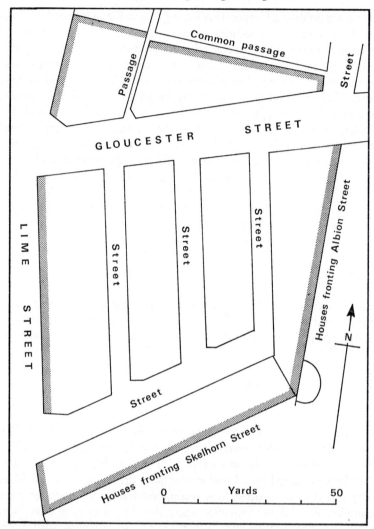

MAP 17. *The Lime Street development*

Apart from Gloucester Street, the roads were planned on this 2-acre development without relation to the adjoining properties (Liverpool R.O. Deeds 719C).

stranger in Liverpool who appears to have joined the partnership for financial reasons. In 1808 they agreed to buy jointly lands in Liverpool for selling in smaller lots to builders, in the usual way. A couple of schemes were considered; one involved the purchase of a large tract of the Mosslake Fields for £10,000: Fitchett was to advance the first third of the purchase money, while the other two handled the land. Then on 15 September Fitchett, on behalf of the syndicate, bought at auction the lease to 2 acres in Lime Street for £2,868, or 5s. 6d. per square yard. There was keen competition at the sale. Afterwards Fitchett wrote to Kirkpatrick that 'several Liverpool attorneys were got together Eden, Bardswell, Griffiths and Crump who all manifested an anxiety to be purchasers of this lot' and claimed that Fitchett had paid too much. Immediately Eyes and Fitchett worked out a street plan to submit to the Corporation. Fitchett wrote to Kirkpatrick that 'we have been laying our heads together as to the best mode of having the land laid out for building on—I believe the Corporation have a plan in view, or something has been said of their wishing the land to be thus disposed in streets but Mr. Eyes proposes it thus as losing less land by 600 yards and making more fronts you see the idea from this rough sketch:'

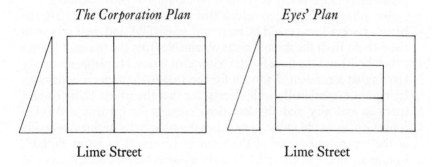

The Corporation Plan   *Eyes' Plan*

Lime Street   Lime Street

This plan of Eyes was similar to the one finally adopted in the lease. But times were not propitious for building, and it was over a year before the formal application for a building lease was made to the Council. In the meantime there were negotiations with Foster, the Corporation surveyor, about the layout of the streets, with the developers hoping to reduce as much as possible the land dedicated to public use. In addition to buying the land, Fitchett paid a £205 returnable deposit to the Corporation to ensure that the street running through the property, Gloucester Street, was paved. On 22 March 1810 Eyes wrote to Kirpatrick that he had received a good many applications for land, but that they all complained of the price; 'in order to keep Mr. F. in good spirits and to induce others to build there we had certainly better to proceed with at least two houses one each for you and me, to build the houses according to the sketch made by me will cost about the sum of £600 each and altho' it is not the best of times to begin yet we must not mind a small sacrifice at the first.' From September 1810 they were receiving payments for plots, Gloucester Street was paved by early 1813, and several thousand square yards, comprising at least half the land not dedicated to streets, had been disposed of in small lots by 1815. Nevertheless, plots were still being sold in 1820 and 1821.[78]

The earliest large planned development in Liverpool, for a 'new town' to be called Harrington, was tried in the 1770s on the estate of the Earl of Sefton in Toxteth Park. Such a scheme was facilitated by the fact that 50 acres were held by one existing lessee. In September 1771, a local surveyor, Cuthbert Bisbrown, approached the Earl with a scheme for a building promotion on the 50 acres, the lease of which he had bought, or contracted to buy, for £1,575. Land development and building were not new for Bisbrown. In 1766 he had paid £2,000 for three closes of 5 or 6 acres, and borrowed nearly £12,000 to finance this promotion and probably other land promotions or house building.[79]

According to the project which Bisbrown proposed to the Earl, the latter's reserved rent could be increased seven-fold, and the Earl would also benefit from the ground rents obtainable from the fronts of houses (when built) and the fines for the renewal of leases. He planned to make Harrington a residential suburb for the well-to-do, especially through laying out exceptionally wide streets 'for that the streets being regular spacious and airy and the lots deep enough for gardens and other conveniences would induce gentlemen not obliged by business to reside in the centre and bustle of the town of Liverpool to resort thither'. Contiguity to the river would allow the construction of docks, quays and warehouses. In 1773 and 1774 twenty-eight lots were leased to Bisbrown and several other head lessees, including three merchants, an iron-monger, silversmith and sailmaker. Bisbrown himself took 14 acres. The leases contained covenants for building houses according to specified dimensions fronting the streets, which were laid out on a gridiron pattern.[80]

The plan for a residential suburb failed. According to a later Earl in 1803 the reason was a lack of a time clause in the leases. As a result, only five or six houses had been built fronting the intended streets. Since the lessees or their assigns were not obliged to build front houses by any

[78] P.R.O. E112/1545/710; Liverpool R.O. deeds 719C; Council minutes XIII (4 Oct. 1809).
[79] Liverpool R.O. deeds 403A.
[80] P.R.O. E112/1533/319 (I owe this important reference to Dr. J. R. Ward); Lancashire R.O. DDM50/23, 'account of the manner of obtaining building leases for building a town to be called Harrington'; H.L.R.O. Main Papers 28 April 1775: Sefton estate bill.

specific date, they had erected poor-quality houses in back streets or passages of their own making where they were not obliged to pay a frontage rent. Parts had been converted into quarries, clay or sand pits or enclosed for pasture. Bisbrown's bankruptcy in 1776 may have been another cause of failure. But the basic weakness is likely to have been a lack of demand for houses in the district from the well-to-do of Liverpool. On the Corporation estate there were residential streets and squares less than half the distance from the centre of Liverpool. For the few wealthy merchants who wish to live outside the town, the village of Everton on a hill to the east was becoming increasingly fashionable. In the early 1800s the land was finally sold to developers, some of whom had been sublessees in the 1780s and 1790s. They included a Chester merchant named John Chamberlain and a Dissenting minister, John Yates, who advanced money to builders out of a trust fund for which he was responsible. While the wide main streets remained in which building according to fixed elevations was still necessary, there was nothing to stop further 'sub-divisions of mean, narrow streets, filled with narrow gloomy courts, into which as many dwellings were packed as it was possible, irrespective of light and air'.[81] This was the opposite of Bisbrown's intention.

On the north of the town, much of the building from the 1790s took place in rows of oblong closes which had once formed Liverpool Town Field. Much of the street layout was shaped by the lines of the lanes and the physical form of the existing closes. On the other hand, several new roads were laid straight through properties in different ownership, presumably by arrangement among the proprietors. One of the most fashionable streets of Liverpool in the early nineteenth century, St. Anne Street, was laid out prior to 1785 about 20 yards wide and 400 yards long, with two parallel streets to the south, across the closes of at least five owners. Street layout on any scale was naturally helped by landholding in single ownership, but this case and other examples on the north side of Liverpool reveal that it was not always essential.

Though many small properties supplied building land, the history of land promotion in these four towns revolves particularly around the larger urban estate. Property ownership gave some landlords and the occasional developer the chance of planning building promotion on blocks of land of at least 20 or 30 acres. When the opportunity was taken,

[81] British Rail Hunts Bank Deed Room, Manchester: Liverpool Central Station deeds; J. Hughes, *Liverpool Banks and Bankers 1760–1837* (Liverpool, 1906), p. 75; Picton, *Architectural History*, p. 60; E112/1533/319.

the typical product was a gridiron pattern of streets of various widths, sometimes centring on a square or a church. In Manchester and Birmingham, where landlords often determined the layout or a few very large parcels passed intact to developers, much of the building land was laid out in this way. In Bath one large property was planned in a formal way at one time by its owner; another, under the same ownership, was

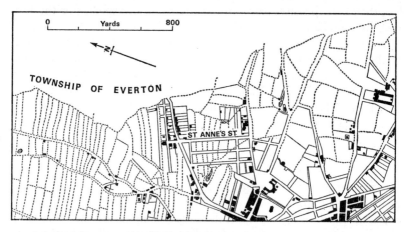

MAP 18. *Land in Liverpool before building, 1785*
The map shows the oblong closes in the former Town Field belonging to different owners on the north side of the town. With the striking exception of St. Anne's Street and the parallel roads, building mostly followed the lines of the closes. The fields to the south were Corporation property, formerly waste (from Eyes, *Plan of Liverpool*, 1785).

laid out in a more piecemeal fashion by developers. Opportunities for planning were greatest in Liverpool with the existence of the 1,000-acre Corporation Estate. Liverpool produced two large formal gridiron schemes, one on Corporation land and the other on the Sefton Estate. The Corporation also developed smaller areas of 20 or 30 acres, according to general plans. But the promotion of part of the Corporation property was influenced by the existing property holdings of individual lessees and their wishes as to the layout of their land. This was in spite of the increasing activity of the Corporation and its paid staff in securing the necessary road links between neighbouring parts of its property, its own work in paving and drainage, and attempts to control the work of developers through the use of covenants in leases.

5
The Smaller Land Promotions: Nottingham, Portsea and Hull

On the edge of some of the major English provincial towns, properties were scattered in small parcels among the estates of other owners. Few or no large territorial blocks existed. This pattern of landownership is illustrated on the edge of Nottingham, Portsea and Hull. It was pre-eminently the case at Portsea, where the building land before 1800 consisted of separately-owned strips in the open field, of about half an acre or 1 acre in size. In Nottingham, too, promoters worked in numerous small closes, gardens or orchards of between half an acre and 2 or 3 acres both within and beyond the physical limits of the town. In Hull a few individually-owned land parcels were much larger, consisting of several closes containing as much as 15 to 20 acres, suitable for a small group of streets, but ownership was still greatly divided.

In each of the three towns nearly all the land was conveyed freehold. The respective Corporations were the chief promoters of plots on building leases, but none of their properties was large. Since corporate bodies expected to last indefinitely, it was natural that their aim should have been a long-term income such as could be produced by ground rents. Local custom clearly played a big part in maintaining the practice of selling land, but it is less easy to explain how the habit became established in each town. Perhaps the most general explanation is that none of the earliest building estates belonged to big landowners with a particular interest in securing a permanent income for their families by creating ground rents. In Nottingham, the Dukes of Newcastle and Rutland sold land in the 1800s, but by then the custom of developing land freehold was well established, and it is understandable that they should follow the general local practice.

Among the three towns, there was much variety in the role of the people concerned, the landlords and developers. In all three, both original owners and developers can be traced as land promoters, but this is the limit of the similarity. In Portsea the role of most landlords was purely passive; in Nottingham most building land was handled by them. In Hull they were both of great importance.

1 NOTTINGHAM

Eighteenth-century Nottingham lay on a sandstone outcrop rising out of marshland adjoining the small River Leen. Despite its population of about 10,000, Nottingham in the 1740s particularly deserved the appellation of 'country town' on account of its physical layout. It was surrounded on three sides by fields and meadows covering about 1,400 acres which could not be built on because they were subject to common rights. Despite attempts to obtain enclosure in 1786–7, 1804, 1806, 1813 and 1833, and in the face of occasional illicit building, the constant vigilance of the burgesses of Nottingham preserved the common fields essentially intact until the middle of the nineteenth century. Within the ring made by these fields buildings were exceptionally dispersed. There was a dense concentration of housing to the north of the Market Place, but the rest of the 2,000 dwellings were well spread out along many dozen roads and lanes. In all they were dispersed over an area measuring about two-thirds of a mile from east to west and about half this distance from north to south. Some of the dwellings were backed by small courts of tenement property, and usually they had gardens. Thus the houses in Narrow Marsh 'had tree-lined avenues and gardens down to the banks of the Leen'. Several large brick houses occupied by local notables were backed by formal pleasure gardens. Particularly in the eastern part of the town and at the west end, whole closes remained intact, used as market gardens or orchards or pasture.[1]

This morphological pattern helps to explain the main locations of building land between the 1740s and 1820. First, all over the town piecemeal development occurred in the gardens and yards of existing buildings, sometimes involving the reconstruction of the front houses as part of the project. The closes within the built-up area, varying in

[1] Chambers, 'Population Change', pp. 101–7; M. I. Thomis, *Old Nottingham* (Newton Abbot, 1968), pp. 52–68.

MAP 19. (*opposite*) *The growth of Nottingham, 1740–1820*

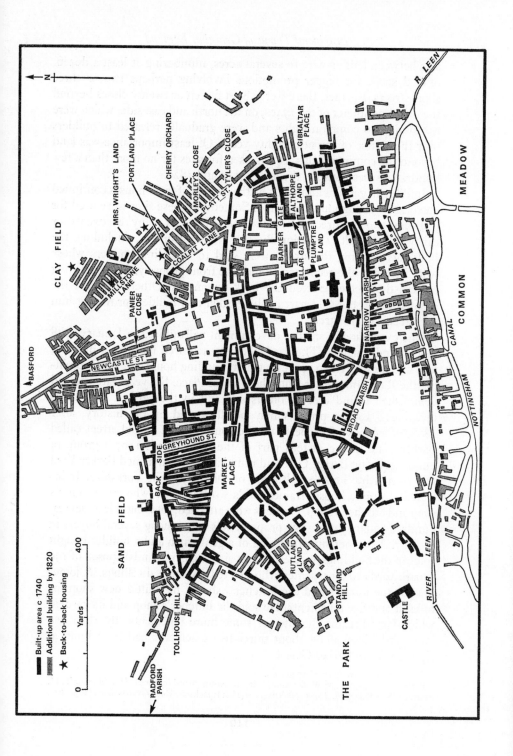

Built-up area c 1740

Additional building by 1820

★ Back-to-back housing

Yards

0   400

R. LEEN

MEADOW

COMMON

CLAY FIELD

BASFORD

MRS. WRIGHT'S LAND

PORTLAND PLACE

CHERRY ORCHARD

MORLEY'S CLOSE

PLATT ST.

TYLER'S CLOSE

COALPIT LANE

MILLSTONE LANE

PANIER CLOSE

GIBRALTAR PLACE

BARKER GATE

ALTHORPE LAND

BELLAR GATE

PLUMPTRE LAND

NARROW MARSH

NEWCASTLE ST.

SAND FIELD

BACK SIDE

GREYHOUND ST.

MARKET PLACE

BROAD MARSH

CANAL

NOTTINGHAM

RUTLAND LAND

STANDARD HILL

TOLLHOUSE HILL

RADFORD PARISH

THE PARK

CASTLE

RIVER LEEN

size between half an acre to several acres, numbering at least a dozen, offered scope for bigger promotions involving perhaps two or three short streets. Further, there were about fifteen or twenty closes beyond the urban perimeter of the 1740s, on the north and east side, which were not subject to common rights and were gradually released to builders over the course of the next eighty years. Of least importance was land beyond the common fields. It was used for sites for no more than a few hundred houses between the later 1790s and 1820.

Infilling in gardens and yards by the owners of front houses continued inexorably throughout the period. Sometimes these sites were used for just one, two or three tenements; sometimes as many as twenty or thirty were built. Occasionally the whole property, including the buildings fronting the street, were sold to intending builders whose work included the reconstruction of the front property. Many existing owners themselves erected the back tenements. Others retained the original house but sold part of the garden to a builder, providing him with access to the street.

One example of a smaller development will suffice. In January 1748 a bellfounder named Thomas Hedderley acquired for £80 'a building now and for many years past used as a founding house and yard' adjoining the Ram Inn not far from the Market Place. Six years later he had demolished it and erected on its site and in the yard at least three dwellings.[2] Larger projects may be illustrated by the history, after 1807, of a block of property on the south side of an old street called Barker Gate in the eastern part of the town. Until 1807 a group of buildings lining Barker Gate and round a courtyard named Barker Yard was owned by Thomas Althorpe of Dinnington in Yorkshire. It included a public house, framesmith's workshop, brewhouse, a joiner's shop and butcher's shop. Gardens were attached, totalling at least several hundred square yards. The property was split among several buyers in in 1807. A partnership consisting of a gentleman and a builder bought some of the buildings, erected at least six tenements, and disposed of 199 square yards to a carpenter who erected six more dwellings. A joiner bought the joiner's and the butcher's shops; he built a new shop for himself and five tenements. He sold the butcher's shop and its garden, which later became the site for some more tenements. By 1820 two long yards lined along about thirty-five tenements had been built, at right angles to Barker Gate.[3]

[2] Nottingham Archives M.17388–92.
[3] *Ibid.*, S.42/2–3, S.48; W. Stretton, 'Map of Nottingham' (*c.* 1800); H. Wild and T. H. Smith, *A New Plan of the Town of Nottingham* (1820); Jackson, *Map of Nottingham*, (1851–61), p. 18.

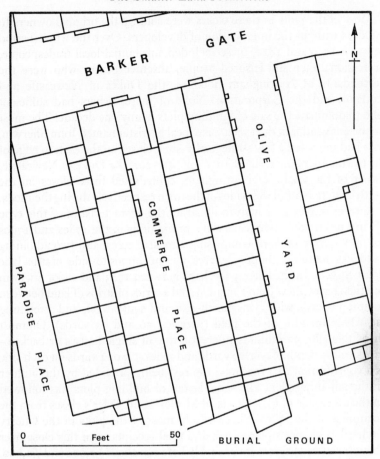

MAP 20. *The Althorpe promotion*
The tenements erected on Althorpe land after 1807 are those lining Commerce
Place and Olive Yard (Jackson's *Map of Nottingham, 1851–61*).

Yet even at Nottingham, what was far more important in terms of the
number of houses erected were developments in closes of 2 or 3 acres
which needed the careful delineation of plots and the layout of access
roads. A few developers were involved in this type of land promotion.
For them the purchase of the land was a major initial cost. In one case a
joiner named Thomas Hutton paid £2,000 for 7,662 square yards at the
east end of the town in December 1791.[4]

[4] Three attorneys (Middlemore, Evans and Green) paid £10,362 12s. od. for 15,352
square yards 200 yards from the Market Place in 1802; Nottingham Archives: TC.2/111/1,
TC.2/90/1.

Most of the plots in these closes were sold by the original owners to builders without the intervention of developers. Over the whole period between 1750 and 1820, these included substantial local tradespeople, professional men and leisured people, absentee gentry who were the descendants of Nottingham notables, the Dukes of Newcastle and Rutland, and the Corporation. None of these owners had sufficient land to dominate the sale of building plots in any one decade. The most important vendor in the 1780s was a local barrister named John Sherwin, who had inherited a few strategically-sited closes on the eastern edge of the town under a marriage settlement of 1726. The Duke of Newcastle, owner of the Castle of Nottingham, contributed three closes on the north-east, north and west sides of the town respectively during the 1800s.

Two examples may help to illustrate the characteristics of this type of land promotion. John Sherwin's promotions in the 1780s and 1790s lay on a cherry orchard comprising almost 2 acres, and two adjoining paddocks totalling about 3½ acres on the opposite side of the lane (Platt Street). In the Cherry Orchard between 1783 and 1800, Sherwin and then his nephew John Longden sold a series of strips of land between 10 and 20 yards wide lying north-east and south-west, and stretching the whole breadth of the field (between 50 and 75 yards). On most strips this allowed builders to erect a row of single houses or back-to-backs with a depth of 9 or 10 yards and to leave 3 or 4 yards on each side as a contribution to a roadway, the rest being provided by the builder on the adjoining plot. The same layout of building plots was followed on the other side of Platt Street in Morley's and Tyler's closes from the beginning of the 1790s. Sherwin sold most of the plots in the Cherry Orchard at 5s. per square yard, and total receipts from this close over about seventeen years were probably between about £2,000 and £2,500. His major expenditure lay in giving the builders financial support. Surviving mortgages and the purchase of houses from insolvent builders suggest that his outlay in this respect regarding the three closes ran to several thousand pounds. For example, a builder in Morley's Close, John Nixon, received £800 on 30 December 1790 and a further £286 on 23 June 1791, by a mortgage secured on sixteen back-to-backs; by 1797, £211 10s. 10½d. more was owing for interest, and Sherwin acquired the property outright at a valuation of £1,320.[5] Sherwin imposed no covenants on the builders regarding the appearance or structure of the houses to be erected.

---

[5] Nottingham Archives M.16433–40; numerous deeds relating to the sale of plots by Sherwin and Longden survive in the Nottingham Archives, including M.19109, 16388, 23141, 23212–16, bdl. 5617, TC.2/19/1–2.

PANIER CLOSE.

PARTICULARS

OF A

VALUABLE

FREEHOLD ESTATE,

IN THE

TOWN OF NOTTINGHAM,

To be Sold by Auction,

BY MR. GASKILL,

ON WEDNESDAY THE 4th DAY OF FEBRUARY, 1807,

At the Blackmoor's Head Inn, in the Town of Nottingham.

(Subject to such Conditions of Sale and Arrangements as will be then produced)

THE SALE TO COMMENCE AT ELEVEN O'CLOCK IN THE FORENOON.

IN FORTY-TWO LOTS.

A

PIECE OF LAND,

IN THE

TOWN OF NOTTINGHAM,

CALLED

PANIER CLOSE,

VERY ELIGIBLY SITUATED FOR BUILDING PURPOSES,

CONTAINING UPWARDS OF

SIXTEEN THOUSAND SQUARE YARDS,

AND ADJOINING TO

PARLIAMENT-STREET.

PLATE 17. *Auction particulars of Panier Close* (Debenham and Co.)

As a second case, in April 1807 the Duke of Newcastle sold a field comprising 16,000 square yards in the north of the town, called Panier Close. According to the deed of covenants with the buyers, the Duke had it 'planned and laid out into building lots so as to form three streets

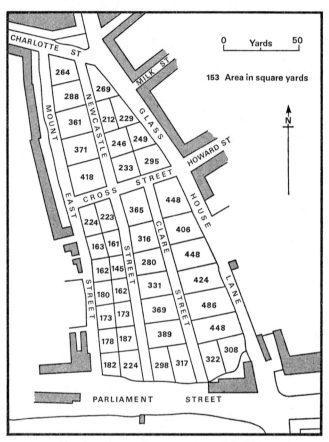

MAP 21. *Plan of Panier Close* (Debenham and Co.)

called Newcastle Street and Clare Street of the breadth of 8 yards each and Cross Street of the breadth of 8 yards'. ⟨*See* plate 17.⟩ The forty-two lots were smaller than those of Sherwin, between 145 and 486 square yards. Their size was more typical of the average building plots found in nearly every provincial town. They were auctioned, instead of the more usual practice at Nottingham of piecemeal private sale. Presumably the excellent position of the land and the timing of the promotion at the height of the boom of the mid-1800s offered the promise of exceptional demand. It was successful, the land selling for between 6s. 9d. and as much as 13s. per square yard.[6]

No covenants were imposed on builders concerning the prohibition of offensive trades or the nature of the houses or buildings to be erected. This was in contrast to a promotion begun by Mary Wright, widow of a Nottingham banker, in 1802 on about 1½ acres about half-way between the former Cherry Orchard and Panier Close. Mrs. Wright required that houses should have an annual value of not less than £8, and forbade some elementary nuisances.[7] It was even more in contrast with the Duke's other promotion in 1807, on thirty-two lots on Standard Hill near the Castle ⟨*see* plate 20⟩, where covenants were not only imposed against nuisances but in order to insist on the construction of houses worth more than £25 a year. Situated on attractive rising ground, this was intended to be, and did in fact become, a select development of large houses.[8] On the other hand, the Estate felt clearly that Panier Close would sell better for artisan housing of the usual kind, without restrictions on the builders.

Undoubtedly the common fields had an effect on land promotion in Nottingham. They prevented the natural outward expansion of the town in several directions, particularly on the north-west, where Sand Field came within 300 yards of the Market Place, and on the south, where the Common Meadow stopped ribbon development along the main road southwards. Land prices were high by Midland standards, though still lower than leasehold fines in Liverpool. Whereas in Nottingham the median price between 1786 and 1794 was about 5s. per square yard and between 1800 and 1815 it was approximately 7s. 9d., at Wolverhampton prices between 1788 and 1807 ranged from 1s. 9d. to 2s. In Coventry, plots were selling for between 2s. 8d. and 5s. 6d., and in the case of the few freehold schemes at Birmingham which were developed freehold between 1805 and 1820, prices were from 2s. 6d. to 5s. 1d. per square yard, being similar to the Coventry prices.[9]

[6] See plan, p. 120; Messrs. Debenham and Co.: deeds re. Victoria Station (for land prices); Nottingham University: Newcastle MSS. D424.
[7] Nottingham Archives M.22142; no necessary house, dunghill, hogsty, cowhouse or any other noxious building was to be erected within four yards of the street.
[8] Newcastle MSS. D425; the 9,000 square yards fetched a total of £7,010; the high price reflected not only the attractive situation but the fact that the land was exempt from paying poor rates: *History, Topography and Directory of the Town of Nottingham* (Nottingham, 1834), p. 33.
[9] For Nottingham land prices, deeds in Nottingham Archives, etc. (see Appendix VII); Wolverhampton Central Library: deeds relating to St. James Square, St. John's Square, Union St., Walsall St.; Coventry R.O.: Town Clerk's deeds, 1959–61; B.R.L. MSS. 249573, 371939, T.C.124, 3789, 9810, 14396, 16723, 17919.

However, this contrast between the price of building land at Nottingham and in other Midland towns relates only to sites within the ring of common-right property. As Dr. Chapman has shown, the Lenton inclosure act of 1796 made available land in the parish of Radford beyond the open fields, but only between half a mile and 1 mile from Nottingham Market Place. In 1796 land was sold for building at 2s. per square yard. As late as the housing boom of the mid-1820s, land was being acquired about 1 mile from the town at between 2s. and 3s. Two miles from the town centre land was available in Basford in the 1800s at 1s per square yard.[10]

There was much more restriction on the choice of builders in Nottingham than in many other provincial towns because of the common rights. Yet even at the height of the building boom in about 1807, there were several land promotions under way within a few minutes' walk of the Market Place, apart from the land beyond the open fields. It is difficult to talk of a general shortage of building land before the 1820s, only a shortage in certain localities.

The most important characteristic of land development in Nottingham was the small size, and large number of land promotions, each involving no more than 2 or 3 acres, sometimes, in the case of back gardens, no more than a quarter of an acre. Basically it was a reflection of the dispersed character of landownership both on the edge and within the town. Amalgamation of land parcels to create larger promotions was difficult because of the dispersal of older buildings between many of the closes, and the ring of common fields which often bounded the remainder.

2 PORTSEA

The whole of Portsea Island is low-lying and flat, and in the south of the island, where building took place in the eighteenth century, the soil is either sand or gravel. The town of Portsmouth, of medieval origin, lay in the south-west corner. Cut off from the rest of the island by fortifications, it covered only about 110 acres. The dockyard lay about 500 yards to the north of the town. The use of the small remaining amount of vacant land within the town provided sites for several hundred more houses in the course of the eighteenth century. Nearly all the new dwellings were erected in the suburb of Portsea. Building spread eastwards and south-eastwards from the dock, near which some 200 or 300 houses were erected during the War of the Spanish Succession.

[10] S. D. Chapman, 'Working-Class Housing in Nottingham during the Industrial Revolution', *Transactions of the Thoroton Society*, LXVII (1963), p. 76; R. Mellors, *Old Nottingham Suburbs Then and Now* (Nottingham, 1914), p. 33; Nottingham Archives TC.10764, 11562-3, 11630.

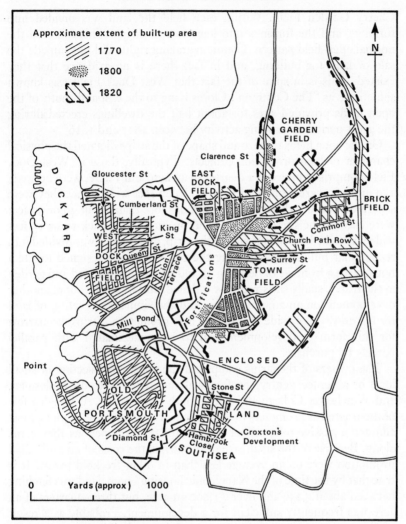

MAP 22. *The Growth of Portsmouth, 1770–1820*

At least half of Portsea Island comprised enclosed fields throughout the eighteenth century.[11] Much of the west of the island, including the part nearest the dockyard, lay in at least five open fields, each comprising well over 100 acres. The sites of the eighteenth-century houses were unenclosed strips in four open fields, West Dock Field (adjoining the yard, and the first to be developed), East Dock Field, Town Field and

[11] *V.C.H. Hants,* III, p. 192: map of Portsea Island, 1716.

Cherry Garden Field. Within each field the land was divided into furlongs, and the furlongs into long narrow strips. This followed the normal open-field pattern. Common grazing rights did not impede the sale of land for building, and in fact there is no evidence that they existed. This is in spite of the fact that West Dock Field was known sometimes as 'The Common'. Closes lying to the east and south of the open fields provided sites for about half the dwellings erected during the great period of building activity between 1807 and 1816.

On the open fields the size and shape of the strips dictated the physical character of land promotion projects. Typically, those in West Dock Field comprised between a quarter of an acre and 1 acre, were between 150 and 180 yards long and from 20 to 80 feet wide. Since they were separately owned, those with a width of more than about 40 or 50 feet were used as the site of a single land promotion. A track 10 or 15 feet wide was staked out on one side of the strip, and the rest was divided into rectangular building plots lining the roadway, each designed to site a house with a frontage of between 12 and 15 feet, with a yard and garden in the rear. Usually the street was widened later by the layout of another development on an adjoining strip and the similar reservation of land for a roadway alongside that on the first promotion. Strips too narrow for this form of development had to be amalgamated with parallel parcels by purchase.

The owners of the strips comprised the usual cross-section of small local or absentee gentry, professional men or well-to-do tradesmen, and Winchester College and Portsmouth Corporation. Although a few of them acted as promoters by laying out a road and a row of plots, most adopted a passive role, selling their strips to developers as they came along. Because of the small size of the strips, the costs of an individual promotion were on an average less than in other freehold towns. It is true that by the time of the Napoleonic housing boom, land was fetching between about £250 and over £1,000 an acre, but three-quarters of an acre was frequently sufficient for a development. Probably as a result of this, the function of developer and house builder was especially closely linked in Portsea. Most developers incurred an additional outlay of several hundred pounds by themselves building a few houses alongside the plots they sold to other builders.

In the 1740s and 1750s, when West Dock Field was the main source of building land, developers included several dockyard workers, at least one building craftsman, and a 'gentleman' who was possibly an attorney. Cumberland Street, created after 1747, provides an example of the method of development typical of these years and indeed for the rest of the century. On 2 June 1747, Richard Davies, scavelman, bought a strip lined east to west in Black Thorn Bush Furlong, measuring about 170 yards by about 83 feet. Reserving 15 feet along the north side for a road, Davies sold a row of plots at 1s. 1½d. per square yard, allowing a frontage of 15 to 17 feet per house, from September 1747. He erected at least one house himself. On the north side Samuel White, gentleman, made up a parallel strip about 49 feet deep, consisting of a parcel bought on 27 October 1743 and more land acquired in August 1747. He reserved 14 feet along the south side to give Cumberland Street a total width of 29 feet. Of the remaining land, he sold the western half in the usual plots in 1749; the eastern part was bought by another shipwright, who subsequently resold it in lots to builders. By the early 1750s, about seventy houses had been erected in the street.[12]

Between the 1770s and the early 1790s, builders began to work several hundred yards further eastwards in East Dock Field and Town Field. At the same time the remaining strips in West Dock Field, some of which adjoined rows of houses constructed in the 1700s and which were used as ropewalks or gardens, were developed one by one. Several of these strips, owned by a family called Swann under strict settlement, were finally released for building when the entail was broken in 1779. Such sites were particularly profitable to the vendors because of their relative proximity to the dockyard compared with plots in the other open fields. Sites on a Swann acre in Gloucester Street fetched over 10s. per square yard in 1782, and the last strip to be released in West Dock Field, King Street in the early 1790s, fetched 18s. a square yard.[13] This contrasts with a price range of 2s. to 6s. in the other open fields.

The number of building plots needed in these decades, particularly during the boom of the early 1780s associated with the American War of Independence, opened an opportunity for many developers. In West Dock Field in 1783 and 1784, one promotion was handled by a broker and a house carpenter, and another street by three men of whom one was a future mayor of Portsmouth, another both a coal merchant and a dockyard official, and the third a baker. The majority of strips were developed by an attorney, Moses Greetham, who was responsible for at least a dozen new streets. Following the normal practice of developers of building to a small extent on each promotion, he erected at least thirty or forty houses in the course of his work as a developer. Several of the strips that he bought in East Dock Field and in Town Field ⟨*see* map

[12] Portsmouth R.O. deeds re. Cumberland St.
[13] Treasury Solicitor's Deeds 2354/62, 2274/62, 2340/62 etc. (re. Gloucester St.); Portsmouth R.O. deeds re. King St.

23⟩ were not disposed of finally until the later 1790s, perhaps reflecting an over-estimation by him of the continued level of demand during and after the American War of Independence.[14]

Greetham had no successor as the leading supplier of building plots. In the unprecedented expansion during the first fifteen or sixteen years of the nineteenth century, when nearly 4,000 dwellings were erected, several scores of people were involved in land promotion. The use of enclosed land for the first time led to promotions on blocks of land of several acres. Each provided the site for a small group of streets. For example, in 1812 a close named Brick Field or the Town Eight Acres, in the middle of Portsea Island, began to be sold off in plots by two Portsmouth residents, a hatter and a shoemaker named Nance and Sheppard respectively. The lots were aligned along five short streets forming a small rectangular block.[15]

The tendency to overestimate builders' needs, which was just detectable at the end of the American War of Independence, was much more important at the end of the boom between 1812 and 1816, and many promoters were left with strips or parts of closes on their hands which were not used for building for decades to come. Speculation in individual building plots (as distinct from land suitable for division into plots) was rare in provincial England during this period. It was a sign of the extent of the land-dealing mania in Portsea that such speculation was visible in a small way between 1806 and 1816.[16]

No evidence survives about the levelling and paving of the roads laid out by developers in Portsea before the 1760s. In 1764 Paving Commissioners were set up by act of parliament, with responsibility for the district covered by West Dock Field and the adjoining western part of East Dock Field, later known as the 'town' of Portsea. This was created primarily to pave existing streets. It also paved the new streets laid out in the 1770s and 1780s, at the cost of the householders.[17] However, the new streets made between the 1770s and 1820 in the other open fields and on the enclosed land, in the districts known as Landport and Southsea, lay outside the jurisdiction of the Commissioners. One of the first promoters on enclosed land, Samuel Wilson, gentleman, who bought a pasture field called Hambrook Close in 1799 and was selling plots in the early 1800s, both made and undertook to maintain the roads

[14] Portsmouth R.O. deeds reRidge; St., Clarence St., Charlotte St., Little Church Path, Marylebone St., Spring St., etc.
[15] *Ibid.* re. Common St., Church Crown St., Lord St.
[16] Portsmouth R.O. deeds D4414, 8736 Brickwoods Brewery deeds re. Southsea Brewery site and C29, W25, etc.
[17] Portsmouth R.O.: Portsea Paving Commissioners Proceedings ICP 1/1–2.

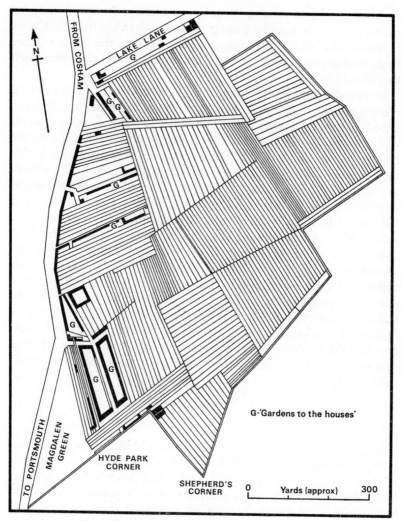

MAP 23. *Town Field, Portsea, c. 1790–95*

One of the open fields that supplied building land in Portsea in the eighteenth
century. A few of the strips have already been used for building. This may
be seen particularly in the south-west corner of the field, where Montagu
Row and Marylebone Street were begun in the 1770s. In this field two or
three adjoining strips were amalgamated to form a street and a row of plots
for building houses (from a map in the custody of the Warden and Fellows of
Winchester College).

he laid out.[18] More usually, the promoter undertook responsibility for the roads but recovered his costs from the builders. On the sale of plots in Brick Field in 1824, Nance and Sheppard bound the builder to pay them their share of making the carriage road and the kerb stones which they should lay.[19]

During the eighteenth century there is no evidence of houses being erected under covenants governing appearance and structure. Builders were free to erect houses or other buildings of any size they pleased ⟨*see* plates 22–3⟩. This continued to be the general practice during the Napoleonic housing boom; only a few terraces were planned in which the builders were required to work to a standard elevation. This reflects the fact that Portsea was primarily a dockyard suburb; the senior officials lived in the yard, and there were also one or two streets of fashionable housing in the town of Portsmouth. Until Southsea grew fashionable as a seaside resort in the 1820s, there was little demand for terraces with architectural pretensions.[20] During the eighteenth century the use of open-field strips for building sites helped to discourage any ambitious planning on the part of the developers. Yet the amalgamation of strips by purchase to form larger promotions with wide streets would still have been possible. Basically the narrow streets and absence of building regulations were acceptable to the type of people from whom the demand for housing came: the dockyard shipwrights and other workmen, and the general craftsmen and petty tradesmen who served their needs.

3 HULL

Before the 1770s, building in Hull was within the medieval town walls, apart from some small ribbon development on the main roads out of the town. ⟨*See* map 4, p. 69.⟩ Defoe had described the town as 'exceeding close built...; tis extraordinary populous, even to an inconvenience, having really no room to extend it self by building.' It is true that there was less vacant space within the old town than at Nottingham, yet the last part of Defoe's comment was far from correct.

---

[18] Messrs. Brickwoods Ltd., Portsmouth: deeds re. Cecil Place.
[19] The developer of a close in Southsea after 1807 undertook to make the road, which was to be 'completed' by the house owners: Croxton was to lay a footpath with kerb stones and to set gutter stones at the cost of the builders: Portsmouth R.O. deeds re. Diamond St., Gold St., etc.; for another development requiring the builders to reimburse the developers for the costs of roadmaking and paving, see Portsmouth R.O. D571 (Fratton Rd., No. 98).
[20] Portsmouth R.O.: D4208 (Lion Terrace); Messrs. Brickwoods deeds: W.25 (Southsea Terrace and Cecil Place); H. and J. Slight, *Chronicles of Portsmouth* (1828), pp. 4–5.

Houses were densely packed on the east side of the town, between the quays on the bank of the River Hull and the Market Place. But particularly in the north and west of the town, large gardens and closes remained behind the houses fronting the streets.[21]

For the first three quarters of the century, new housing consisted of piecemeal development on back gardens, the occasional small close or vacant front site, or the redevelopment in a more intensive form of the sites of old buildings.[22] The opening of the first dock in 1778 on the site of the old northern defences of the town and the faster population growth from the 1780s led to rapid outward expansion. Houses spread over the closes on the plain to the north and west of the town. Building still continued in the remaining closes and gardens in the north-west corner of the town, but by the second decade of the nineteenth century the new buildings beyond the line of the old walls covered about twice the area of the original town. Apart from the Humber on the south, there was no obstacle to the development of building land.

As at Nottingham and Portsea, there was no single large landowner in the outskirts of the town. Single closes or a contiguous small group of closes, comprising individually-owned blocks of land varying in size from 2 to 20 acres, were held by trading or professional or gentry families mainly resident near Hull, as well as by the Corporation and the Dock Company. Some of these original owners, such as the Corporation, the Company and several private proprietors promoted building schemes themselves. The work was also done by developers. For example Richard Baker, merchant, bought about 8 acres in September 1787, over which five short streets were laid out and the plots sold off in the 1790s. Some 200 yards to the east of the Baker promotion, Joseph Sykes of West Ella, a member of a prominent merchant, banking and landowning family in Hull and the East Riding, bought 11 acres called 'French's Garden' in 1796, and was selling off sites along four streets in the early 1800s.[23] Most of the plots sold by the land promoters were the typical building sites of a few hundred square yards suitable for one or two front houses and (if required) a small court of tenements in the rear. There was also some speculative dealing in larger plots, usually between 1,000 and 5,000 square yards, by men intervening between the land promoters and the typical small builder of between one and half a dozen dwellings.

[21] Jackson, *Hull*, p. 2 and map p. 286; Hull R.O. map of Hull (1715) (F1/7); R. Thew, *A Plan of Kingston upon Hull* (1784).
[22] E.g., P.R.O. C110/80; Hull R.O. L.77; Trinity House deeds.
[23] A. G. Chamberlain, 'The Northern Suburb of Hull. Historical and Architectural Notes for the Victoria County History' (1966), pp. 11, 14.

This often involved the construction of a few houses by the middlemen as well as the sale of plots to other builders.[24]

Since the developers bought their land, its cost was a major item of expenditure. Before the inflation at the end of the century, its price was well over £100 an acre. Baker paid £300 an acre, or a total of about £2,500, for his land in 1787.[25] Further to the west, where land was cheaper, a syndicate consisting of a watchmaker, a gardener and two joiners paid £1,029 4s. 9d. for 6 acres in March 1789.[26]

Sometimes credit was given to builders for the land and loans made towards construction. In 1803 an ironfounder named Todd advertised 5 acres for sale in lots, and offered credit for the purchase money 'for a limited number of years'.[27] R. C. Broadley, underwriter, shipowner and landowner, who undertook at least four or five promotions both within and outside the old town between 1786 and the early 1800s, lent money on mortgage to builders. For example, in July 1790 he lent a joiner £450, secured on two houses the latter was erecting on a site conveyed to him by Broadley a few days earlier at a price of £207 17s.[28]

Paving and the making of drains were normally undertaken by the land promoters. The syndicate just mentioned advertised as follows on 30 September 1788:

'Notice to stone masons and pavers: that the new street . . . called West Street is intended to be flagged on each side and paved in the middle the whole length thereof by the 1st of October 1789. All persons desirous of contracting for the same are requested to deliver in their proposals on or before the 13th October next . . .. For further particulars enquire of Messrs. Mann and Beaumont [two of the developers].'[29]

In Hull the cost was often borne by the promoter; less usually the deeds conveying the land plots stipulated that they were recoverable from the builders. Thus, as part of the conditions of sale of his building plots, Sykes undertook to lay out and make the streets and dig the drains 'at his

[24] E.g., British Transport Archives, York HDC1/1 Dock Commissioners minutes, pp. 247–51 (now in the custody of the P.R.O.); Chamberlain, 'Hull', pp. 3–7.
[25] Hull Local History Library: *History of the Streets of Hull*, collected by W. Sykes from J. Richardson MSS., (1915), p. 6.
[26] Hull R.O.: deeds re. Clarence Inn, 22 Brook St.
[27] *Hull Advertiser*, 1 Jan. 1803.
[28] Hull R.O. GC147–9; also manor of Tupcoates with Myton court book 2, pp. 57, 222 etc.
[29] Sykes, *Streets of Hull*, p. 13.

own expence'. He also laid flagged pavements, though the cost of these was recoverable.[30]

Covenants attempting to control the character of building were used on several of the promotions. In 1781 the Dock Commissioners laid out a long street, Charlotte Street, and its continuation, George Street, running parallel with the new dock. It was intended for larger houses, presumably for merchants and others connected with the commerce of the dock. Purchasers of the adjoining lots were to 'errect and build a dwelling house not less than 30 feet high upon each lot to be purchased agreeable to the direction and Elevation in the Plan hereunto annexed'. Some of the houses erected were as wide as five bays and formed what has been described as 'the finest architectural group of eighteenth century houses in the city'[31] ⟨*see* plate 28⟩.

The Corporation also used covenants to control the construction of smaller terrace houses on several acres it owned on the western edge of the town. ⟨*See* Plate 12.⟩ According to leases made in September 1795, builders in Waterworks Street were required to erect one or more brick and tiled houses with the facade uniform to the elevation drawn by the Corporation architect and exhibited at the auction, subject to his inspection.[32] Other promoters may have felt that they would attract more builders by not insisting on construction according to rigorous specifications. Thus one major developer of land near the Humber, Thomas English, shipbuilder and merchant, advertised that 'the purchasers will not be obligated to build to elevation'[33] ⟨*see* plate 26⟩.

In Hull, land promoters had more space in which to design a street pattern than in the tiny closes at Nottingham or on the open-field strips of Portsea. The effect may be seen in the Sculcoates districts to the north of the dock, which particularly attracted merchants, shipowners and well-to-do professional people as a place of residence. The Dock Company laid out the long Charlotte and George Streets, and on 11 acres to the north an original owner, John Jarratt, planned Kingston Square.[34] Yet no general scheme for the district emerged. At least

[30] Hull R.O. deeds re. French's Garden; an act of 1801 (41 Geo.3 c.30) established Commissioners for paving, lighting, watching and nuisance removal in Sculcoates, with the power to order owners or occupiers to make, pave and cobble the roads in front of their houses; the Commissioners were themselves empowered to make the sewers; presumably these powers were used only in case of neglect by the promoters, since both Sykes and Todd provided these amenities subsequent to the act. An act with wider powers was obtained for the Myton district in 1810 (50 Geo.3 c.41), which was inspired partly by inadequate paving in the new streets of the previous decade.
[31] Chamberlain, 'Hull', pp. 2–3.
[32] Hull R.O. B.R.N. 667.
[33] *Hull Advertiser*, 30 July 1804; Todd only required building according to a certain value.
[34] Chamberlain, 'Hull', p. 13.

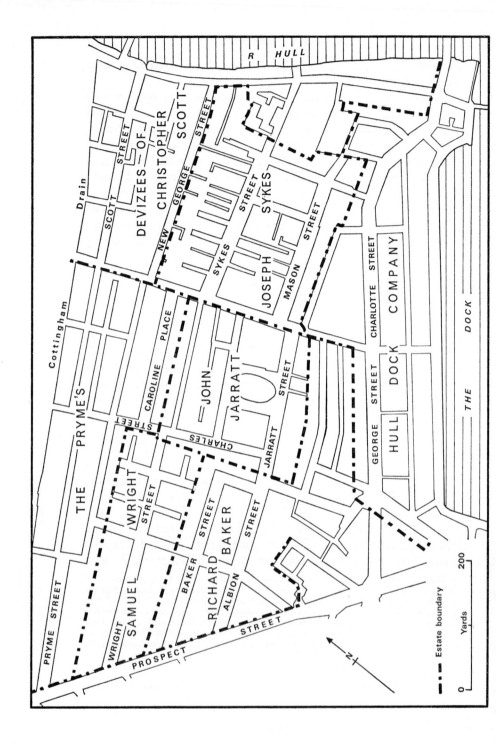

R HULL

Drain

Cottingham

SCOTT STREET

DEVIZEES — OF — CHRISTOPHER — SCOTT

NEW — GEORGE — STREET

SYKES STREET

JOSEPH SYKES

STREET

MASON STREET

THE — PRYME'S

CAROLINE PLACE

CHARLES STREET

JOHN JARRATT

JARRATT STREET

JARRATT STREET

CHARLOTTE STREET

GEORGE STREET

HULL — DOCK — COMPANY

THE — DOCK

WRIGHT STREET

SAMUEL — WRIGHT

BAKER STREET

RICHARD — BAKER

ALBION STREET

PRYME STREET

WRIGHT STREET

PROSPECT — STREET

N

— · — · — Estate boundary

0   200
          Yards

eight promoters were responsible for the layout of about 120 acres, not all of which had been used by builders by 1820. The result was a series of blocks of streets determined by the original ownership pattern with only the minimum communication between them.

In Nottingham, the miniature nature of the individual land promotions was determined partly by the pattern of landownership. It was also affected by the scattered layout of closes between old buildings and lanes, and the existence of common fields hemming in the available closes lying beyond the old urban limits. But in Portsea and Hull, one is left with the impression that the pattern of ownership moulded the physical form of land developments because it suited the promoters that it should do so. In Portsea, throughout the eighteenth century there were plenty of cases of strip amalgamation by piecemeal purchase, but only in so far as it was necessary to provide a parcel of land wide enough for a narrow roadway and line of building plots. As we have seen, a few parcels were not available for building for legal or other reasons, but they were in a small minority. In Hull, there was only one known example of amalgamation by purchase of two separately-owned groups of closes for building development.[35] Yet if the total demand for new housing had been greater in these towns, or if a sufficient number of well-to-do residents had created the need for a planned residential estate, it is difficult to see why amalgamations or joint schemes should not have been carried further, as happened in a part of Liverpool Town Field. It is likely that the land pattern determined building layout as a matter of convenience rather than compulsion.

Freehold promotions differed from those based on the disposal of land by building lease, in that the developer was faced at the outset with a capital liability for the purchase of his land. He also received his profit in the form of cash payments for land plots instead of rents: on the other hand, landlords or developers on leasehold estates could convert rents to similar cash sums by the sale of ground rents, as was sometimes done. There was no perceptible difference in the outlay by developers on the basic amenities, on loans to builders, or the occasional house construction. As we have seen, owners and developers sometimes inserted covenants in their conveyance to builders, as on leasehold

[35] Hull Guildhall: deeds re. Middle and Brook Sts.: this was done by the syndicate of four developers.

MAP 24. (*opposite*) *Building land promotions in the Sculcoates District of Hull, c. 1780–1835.* Names refer to landowners. (Based on Chamberlain, 'Hull', see p, 129 note 23.)

estates, to enhance the character of the building or the general environment on the whole promotion, and the sale value of each site. Since the interest of the owner or developer ended with the sale of the last plot, there was no long-term interest in the quality of the estate. While covenants are particularly characteristic of promotions designed for large houses for the well-to-do, they were occasionally used towards the end of the period for more modest terrace property.

4 A BIRD'S-EYE VIEW OF BUILDING DEVELOPMENT

A principal theme of these studies of the seven towns has been the work of original owners and developers in building land promotion. It is difficult to see a pattern in the extent to which developers acted as middlemen between owners and builders, assuming at least some of the functions involved in disposing of building land. It is even more difficult to explain it. Developers were prominent at all times during the eighteenth and early nineteenth centuries, and particularly as the demand for houses grew towards the end of the eighteenth century. Nevertheless, the extent of their activity fluctuated in the short run, sometimes to a considerably greater extent than the demand for houses. Boom years in building activity, which created a keen demand for sites and pushed up land values, tended to encourage numerous well-to-do townsmen in many places to speculate in land development. The phenomenon is visible in Portsea during the American War of Independence and particularly during the later stages of the Napoleonic Wars, when parcels of an acre or more fetched unprecedented prices (even taking into account the general inflation). In Manchester and Liverpool it is noticeable in the 1770s. But this was most striking nationally during the great building boom at the end of the 1780s and beginning of the 1790s. The prominent role of developers in Birmingham and particularly in Manchester in these years has been shown. By 1792 more land was being prepared for building, in Bath and Bristol, than a realistic assessment would have estimated as being necessary for several years. Everywhere prolonged trade prosperity at once created an unprecendented demand for houses, thus raising land values, and the wealth and credit which made extensive land promotion possible. Such a feature did not reappear again on the national scale before the 1820s.

We have also seen that towns differed over the whole period in the extent to which developers acted as middlemen between the original owners and the builders. A partial explanation may lie in the extent of the financial incentive to potential developers to act as middlemen. For example, expectations of profit from land development were particularly high almost everywhere in the later 1780s and beginning of the 1790s. Owners with no fixed ideas on how to dispose of their land are likely to have been persuaded to sell or lease large parcels by the high prices which developers were willing to offer. But differing financial inducements do not explain why Nottingham throughout the period, and Birmingham before the 1780s, were towns in which the role of the developer was small, by contrast, say, with Portsea and Manchester. In both towns the increment on the conversion of agricultural land to building use was of a size sufficient to yield a handsome return both to the owner conveying to a developer and to the developer conveying to the builder.[36]

An explanation is more likely to lie in the attitude of the original owners. However, it is easier to show what was *not* an important influence on their approach to land promotion than what *was* significant. One might expect that absentee owners would prefer to sell or lease to developers and avoid the burden of dividing the land into plots and of providing the basic amenities. But at Birmingham both the Colmore and Gooch families and two or three smaller owners who leased direct to the builder were absentees, and in Nottingham the landlords who developed the land themselves included John Plumptre, a landed gentleman who lived in Kent, in 1797, and the Duke of Newcastle.[37] The reason was probably that the land conveyed for building was part of a larger local estate consisting of farmland or houses already administered by a local agent or steward who could supervise or partially carry out the surveying, legal and financial work involved for himself. Both the Duke of Newcastle, who owned the Castle at Nottingham, and the Gooch family, who held the manorial demesnes of Birmingham, were important local property owners.

Nor does the usual local method of land conveyance, whether by sale or by lease, appear to have affected the extent to which developers intervened in the handling of the building land. There is no indication that one type of promotion was more attractive than the other to developers, or that landlords were more inclined to deal directly with builders in the case of one method of promotion than in the other.

Yet again, the type of owner was not of crucial significance: in Nottingham after 1800 the Duke of Newcastle's agent auctioned the building plots himself, while the Duke of Rutland sold in one piece the biggest amount of land to pass to any Nottingham developer, 15,352

[36] For the size of this increment in Birmingham, see below, p. 145; for the high price of building land in Nottingham, see above, p. 121.
[37] For the Plumptre property, a 'paddock' between Bellar Gate and Stoney St., through which Plumptre St. was laid, Nottingham Archives: S.42/3.

square yards.[38] In Birmingham Sir Thomas Gooch of Suffolk leased direct to builders, while in Liverpool the Earl of Sefton and in Manchester Sir Ashton Lever conveyed to developers. Among private owners lower down the social scale the pattern is similarly mixed.

The same is also true of the corporate holders of land. In the case of one or two corporate bodies their general method of leasing land for agricultural and other non-building use may have affected their approach to building promotion. We have seen that Liverpool Corporation granted non-building leases for three lives and twenty-one years, the lives being replaceable on payment of a fine. This gave the lessee a stronger financial interest than the normal tenant leasing for a limited number of years, and it was thus natural that the lessee should share in the profits by acting as the developer when the land became suitable for building promotion. It would also have been costly for the Corporation to have bought out the interest of the lessee. This may also have been true of the Bath Corporation Estate. Other corporations, such as those of Hull, Newcastle and Nottingham, conveyed land direct to builders. They were able to plan and control their promotions through committees and a professional surveyor.

Thus the Common Council of Newcastle had a viewing committee for its property throughout the eighteenth century and a surveyor was being employed at least as early as 1746.[39]

Despite the absence of any obvious pattern in the types of owners or the legal methods of conveying land, it still seems most likely that the basic reasons for the presence or absence of developers lie in the attitude of the landowners. Some probably lacked any sort of policy and responded passively to the varying demands of developers and builders, such as—probably—Ashton Lever in Manchester. Others, no doubt, naturally followed earlier custom on their own property or adopted the practice of neighbouring estates. However, at least a few deliberately adopted the practice of disposing of land in small individual plots. For instance, this appears to have been the case with the Colmore property in Birmingham when land began to be leased after 1746; there were many precedents for disposing of one or more parcels of several acres to developers in the town earlier in the century. In some cases involving leasehold developments, the estate may have feared that the grant of too much land to one person might put at risk the securing of the ground rent. Thus when the Governors of the Grammar School in Birmingham

[38] For the Rutland Estate, Nottingham Archives: TC2/90/1.
[39] Newcastle R.O.: Common Council minutes 1699–1718 etc., and especially 1743–65, pp. 70–71.

considered the lease for building on a croft in New Street in 1739 and 1740, they first agreed to lease it in one lot to a local carpenter, and then revised their decision because they felt that the anticipated building would be too much for one person to undertake.[40] Again, in some instances sites were disposed of by the original owners because of the higher prices obtainable if no developer acted as a middleman. In 1844, it was said that the small amount of available land within the common fields surrounding Nottingham had encouraged the owners, such as the Corporation, to dole them out cautiously in diminutive lots, so that the highest prices might be obtained.[41] Further, the extent of the probable outlay for basic amenities may have influenced the decision of some landowners: thus at Bath, where the need for housing for wealthy visitors and residents made the expenditure on amenities particularly high, it was normal for the original owners to convey to developers. Alternatively, the offer by a developer of an enhanced price or ground rent with no trouble or expense was attractive to some landlords, even though they may have been aware of the likely ultimate gain that would accrue to the developer. But whatever their motive, and whether they made a positive decision or instinctively followed other local practice, the view of the landlords appears to have been the paramount factor.

Another recurring topic in the study of the seven towns has been the increasing use of covenants to control the work of builders. One way of evaluating the success of land promoters is to decide how effective these were. To what extent did builders pay attention to the requirements of those who supplied their land?

How successful the covenants were is difficult to say. Evidence is largely restricted to disputes between landlord and building tenant over alleged broken covenants. Much depended on the nature of the covenant. In the case of the usual requirement to build within a certain period, it is likely that the landlord or developer inserted the time limit to give himself the legal right to evict the builder if circumstances warranted it. It was available if he felt that he could find another builder who promised to make a quick start. Building tenants took the clause seriously. In Bath in 1808, the intending lessee of a field on which he was expected to spend £800 in building wrote to the owner that 'you will, I well know, grant me as long a time as you *possibly can* (consistent with your own

---

[40] P. B. Chatwin (ed.), *The Records of King Edward's School Birmingham*, IV, Publications of the Dugdale Society, XX, pp. 69–70.
[41] *B.P.P.* 1844, XVII, *First Report of the Commissioners for Inquiring into the State of Large Towns*, p. 670.

engagement under your purchase deed) for my expending the £800 in the buildings to be erected on the ground.'[42]

In practice, the landlord or developer was often willing to ignore the requirement for the time being if the rent was regularly paid, and particularly if the general demand for building land and building activity was at a low ebb. It has been shown that much land in Manchester acquired by developers and intending builders in the year or two prior to 1793 was unbuilt on for many years. Generally, the vendors did not resume possession as long as the rent was paid. In more normal times instances may be found of the land promoter allowing the tenure to run on. In April 1800, Nottingham Corporation leased 1,381 square yards to a builder named Stocks, requiring him to use the front of the site within three years. Stocks built on part of the rest of the plot and failed to use the frontage, but only in 1819 did the Corporation enforce its surrender, although it had frequently called upon him to relinquish this part of his land.[43] The case of the Sefton Estate in Toxteth Park, Liverpool suggests that, although the time clause was often not enforced, it provided the landlord with a vital legal safeguard. According to the Earl of Sefton, the absence of such a clause was the reason for the failure to build along the street frontages.[44]

The covenant naming the minimum sum to be spent (usually in conjunction with the requirement to build one or more houses) may have been too vague to be effective.[45] Where covenants were detailed, especially in the case of better-class housing, there is almost no evidence to show to what extent the estate or the developer supervised construction to see that the covenants were implemented. Adherence to the specifications for the facade could easily be watched, and many of the surviving squares and streets in towns such as Bath, Bristol and Liverpool are evidence of their success. The remaining construction was probably much less adequately supervised. At least occasionally inspection did

---

[42] Bath Guildhall: Hensley deeds.

[43] Nottingham Archives M19657-8; for a Manchester case in the early nineteenth century, see P.R.O. PL.6/109 f.20.

[44] See above, p. 110; for a Bristol case in 1781 in which legal action for non-compliance was taken without a long delay, see P.R.O. E112/1929/261-3.

[45] It is doubtful how legally effective were clauses just to spend a stated sum on one or more houses. In 1788 the Mosley Estate in Manchester conveyed 6½ acres to developers under a covenant to spend £1,000 'in building'. Chancery ruled in 1796 that this was too vague to be enforceable because only 'building' was mentioned; even if 'houses' had been said in general terms enforceability would have been difficult; on the other hand the courts were able to enforce specific covenants regarding the facade of houses: F. Vesey, *Reports of Cases in the High Court of Chancery*, III (1814), pp. 184-7 (usually quoted as *3 Ves.184*); H. Maddock, *Reports of Cases in the Court of the Vice Chancellor of England*, V (1822), p. 469 (*5 Madd.469*); A. B. Emden, *The Law about Building Leases and Building Contracts* (1882), pp. 169-74.

take place. In 1766, John Seely, carpenter, agreed to lease land outside Frankfurt Gate in Plymouth from a local mercer, Courtenay Connell, for a row of substantial houses; then he dug the foundations 'with the privity and almost daily inspection of the said Courtenay Connell'.[46] The *intention* of supervision was sometimes inserted in a covenant. At Bath in the case of one of the elder Wood's promotions, North Parade, Wood agreed with the builders that he would 'inspect and direct the carrying on and building' of the houses.[47] In so far as it was done, inspection was probably in most cases intermittent: in general, urban estate owners in the eighteenth century are unlikely to have had the staff to watch building systematically.

Covenants regarding the *use* of the premises erected were particularly difficult to enforce. We have seen that the Liverpool Corporation covenant regarding separate occupation of cellars was widely disregarded. The financial advantage to the lessee was too strong. Nuisance clauses were also a problem.[48] Several cases have been traced of attempts by promoters to enforce restrictions against the erection of butchers' shambles.[49] At least in the years of first building, when the success of a promotion through the disposal of the remaining lots may have depended on nuisance covenants being obeyed, the owner or developer was sometimes successful in this respect. In the case of Mrs. Wright's promotion at Nottingham, begun in 1802, she was able to advertise a few lots still unsold in 1806 with the inducement that 'the houses in these streets are very respectable, having been erected under a deed of covenant to prevent nuisances, or improper buildings'.[50] Once the land had been fully covered with houses, the inducement to enforce such covenants would have been less strong.

It is easy to underestimate the effectiveness of restrictive covenants in this period. The remark of the Liverpool developer James Gill that 'there was scarcely a lease under the Corporation of Liverpool in which all the covenants have been complied with' has already been quoted. Clearly some covenants were almost impossible to enforce, and some others promoters often did not try to get obeyed. Yet, where compliance was essential to the completion of a scheme as originally planned, as in the case of covenants regarding the facades of houses, a real degree of success was achieved.

---

[46] P.R.O. E112/1412/126.
[47] Bath Guildhall: deeds re. North Parade; in 1796 Nottingham Corporation decided to give itself the power in building leases 'to inspect the progress' of erections: *Records of the Borough of Nottingham*, VII: 1760–1800 (Nottingham, 1947), p. 340.
[48] See above, p. 121.
[49] E.g., P.R.O. E112/1548/831 concerns a Manchester case.
[50] *Nottingham Journal*, 16 Aug. 1806.

6
Land Prices, Outlay and Profits

I BUILDING LAND VALUES

It is easier to say who supplied the building land than to write about the financial transactions involved in land promotion. The size of the project, the increase in the value of the land following its conversion from agricultural to building use, the length of time needed to dispose of all the sites to builders, and in particular the initial outlay by landlords or developers on the basic amenities, differed greatly not only between towns but also between individual schemes. Even if the evidence available were plentiful—which it is not—it would be impossible to generalize on such matters as outlay and returns.

The amount of the increase in the value of the land on its conversion to building use was crucially important for the profit of the landlord and developer. Three factors helped to determine the extent of the increase. One was the value of the land while still in non-building use; the second was its precise urban location; and the third was the point in time at which it was marketed.

In the case of the larger towns, farmland near the outskirts was highly rented, whatever its precise use, compared with most agricultural land, because of the great market for meat, milk, fruit and vegetables. At Hull in the 1790s, land on the outskirts was worth two or three times more than land of similar quality several miles from the town.

'The land, for two or three miles round Hull, is in grass, for the convenience of the inhabitants. The rent of that which is contiguous to the town, is from £4 to £5 an acre. The rent decreases in proportion to the distance of the land from the town. At four or five miles from Hull, it is about 30s. an acre.'[1]

Rich soils used for market gardening, and in particular land parcelled out into small allotments for the use of the inhabitants, yielded large

[1] F. M. Eden, *The State of the Poor*, III (1797), p. 830.

rents. On the outskirts of Birmingham in the early 1780s, the land on six or eight farms rented for about £2 per acre, other ground in detached parcels (probably grazing accommodation land) at about £4, while little gardens of a few hundred square yards each let at the equivalent of about £16 an acre.[2]

The location of land on the edge of the town was another important influence on building land values. The relative demand for the various sites on offer naturally influenced the price which land promoters were able to ask. Plots lying near lines of communication or sources of employment, or sites on rising land, suitable for housing the well-to-do, commanded higher prices or ground rents than land which did not enjoy such benefits. Land within the physical limits of the town attracted the biggest premium. Higher land prices near the business heart of a town seem to have been a universal characteristic. An example has already been given for Portsea, relating to the open field strips in the 1780s and early 1790s. The contrast is observable well before the great urban expansion of the 1780s. In Nottingham in the 1760s, land in the Greyhound Yard between the Market Place, the business centre of the town, and the Backside (now Parliament Street) sold for 7s. 7d. and 8s. per square yard, while land in closes on the edge of the town or further from the Market Place fetched between 2s. and 3s.[3]

The size of the increment on building land also depended on the date at which it was used. Although land on the edge of a town was generally available to builders, the unprecedented expansion of the later eighteenth century was accompanied by rising prices for sites in comparable situations in the outskirts.[4] They rose at least two or three times in every town during the course of the period. The trend was moving unmistakeably upwards from the middle of the eighteenth century. Though local factors affected the degree and timing of the changes, the same general pattern is visible everywhere.

Birmingham, Manchester and Sheffield were all centres where no large entailed estate or common field blocked expansion between the

[2] W. Hutton, *A History of Birmingham*, 2nd edn. (Birmingham, 1783), p. 8.
[3] For the Portsea case, see above, p. 125; for Nottingham, see Nottingham Archives: M.17523-30, 17783-6, 18021-4; Debenham and Co.: deeds re. site of Victoria Station, Nottingham: C.249, H.308, N.107, B.378, B.329, B.340. As another later example, in Hull in the boom of the later 1780s and early 1790s, land within the town wall in Broadley St. sold at prices between £1 10s. 0d. and £1 15s. 0d. per square yard, compared with prices in Dock St., adjoining the new dock outside the wall, at between 8s. 3d. and 9s. 3d., and in some streets further from the old town to the north-west as low as 1s. 6d. to 3s. 0d.: Hull R.O. deeds re. Dock St., West St., Middle St., and Gas Company deeds.
[4] The following analysis of land prices is based on prices given in the almost innumerable surviving building leases and sale conveyances, used in conjunction with contemporary town maps (*see* Appendix on Sources). It should be stressed that the prices given are for land on the edge of the town at the dates quoted.

1760s and 1820. They were also inland towns and none lay beside rivers which posed obstacles to building. Expansion could take place on all sides. In all three towns the price of land appears roughly to have doubled between the 1770s and 1820. In Birmingham and Sheffield, where the evidence is available from the early eighteenth century, the price seems to have increased about three times between 1740 and 1820. It is true that prices in general were rising sharply between the early 1790s and about 1810, but the earlier rise in prices of building land represents at least a doubling of land values in real terms on the urban perimeter.[5]

In Birmingham, the tendency for the major landowners to lease direct to builders and to adopt a standard price per square yard on their respective estates gave some uniformity to site prices. On the perimeter in the 1740s and 1750s, most land on a 99 or 120-year tenure was let at between ¾d. and 1d. per square yard. At the beginning of the long period of activity from 1764, prices were raised from under 1d. to 1½d. on the Colmore Estate, and this was the price fixed in 1766 and 1768 by the Gooch and Inge Estates respectively. The remaining properties followed suit during the boom of the 1770s, and 1½d. remained the general price for the decade. The big owners had more than enough land to meet the unprecedented demand. During the mid and later 1780s, the Colmore, Inge and Gooch Estates raised their prices in turn from 1½d. to 2d., reflecting the renewed surge of building activity. By 1789, 2d. had become the common price, as it was to remain until the end of the boom in 1793 and 1794. When building recovered well after 1800, 2d., 2½d. and 3d. were the usual prices.

In the case of Manchester the evidence is less plentiful. The common practice for land developers to act as middlemen between original landlord and builder led to a more varied price range for building sites. The available material suggests that builders on the edge of the town paid between about 1½d. and 5d. per square yard between the early 1770s and 1788, as a fee-farm rent or on a long lease of 999 years. The great surge of building at the end of the 1780s and the beginning of the 1790s drove up prices, and prices created between 1789 and 1800 lay between about 2d. and 8d. per square yard, or more. In the rising activity after 1800, prices rose again to between 3d. or 3½d. and 10½d.[6]

---

[5] The Sheffield conclusions were based on Sheffield Archives: Arundel Castle MSS. S382, 383, 391; register of Capital Burgesses' leases.

[6] Manchester Town Hall: deeds; British Rail: Hunts Bank deed room: Manchester Piccadilly Station deeds. In the case of Manchester the deeds of site conveyances available were only a tiny fraction of the total number made, but related to most parts of the edge of the town: thus the evidence for 1771–88 related to *c.* 30 streets, that for 1788–1800 to *c.* 35 streets, and that for 1801–20 to *c.* 40 streets. Again it should be stressed that the prices are those paid by builders, not developers.

In some of the coastal towns prices rose even faster, for reasons already suggested. In Portsea, where sites were sold freehold, rates increased in each period of building activity. By the great Napoleonic boom after 1806, prices for land on the edge of the town were at least four times what they had been in the War of the Austrian Succession and the Seven Years War. The median price was about 6s. 2½d. compared with 1s. 6d. in the 1740s and 1750s.

In the port of Liverpool, where most land was let for three lives and twenty-one years at an almost nominal rent of 1s. per yard frontage, the fines paid at the time of the granting of the lease rose at least three times between the early 1770s and the 1810s:

1771–6[7]	3s.–7s. 3½d.
1781–90	3s. 3½d.–12s. 3½d.
1791–1800	4s. 8d.–18s. 7d.
1801–10	8s. 2½d.–£1
1811–20	10s.–£1/£2[8]

The leasehold estate owners in Birmingham sometimes raised their land prices during years of heavy building activity, but generally did not reduce them in years of depression. The ample resources of these estates made a lowering of prices to attract more builders a marginal benefit in relation to total income. The owners and their agents probably preferred to hold their land until construction recovered.

When land was in the hands of developers, as at Manchester, Liverpool or Portsea, prices were pushed up in the boom years, but in the ensuing period they might fall temporarily if the change in building conditions was great. The financial resources of most developers were smaller than those of the landowners. In a period of building depression, at least a few preferred a quick sale at a reduced profit, or even some loss, to holding land with uncertain prospects. As the great Napoleonic building boom was drawing to a close developers in Portsea were receiving lower prices for plots between 1815 and 1818.

In Manchester in the later 1790s the position was rather different. By the beginning of 1795 there was a fall in the value of land intended for building development consequent upon the collapse of the housing boom of the early 1790s. In January 1795, a timber merchant and iron turner who had acquired local property subject to the payment of large

---

[7] Liverpool R.O.: deeds. While the evidence is drawn from a large number of streets, it is insufficient to suggest a median price.

[8] Again at Brighton, where the sea prevented expansion to the south, land prices were high, ranging from 4s. 4d. to 25s. od. over the whole period 1780–1820; East Sussex R.O. D297, 527, 530, 628, 921; Sussex Archaeological Society: deeds: BR, HC, L, N: Brighton Town Hall deed bdl. 84/9.

chief rents, found that these 'rents by reason of the then late reduction or fall in the value of lands were considered to be more in amount than the then present worth' of the property. But this fall did not affect the sale prices of individual building lots between 1795 and 1800. They stayed at much the same level as those of 1790–93. Presumably they remained steady because many developers were prepared to hold land until they could obtain a good price. The earlier long rise in land values may have encouraged them to wait for the market to brighten, as it certainly did a little in the later 1790s,[9] and by 1804–5 prices had moved up more. In Liverpool between the 1780s and the 1820s, many developers held land for as long as one or two decades. This may help to explain the failure of the depressions of the mid-1790s and 1808–10 to prevent a long-run rise in land prices.[10] It was fairly general for prices to rise in times of high activity and not to fall more than temporarily in years of depression.

With the brisk disposal of plots at rising prices returns to land promotion were generally good in a boom. In a building depression promoters were hit not so much by declining site prices as by the small number of buyers and the consequent delay in completing the promotion. In the long run, although land prices were highest in money terms about 1810, profits on land promotion had probably reached a high point earlier. The twenty years after about 1791 were a period of inflation: agricultural land prices rose sharply with the rising demand for foodstuffs, and climbing wage rates (which rose at least as fast as plot prices) also drove up the cost of amenities. On the other hand, site prices were rising sharply between mid-century and about 1790 without corresponding growth in the wage level, though rents on agricultural land in the neighbourhood of towns also increased with the expansion of the urban food market. On the whole, potential profits on the conversion of land to building use were probably climbing until about 1790, and in the long run tended to level off thereafter.[11] If returns were at a peak

[9] Manchester Town Hall: P.30, C.30, box 55 pcl. 2, box 349, G.2, P1/324; B.R. Mornington Crescent: Piccadilly Stn. deeds 44, 64R, and B.R. Hunts Bank: Central Stn. deeds 3, 47, 67, 6(d), 30(b). It is possible that a further factor may have been that there was little encouragement to reduce land sale prices because land was a relatively small element in building costs; cheaper land alone would have been insufficient to persuade builders to erect houses. See also C. D. Long *Building Cycles and the Theory of Investment* (Princeton, 1940), pp. 201–2.
[10] See below, pp. 283–4, 290.
[11] Apart from the general factors just discussed in this chapter, it has also been shown that the value of plots was affected by the type of housing project involved: the estate intended for bigger houses for the well-to-do often charged higher rents or payments per square yard, but from the point of view of profit this was offset at least in part by greater outlay on amenities and a loss of income from the dedication of a higher proportion of land to streets and open spaces; see above, pp. 62, 64; estates might also obtain varying prices for sites by auctioning land instead of making private sales at a fixed price.

about 1790 it may help to explain, with other factors such as the easy availability of credit in most towns, the great land promotions of the time.

Most land on the edge of towns increased in value several times on its conversion to building use. Birmingham, where building land values were lower than in some of the major provincial towns, offers some examples. In 1746, witnesses for the Colmore Estate Bill told a House of Lords committee that land on the Estate would increase in value from 30s. to £15 an acre if converted to building use.[12] Such an estimate proved roughly correct: after allowance had been made for land used for streets, the Estate received the equivalent of between about £12 and £16 an acre from builders between 1747 and 1750.[13]

Again, at the beginning of the 1780s owners letting land for building in Birmingham generally received an equivalent of about £24 an acre. As we have seen, farmland on the outskirts was worth about £2 an acre, land in parcels (probably grazing accommodation land) £4, and allotments £16. Because of the costs involved, it would hardly have paid to convert the little gardens into housing sites, but the other land would have increased in value between six and twelve times.[14]

In Portsea, at the height of the building boom in 1813, land in use for market-gardening in the suburbs was worth between £2 and £4 and accommodation land between £7 and £10. In terms of capital value at thirty years' purchase, these figures corresponded to £60–£120 and £210–£300 respectively. The sums received for sites from builders were the equivalent of about £600–£1,800 an acre, with a median of about £1,200. Even accommodation land would have been worth converting to building, and some of the garden land may have increased in value over ten times.[15]

When the landlord leased or sold direct to builders, the whole of the increment naturally passed to him. On the other hand, if the layout of the land and provision of the amenities was partly or wholly done by one or more developers, it was shared. Occasionally this was done by prior agreement. We have seen that in a building lease of 30 August 1774, conveying about 2 acres to Richard Atwood, Bath Corporation reserved to itself one-third of all the ground rents the developer was

---

[12] It should be stressed that the amounts referred to as applying to building in the following cases are those received (or expected to be received) from *builders*, not *developers;* British Museum 357.d.2(50).

[13] Based on ground rents actually received per square yard, making a deduction to allow for the area of the streets: B.R.L. Colmore MSS.

[14] See above, p. 141; based on Colmore and Gooch MSS. etc.

[15] C. Vancouver, *General View of the Agriculture of Hampshire* (1813), p. 86; Portsmouth R.O. deeds.

expected to get from his tenants.[16] More often the developer paid a fixed sum upon the conveyance of the land (or covenanted to pay it after a certain date), or agreed to pay an agreed rent. The amount varied, but tended to be more than the agricultural value of the land, and of course much less than the developer hoped to obtain from the conveyance of individual plots to builders. For example, in Portsea between 1810 and 1814, prices paid by developers for parcels of half an acre or 1 acre for building promotion varied between £250 and over £1,000, in other words between the agricultural and building site values just quoted.[17]

2 THE COSTS OF LAND PROMOTION

The big rent increases or capital gains received by the original land-lord alone, or shared by him with one or more developers, were naturally realised in full when all the land had been conveyed to builders. We have seen that schemes often took many years to complete. Developers were hit more by delays than promoter-landlords because they either paid a capital sum for the land initially (in the case of freehold projects) or, in leasehold or perpetual-rent schemes, they contracted to pay a rent which usually took account of the building potential of the land. The case of the Lime St. project, in which the land was purchased in 1808 but receipts for the sale of plots did not begin to be received until two years later, has been described. One Manchester development, in which the delay in disposing of land was the result of unexpected legal difficulties rather than the more usual lack of demand, provides rare contemporary comment on the ensuing financial difficulties. In December 1798, Henry Philips, merchant, John Leigh Philips, merchant, Oliver Ormrod, plumber and glazier, William Tate of Manchester, portrait painter, and Thomas Moss Tate, Esq., of Liverpool, acquired 29,936 square yards 'for the purpose of granting and selling the same in fee in small lots or parcels to persons willing to build upon and improve the same'. Henry Philips's quarter share of the perpetual rent charges was £217 19s. 7½d. The total rent was thus nearly £150 an acre, but in January 1800 he died intestate. Because of the infancy of his heiress, no grants could be made for building from her share of the ground. To overcome the difficulty, parliament was petitioned for a private act in 1802. The petition stated 'that until such grants and sales can be made, the said lands must in great measure be useless and unproductive and not nearly adequate to the payment of the rents to which the same were originally made subject and liable'. Letting the land for grazing or market

[16] See above, p. 79.
[17] Portsmouth R.O. D197, 402, 1912, 1966, 1984, 2122, 2398.

146

gardening would have been unlikely to have earned more than about £5 or £10 an acre at the most.[18]

More often in the case of a promotion which lasted many years, the developer was able to dispose of some lots at any early stage. But this involved him in expenditure on the preparation of the land and supply of amenities. Evidence on this important topic is generally sparse. Only on one point is it possible to be relatively clear: that of the cost of securing an act of parliament to grant a legally binding building lease or to sell land. We have seen that in the later eighteenth century the legal expenses were usually between £150 and £300.[19] But many owners did not need an act.

One inescapable charge was expenditure on measuring the projected building land, drawing plans and staking it out, but total costs were modest. One detailed case may help to make this clear. Between November 1792 and February 1793, the Corporation of Nottingham was planning the sale for building of several closes in the west end of the town at a place called Tollhouse Hill. The following were the items charged by William Stretton, the Corporation surveyor:

Nov. 22	attended Committee to view Tollers Hill, Sandhills, Smarts, Butchers Close, etc.	10s. 6d.
24	drawing plan of Tollhouse Hill and staking and measuring the ground	£1 1s. 0d.
Dec. 30 and 31	measuring the Sandhills and making general plan of the 17 lots of land, staking out the same and attending Committee with it sundry times	£2 12s. 6d.
	paid for 12 stakes for Sandhills	2s. 0d.
Jan. 8	attending Committee and altering Sandhills plan in consequence of a view with Mr. Oldknow	5s. 0d.
22	attending Common Hall to confirm preceding business, making new plan of Toll House Hill dividing into two lots and attending to draw up advertisements	5s. 0d.
29	making plan on large scale of 5 first lots on Sandhills	5s. 0d.
Feb. 20	making plan on large scale of 12 lots on Sandhills	5s. 0d.[20]

[18] The evidence provided by this instance is available because the cause of the delay was legal and was thus curable by act of parliament: H.L.R.O. Main Papers, 26 April 1802: Philips estate bill; J. Holt *General View of the Agriculture of the County of Lancaster* (1795), p. 22.
[19] E.g., H.L.R.O. draft acts 1764, 1766, 1786.
[20] *Records of the Borough of Nottingham*, VII, 1760–1800 (Nottingham, 1947), pp. 304–7.

Thus the total surveyor's bill was only £5 6s. od. for the nineteen building lots, which included numerous attendances, some alterations, and the preparation of large-scale plans; by comparison the sale price of the two Tollhouse Hill plots and the first five Sandhills plots alone was £937 6s. 7d.[21]

In the later eighteenth century some landowners prepared elevations of the facade of intended houses which builders were expected to follow, but the cost of these was small. In 1786 Liverpool Corporation paid Samuel Hope, the Manchester architect, £20 for his designs and elevations for rebuilding the west side of Castle Street.[22] As the sum related to a row of plots, the amount was tiny in relation to the size of the project. Architectural fees are unlikely to have been a major item in the outlay of any of the major building projects of the period.[23]

Far greater was expenditure on levelling the streets, paving the road surface and the footpaths, and the making of drains. Evidence on this subject is meagre, and the value of some of the brief references to expenditure on these items is reduced by the impossibility of relating them to the size of the whole project. There is a little material for Manchester and Liverpool after 1800. In the case of the Mallalieu and Outram property a Manchester surveyor said in 1806 that the unsold land comprising 10½ statute acres would need to have between £2,700 and £3,000 spent on it in levelling the ground, making streets and sewers and sluices before it could be sold for building.[24] This implies an outlay of over £250 an acre. The amount spent per acre varied according to the quality of the paving, the size of the streets, and whether sewers were laid. Expenditure at the beginning of the nineteenth century on the typical project in Manchester and Liverpool was well over £100 per acre, and reached in some instances as much as £200 or £250.

[21] Though the sale prices were agreed with intending purchasers, the sales may not have been completed; *ibid.*, pp. 285, 289.

[22] Mathias, 'The Liverpool Corporate Estate', pp. 112–15.

[23] The architect and builder John Eveleigh of Bath, who was active in the great boom of the later 1780s and beginning of the 1790s, charged architectural fees which have been described as 'ridiculously small'; for the central feature of a major block of houses, Somerset Place, he is reputed to have been paid a guinea. Cf. Ison, *Bath*, p. 41 re. architectural activities of John Eveleigh.

[24] H.L.R.O. Committee book, 1806, pp. 274–5; in another Manchester case £149 18s. 8d. was owed in 1807 for the expence of 'soughing and paving' streets with reference to 5,740 square yards in Chorlton Row, the land having been acquired in 1799; this is about £125 a statute acre, but it is not clear whether it represents all the money payable: P.R.O. B1/109, p. 157; for Liverpool evidence concerning just paving, see Liverpool R.O. deeds 865A and P.R.O. E112/1545/710; the former reference concerns a bill for paving in Seymour and Vincent Sts.; suggesting a cost of about £150 or £200 per acre of building land; the latter refers to a returnable deposit of £205 required for the paving of Gloucester St. on the 2-acre Lime Street development; the Liverpool Corporation ledger 1789–98 suggests that opening and levelling streets was also expensive, though costs per acre cannot be measured from this source (*see* ledger 19 Sept. and 5 Nov. 1791).

Land Prices, Outlay and Profits

It is of course true that basic amenities such as pavements and drains were not always supplied. Most streets were roughly levelled, but not all were necessarily paved nor sewered, even in the 1800s. Despite covenants in land conveyances in Liverpool and Manchester, not all back streets were paved, still less drained. On these points the evidence in our period is small. Reports made one or two decades later comment on the number of unpaved and undrained roads. In Manchester in 1832, out of 687 streets inspected, 248 were unpaved and 53 partially paved. It was reported of Liverpool in 1842 that many of its main streets were still unsewered, and that most of the working-class thoroughfares were in this condition.[25] Road surfaces deteriorated rapidly in the later eighteenth and early nineteenth centuries from sheer neglect. Some roads thus described as 'unpaved' may in fact have been laid with cobblestones or flagstones at the time of building two or three decades earlier. However, as the dispute between James Gill and the Corporation of Liverpool has shown, some roads were not paved and more not sewered before 1820.

In better-class promotions, costs were generally higher than on more typical developments. The streets and pavements were wider and more care was taken with the provision of the sewers; a piped water supply was occasionally created. At Edinburgh in the New Town, the Council spent £14,910 between 1767 and 1783 on levelling and paving streets, providing drains and laying sewers on a site that was under 50 acres, or over £300 an acre—and that before the inflationary years at the end of the century.[26] Sometimes squares and gardens were planned as an additional attraction.[27]

In Bath and Bristol the preparation of the ground and levelling on uneven sites was sometimes a heavy initial charge for developers. On a 5¼-acre site in Bath, bought in 1765, two developers spent £1,881 19s. 0d. (about £360 an acre) in the first seven years in constructing substructures of vaults and arches, levelling and pitching, as well as demolishing and rebuilding stables and a coach-house.[28]

[25] *B.P.P.* XXVII, 1842 (Lords), p. 307; M. W. Flinn (ed.), *Report on the Sanitary Condition of the Labouring Population of Great Britain, by Edwin Chadwick, 1842* (Edinburgh, 1965), p. 104.
[26] A. J. Youngson, *The Making of Classical Edinburgh* (Edinburgh, 1966), pp. 104–5.
[27] C. W. Chalklin, 'Urban Housing Estates in the Eighteen Century', *Urban Studies*, V, no. 1 (1968), p. 72; Dr. Kellett has shown that at Glasgow at the end of the century, one speculative developer spent £9,000 in converting a piece of waste known as the 'Washing Green' into an embankment and avenue: J. R. Kellett, 'Property Speculators and the Building of Glasgow, 1780–1830', *Scottish Journal of Political Economy*, VIII, no. 3 (1961), p. 226.
[28] Bath Guildhall: Corporation leases, 29 Sept. 1772. In the case of the spectacular Royal York Crescent at Bristol, the promoter James Lockier is said to have spent 'an immense sum' (possibly £20,000) in 1791 'in erecting the deep sub-structure of vaults and basements required to raise the houses and terrace-walks to a constant level': Ison, *Bristol*, p. 228.

Responsibility for all this expenditure varied. At least a few roads in some provincial towns were made up by the local improvement commissioners or turnpike trust. It has been shown that in Portsea in the later eighteenth century, a few streets were paved by the Paving Commissioners.[29] But of far more general importance was the contribution of landlords and developers. In Liverpool, Manchester, Hull and Portsea there is evidence of their work in this respect, particularly towards the end of the period.[30] Sometimes the cost was borne by the land promoter. More often he paid for the work and presented each builder with an account for his share of the costs when the sites were conveyed. In fact the precise practice made little difference, since the provision of amenities without specific charges on the builders was presumably taken into account in fixing the amount of the ground rent or sale price for the plots.

The promoter began to spend money on these amenities when the first plots were conveyed and as builders began work. Since promotions usually took many years to complete, heavy expenditure was involved before the majority of plots were conveyed. The financial involvement often did not end here. Original owners almost never built houses, but it was probably done by the majority of developers. Further, lending of capital by landlords and developers occurred often, though its extent and importance is not clear. Evidence of the granting of short-term credit is relatively sparse, coming chiefly from lawsuits in the Exchequer and Chancery Courts, and these cannot reveal its full extent. Material on longer lending by mortgage is more abundant, but many landowners and developers who were prepared to make temporary advances were unwilling to convert them into indefinite loans, and they only indicate a part of the total lending to builders.

Lending of this kind was greatest in towns or in periods where the building craftsmen were predominant among the speculative builders, because they were more likely to need borrowed capital than other builders, who tended to be investing their own savings. Thus at Liverpool in the early nineteenth century, credit from developers was an important aid to the joiners and other craftsmen who comprised the

[29] See above, p. 126.
[30] See above, pp. 104–6, 97, 130, 126–8; in the absence of estate accounts, there is no evidence for Birmingham about the role of landowners and developers in paving etc.; and act of 1812 (52 Geo. 3c.113) gave the Improvement Commissioners some powers in this respect, but earlier they had no authority in this field; the local Lench Trust made grants for paving, but not for new streets. In Sheffield the Norfolk Estate spent money on road-making in the 1780s and 1790s: Sheffield Archives: Arundel MSS. S185/24, and 1793–4.

majority of suppliers of new houses.[31] On the other hand, in Manchester only one of the developers has been traced as lending money on mortgage to builders, and in Birmingham none of the major landowners has been traced as lending in this way.[32]

It is clear that the offer of capital was some inducement to builders. The attitude of the attorney-developer Bowsher at Bath in 1792 has already been mentioned. In another case occurring in April 1823, Lord Fitzwilliam received a letter from this steward regarding applications for building lots on his Sheffield Estate: 'the applicants are merchants or traders who find it inconvenient to withdraw so much capital from their trade, and they request me to ask, if your lordship would consent to advance them one half of the money expended on the premises, upon mortgages, at 5 per cent . . . .' Fitzwilliam replied: 'I think an arrangement of this nature would soon bring the land to the market.'[33]

The relatively small contribution made by landowners and developers to the total supply of builders' capital may be explained in several ways. Much construction was undertaken by men outside the building trade who erected houses as an outlet for savings and were not in need of credit, particularly in some of the industrial towns as Manchester and Birmingham. There were other local sources of loan capital.[34] Further, because of expenditure on amenities and in the case of developers on land and probably a few houses, some land promoters would have been reluctant or unable to extend their commitments further. Though advances to builders were desirable, and tended to speed up a promotion, they were not essential to most undertakings.

The amount of capital sunk in a building project varied almost endlessly from scheme to scheme. This was due to the difference in the size of each project, the extent of outlay on amenities, and whether money was spent on house construction and advances to builders. On the whole, promotion was a greater gamble for the developer than for the landlord who conveyed direct to the builders. The estate of the landlord was likely to be greater, and the developer not only had to make payment for the land but also often erected houses. Freehold development or promotion involving the payment of a fine was a bigger financial burden to the developer than leasehold projects, because of the initial payment.

---

[31] See above, p. 101. Dr. Ward has drawn my attention to the fact that at Bristol in the beginning of the 1790s, building craftsmen depended heavily on credit supplied by attorney-developers.

[32] Based on a large quantity of mortgage evidence for Manchester and Birmingham: the single case for Manchester is from P.R.O. C110/178.

[33] Sheffield Archives: F107/143: I owe this reference to the Archivist, Miss Meredith.

[34] See below, ch. 9.

However, it is likely that even during the Napoleonic Wars, when prices were highest, developments involving the use of just an acre or two of land would have involved the expenditure of only about £1,000 or perhaps £2,000. This would have been the case in projects which used the open-field strips in Portsea: the land cost between about £200 and £1,200, three or four dwellings to begin the scheme could be built for £100 to £150 each, and only one narrow street would have been needed. On the other hand, the Liverpool developers of the same period probably spent several thousand pounds almost as a matter of course, since often the land alone cost more than £1,500 or £2,000. Some of the biggest outlays were incurred during the boom years at the end of the 1780s and beginning of the 1790s, and outlays of £10,000 or even £20,000 were common among the biggest developers in some of the major provincial towns at this time.[35]

3 DEVELOPERS' PROFITS

Clearly the developer's potential profit was large on account of the increase in the value of the land when it was conveyed in small lots to builders, despite the initial expenditure. Expectations of the capital gains to be made, or the greatly increased rents to be obtained, were high. The Liverpool developer Kirkpatrick hoped that land which he negotiated to buy for £10,000 in the Mosslake Fields in April 1808 would yield about £80,000 profit if he gave careful attention to its sale. His partner Eyes said that the much smaller speculation in Lime Street might 'clear £1,500 in three years', that is, presumably, while part of the land remained unsold.[36] In the case of the Outram and Mallalieu property in Manchester, a local surveyor estimated in 1806 that the remaining 10½ statute acres would produce an annual income of £1,696 when fully let. He did not give enough information to allow us to calculate the potential return on the developers' outlay. It is not clear whether part of the reserved rents of nearly £700 payable by the developers should be deducted from the figure of £1,696. They had to spend between £2,700 and £3,000 on amenities, and rent payments over the previous years may have cost them another £2,000 or £3,000. Even so,

---

[3]; See the Birmingham, Manchester and Bath instances cited above, pp. 78, 88, 92; in Bristol in 1792, what was perhaps the biggest project of the eighteenth century in provincial England involved the acquisition of 78 acres of freehold and leasehold land laid out for 'a crescent, square, circus and several streets and other buildings upon a regular plan', the freehold land of 54 acres alone costing £40,000; but the scheme collapsed in 1793: H.L.R.O. Main Papers 5 March 1792, and information from Dr. Ward.
[36] P.R.O. E112/1545/710.

Land Prices, Outlay and Profits

an annual return of about £1,000 on a total outlay of, say, £5,000 or £6,000 would have been handsome.[37]

Unfortunately no precise figures are available for returns on finished building-land projects. In one instance, that of Thomas Croxton on about 8 acres in the Southsea district of Portsea during the great Napoleonic boom, some indication of the profit has survived. He claimed to have 'netted £17,000', a reasonable figure when judged against site sales on his property of between 8s. and 15s. a square yard.[38] Contemporary prices paid by developers for large parcels in Portsea suggest that the land may have cost him between £1,500 and £4,000; at the very most, bearing in mind that he created tiny back streets for his plots, amenities cost him £500 an acre, or another £4,000, and part of this was recoverable from builders. As he does not appear to have lent to builders or constructed dwellings himself, his outlay can have been no more than £7,000 or £8,000, and could well have been half such a figure. On this basis his net gain was at least twice, and probably three or four times, his expenditure.[39]

It is likely that the Lime Street project was rather less successful, even if all the land was ultimately sold. From what is known of the prices received for the plots, total receipts are unlikely to have exceeded £5,000 or £6,000, and some were still being sold after 1820. On the other hand, there were non-recoverable charges of £3,027 12s. 6d. involved in the land purchase. The partners also laid out several hundred pounds on the amenities, and agreed in 1810 to erect two houses costing about £600 each, though both these outlays were presumably recovered at least in part. Two things helped to reduce the profits of this

[37] H.L.R.O. Main Papers 28 April 1806: Outram estate bill, and Committee book, 1806, pp. 274–5; the developers had obtained the lands between 1796 and 1803, rent payments by them being nearly £700 annually; by 1806 they were receiving about £360 in income from the whole property, which was expected to rise to about £600 a year when some contracts were executed.

[38] H. Slight, The History of Portsmouth (1838), Southsea, p. 1; Portsmouth R.O.: deeds re. Kings Rd, Copper, Flint, Stone, Gold and Diamond Sts., and Little Southsea St.

[39] A similar success story is provided by Hull during the boom of the mid-1800s. According to a local historian, Osborne St. was laid out in 1802 and houses began to be built in 1803, the landowner being Robert Osborne. On his marriage his father-in-law had given 'him his choice whether he would have £5,000 as a marriage portion or the fields on which Osborne St. now stands. Robert Osborne most wisely selected the fields, and soon laid them out for a street running from Water House-lane, and soon realised by the sale of small allotments more than £15,000'; his outlay is unknown, and it is not clear whether the figure represents gross or net profit, but the implication is that the promotion was highly successful: Hull Reference Library: History of the Streets of Hull, collected from the J. Richardson MSS., reprinted from The Hull and East Yorkshire Times, 1915, p. 11; this also contains a local tradition about Cent-per-Cent St., developed at the same time by the auctioneer William Bell, who is supposed to have realized 100 per cent on the scheme, from which the name was said to have derived (p. 7); but deed evidence shows that the name was in use while the sites were being sold!

153

development. The proportion of the land devoted to streets was exceptionally high, expecially with the 14-yard Gloucester Street running through the parcel; more important, Fitchet had obtained the land at auction against keen competition, and the price was thought by the Liverpool attorneys to have been dear.[40]

Croxton and the Liverpool syndicate were fortunate in that their projects were well timed. Croxton began to put sites on the market just as local building activity was gathering pace. The Liverpool partners were able to sell their first plots in the rising activity after 1810. The fate of the Ancoats Lane scheme is unknown. Unless all the lots were sold within the next two years the developers would have been caught by the onset of the building depression in 1808 and 1809, which lasted for several years. Brooke of Ashted was bankrupted as a result of the financial difficulties of 1792 and 1793. The rewards of land speculation might be outstanding. But failure, leading to bankruptcy, was a real possibility for developers, because of the initial outlay on land, amenities, and perhaps building and credit.

[40] P.R.O. E112/1545/710; Liverpool R.O. deeds 719C.

18 Commerce Place, Nottingham. Tenements erected by several builders on land sold by Thomas Althorpe in 1807 (*see* map 19). Six dwellings were sold for £420 in 1813.

II THE FREEHOLD TOWNS

19 (*left*) Crosland Place, Nottingham, in The Red Lion Street area.

20 (*above*) Standard Hill, Nottingham: two houses erected on land sold by the Duke of Newcastle in 1807 for larger houses. No dwellings were to be erected worth less than £25 per annum.

21 (*opposite*) Nile Street, Nottingham: back-to-backs erected in the early 1800s. The builder of some, or all, of the dwellings was probably William Johnson, victualler, who bought the land from the guardians of the Duke of Newcastle in 1801, and was also responsible for several houses on the Sherwin Estate and for property elsewhere in Nottingham.

22, 23 Stone Street, Southsea (*above*): houses erected on the Croxton development during the Napoleonic boom. The two built as a pair were sold for £410 in 1811 by the builder James Freeman, stonemason. The dwellings were typical of those erected in this period without covenants controlling the façade. Ridge Street, Portsea (*below*): a row of houses developed by the attorneys Moses Greetham and Thomas Binsted in the early 1790s. The houses fetched between £120 and £160 each.

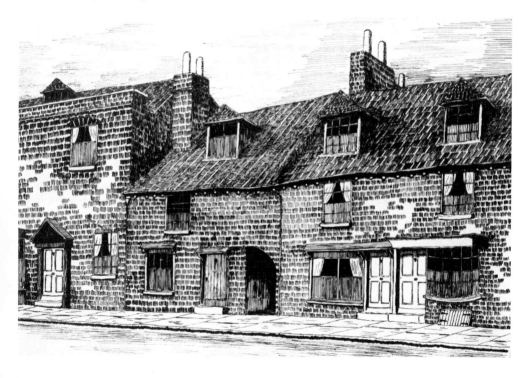

24, 25 Union Street, Portsea (*above*): a typical street in West Dock Field, where most of the open-field strips were developed between 1702 and 1784. Union Street was built partly in the 1700s and partly in the years after 1736. Surrey Street, Portsea (*below*): houses erected in the later 1790s. No. 58 was built by John Edmunds, blacksmith, on a site bought in 1797; No. 62 was erected by Benjamin Calcott, joiner, with the help of a mortgage for £120 from William Hurst, probably a pawnbroker, and sold in 1803 for £180.

26, 27 Scott Street, Hull, *c.* 1800–1805 (*left*): houses erected in one of the smaller streets in the Sculcoates district without covenants relating to the facade. The land was developed by the devizes of Christopher Scott. Stubbs Buildings, *c.* 1800 (*below*): a typical Hull court. Seven of the tenements were conveyed in 1801 to Samuel Stubbs, the builder, after completion. They were promptly mortgaged to a Lincolnshire farmer.

28, 29 Houses on the Dock Company Estate, Hull, *c.* 1782 (*above*). The nearer house was erected by Philip Green, merchant and shipowner, the further one by William Osborne, timber merchant. The sites were bought from the Company at auction on 11 October 1781. Terraced houses in Albion Street, *c.* 1794–6 (*below*), erected on land sold by Richard Baker, merchant. Among the builders were a stone mason, Daniel Hopewell, a bricklayer, George Jackson, and a joiner, Joseph Clarkson.

30, 31 Regency Square, Brighton, built after 1818 (*above*): one of the most ambitious developments in the housing boom of the end of the 1810s. The owner, J. F. Hansom, laid out the garden enclosure and seventy building plots which he leased with an option to purchase. Each builder was to complete his facade according to an approved pattern, with a balcony, area and pavement. Most of the houses had been built ten years later. Portland Square, Plymouth (*below*): houses developed between 1809 and 1815 when the Napoleonic building boom was at its height. The developer was a local tanner, John Allen, who sold the lots to builders of the usual varied occupations. It was agreed that the facades should be built to a uniform plan and that owners should contribute to the upkeep of the square.

Part III
The Builder

7

The Building Owners

I HOUSE OWNERSHIP AND BUILDING AS AN INVESTMENT

Several groups of people contributed to urban building in the later eighteenth century, First, there were those who made the decisions to build, the 'building undertakers' or 'building owners', who leased and bought the site and arranged and financed the erection of one or more houses, which they let, sold, or occupied personally. It is with this group of 'builders'[1] that the following chapters are especially concerned. Capital also passed indirectly into building from those who bought houses soon after construction; the capital of the men responsible for their erection being freed for further projects. A third source of funds came from the suppliers of loan capital to builders, and lastly there were the craftsmen—the carpenters, bricklayers, plasterers and the like—who actually built the houses. Sometimes they were the same men as the building owners.

It is generally accepted that there was more than sufficient capital in the community to meet the needs of the growing investment of the eighteenth century. The long-term fall in the rate of interest preceding the 1750s suggests that the supply of capital was increasing in relation to demand. Savings were accumulating as a result of the expansion of inland and overseas trade, of higher productivity in agriculture and the development of the dependent processing industries, and in some branches of manufacturing industry. Its continuation at a relatively low level implies that investment needs in agriculture, transport and industry were being met without undue difficulty.

It has been argued that 'there were enough rich people in the country to finance an economic effort far in excess of the modest activities of the leaders of the Industrial Revolution'.[2] Large capitals did exist in the

---

[1] Throughout the book, 'builder' refers to the building owner, or undertaker, who acquired the site and paid for the construction of one or more houses.

[2] M. M. Postan, 'Recent trends in the accumulation of capital', in F. Crouzet (ed.), *Capital Formation in the Industrial Revolution* (1972), p. 71.

eighteenth century, particularly among landowners and a few merchants engaged in foreign trade and occasionally in industry, at least towards the end of the period. But, outside London at least, much of the wealth of the country consisted of countless small estates with a mixture of personal and real assets worth between a few hundred and two or three thousand pounds. In the towns these were held by some of the more substantial artisans and craftsmen, general tradesmen, victuallers, processors of agricultural products, a few professional people, and leisured men, widows and spinsters.

In the Medway Towns between 1687 and 1740, probate assessments were made in the local ecclesiastical courts for 478 people who were believed to have left goods and money worth valuing: 178 had personal property worth more than £100, and sixty-seven more than £300. Those in the latter category included shipwrights, maltsters, fisherman, vintners, drapers, carpenters, bakers, cheesemongers, tallow-chandlers, tobacconists and other retailers.[3] Probably wealth per head of the population was higher in these towns than in most other regions outside London on account of the presence of Chatham dockyard, but everywhere the wealth at the apex of urban society was considerable. In the little Sussex market town of Petworth, 40 per cent of the inhabitants for whose estates inventories were made after death in the seventeenth and early eighteenth centuries had over £100 in personal estate.[4] Even in south Wales, where one would expect wealth *per capita* to be lower than the national average, there were people with goods and money of similar value. Thus in Swansea, twelve out of seventy-three inventories exhibited in the diocesan court between 1705 and 1720 consisted of personal estates worth more than £100, including those of an apothecary, two mercers, an innkeeper, a doctor, a clergyman and several women.[5] Many of the people appearing in probate inventories also owned real property, especially houses. No similar evidence exists for the later part of the eighteenth century, though it is safe to assume that with the general increase in the national product and the growth of trade and industry, the capital held by this type of townsmen grew at least proportionately.

[3] A. J. F. Dulley, 'People and homes in the Medway Towns: 1687–1783', *Archaeologia Cantiana*, LXXVII (1963), pp. 173–5; these inventories comprise all those exhibited in the archdeaconry and consistory courts of Rochester diocese, but not those for a few rich people, whose estates were handled by the Prerogative Court of the Archbishop of Canterbury.

[4] Kenyon, 'Petworth Trades', *Sussex Archaeological Collections*, XCVI, p. 66; again, P.C.C. inventories are not included.

[5] National Library of Wales, Aberystwyth, probate inventories relating to Swansea; see also M. I. Williams, 'Cardiff—its People and its Trade, 1660–1720', *Morgannwg*, VII (1963), pp. 84–5.

For such people, a local investment was the normal outlet for their money. Apart from the aristocracy and gentry, people in the provinces rarely invested in Government securities or the stocks of the Bank of England or in the great trading companies, in the early eighteenth century. The probate inventories suggest that the practice was adopted occasionally in towns within twenty or thirty miles of London, but that further afield it was practically unknown. Most of the owners lived in and around London as late as 1750.[6] Later in the eighteenth century the habit of investment in the Funds became more usual outside London.[7] It may have grown during the American War of Independence, when the total size of the Debt expanded sharply. It certainly increased with the growth of the National Debt during the French Wars after 1793, when, according to Lowe, 'the general ardour of our countrymen in the contest, their confidence in government, and the comparatively high interest then given by the Treasury, led to the deposit in that ready absorbent of sums of which the magnitude would have startled the caution of our forefathers'.[8] But even at the end of the Napoleonic War, some provincial townsmen were still suspicious of the Funds and preferred a local investment.[9]

In the later eighteenth century local transport schemes offered one outlet for funds. According to Professor Mingay, writing on canal investment:

'Towards the end of the century, . . . people such as shopkeepers and professional men not directly concerned with the transport question, were drawn in by the prospect of a rich investment . . . The shareholders in the Sleaford Navigation Company in 1792, for example, included besides landowners and merchants, six attorneys, three surgeons, three clergymen, three graziers and two farmers, two widows, and three innkeepers (one of whom put up £625), a brewer, a tanner, a miller, a hairdresser, and a grocer who could spare £1,000.'[10]

Yet although canals provided a useful investment medium, especially in the 1790s, the amount of capital that they could absorb was relatively limited. It has been estimated that about £15½ million was invested in

[6] P. G. M. Dickson, *The Financial Revolution in England* (1967), pp. 297–8.

[7] For example, several references to money in the stocks were noted in Portsmouth wills proved in the local ecclesiastical courts in the early 1770s: Hampshire Record Office, Winchester archdeaconry and consistory wills, 1770–75.

[8] J. Lowe, *The Present State of England in Regard to Agriculture, Trade and Finance; with a Comparison of the Prospects of England and France* (1823), p. 364.

[9] See below, p. 290.

[10] G. E. Mingay, *English Landed Society in the Eighteenth Century* (1963), p. 200.

canals between 1760 and 1820, or an average of not much more than £250,000 per annum.[11] In fact canal investment was bunched in certain years in the later 1760s and the 1770s and the early 1790s, when its share of the national capital formation was considerable. In other years it is unlikely to have made considerable inroads into local urban capital.

Small landed properties outside towns also attracted some townsmen. The amount of land that could be bought for less than £1,000, or a little more, was small. It only came on the market occasionally. The return on landowning was also low: at the beginning of the eighteenth century, land yielded on average no more than 5 per cent gross, and towards the end of the century the figure was about 4 per cent. A potentially larger outlet for money lay in a local business activity. Funds could be lent at the going rate of interest on bond, and this was a favourite investment among those who desired a regular return on their cash. Those looking for a higher yield might make a direct stake in a business activity. This involved setting up on their own or taking up a partnership with either an active or a passive role. Returns on capital employed in manufacturing are known to have been high, at least 10 per cent and often as much as 15 or 20 per cent and even more.[12] In the ports, trading ventures, though sometimes involving considerable risk, might bring even higher returns.[13] Local directories show that it was not uncommon in the eighteenth century for men to undertake more than one business activity, but there must have been many involved in one occupation, either a trade, craft, manufacture or profession, or even leisured people, who had money to invest but did not want to take an active role in a new trade or industry, and who felt that a sleeping partnership involved too

[11] H. J. Habbakuk and P. Deane 'The Take-off in Britain', in W. W. Rostow (ed.) *The Economics of Take-off into Sustained Growth* (1964), p. 73.
[12] Towards the end of the period all the textile manufacturers whose profit rates are known enjoyed high returns in good years; firms such as Gott and Marshall of Leeds, J. and T. Clark of Trowbridge and the Pleasley Mill took profits superior to 15 or 20 per cent on their capital. Even the common practice in the east Midlands of owning knitting frames and letting them to knitters in the hosiery industry brought good rewards: referring to the two generations before he wrote in 1831, Gravenor Henson noted that 'the average price of the frames being £18, they paid 14 per cent, and the wear did not exceed 4 per cent, consequently this description of property paid a clear 10 per cent . . .'; F. Crouzet, 'Capital Formation in Great Britain during the Industrial Revolution', in Crouzet (ed.) *Capital Formation*, pp. 195–6; G. Henson, *History of the Framework Knitters* (1931), pp. 385–6n: I owe this reference to Dr. Chapman.
[13] According to Professor Hyde, for Liverpool traders 'from 1700 onwards, the profit-ability of merchant voyages saw a net return of double and more often than not, treble the original outlay of capital': Hyde, *Liverpool*, p. 25; Liverpool newspapers after 1800 include tempting advertisements stressing the high profit rate as an inducement to partnerships: in February 1805, a partner was asked to advance £2,000 in a concern yielding about 40 per cent; in January 1815 a partner was sought in a firm yielding 20 to 25 per cent: *Gore's General Advertiser* (1805), *Liverpool Mercury* (1815).

great a risk. In any case some of these opportunities were open only to the wealthier of the capital-owning townsmen. Such returns often needed the outlay of considerable sums (say £1,500 or £2,000 or more) which were larger than most townsmen were able to invest.

For such people there remained house property, either in ownership or through the holding of a mortgage. Wills throughout the century show the extent to which the ownership of houses was spread among the substantial urban inhabitants. One example may suffice: the wills of men and women dying in Portsmouth early in the eighteenth century. Although real estate is often not mentioned in wills because it had already been settled by other means, forty-nine out of 158 wills proved in the archdeaconry and consistory courts of the diocese of Winchester relating to Portsmouth (including Portsea) between 1705 and 1711 (inclusive) and 1721 and 1724 (inclusive) contain references to houses owned by the testator, the number of dwellings totalling 115 and the majority having more than one dwelling.[14] It was the typical pattern of house property ownership by many people in all the large towns, with houses being owned in ones, twos and threes, and occasionally in larger groups.[15]

It is also shown by a study of surviving local title deeds, which forms the basis of this part of the book relating to house building. For example, in Birmingham between 1781 and 1820, 140 people bought the 470 new houses sold in the period whose full history it has been possible to trace. They included all the people one would expect to find among the more substantial townspeople. There were numerous men in the metal trades, such as gunmakers, platers, button manufacturers, brassfounders and toymakers; a big group of men from the other trades and crafts, such as the building trades (in these years), numerous victuallers, and grocers, tailors, butchers, coal merchants, and a smaller number of gentlemen and women. The occupational spread of these people compares roughly with the occupational pattern in the section of the *Universal British Directory* for Birmingham which relates to the 1790s.[16] Similarly, in Liverpool between 1745 and 1800, 145 people were involved in the purchase of the 269 houses sold within twenty years of the formal lease of the site to the builder, whose history has been traced by

[14] Hampshire Record Office: Winchester archdeaconry and consistory wills; wills proved in the Prerogative Court were not included. Again, sixty-five out of a total of 115 Portsmouth wills proved in these courts between 1770 and 1775 inclusive contain references to one or more houses owned by the testator.
[15] The phrase 'owned' here covers those holding property under building leases.
[16] This is based on surviving Birmingham title deeds (*see* Notes on Sources); Barfoot and Wilkes, *Universal British Directory*, II, pp. 206-41.

me. They included men in shipbuilding and mariners, merchants, bakers, brewers, and other general tradesmen and craftsmen, those described as gentlemen—including attorneys—and some women.[17]

A further form of investment in house property lay in lending money on mortgage. This naturally increased even further the number of people in every town with capital linked to real estate. The rate of interest on mortgages varied from 4 to 5 per cent. In Nottingham in the 1760s (when most of the surviving mortgages record the rate of interest), the price of these loans was 4, $4\frac{1}{2}$ or 5 per cent. In Birmingham between 1750 and 1776, four mortgages have been traced which paid 4 per cent, one $4\frac{1}{4}$, five $4\frac{1}{2}$ per cent, and seventeen at 5 per cent. In both towns and in Manchester 5 per cent was the usual return in the 1780s and 1790s, with the occasional loan dropping to a price of $4\frac{1}{2}$ or 4 per cent between about 1789 and 1793. From the middle of the 1790s until after the end of the Napoleonic Wars, 5 per cent was the normal rate in all the major provincial towns.[18] Except in some years during the American War of Independence and during the French Wars, a mortgage not only had the attraction over the Funds of being a local investment, but the yield was also higher. Thus, 3 per cent stock provided an income of less than 4 per cent between 1763 and 1777, and just above or below 4 per cent for most years between 1787 and 1794.[19] Again, unlike the Funds or even houses, the money value of mortgages did not fluctuate, with the possibility of the loss of part of the capital. Mortgages offered a regular income without the responsibilities of property ownership, and the ability to secure a sale to recover the capital if the interest was not paid.

An investment of a rather similar kind, though much less often available, was the ownership of ground rents. Landlords, and occasionally developers who disposed of land on building lease, sometimes sold the rents after houses had been constructed. Again, they provided a regular income without the administrative problems of house ownership. Their advantages were spelt out in the following advertisement in the *Hull Advertiser* of 30 May 1801 regarding the sale of the ground rent on a house and shop in Hull:

'Such a ground-rent is unquestionably the best of all securities, for whether the premises are let or not, the proprietor of them is

[17] For the Liverpool title deeds on which this is based, *see* Notes on Sources.
[18] These figures are taken from those surviving mortgages on new property in which the rate of interest is stated; in the southern towns, the interest pattern with regard to mortgages appears to have been broadly similar, though mortgages at 4 and $4\frac{1}{2}$ per cent between the 1750s and 1770s may have been more common at Bath than elsewhere among the major provincial towns. For specific examples, *see* Appendix III, and for the general deed evidence, which contains innumerable mortgages, *see* Notes on Sources.
[19] T. S. Ashton, *Economic Fluctuations in England 1700–1800* (Oxford, 1959), p. 187.

liable to pay the ground-rent, and when they are let, the owner of the ground-rent can distrain for it. *This will be sold to pay 6 per cent.*'

The ownership of tenement property offered a rather higher return as a compensation for the administrative problems involved. New working-class property in the major provincial towns generally yielded between about 7 and 12 per cent gross, with 8, 9 or 10 per cent being the most usual figures. Evidence may be found occasionally in advertisements in the local newspaper: these sometimes state the rents paid on property for sale, which may be compared with the sale price noted in the relevant title deed, where this is available. Alternatively, the yield that the purchaser of the property might expect to receive from rents is occasionally mentioned in the advertisement.

In Birmingham this type of property paid about 9 or 10 per cent gross in the later 1780s and early 1790s; for example, on 3 July 1786, four new houses in Aston Street consisting of two front and two back tenements let for a total of £25 16s. od. were advertised, fetching £267 15s. od. at auction on 14 July.[20] The evidence between the 1750s and the 1770s for Birmingham does not enable one to estimate the precise gross return except in a few cases, but there is little doubt that profits on tenement property were quite similar. The cheapest new houses sold for between £35 and £60, while the lowest rents on this type of property were about £3 10s. od. or £4 10s. od. On 19 September 1777, three 'modern' houses in the new Vale Street, with five tenements, a shop and two brew-houses behind, let for £46 16s. od., fetched £470 at auction.[21] Thus, in the long run at least, gross returns on house property appear to have been reasonably stable in Birmingham between the 1750s and the early 1790s. They remained similar in the 1810s.[22]

Returns were much the same in Nottingham in the early 1790s and the 1800s, despite the prolonged period of inflation beginning in the early 1790s.[23] In the Nottingham area, new house property was fetching about 7 or 8 per cent in the early 1790s: between 1806 and 1809, advertisements in the *Nottingham Journal* were offering houses for sale to yield between 7 and 10 per cent.[24] As a final instance, this time for a port, returns on working-class tenements at Liverpool were about 8 or 10 per

[20] Sale price in B.R.L. TC.111688–97; advertisement in *Aris's Birmingham Gazette.*
[21] Advertised 8 September in *Aris's Birmingham Gazette*; sale price in British Rail: Mornington Crescent deed room B.E. 137.
[22] *Birmingham Gazette*, 28/1/1811, 28/10/1811; *Birmingham Chronicle* 24/8/1820.
[23] For a general comment on yields in the East Midlands, *see* Henson, *Framework Knitters*, pp. 385–6.
[24] *Nottingham Journal*, 15/9/1792, 20/10/1792 (and Nottingham Archives M.23141–57), 14/12/1793, 30/8/1806, 23/11/1807, 24/12/1807, 9/4/1808, 15/4/1809, 1/7/1809.

cent in the 1810s: for example, on 1 May 1818, the *Liverpool Mercury* advertised 'two front and seven back houses, in Jordan-street, Park-lane, and a lot of land adjoining, to be sold to pay 10 per cent'.[25]

It is impossible to determine exactly the net yield on artisan property investment. Probably between 1 and 3 per cent should be deducted from the gross return to cover the cost of repairs and maintenance, bad debts and periods when tenements were empty.[26] Further, in the case of houses erected on building lease, account must be taken of the ground rent; in Birmingham this was normally less than one-tenth of the house rent: thus the eight houses in Vale Street auctioned in 1777 rented at £46 16s. od. were subject to a ground rent of £2 11s. 6d., and six more sold in the same street in April 1790 for £330 were rented at £31 17s. od. and were subject to a ground rent of £1 5s. 2½d.[27] Probably most working-class housing yielded between 6 and 8 per cent net, at least between 1780 and 1820.

In most cases it was profitable to pay for part of a purchase with borrowed money, and many buyers did so. To take a hypothetical example: a group of tenements bought for £300 might provide a net yield of 6 per cent; if half this sum were borrowed at 5 per cent, then the return on the £150 of personal capital invested would be almost 7 per cent; if (as often happened) £200 were borrowed, then the return on the £100 invested would have been 8 per cent. If the gross yield was as high as 9 per cent, it is easy to see that the net return on a geared investment might be 10 or even 15 per cent. To take an actual case: in August 1790, six houses in Vale Street, Birmingham fetched £305; rents were £30, and

[25] Also *Liverpool Mercury*, 16/9/1814.

[26] No contemporary evidence has been traced to indicate the likely difference between gross and net yield on tenement property. Some scattered material for the 1830s and 1840s suggests that it may then have varied between as much as 1 and 3 per cent of the property value. In 1837 a Liverpool joiner said he had made 5 per cent net and 8 per cent gross on houses he had built and let: *B.P.P.* 1837–8, xxi, *Report of the Select Committee on Rating of Tenements*, QQ.2057–64; contrast with houses erected in Sheffield costing £60–£75, let at £6 10s., for which repairs, insurance, loss of rent while empty and bad rent was only estimated at 10s. annually: *B.P.P.* 1845, xviii, App. Part II, p. 347, *2nd Report of the Commissioners for Inquiring into the State of Large Towns and Populous Districts*; for Leeds (repairs only) *B.P.P.* 1842, xxvii, Lords, *Sanitary Condition of the Labouring Population, Local Reports*, 'On the State and Condition of the Town of Leeds', p. 358. Loss of rent on account of the poverty or unannounced departure of tenants was a constant problem in the case of working-class property. In a group of instances in a lawsuit about rents claimed to be owing from seven tenements in Manchester in 1817 and 1818, the collector stated that one tenant had paid nothing because 'he always pleaded extreme poverty which no doubt was too true'; in a second case, 'an attempt was made to distrain upon this man's goods, but he contrived to abscond and carry them away with him'; and in a third, 'this man absconded and afterwards sent to Chester Castle for debt'. The remaining occupiers were 'good tenants': P.R.O. E134/59 Geo.3 Hil. 3.

[27] Price in B.R.L. MS. 372546.

ground rent £2 15s. 2½d.[28] If an allowance of 2 per cent is made for other deductions, there would have been a net yield of 7 per cent. If the purchaser had borrowed £150 at the rate of 5 per cent usual in the town, then the net return would have been about 9 per cent; if he had borrowed £200 it would have been about 11 per cent.

Returns tended to be smaller, between about 5 and 7 per cent, on more substantial houses costing, say, more than £150 or £200. In Liverpool gross returns in the 1810s on this type of property were 6 or 7 per cent. Thus the following advertisement appeared in the *Liverpool Mercury* on 23 May 1817:

> 'Advantageous Investment of Money: TO BE SOLD, A house in Bold-street, Price £900, Rent £65. £400 may remain on mortgage.'[29]

If the price paid was in fact £900, then the gross return would have been just over 7 per cent. In November 1814, John Gladstone valued the ten houses which he owned in Rodney Street at £18,200; since the total rent was £1,088, the gross yield was about 6 per cent.[30] It is true that a landlord's expenses or losses would have been smaller with this type of property, since bad debts would have been fewer and rent collection no problem but the considerably smaller gross yield suggests that net returns probably did not exceed 5 or 6 per cent. Another reason for the difference in returns between the various types of housing may have been that tenants paid poor rates on the bigger houses, while tenement property was exempt; according to contemporaries this allowed higher rents. It was the view of Birmingham parish officials that 'the [small] houses not paying poor rates are almost universally let at increased rents'.[31] Presumably the attraction of larger houses was the smaller administrative burdens afforded by fewer and more reliable tenants.[32]

There is thus a little material relating to returns to *purchasers* of new

[28] *Aris's Birmingham Gazette*, 9/8/90; B.E. 208.
[29] *Liverpool Mercury*, 23/5/17.
[30] S. G. Checkland, *The Gladstones: A Family Biography* (Cambridge, 1971), p. 80; cf. also *Aris's Birmingham Gazette*, 31/5/90, suggesting a 7½ per cent return on four houses selling for over £250 each.
[31] *Birmingham Chronicle*, 20 January 1820.
[32] One would naturally expect changes in house prices and sometimes in rents during booms or recessions in construction to cause some temporary changes in returns on new houses, particularly as the contractual element in some rent payments would mean that some rents would have been more 'sticky' than prices. However, in the case of returns in depressions, several contemporary comments refer to sharp falls in rents, and one, that relating to Liverpool in 1751, explains a fall in house values as a result of a decline of rents (see below, p. 261). Further detailed research might clarify the position in recessions between about 1793 and 1820 in one or two of the towns, but the decline in the number of property sales in these periods makes the search for evidence especially difficult.

houses. The profits of builders is another matter. Much housing was erected under contract with craftsmen by building undertakers outside the trade. Their returns appear to have been very similar to those of purchasers. The members of Northwood's Building Society in Birmingham, formed in 1783, were charged just over £84 for the construction of each house on their estate, receiving rents of £6 10s. od. per dwelling after completion in 1788, a gross return of about 7½ per cent.[33] In Liverpool in November 1807, the proprietors of the Herculaneum Pottery were told that the cottages just erected for employees yielded about 10 per cent in rent on the amount spent.[34] It is impossible to estimate the profit margins of craftsmen-building undertakers who erected for an early sale, or the annual return on the initial outlay for such men who built for long-term investment:[35] this is because of lack of evidence about construction costs for houses of which the sale price or rent is known.

The principal object of most purchasers of new houses and even of many of the builders was a steady and reasonably secure income. Advertisements of property for sale sometimes mentioned the names or respectability of the tenants, the amount of the rents, the good state of repair of the property, or that considerable improvements might be made. These characteristics of property advertisements may be seen for example in the *Birmingham Gazette* in 1766. On 7 July there was a note of an auction of

> 'a new house, well built, with warehouse and shops, at the further end of Paradise Row . . . late occupied by Thomas Cater, owner, now let to Richard Walker at £23 per annum';

there was also an advertisement of the sale of

> '12 new houses in Lovely [Loveday] Street . . . let at £70 per annum, all well tenanted'.

Some fifty years later there was little difference in the quality of advertisements, though they were sometimes fuller. On 1 April 1814, the *Liverpool Mercury* advertised four front houses and five back dwellings, 'well tenanted and in excellent repair', yielding a 'clear rental' of £54 19s. 6d.

The changes in house prices and rents, whether short- or long-term, offered the possibility of capital appreciation or rising incomes, both

---

[33] B.R.L. MS.260742.
[34] Liverpool R.O.: Herculaneum Pottery MS. p. 19.
[35] This is of course also true of later periods: cf. A. K. Cairncross, *Home and Foreign Investment 1870–1914* (Cambridge, 1953), p. 15.

for purchasers and builders. Naturally they were aware of these possible advantages. Newspaper advertisements occasionally stressed the low level of existing rents on houses for sale as a bait to intending purchasers. On 4 February 1811 the *Birmingham Gazette* advertised for private sale

> 'the lease, in which 81 years are unexpired, of eight well built dwelling houses . . . occupied by good tenants, and produce the annual rent of £44 14s 6d. (but are much underlet)'.

In September 1808, Ann Loxdale from Buxton decided to buy the building lease (costing £900) and freehold reversion of a house in Clarence Street, Liverpool, to live in, and explained her motives in a letter to her brother at Shrewsbury:

> 'I think I never acted much upon speculation. At Liverpool houses are reckoned a very good one and at present they are lower than they generally are and should trade revive which is the general hope and expectation they will be as high as ever; therefore as the present purchase is much for our accommodation I think it will turn to good account . . .'.[36]

Rising prices and rents brought a speculative element into construction in time of peak activity. During the American War of Independence, when the demand for accommodation in the dockyard towns was unprecedented, a contemporary referred to 'the rage for extending the buildings, and the speculations of mechanics being at that time very prevalent' in Dock.[37] But house ownership and its natural extension in the rapidly-growing towns, house construction, especially by men outside the building trades, was usually aimed at providing a sound rather than rapidly-growing income-yielding investment and an asset which could be realized for a reasonable price when the capital was needed.

2 BUILDING OWNERS IN THE INDUSTRIAL TOWNS

Everywhere the purchase or leasing of a site and the erection of one or more houses for an early sale, for letting or for self-occupation, was usually undertaken by one person. There was the occasional formal partnership and probably in at least one or two provincial towns associations of building craftsmen working on a group of adjoining

[36] Liverpool R.O.: deeds D468B.
[37] Quoted in Worth, *Devonport*, p. 21.

sites.[38] The typical building project of the eighteenth century was small in financial terms, costing between several hundred pounds and £1,000 or £2,000. It might mean the construction of a small block of tenements for the artisan or labouring class or one or two substantial terrace houses. The rising demand for accommodation involved more and more townsmen from a wide range of occupations as building undertakers.

These men fell into two groups. There were the craftsmen-builders—bricklayers, carpenters and the like—who acquired a site, themselves performed part of the building, and contracted the rest of the work to other craftsmen. Secondly, there were the building owners from outside the trade who had to contract with craftsmen for the whole of the work of construction. For both kinds of undertaker, housing speculations were far from being a full-time occupation.

In the case of the craftsmen, private contract work was usually available. It came from the building owners outside the trade and from other craftsmen who needed to sub-contract work in which they themselves were not skilled. There were also the innumerable large and small house-repair jobs. Periodically they did construction or repair work on public buildings. For example, a Liverpool bricklayer, Robert Waln, was responsible as building owner for at least one of the larger houses in St. Pauls Square, which he sold in 1768 for £500.[39] He was employed by the Corporation on a number of minor jobs on two churches in 1770, and received £128 4s. od. for work on a new house in Castle Street in 1773.[40]

Other craftsmen who were building owners also dealt in building materials. In Birmingham, a carpenter named Josiah Deeley undertook at least two building projects, in 1767 and 1771 on the north-west of the town.[41] In between he opened a timber yard in the same neighbourhood, according to an advertisement in *Aris's Birmingham Gazette* for 17 July 1769:

'Josiah Deeley, carpenter and joiner, takes this method to inform the public, that he has opened a timber yard opposite the Verulam

[38] In Part III I have used the word 'site' to refer to a plot of land leased or purchased for the erection of one or more houses, usually by one person, but occasionally by two or more builders acting as partners; the adjoining plots were conveyed normally to other builders, but in those cases in which the same undertaker took an adjoining plot, it has been treated as a separate site if the second plot was obtained more than two years after the first, but otherwise as part of the same undertaking; the words 'project' and 'undertaking' have been used in connection with investment on a single site.
[39] B.R. Manchester Deed Room L. and Y. 3022R.
[40] Liverpool R.O.: Corporation ledger 1769–73, ff. 35–48.
[41] B.R.L. MS.410003; B.R., Mornington Crescent O.B.R. 869.

Printing-Office in Great Charles-Street, Birmingham, where Gentlemen and Tradesmen may be supplied with the following articles upon the most reasonable terms, viz. Building Timber of all Sorts; English and American Oak Boards and Planks; yellow and white Dale, and Packing Boards; he likewise has to dispose of a quantity of 2 inch walnut plank, and barrel staves.'

This type of business remained the usual pattern throughout the period, even among craftsmen who were most active as building undertakers. In Birmingham, Jonathan Johnson, a carpenter who was possibly the biggest builder in the town in the 1730s and 1740s, also erected houses on contract, and did the carpenter's work involved in the rebuilding of the School after 1731, and in the construction of the Workhouse in 1734.[42] In Hull about 1800, a stonemason called Appleton Bennison, who erected substantial terrace housing in the Sculcoates district, also acted as an architect. On 31 January 1801, he advertised for sale in the *Hull Advertiser* two houses in Storey Street, 'also one in Albion-street, now finishing ... PLANS and ELEVATIONS drawn at the shortest notice; MARBLE CHIMNEY PIECES and MONUMENTS, executed in the neatest manner'.[43] Naturally, because of their particular skills and experience of building work, construction on their own account was attractive to craftsmen. Yet they may often have been restricted by the size of their own capital or the credit available to them—except in the temporary period of massive credit expansion at the beginning of the 1790s. Again, the alternative of contract building had solid advantages, since payment was received during or immediately after construction. For whatever reason, the typical craftsman continued to mix small speculations with contract and repair work.

For most of the undertakers from outside the building trades, a speculation involved the investment of an occasional legacy or of savings. Compared with their main occupation, it was essentially a minor project, often not repeated. Biographical details of such people are almost non-existent, but the case of a Portsmouth widow may serve as an example of countless non-craftsmen builders at the beginning of the nineteenth century:

'The said Eliza Stuart was the widow of a warrant officer of the Navy who was believed to have left her some property with which she set up an upholsterers shop in Portsea ... where she continued

[42] B.R.L. MSS.329284, 372112, 372221 etc.; Chatwin (ed.), *The Records of King Edward's School Birmingham* IV, pp. xx, 53, 69–70.
[43] East Riding Registry of Deeds: registers CC–CK.

some time when she took the Fortitude Public House on Portsmouth Point and [by 1813] she had quitted the said public house and returned to the upholstry business and she had also laid out a considerable sum of money in building on some pieces or parcels of land in or near Commons Street Portsea . . . and two houses had been actually built by her . . . .'[44]

Despite its vital role in urban expansion, the organization and financing of house construction remained for nearly everyone a part-time activity.

The wide occupational range of people attracted into building undertakings in the industrial towns is well illustrated in the case of Birmingham between 1746 and 1780, when its stock of houses increased from about 3,000 to 8,000. Naturally, one group of entrepreneurs were the building craftsmen. Carpenters and bricklayers, the most common of these trades, comprised most of the men in this category; there were also a few brickmakers, glaziers, plumbers and joiners, and several men described as 'builders'. These were normally craftsmen who had acquired this description as a result of handling the construction of whole houses under contract or as their own speculation over a number of years. Even more of the undertakers were men whose principal livelihood came from work in one of the metal trades, the major industry of the town. These builders' occupations give a good cross-section of the crafts which gave Birmingham its industrial reputation and prosperity, with brassfounders, buckle-makers, buttonmakers, gunsmiths and gunstock-makers, and most numerous, toymakers. Rather fewer among the undertakers belonged to the group of the general tradesmen and craftsmen who were so common in urban communities of the time. Victuallers were particularly prominent, and there was more than one baker, shoemaker, merchant and brushmaker. A few leisured men and women complete the picture.[45]

The contribution of each of these main occupational categories may be illustrated by a study of the builders on the Colmore Estate, for which most of the lessees of building sites have been traced. In the period 1746–80, the names and occupations of some 132 of these people have been found. Fifty were craftsmen in the trade; no fewer than fifty-six were in the metal trades; eighteen followed other trades and

[44] P.R.O. B1/138, pp. 81–4.
[45] The names and occupations of the builders are derived from contemporary title deeds (*see* Appendix III and Note on Sources). The occupations of 166 people who are *known* to have built houses between 1746 and 1780 have been traced in the deeds. The occupations are known for another 138 people who leased building sites, but for whom there is no specific evidence about the houses they erected; in this case they may be assumed to have been building owners, since in Birmingham it was rare in these decades for people to lease plots without building on them.

crafts, and there were five women, four gentlemen, a surgeon and a clergyman. In the case of the first houses erected on the Estate along Colmore Row between 1747 and 1750, the majority were craftsmen, but there was also a stationer, an ironmonger, a hingemaker, a gunlock-maker, and two toymakers on adjoining sites. On the other hand, Great Charles Street, built in the 1760s and 1770s, attracted more metal manufacturers as undertakers than craftsmen.[46]

A roughly similar distribution of occupations existed among the builders between 1780 and 1820. The main difference was that building craftsmen were less prominent, and those in the metal trades even more important as undertakers than before 1780. For example, in Bartholomew Street on the south-east of the town in the mid-1780s, the builders included at least six brassfounders, a caster, two button-makers, a steel toymaker and engraver, a butcher, a baker, a publican, a builder, a gentleman, a widow, and four spinster sisters who were partners in a single project.[47]

With the obvious difference that people in the textile trades replaced the metal workers, the range of occupations among the undertakers was much the same in eighteenth-century Nottingham and Manchester as it was in Birmingham.[48] In neither town were people connected with textile manufacture as important as representatives of the metal trades in Birmingham. Probably this reflects the fact that most people in hardware manufacture were men of small capital, for whom building speculation was particularly attractive. In Nottingham throughout the period, and in Manchester particularly from the 1780s, men in the general trades and crafts were especially important as undertakers.

Prominent as builders in Nottingham were victuallers, innkeepers, maltsters, bakers, grocers, and other shopkeepers. Among those linked to the textile trades were a few hosiers and needlemakers; framework knitters and framesmiths were numerous. The long rows of back-to-back tenements erected on the eastern edge of the town from the mid-1780s on the land of John Sherwin were mainly the responsibility of bricklayers and joiners.[49] A wider occupational range were concerned in building on Panier Close, marketed in 1807. The builders included at least half-a-dozen joiners, a lace manufacturer and two framework knitters, a cowkeeper, two tailors and a cordwainer, as well as a small

---

[46] B.R.L. Colmore MSS. etc.
[47] B.R. Mornington Crescent Deed Room: B.E. 11, 13, 14, 15, 18, 21, 23, 24, 28, 275; B.R.L. Gooch MSS.
[48] Based on surviving title deeds for Nottingham and Manchester: *see* Note on Sources.
[49] E.g. Nottingham Archives M.23183–5, TC.2/10, 2/51.

building society.[50] Some of the biggest new houses erected in Nottingham in these years, on Standard Hill near the Castle, were built by an architect, a hosier, a dyer and several others.[51]

In Portsea, the occupations of at least one quarter of the builders have been found for the whole period between the later 1730s and 1820.[52] Craftsmen were responsible for about half the undertakings; some of these men, such as the bricklayers, probably worked principally in the Dockyard and may not have been concerned with house construction except in the case of an occasional speculation. In Portsmouth, the dockyard took the place of the metal industries of Birmingham and the various branches of the textile trades in Manchester and Nottingham, and it is natural to find dockyard workers—such as caulkers, scavelmen, and especially the shipwrights—investing in building. There were also mariners and gunners, presumably employed by the Navy, among the builders. As usual, victuallers and the more substantial tradesmen such as bakers and butchers and a few leisured people also made a contribution. For example, the builders of Surrey Street on the east of the town in the later 1790s ⟨*see* plate 25⟩ included six joiners, a bricklayer, a shipwright, a victualler, a blacksmith, a baker, and the attorney Greetham.[53]

Much new property in the industrial towns was held by the building owners for many years after construction. In the case of Birmingham, the date of sale has been found for 652 of the houses of which the site was conveyed between 1746 and 1780. They included all types of dwellings, from the tiny courtyard tenements to large houses of twelve or fifteen rooms. Nearly four-fifths of the houses were still in the builders' hands five years after the site conveyance, and half after twenty years. It is true that we do not know the date of construction of the houses. Although nearly every builder began work within a year or two of acquiring the site, construction of a group of dwellings sometimes spanned a number of years. The builder may have begun by erecting one or more front tenements, adding to them later, or erecting the front houses first and the back tenements afterwards. Even so, the majority of houses were held for many years, mostly for letting. A small number were occupied by the owner. A few of the larger single houses were erected for self-occupation, and sometimes an undertaker responsible for a group of dwellings occupied one himself, drawing an income from the others.

[50] Nottingham Archives TC.2/19/1–4, M.19137–50, M.23211–16, M.23141–57; Debenham and Co.: Victoria Station Deeds.
[51] Nottingham University Hospital Management Committee deeds.
[52] Based on surviving title deeds for Portsea: Note on Sources.
[53] Portsmouth R.O.: D.7127, 7394, 7479, 7843, 8007, 9833/2, 10008, 10075 etc.

Building craftsmen were more likely to erect for an early sale than builders outside the trade, so as to release the capital for further speculation. Craftsmen were responsible for 125 out of the 145 dwellings sold within five years of the site conveyance, between 1746 and 1780. It was still not unusual for craftsmen to hold houses for much longer, as an investment. Among the carpenters who leased or bought lots in 1749, Anthony Spicer erected two houses on the newly-developing Colmore Estate which he sold for £154 7s. 6d. less than two years later. The two houses built by another carpenter, Robert Griffiths, on a site in the east of the town were part of his estate at his death in the early 1750s, and his family held them until 1775. On the other hand, construction for letting with the likelihood of the retention of the houses indefinitely must have been the aim of nearly all builders outside the trade. A wireworker named George Caulton leased a site measuring 13 by 42 yards in Park Street in March 1777. Four years later he borrowed £300 on the security of eleven dwellings, one of which he occupied; in 1788 there were seventeen tenements, and when they were sold in 1797 after his death there were twenty.[54]

Building for long-term investment was also characteristic of Manchester and Nottingham in the eighteenth century. The great increase in the number of houses erected in each of the three towns after 1780 brought no change to this pattern. Most of the houses sold within three or four years of construction were built by the craftsmen. In Nottingham one of the biggest builders on Sherwin's Cherry Orchard, Thomas Woolridge, bricklayer, bought land in August 1785 and had sold forty-five tenements by 1 May 1788.[55] In the case of the houses erected on Panier Close after 1807, at least fifty-one were built by men outside the trade, all of which were held for more than five years after the site purchase. Craftsmen are known to have been responsible for sixty-seven dwellings in the Close, of which twenty-three were sold within five years of the site conveyance.[56] Even in Manchester, where the addition to the housing stock increased enormously from the 1780s, there was no major change in the speed of turnover of new house property. Building for indefinite investment remained a general custom.

The great extent to which people from outside the trade acted as building owners in the industrial towns may be partly explained in terms of the attraction which building had for them. In Birmingham, wealth

[54] B.R.L. MSS. 372230, 371945, 409187; B.R. Mornington Crescent Deed Room O.B.R. 736.
[55] Nottingham Archives M.23185, 23211–16, and bdl. 5617.
[56] Debenham and Co.: Victoria Station deeds.

was more evenly distributed than in most other towns, particularly among the numerous small metal manufacturers, who constituted as many as one-third of the builders in the great expansion between about 1781 and 1795. This workshop industry was based on small capital; naturally the profits and savings it generated tended also to be modest. For such people, the building of a block of six or eight tenements costing several hundred pounds was an ideal investment. By the 1780s, interest in building reached a peak. Hutton noted that 'the itch for building is predominant: we dip our fingers into mortar almost as soon as into business'.[57] In January 1795, after nearly two years of the biggest business depression of the century, it was reported that 'although there is now supposed to be a thousand houses untenanted in the parish of Birmingham, yet such is the passion for speculations in building, that upwards of 60 acres of the common land, lately enclosed in the parish of Handsworth . . . is already taken or purchased, and intended to be built upon.'[58]

In the case of Manchester, the parliamentary committee investigating the rating of tenements in 1837 was told that the small man speculated in cottage building because the size of outlay needed debarred him from entering the cotton trade.[59] By the beginning of the nineteenth century, the general tradesmen in the town were particularly important as builders, and this later comment suggests a probable reason for it. In the east Midlands, the hosiery industry may have presented similar difficulties to the intending investor, though here the ownership of stocking frames offered a possible outlet for small sums.[60]

3 THE ORIGINS OF BUILDING SOCIETIES

A major innovation among building undertakers in manufacturing centres in the last quarter of the eighteenth century was the development of building societies based on the device of the equitable trust. This allowed a joint project by more than six people without the need for a private act to create a joint stock company. The basic features were the aim to provide the members with their own houses, and the temporary nature of the project, the societies being dissolved when the dwellings were paid for.[61]

[57] Hutton, *Birmingham*, p. 70.
[58] Langford, *Birmingham Life*, II, p. 6.
[59] *B.P.P.* 1837–8 xxi, Q.1565.
[60] Henson, *Framework Knitters*, pp. 385–6.
[61] The following paragraphs rely partly on E. J. Cleary, *The Building Society Movement* (1965), and S. J. Price, *Building Societies: their Origin and History* (1958); the deeds I have examined have revealed many more societies in a number of towns.

While their methods differed in detail, there were two basic types, the society which erected houses itself, and that which loaned money to members for their own undertakings. In this study of building owners we are concerned with the first type. Regular subscriptions of at least several shillings a fortnight were the means of raising money from the members. For those prepared to wait several years until the houses became their sole property, subscription to a society avoided an initial down payment.

The societies grew out of the habit among artisans and tradesmen from the middle of the eighteenth century to form clubs for mutual aid. All relied on subscriptions and regular social meetings at inns. Their emergence is usually linked with the spread of friendly societies, which were designed to give protection against illness and unemployment, and involved social activities at inns. Building clubs comprised a smaller number of people, and their subscriptions were much higher. They also probably originated in part from 'money clubs', in which 'groups of people agreed to subscribe weekly sums and ballot for the right to borrow the week's proceeds'.[62]

On present evidence, clubs which erected houses originated in the Black Country. It is here that the earliest societies are known, and they were certainly most common here before 1800. In Birmingham they were merely one of several types of co-operative associations, such as friendly societies, rent and capital clubs, as well as a host of smaller clubs for buying books, clothes, watches and clocks. This aspect of the town's life was noted by contemporaries: in 1797, Eden mentioned that 'there are innumerable Friendly Societies, and Clubs (in the nature of raffles) for the encouragement of particular trades in this town', and five years later, Nemnich wrote that 'the inhabitants of Birmingham are fonder of associations in clubs than those of almost any other place I know'.[63] Early building societies are known to have existed not only in Birmingham, but also in Dudley, Wolverhampton and Handsworth. The spread of the habit of forming clubs was presumably helped by the even distribution of income in the Black Country communities. With the growing popularity of building investment in Birmingham (and probably elsewhere in the Black Country on a smaller scale) in the later eighteenth century, particularly among the small manufacturers and tradesmen, the early emergence of building clubs in this area is readily understandable.

The first known society in the Black Country, Ketley's in Birmingham,

---

[62] Cleary, *Building Society Movement*, p. 9.
[63] F. M. Eden, *The State of the Poor* III (1797), p. 739; Gill, *Birmingham*, p. 127; *V.C.H. Warks*, VII, p. 100.

began about 1775, during the boom of the mid-1770s. At least three more had appeared by the end of 1781. Altogether nineteen societies have been traced in Birmingham between 1781 and 1795, mostly erecting between twenty and fifty dwellings each. The first and very successful association in Dudley was formed in 1779, and another to build houses was formed in the town before 1795.[64] One existed in Wolverhampton in 1788, and several were active in Handsworth near Birmingham in 1795.[65] In Birmingham, the long depression in building after about 1795 appears to have killed the habit. No associations have been traced in the revived activity towards the end of the Napoleonic War.

The Birmingham societies required their members to pay subscriptions of between 4s. 0d. and 6s. 0d. per month, and sometimes an additional quarterly payment. The Amicable Building Society formed in 1781 was based on a subscription of 5s. 0d. a fortnight per share and £1 1s. 0d. a quarter. [66] Since they intended to build houses at prices varying between £80 and £140, societies might last for many years. Northwood's Building Society was planned in 1781, the articles were signed in 1783, the land was leased in 1785 and the dwellings assigned to members in 1792.[67] In fact various methods were used to hasten the conclusion of the work of a society. They included borrowing money to get the houses erected quickly and then letting them, or raising the subscriptions at a later stage. Thus Lundy's Building Society (begun about 1794) borrowed £350 to finish six houses.[68] The Amicable Building Society (formed in October 1788) leased a site on the estate of the Rector of Birmingham near Five Ways and completed the houses by 1792; some of the members paid their remaining liability in a lump sum, and eight others increased their subscriptions from 4s. 0d. to 5s. 0d. per fortnight, and two guineas instead of one guinea monthly.[69] Yet another means of ending a society once the houses had been built was to allow members to discharge their debt to the society if they wished, and to sell any remaining houses: this was done by a society formed in Woodcock Lane in 1793 which was wound up in 1803.[70]

Some societies were managed by a treasurer. In others a committee held the main responsibility. Some employed their own members to do jobs if they were craftsmen or had a useful skill. The Islington Building

[64] Price, *Building Societies*, pp. 24, 62.
[65] Wolverhampton Central Library: deeds re. St. James Square; Price, *Building Societies*, p. 21.
[66] B.R.L. MS.324353.
[67] B.R. Deed Room, Manchester: B.W.R. 9, 50.
[68] B.R.L. Lee, Crowder 653.
[69] *Ibid.*, 18.
[70] B.R.L. MS.250251.

Society, formed in July 1793, gave the building work to its member Abraham Lee, who was to be paid afterwards according to value; another was to do the painting and glazing, and a third was to be the Society's attorney.[71] Sometimes a contract for the whole work was given to an outsider: in February 1782, the first Amicable Society advertised in *Aris's Gazette* for a person willing to contract to build ten houses.[72] Sometimes the owner of the site was a member of the society, and he may have intended to use it to encourage building on his estate: in October 1791, John Pritchit, timber merchant, helped to form the 'Union Freeholders Society' to erect forty houses on his land in Pritchit Street.[73] More often the site had to be sought by the society.

Generally one house was built per share. Some articles of association stated explicitly that there was to be no restriction on the number of shares held by each member, and there is no evidence that the other societies limited their members to one share. This suggests that the purpose of building was for many similar to that of those people who built their own houses, for letting rather than self-occupation. In the case of Northwood's Society, several members ultimately received two, three or four houses each. Among the assignments of houses made to members in 1792, a Birmingham husbandman, Thomas Fisher, received two front houses and two in the rear on 331 square yards, and a maltster from Aldermaston (Warwickshire) received two dwellings on 356 square yards. Several people received one house each, and two others probably had three and four respectively.[74]

Subscribers came from similar occupations to those who erected houses. The Union Freeholders Society in 1800 included a timber merchant, two gentlemen, two jewellers, a silversmith, three victuallers, a builder, plater, stonemason and other tradesmen and craftsmen.[75] The second Amicable Society near Five Ways comprised two pocketbook-makers, a pocketbook lockmaker, two hairdressers, a button turner and the widow of a japanner.[76] Although building societies contributed more than 10 per cent to the stock of new houses in the 1780s and early 1790s they did not tap a fresh source of savings. The poorer artisan classes were unable to afford the large regular subscriptions. Instead the clubs offered a different way of investing for persons on the same income level as the individual building owners.

[71] B.R.L. MS.453531.
[72] Price, *Building Societies*, p. 28.
[73] B.R.L. Lee, Crowder 1017.
[74] B.R. Manchester Deed Room: B.W.R. 9, 50, 58, 60, 61.
[75] B.R.L. MS.256353.
[76] B.R.L. Lee, Crowder 18.

Apart from the Rowley Regis Building Society in Staffordshire, the other societies which are known to have existed before 1800 were all in the West Riding and Lancashire. Two early building societies have been traced in Leeds, one in 1787 and the other in 1788.[77] There was at least one small society in Sheffield before 1790, as at Birmingham comprising the sort of people who provided the bulk of the building undertakers: there were six cutlers, one weaver, one baker, a shearsmith, a scissorsmith, a grinder and one woman.[78] Since industry in Sheffield was organized on the workshop basis as in Birmingham, and wealth was well spread, a detailed sifting of deeds and newspaper advertisements might well reveal the existence of several other societies. In Lancashire, apart from a society which built in Liverpool in the 1790s, the other known societies were all in the industrial districts, and as much in the villages as in the big towns. At least two or three small societies were formed in Manchester itself, in the early 1790s.[79]

After 1800 building societies spread to other parts of the country. The first association found in Nottingham appeared in 1803. Societies were not known in the south of England before 1800. There was one small society at least in Portsmouth during the Napoleonic boom, founded to erect twenty houses in 1813.[80] The first society known to have existed in the London area was the Greenwich Union Building Society in 1809.[81] These societies seldom made a sizeable contribution to the stock of new houses. None at all are known in Liverpool, Birmingham, Hull and Newcastle during these decades.

While the only building societies that can be discovered in Manchester between 1800 and 1820 were lending, not *building*, associations, outside Salford at Pendleton in about 1803 it was said that 'a general mode of facilitating the sale of lands in and about the parish of Pendleton is the forming of a club or association of... persons who join together in building a certain number of houses....'[82] In Nottingham three societies have been traced, one after 1803 (which undertook two projects in 1803 and 1806), another formed in 1807, and a third in 1811.[83] As in Birmingham, their work took many years. The first group assigned its

[77] Beresford, 'The back-to-back house in Leeds', in Chapman (ed.), *Working-Class Housing*, p. 102.
[78] Sheffield Archives: She S 1669.
[79] P.R.O. B1/88, pp. 322–7; Green, *Map of Manchester* (1794), and Pigot, *Map* (1819); Manchester Town Hall bdl. 53/138: re. society created in 1790 to build twenty houses at Ardwick: shown on Green's map.
[80] Portsmouth R.O. D1595, 1737, 1738/2, 1897, 1938, 2453.
[81] Price, *Building Societies*, p. 53.
[82] P.R.O. E112/1537/444: I owe this reference to Dr. J. R. Ward.
[83] Nottingham Archives: M.18806–7, 19091–19102, TC.2/90/1–6, TC.2/98/4–5; Debenham and Co. P.150.

houses to members in 1815 and the last in 1818 and 1819. Members came from similar occupations as those who built individually: the society which began in 1803 included a joiner, victualler, maltster, gentleman and lace manufacturer; that in 1807 a joiner, baker, cordwainer and two framework knitters; and the last a grocer, trimmer, engineer and three framework knitters. Again, at least some of the members were building for long-term investment. In the case of the first society, a draper named Samuel Cullen received two-and-a-half houses and a stonemason two dwellings. Together the associations built about 15 per cent of the new housing during these two decades.

Various other types of associations for building appeared at the end of the eighteenth century and in the 1800s. Occasionally undertakers secured intending house-purchasers by obtaining regular subscriptions from them as construction proceeded. In Birmingham in 1795, the builder Charles Norton proposed to continue the ill-starred Crescent scheme in this way. Subscriptions were to be £25 quarterly per share; Norton was to build according to detailed specifications and the interests of the subscribers were to be watched by a committee of three.[84]

Another type of association to appear in these years were societies building houses for long-term-letting or sale. In Swansea in 1779, the vicar and four others formed the Union Society to build fifteen houses to let. Most or all the houses were kept at least until 1797.[85] In Leeds in March 1807, a building association was proposed, the subscriptions to be used by the directors in building and buying houses.[86]

A variation with a gambling element was the tontine which was particularly popular in the 1790s. One such undertaking in Bristol in 1791 was intended by a builder-developer to enable him to raise the money to finish a building project. This was James Lockier who tried to solve his financial problems 'by promoting a tontine subscription to raise £70,000 in £100 shares, this sum being required to finish [the Royal York Crescent] on which some £20,000 had already been spent.'[87] Subscription associations and tontines were obviously helpful for building undertakers who were unable to raise money for building by other means. But in general such projects were few.

[84] C. Norton, *Proposals, with Plan and Specification, for Building the Crescent in Birmingham* (Birmingham, 1795). In Preston, two cabinetmakers and a plumber and glazier received subscriptions beginning in 1796 to build thirty houses, which were balloted for by them and the subscribers upon completion: P.R.O. PL.6/91, m.20.
[85] Swansea Guildhall: Swansea Hall Day minute book, 1783–1821, p. 257.
[86] Price, *Building Societies*, p. 50.
[87] Ison, *Bristol*, p. 228; a tontine was set up to build houses near Hanover St., Manchester, in 1790: Co-operative Wholesale Society, Manchester: deed bdl. 9/226. For a St. Helens case about 1797, see T. C. Barker and J. R. Harris, *A Merseyside Town in the Industrial Revolution: St. Helens, 1750–1900* (1959), p. 169.

The geographical distribution of early building societies suggests that they were above all the creation of the industrial town. In the north, societies existed in Manchester, Leeds and Sheffield before 1793. None has been discovered in Hull or Newcastle before 1820, and only one has been found in Liverpool. They were also almost unknown in the south before 1820. They tended to appear in the north and the Midlands in towns and at times when the predominant contribution to house-building was coming from men outside the building trades. It is likely that where craftsmen supplied the majority of houses, they sometimes made their own informal arrangements to pool skills and labour on neighbouring sites. Building societies emerged in Birmingham at the same time as the contribution of craftsmen as building owners began to decline, at the end of the 1770s. In Nottingham they appeared in the boom of the 1800s, when the majority of the houses were built by men outside the building trades. Since societies were largely intended for the same purpose as the projects of individuals outside the trades—that is, to supply houses to members for long-term letting or self-occupation —they may best be seen as an alternative means to this end for those without the capital or the credit to begin a project of their own, or for those who wished and had the means to save regularly.

For landowners or developers with building land on their hands, or for builders lacking credit, building societies or tontines offered the means to get new projects started. Thus, in some individual cases an association of this kind was a way of overcoming financial problems. It is less clear that the existence of several societies at any time reflected a general shortage of capital. Not enough is known about the history of individual money markets to help on this point. In Lancashire their popularity in the mid-1790s, including that of the various types of subscription society, may reflect a shortage of capital with which to begin building. On the other hand, Birmingham societies reached the height of their popularity at the beginning of the 1790s, when capital is believed to have been plentiful. In such boom years building societies may have flourished just because the interest in building was spreading among more and more people.

4 THE BUILDING OWNERS OF THE SEAPORTS AND OF BATH

To what extent were the types of people who handled building undertakings in the industrial towns also at work in the seaports and in Bath ? In Liverpool between about 1740 and 1780 craftsmen, particularly joiners and bricklayers, may have made a bigger contribution to the stock of new houses by speculating on their own account than they did in the industrial towns. Mariners and craftsmen linked to the making and repairing of ships and their accessories, such as shipwrights, block and ropemakers, and the usual general tradesmen and occasional professional or leisured person contributed the rest of the houses.[88] For example, the undertakers in Drury Lane near the docks, developed in the early 1750s, included at least one bricklayer, two plumbers and glaziers, a plasterer, a mason, two mariners, a boatman, anchorsmith, ship's carpenter, surgeon and a woman.[89] Again, the builders of Sparling Street on the south of the town in the later 1770s included a wide range of craftsmen, including bricklayers, cabinetmakers, joiners and painters, and at least one slater and plasterer and a mason.[90]

From the 1780s the role of the craftsmen becomes more important. Most houses built by them were as undertakers, often on credit supplied by local attorneys. This dominance of men in the trade, particularly the joiners, is especially marked after 1800, though the majority were not Welshmen, as Ashton led us to believe.[91] This was true of the construction of all types of housing, from the courtyard tenement property in such areas as Toxteth Park to the substantial terraces in roads such as Great George Street and Clarence Street. Although general tradesmen, craftsmen and mariners still built in a small way, and merchants contributed to the stock of fashionable housing, sometimes for personal use, joiners and smaller number of bricklayers, masons, painters and other craftsmen were ubiquitous. The builders on the plots in Gloucester Street sold by John Fitchett and his partners between 1810 and 1812 included at least five stonemasons, four joiners, one bricklayer, one paviour as well as two excise officers.[92]

The growing predominance of the craftsmen-builders was accompanied by a more rapid turnover in the market for new houses than in the manufacturing towns. More were sold quickly than were kept for long-term investment. In 1784 a Liverpool writer, commenting on the inadequate dwellings of the poor, blamed 'builders who erect most of the new houses on their own accounts upon speculation for sale'.[93]

[88] Out of 211 houses erected on sites acquired between 1746 and 1780 of which the occupation of the builder was traced, 124 were constructed by craftsmen-undertakers: for sources *see* Note on Sources.
[89] Liverpool R.O. deeds 554C, 555A and B.
[90] *Ibid.*, 885B and C, 886A, B and C, 887A.
[91] T. S. Ashton, 'The Treatment of Capitalism by Historians', in F. A. Hayek (ed.), *Capitalism and the Historians* (1954), p. 47.
[92] Liverpool R.O. deeds 616B, 617B, 618A.
[93] I. C. Taylor, 'The Court and Cellar Dwelling: the Eighteenth Century Origin of the Liverpool Slum', *Transactions of the Historic Society of Lancashire and Cheshire*, CXXII (1971), p. 71.

It was also true of the larger houses. A majority were sold within five years of the acquisition of the site. Nearly all the dwellings which were sold quickly were the responsibility of craftsmen. With the help of credit from attorneys, they moved from one building project to another. Most of them remained part-time speculative builders, handling contract work and perhaps supplying materials. Samuel and Thomas Franceys, 'plasterers and builders and marble masons and sculptors', were traced in connexion with nine speculations on the Corporation Estate between 1792 and 1808, and were doubtless involved in others. They also dealt in chimney pieces and statuary. Less than fourteen months after acquiring a large building site in Russell Street, they advertised for sale on 31 January 1805 'an extensive assortment of Italian marble chimney pieces . . . with every other article in the marble business. Also statuary, veined and dove, in blocks, slabs, or scantlings. And at the latter end of March, they will have on sale, dry hair, in packs, for plasterers use.'[94]

Even among the ports, Liverpool may not have been typical in the concentration of building undertakings in the hands of craftsmen by the beginning of the nineteenth century. At Hull, at least half the builders were not craftsmen. There was a small proportion of shipwrights, ropemakers and especially mariners, but far more numerous were the general trades and crafts, such as merchants, victuallers, grocers, tailors, cordwainers and millers. For example, on the north side of the town, Scott Street ⟨*see* plate 26⟩, consisting of small terrace houses and courtyard tenements, was largely built between 1800 and 1805. Among the builders in these years were three joiners, two bricklayers, a builder, a sawyer, a cooper, a victualler, a cowkeeper, a yeoman, a tailor and a shoemaker.[95]

In Bath, the majority of substantial terrace houses, designed particularly for the well-to-do residents and visitors as well as some of its own professional men and tradesmen, were handled by craftsmen undertakers. This is true of the whole period between the 1730s and the beginning of the nineteenth century. Out of thirty-seven houses in Milsom Street erected about 1764, twenty were contributed by craftsmen in the trade.[96] Among about sixty houses built in St. James Parade after 1767, only fourteen were handled by men outside the building trades.[97] The taking of adjoining plots by craftsmen of different skills probably led to a pooling of labour in some cases. This is likely in

[94] Liverpool R.O. 427B, 468B, 734B, 820B, 845, 846C; *Gore's Liverpool Advertiser.*
[95] East Riding Deeds Registry: registers CC–CK.
[96] Bath Guildhall: leases re. Milsom St.
[97] *Ibid.*, lease colln., 14 Aug. 1772.

the construction of Bennett Street about 1774 ⟨*see* plate 3⟩, in which all the builders whose names have been discovered were craftsmen, comprising six carpenters (two of them partners in the erection of a single house), four masons, two plasterers and a tiler: between them they supplied all the skills except those of plumber, glazier and painter.[98] The smaller houses were also mainly built by craftsmen. During the great boom of the later 1780s and beginning of the 1790s, they largely monopolized the supply of new housing. For example, all the fifteen builders of Lansdowne Crescent in 1788 and 1789, whose occupations were stated in a Chancery suit in 1794, were craftsmen, most of them carpenters.[99]

Craftsmen-builders in Bath commonly retained newly-constructed houses for letting, possibly on account of a disinclination on the part of leisured residents to buy. Long-term loans supplied the necessary capital. One carpenter, timber merchant and coach builder, John Hensley, began his working career in the later 1760s and died in 1802. He was among the larger building undertakers and was also a developer. When his estate was auctioned in 1803, it included thirty-seven dwellings, of which eleven lay in fashionable terraces and twenty were court tenements. The thirty-four which were sold fetched £11,010, and the other three were worth about another £750. Among his mortgages, in 1786 he had borrowed the large sum of £3,000 from a Bristol man on the security of several building projects in progress and ground rents, finally paid off in instalments by him and then his executors between 1799 and 1803.[100]

One reason for the predominance of craftsmen among the building owners in Bath may have been a relative lack of other undertakers. Seasonal visitors and even permanent leisured residents were reluctant to build. As elsewhere, general tradesmen and craftsmen provided some new houses, but most of the demand had to be met by craftsmen.

The question still remains why building owners in Liverpool were mainly joiners and other craftsmen, in contrast to the industrial towns. As we have seen, in Manchester, the other of the two largest Lancastrian centres, houses were largely erected by men outside the trade. In both towns the same type of building owner seems to have been concerned with all sizes of houses. There is no indication in either place that artisan tenements tended to be built by men outside the trade *in contrast with* the construction of substantial housing by the craftsmen. Apart from

[98] *Ibid.*, deeds re. Bennett St.
[99] P.R.O. C12/202/30: I owe this reference to Dr. Ward.
[100] Bath Guildhall: Hensley MSS; deeds re. Alfred and Russell Sts.: the rents in the sale particular of 1803 and the prices obtained suggest that the purchasers of the big houses would have received gross returns varying between 7 and 9 per cent.

the special explanation already suggested for Manchester, there is also the possibility of the differing availability of capital, either short or long-term, or both. Craftsmen-undertakers were more inclined to gear their building projects than men from outside the trade. Short-term credit was often needed while dwellings were being erected, and then they might require mortgages to bridge the period—varying between a few months and several years—while a purchaser was obtained, or if the houses were being kept as an investment. They thus benefited particularly from the great credit expansion in the provinces at the beginning of the 1790s. This is apparent in Nottingham and Manchester. In Manchester, the years 1789 to 1793, in which building activity was at its height was the only period in which craftsmen have been found to have played a prominent role. Such a pattern does not reappear in the next great boom after 1804. In Nottingham heavy borrowing by craftsmen began about 1785 and reached its peak after 1790, when the loan of sums between £1,000 and £2,000 was not unusual. This did not reappear after 1800.[101]

It is thus likely that financial conditions were exceptionally favourable to craftsmen in the later 1780s and beginning of the 1790s. It raises the further question as to whether loan capital was short for builders in the industrial towns in some other periods, such as after 1800. In the case of mortgage loans, since both Manchester and Nottingham were metropolitan centres it is difficult to imagine that sums of £100 or £200 would have been unobtainable in most years. Yet the competition of local industry for loan funds during a period of rapid manufacturing expansion may have made it difficult for builders to borrow larger sums. The *Nottingham Journal* between 1806 and 1808 includes numerous advertisements inviting sums of £500 or more on landed securities, while offers of money on mortgage were generally restricted to a few hundred pounds at the most. Some of the largest sums required were stated to be in connexion with industrial investment. It is thus possible that a limit on the amount of long-term credit available to craftsmen gave men outside the trade, who relied more on their own funds, more opportunity to speculate in building.

Craftsmen-builders also had a special need of short-term credit. Some was usually obtainable from builders' merchants. More certainly one can link an important role played by craftsmen as undertakers with the presence in the town of professional financiers able and willing to supply it to them. In Liverpool the particularly important role of joiners as undertakers after 1800 appears to have been linked to the

[101] A conclusion based on the deed evidence for Manchester and Nottingham.

efforts of attorneys to provide finance. Such a habit had been developing since at least the 1770s. On the other hand, except at the beginning of the 1790s there is no evidence that bankers or attornies were much interested in house building for loan investment in Manchester or Birmingham. In Hull after 1800, where craftsmen were important but not predominant as builders, attorneys and bankers lent money to builders, but on a small scale compared with the sums supplied by the attorneys of Liverpool.[102]

Another factor may have been the extent to which land developers provided credit. In Liverpool, many attorneys combined land development with lending to joiners and craftsmen on their own schemes. In Hull in the early 1800s, one or two of the landlords or developers provided at least small amounts of credit. In Nottingham in the 1780s we have seen that one developer, John Sherwin, provided financial help to the craftsmen-builders who bought his land.[103] Yet in Manchester only two cases of lending by developers have been traced over the whole period. This is in spite of the great extent to which developers intervened between original owners and undertakers in the supply of sites.[104] On the whole, it is likely that the amount of short-term credit available provides a partial explanation of the extent to which craftsmen acted as undertakers rather than contract builders in the three or four decades after 1780.

In varying numbers in each town, building speculation attracted craftsmen in the trade, some general tradesmen and more substantial artisans, small manufacturers, mariners and shipwrights, and a few professional people and leisured men and women. However, in none of the centres do the very wealthiest members of the community play a prominent role as builders, despite their financial resources. Those with easiest access to large amounts of capital, such as local landowners, leading industrialists, ship-owners or attorneys, sometimes handled building land. They tended not to construct houses in any number.

None of the landowners (as distinct from developers) on the edge of the town, whether resident or absentee, appears to have gone further than the provision of the land, some of the basic amenities for building, and the occasional loan to builders. None of the original owners in Birmingham, such as the Colmore, Gooch, Inge and Legge families,

---

[102] East Riding Deeds Registry: registers of deeds CC–CK; Hull R.O. Manor of Tupcoates with Myton court book 2, and various deeds. In Bath the craftsmen-builders of the beginning of the 1790s were extensively supported by the banks, and Dr. Ward has drawn my attention to the importance of attorneys in Bristol in this connexion at this time, but evidence is insufficient to show how important they were in either town before this date.

[103] See above, p. 118.

[104] See above, pp. 93, 151.

has been traced as builders. In Portsea, in the whole period between the 1730s and 1820, one landlord alone is known to have erected one or two houses, about 1799.[105] In Bath one of the smaller crescents, Widcombe Crescent, was partly erected by the original owner of the land, after 1800.[106] Again, no other case has been discovered.

In some of the smaller manufacturing towns the leading industrialists made an important contribution to new housing stock. In Merthyr Tydfil about 1800, a quarter of the cottage accommodation was supplied by the leading ironmaster.[107] There were many cases of rows of cottages being built near the factories and collieries of Lancashire by their owners.[108] Instances of this practice have been traced in the major towns. In Nottingham a framework knitter and hosier named John Crosland built over forty tenements in Narrow Marsh between 1788 and 1790.[109] At Handsworth, outside Birmingham, Boulton and Watt were responsible for several terraces adjacent to the Soho works after 1796.[110] In aggregate this contribution was probably small. Many of the biggest manufacturers did not build. In Birmingham, John Baskerville, the famous japanner and printer, is only known as a builder in connection with the house erected for his own use outside Birmingham on Easy Hill on land obtained in 1747. John Taylor, 'the most considerable maker of gilt-metal buttons and enamelled snuff boxes' around the 1760s, has not been traced as a builder. At the same time, he became a partner in Taylor and Lloyd's Bank in 1765, and a landowner by the purchase of the manors of Bordesley and Yardley.[111] In the industrial villages and smaller towns, one reason for building by an industrialist was to provide accommodation for the workpeople. In the biggest centres, supply by other people, such as the numerous general tradesmen, made this service less necessary.

Similarly, the leading merchants and professional men do not figure prominently as builders. In Birmingham, none of the Lloyd family, who were iron merchants, has been traced as an undertaker. Instead they became partners in the Bank and local landowners. In Liverpool,

[105] Portsmouth R.O. D4848.
[106] Somerset R.O. deeds re. Widcombe Crescent.
[107] Glamorgan R.O.: list of cottages etc. on the Cyfarthfa Estate etc.
[108] P.R.O. B1/113, pp. 175–6; Barker and Harris, *St. Helens*, p. 170.
[109] Nottingham Archives M.23361–2, 23282–92.
[110] S. D. Chapman and J. N. Bartlett, 'The contribution of building clubs and freehold land societies to working-class housing in Birmingham', in Chapman (ed.), *Working-Class Housing*, p. 236. The biggest building owner known to me who was also a manufacturer by trade was Richard Paley of Leeds, soapboiler, the subject of a forthcoming paper by Professor Beresford: he was responsible for several hundred dwellings before 1805.
[111] Gill, *Birmingham*, pp. 90–93, 101–4; R. S. Sayers, *Lloyds Bank in the History of English Banking* (Oxford, 1957), pp. 7, 28.

the contribution of wealthy merchants to building undertaking was small.[112] Their money went into land or industrial concerns in south Lancashire or Cheshire. Some erected saltworks in Cheshire in the 1780s and 1790s, and by 1804 held two-thirds of the total interest in the industry. In 1801 Liverpool merchants opened a new colliery at St. Helens.[113] The attorney William Roscoe bought 153 acres and a country mansion for his residence in 1799; he became a local banker, and had interests in a local colliery and smelting works at Bagilt. [114] As far as Liverpool property was concerned, it was speculation in building land rather than housing that attracted Liverpool notables. Roscoe was an important land developer, his projects including much of the land on the south-east of the town in the neighbourhood of Rodney Street: among his many activities, legal, commercial, literary and political, building seems the only conspicuous omission. Earlier, the prominent Virginian merchants Sparling and Bolden were conspicuous land developers in the 1770s. Sparling Street was one of their ventures. There is no trace of them as builders in the Street. The local notables invested in rural land, because of the social prestige it conferred, or in urban land development or local industry, because of the potentially high returns. The supply of new houses was largely undertaken by people with smaller capital.

[112] John Gladstone was responsible for a number of houses in the fashionable Rodney St., some of which were occupied by his relations: Checkland, *The Gladstones*, pp. 44, 53, 80; his building is noticeable in the deed evidence which I have examined, but this material as a whole suggests that the size of his operations as a builder was exceptional for a merchant.
[113] T. C. Barker, 'Lancashire coal, Cheshire salt and the rise of Liverpool', *Transactions of the Historic Society of Lancashire and Cheshire*, CIII (1951), pp. 96–7.
[114] Hughes, *Banks and Bankers*, pp. 61–4.

8

Houses and House Prices

The last chapter discussed house building in the provincial towns as a form of investment, and the people who acted as building owners. This chapter is concerned with the houses they erected, from the tiny two- or three-roomed tenements occupied by most of the artisan and labouring classes, to substantial terraced property of ten or fifteen rooms or even more, occupied by merchants, manufacturers or professional men. They are discussed particularly in relation to their price. Something is also said as a preliminary about the costs of land, labour and various materials in building, and the way the crafts contracted to do the work of construction.

Except in Bath, not much now remains of the eighteenth-century buildings of the seven towns which are the main subject of this study. Bath is a special case. Here, Georgian urban architecture may still be seen at its most splendid. Elsewhere, piecemeal commercial rebuilding, successive slum-clearance schemes and urban redevelopment projects have taken a devastating toll. Apart from continual losses as a result of business enterprise, the destruction of Georgian Birmingham began with a municipal improvement scheme in the 1870s. It has been completed ruthlessly in the massive redevelopment of the town centre in the last fifteen years. In Portsmouth, some of the main streets of the old town have been carefully preserved. The blitz and urban redevelopment schemes have swept away all but a handful of the innumerable rows of modest two- and three-storey dwellings in Portsea originally built for the workers in the dockyard and the tradespeople who served them. In Manchester and Hull, a few isolated rows of substantial Georgian housing remain. In Liverpool, part of the substantial terraced housing built between the 1780s and 1820 still exists. Nearly all the smaller dwellings have long since disappeared. Altogether, what survives in these seven towns is far from typical of the whole range of eighteenth- and early nineteenth-century housing. Of the courtyard or back-to-back tenements, innumerable in every Georgian town of any size, there is almost no surviving evidence.

Some idea of what the smaller dwelling looked like can be gained from photographs. Some of them have been used as illustrations in this book. Yet they are all too few, and they relate principally to houses built from the 1780s, and particularly after 1800. For some towns, detailed early or mid-nineteenth-century town maps reveal the ground plan and layout of the smaller dwellings. In other cases, such as Birmingham, they were drawn too late to be helpful, particularly for building done before 1800. Where they exist, the earlier maps have been used as the basis of some of the drawings in this chapter. In fact much more can be discovered about the builders and prices of new houses than about their physical structure, particularly in the case of dwellings erected before the boom of the 1780s.

The absence of evidence about the size and appearance of early and mid-eighteenth-century housing, particularly smaller tenements, is well illustrated by the fact that one cannot be explicit about the predominant building materials. Outside the stone-bearing areas, in which lay Bath, Bristol and Plymouth, the main choice of material for the external structure lay between timber and brick. By the 1780s, brick building was predominant in all the major towns included in this study. It is less easy to be definite about the early and mid-eighteenth century. Large town houses were built of brick fairly generally by the end of the seventeenth century. This does not mean necessarily that the same was true of tenement property. Owners and occupiers of substantial housing were influenced by such motives as prevailing fashion and the need for protection against fire, as well as by price. For dwellings occupied by the artisan and labouring classes, cost alone was the crucial factor. Clearly, as pressure on timber supplies grew in the course of the seventeenth and eighteenth centuries, there came a time when it was more economical to build in brick than in wood, but this chronological point naturally varied from town to town.

In Birmingham brick building was probably fairly general for all types of housing by the early eighteenth century. It is suggested by the number of bricklayers who were building undertakers. Local clay was abundant. Grants of 'free liberty to dig and take clay' on the site 'for the making of bricks, tiles or otherwise to be used in building' often accompanied building leases.[1] Photographs and drawings of houses erected in these years tell the same story.[2]

---

[1] Wise, 'Birmingham and its Trade Relations', p. 54; W. F. Carter (ed.) *Records of King Edward's School Birmingham*, II, Publications of the Dugdale Society, VII (1928), pp. 46, 109–10, 132.

[2] B.R.L. Birmingham Improvement Scheme Photographs (1875), re. Lichfield St. and Thomas St., etc.; A. and W. Tarlington and W. Blackham, 'Original Water Colour and Sepia Drawings of Old Buildings and Streets in Birmingham' (*c.* 1870–80).

The same pattern was probably true of Nottingham. Brickmaking began on the outskirts of Nottingham in the beginning of the seventeenth century. Bricks began to be used as the normal building material in the east Midlands after 1660. By the mid-eighteenth century Sherwood Forest, the main local source of supply of oak, was almost exhausted.[3]

In Manchester and Liverpool, brick construction was the fashion for larger houses by 1700. In the case of Manchester, 'about the year 1690, the manufacturers and traders having accumulated capital, began to build modern brick houses in the place of those of wood and plaster, which had prevailed so generally since the former era of improvement in the reign of Elizabeth . . .'.[4] When Celia Fiennes visited Liverpool in 1697, she found 'mostly new built houses of brick and stone after the London fashion'.[5] Particularly in Liverpool, the number of bricklayers among the undertakers suggests that bricks were used in small as in the larger houses. All the evidence points to a general use of bricks in most, if not all, the seven provincial towns (except Bath) by the early eighteenth century.

The substitution of bricks for timber in the external structure was accompanied or followed by the use of foreign softwoods for internal construction. By the beginning of the eighteenth century, the quantity imported was considerable. Its use was widespread in Birmingham in the 1740s. In 1746, one John Collins advertised his services as an architect and engineer, and mentioned that 'gentlemen may be furnish'd with building timber, or deals and Norway-oak, as cheap as in the deal-yards . . .'. Later in the year, a cooper and timber merchant advertised that at his deal-yard 'is lately laid in a large quantity of well-season'd deal, of all lengths and thicknesses, Norway oak, etc., which may be bought either by measure or number', from the 'Agent for the Importer, Cornelius Gardiner, of Gloucester'.[6] Imported deals would have been expensive in Birmingham, since costs of water transport via the Severn and then overland would have been high. Their general use in the town makes it probable that they were widely used in the other major towns more accessible to Scandinavian imports at the beginning of our period.

I THE COSTS AND ORGANIZATION OF HOUSE BUILDING

Of the three elements in the cost of house building, land may be considered first. Its proportion naturally rose with its increasing

---

[3] Chapman, 'Working-Class Housing in Nottingham', p. 138.
[4] Axon, *Annals*, p. 71.
[5] Fiennes, *Journeys*, p. 183.
[6] *Aris's Birmingham Gazette*, 24 March and 9 June 1746.

cost over the whole period between 1750 and 1820. It also varied according to location. The rising price of the sites of artisan dwellings might be contained in part by a more economical use of land, through the dense packing of courtyard or back-to-back tenements. But there was a limit to this development. Part, at least, of the rising price had to be recovered from the house purchaser or allowed for in higher rents from tenants.

Builders taking land leasehold were faced merely with an annual ground rent. The purchase of sites involved a down payment. The effect of rising land prices is well illustrated by a study of the relationship of site cost to the selling price of houses in the freehold towns of Portsmouth and Nottingham, and in Liverpool (where fines were paid). In Portsea, between about 1740 and 1770, the plots cost on average about 10 per cent of the selling price of the new houses. In the next two decades there was an increasing difference in land costs between the remaining strips in West Dock Field near the dockyard and those situated further away. At the end of the early 1780s boom, some inner sites cost about 24 or 30 per cent of the selling price of finished houses. On the outskirts, the proportionate cost in the 1780s and 1790s was normally between 10 and 20 per cent.[7] Land costs were between about 15 and 25 per cent of the selling price during the great house boom in the later stages of the Napoleonic Wars. Although plot prices on the edge of the town had risen two or three times since the 1780s, the effect was reduced partly by a rise in house prices. Further, on some developments land was being used more intensively, with more courtyard tenements. In other cases garden plots were shorter, because the use for the first time of closes instead of open-field strips made possible a more economical estate layout.

In Nottingham, land costs rose from between about 5 and 15 per cent of the price of new houses in the 1760s and 1770s to between 15 and 25 per cent in the 1800s. The construction of large blocks of tenements, particularly the typical rows of back-to-backs at right-angles to the streets, economized on land use, but houses with a street frontage could not avoid the full effect of rising land costs. At Liverpool, land prices rose from between about 10 and 15 per cent (with a few as high as 20 per cent) in the 1770s to a possible range of 15 to 30 per cent between 1810 and 1820. Again, rising house prices from the 1790s helped to reduce the effect of land costs, which increased at least three times

---

[7] Portsmouth R.O.: deeds re. Unicorn St. and Southampton Row, All Saints Rd., etc. The estimates in this and the following paragraph are based on contemporary title deeds: *see* Appendix III and Note on Sources.

between the 1770s and the 1810s. A further factor in limiting the growth in the land element in the price of new dwellings was the more economical use of plots, particularly in the more systematic grouping of courtyard tenements at the back of front houses. It is revealed in the increasing housing density in Liverpool: as early as 1774, it could be said that (presumably at least in part because of high land prices) 'the inhabitants of Liverpool live more closely together than in most towns . . . its whole area . . . is not so large as Birmingham or Manchester, yet it has a greater number of inhabitants than either of them.'[8] In 1765 there were about twenty-two or twenty-three dwellings per acre, but by 1821 the figure had risen to about twenty-six or twenty-seven.[9]

Accounts and estimates of building costs relating to housing are surprisingly rare for the major provincial towns in the eighteenth and early nineteenth centuries. The cost structure is still reasonably clear. The big contributions to building work were made by bricklayers (or masons in stone-building areas) and carpenters. One contemporary estimate gives the breakdown of expenditure for a Birmingham house erected in 1794. The total cost was £388 1s. 1d. Of this sum the brickwork contributed nearly one-third.

'77,400 new bricks laid with all materials and
    labor   29s. 0d.   £112 5s. 0d.
12,000 of old bricks laid w. morter and labor   £6 0s. 0d.'

The carpentry and joinery cost about £140, the plastering between £20 and £25, and 'plumbing glazing and painting' £23 4s. 3d.[10] Other estimates confirm that the brickwork (or stonemasonry) and carpentry and joinery formed at least two-thirds of the total cost, and that (as one would expect) plumbing, painting, ironwork, glazing and plastering were all relatively minor items.[11]

Although wages was the major element in the price of bricks, the charge for laying them was well below their prime cost. This was also true of carpentry and joinery. Two estimates made in 1792 and 1806,

---

[8] W. Enfield, *An Essay Towards a History of Liverpool* (Liverpool, 1774), p. 24.
[9] J. Eyes, *Plan of Liverpool* (1765); *Plan of the Town and Township of Liverpool* (1821).
[10] B.R.L. Lee, Crowder MS. 11A; cf. also an account for building two houses in Brighton in 1809: bricklaying and plastering cost £158 10s. 1½d., the carpentry £229 11s. 0d., stonework £6 2s. 8d., and painting and glazing £20 18s. 2d.: P.R.O. C.217/68/9.
[11] E.g., P.R.O. E112/1516/576 re. house erected in Deal in 1803, for which the bills submitted totalled £853 17s. ½d. (carpentry £424 0s. 7¼d., bricklaying and plastering £361 14s. 5½d., painting and glazing £38 0s. 11¼d.); the same also applies to rural buildings: N. Kent, *Hints to Gentlemen of Landed Property* (1775), pp. 247–55, re. two pairs of cottages costing £132 and £140 respectively, and A. Young, *General View of the Agriculture of the County of Lincoln* (1799), re. cost of new farmhouse at Osbornby, Lincs., for £919 18s. 11½d.

using a cottage at Stockport as an hypothetical example, suggest that the labour cost in both bricklayers' and carpenters' work was about one-fifth of the total outlay. For a rod of brickwork, labour in 1792 amounted to 15s. 4d. out of £4 os. 1od., the rest being spent on bricks, lime and sand; in the case of the carpenter's work for a square of roofing, labour cost 5s. 6d. and materials £1 4s. 9d.[12]

A similar pattern is shown in an 'estimate of new houses July 1810' constructed for Boulton and Watt in Handsworth near Birmingham. Out of a total figure of £1,083 19s. 6d., timber alone cost almost one-quarter of the amount (£251 5s. 9¼d.), and bricks, lime and sand more than a quarter at £289 11s. 7d. On the other hand, the main labour charges totalled only £246 10s. 3d., most of the remainder representing other materials.[13] Thus, so far as costs on the site were concerned, the chief charge was that for materials.[14]

The key function of carpenters and bricklayers in the physical work of house construction was naturally paralleled by their important role in the organization of building. This was true whether a craftsman was speculating on his own account or if the building owner was not a craftsman, and he had to arrange for all the work to be done by other people.

We have seen that in every provincial town, many building undertakers were not themselves in the trade, and paid one or more craftsmen for the whole construction. In this case there were various ways in which the actual building work might be organized. For more expensive houses, the building owner or his agent occasionally bought the materials himself and the craftsmen were paid just for labour. The building of a substantial house costing £3,390 in Mosley Street, Manchester between 1783 and 1787 for J. R. Pease of Hull involved the purchase of materials independent of payments for labour.[15]

Another way of having houses erected was for the site owner, or an architect or surveyor employed by him, to contract with different craftsmen for completing only the work which they could handle themselves, each being paid a sum agreed in advance or according to a

[12] See Appendix IV; labour was less than one-quarter of the outlay in the following estimate for a rod of brickwork, presumably in the London area, *c.* 1749: 4,500 bricks at 16s od.: £3 12s. od.; 1¼ hundred lime at 10s. od.: 12s. 6d.; 2½ loads sand at 3s. od.: 7s. 6d.; labour and scaffolding: £1 8s. od.; total, with profit £6: J. Noble, *The Professional Practice of Architecture* (1836), p. 139.
[13] B.R.L. Boulton and Watt MSS. box 43: I owe this reference to Dr. S. D. Chapman.
[14] See also Dickson, *Lancashire*, pp. 108–10: estimates of building costs of rural cottages in Lancashire before 1815. In general, estimates distinguishing the charges for labour and materials are few, as the various craftsmen often supplied materials with their labour.
[15] Wilberforce House, Hull: Pease MS. 97; this method was used by Boulton and Watt in the case just quoted.

measurement of their work after completion, with the craftsmen supplying the materials. In June 1814, Henry Griffith of Liverpool contracted
with a local silversmith to do the joiners' and carpenters' work for eight
houses in Soho Street, for £780 according to a plan and specifications.[16]
Construction by several craftsmen, with no one of them undertaking
responsibility for the whole, clearly offered opportunities for fraud or
skimped building, and sometimes one of the craftsmen agreed to supervise the work of others. In Ormskirk in 1744, Thomas Cropper, carpenter and joiner, said he had offered to do the wood work on a house for
William Knowles, and that he would also superintend the stone and
brickwork as well as all the other tasks, to prevent Knowles being
defrauded by the workmen; in the accounts which he submitted upon
completion were not only the items involving his carpentry work but a
charge of 10s. 6d. a week for superintending the building for eighteen
weeks.[17]

Much more usual was a contract with one craftsman, or with two
acting jointly. This method of building was used long before the middle
of the eighteenth century. Instances have been found of master masons
contracting for the construction of whole buildings in the sixteenth and
early seventeenth centuries.[18] The practice was used extensively in the
rebuilding of Warwick after the fire of 1694.[19] It might either involve an
agreement to build for a fixed sum, or for the price to be calculated by
surveyors according to the usual rates for building craftsmen's work
after construction was completed. Several lawsuits in the Exchequer
Court in the late eighteenth and early nineteenth centuries turned on the
question whether the original agreement involved payment of a fixed
sum or was contracted for a price according to measurement. This
suggests that both practices were in use at least in those localities. For
example, in 1806 a baker in Dock named Stephen Hawkins contracted
for the building of a house with William Tremearn, at a price (according
to him) of 300 guineas; while building was being done, Tremearn tried
to induce him 'to submit the building to be paid according to measure
and value', but Hawkins stuck to his version of the contract.[20]

[16] P.R.O. E112/1547/789; other examples, P.R.O. B1/138, pp. 81–4; E112/1514/484
and E112/1547/791; for an example relating to a house erected in Ormskirk in 1724, see
E112/1148/27.
[17] P.R.O. PL.6/77 m.5; another similar example in E112/1506/164.
[18] E. W. Cooney, 'The Origins of the Victorian Master Builders', *Econ. H.R.*, 2nd ser.,
VIII (1955–6), p. 169.
[19] Warwickshire Record Office: CR.556/364, W.A.6/116, Warwick Corporation order
book, 4 July 1709.
[20] P.R.O. B1/114, pp. 25–30; see also E112/1422/481 and E112/1516/576.

Much more usually, the contract specified the payment of a fixed amount for construction. Especially in the case of cheaper houses, it was clearly more satisfactory for the undertaker with usually limited means to know the price he was expected to pay at the outset: particularly in the growing towns, where all except the most expensive houses tended to follow several fairly uniform types, craftsmen could estimate easily the approximate cost of a building project. Part of the money was paid during the course of construction, sometimes in several instalments, and the rest on completion. The practice was common, though not invariable in Birmingham in the middle of the eighteenth century: in February 1757, Richard Best, bricklayer, agreed to build six houses with two brewhouses and two workshops for Thomas Chapman of Birmingham, salesman, on a plot with a frontage of 26½ yards for £255:[21] £130 was to be paid when the roofs were tiled, and the rest on completion. William Hutton, the Birmingham antiquary, wrote in 1781 that 'the proprietor generally contracts for a house of certain dimensions at a stipulated price'.[22] Again, Hull Trinity House used this method for building houses on its local estate throughout the later eighteenth century: in 1752, the proposal of John Meadley to charge £900 for building five houses according to an agreed plan and specification was accepted by the House; in 1781, it received seven proposals for erecting some small tenements for its pensioners, and understandably accepted the lowest of £618.[23] It is likely that contract building for an agreed amount was a common practice all over England, and probably in the country as well as the towns, for most of the eighteenth century.[24]

Whether or not a craftsman was acting as a contractor for building a whole house, or whether he was speculating on his own account, he still needed to use a range of craft skills in the course of construction. There is little direct evidence as to how this was organized in the provincial towns of the eighteenth century. Numerous local newspaper advertisements for one, two or three craftsmen in the trade of the advertiser alone suggest that it was customary for craftsmen to employ men in their own skill alone. Thus sub-contracting to other craftsmen of the work in which the contractor or craftsman undertaker was not himself trained

[21] B.R.L. MS. 491073; see also B.R.L. T.C. 6292.
[22] W. Hutton, *A History of Birmingham* (1781), p. 71; for a case of a house which was priced according to measurement and value on completion, see below, p. 198.
[23] Hull Trinity House: vote books 1749–84.
[24] The Duke of Chandos had several houses erected for him in Bridgwater in 1726 by this method, and two years later the elder Wood built a house for him in Bath at a tender of a little over £2,345: C.H.C. and M.I. Baker, *James Brydges First Duke of Chandos* (Oxford, 1949), pp. 225, 318–19.

would have been the normal practice. This method is explained by a carpenter and builder in Cambridge in the 1790s, John Carter, who

'used to enter into contracts as is usual in his line of business to build or repair houses and other buildings for a given sum agreed upon and upon such occasions [he] used to engage with . . . David Bradwell to perform that part of the contract which was to be done by persons in his business of a bricklayer at a given sum and used to employ Mr. Wm. Coe to perform the smiths work and Mr. Jn. Favell to do the painting.'[25]

The great expansion of demand for housing in the provincial towns from the 1770s and 1780s brought no obvious change in the organization of the building industry.

2 NEW HOUSING IN THE INDUSTRIAL TOWNS

It is convenient to discuss the various types of houses and their prices first in the manufacturing centres and secondly in the ports. Housing in Bath and Portsmouth had special features, and are considered last In Birmingham, about 5,000 houses were erected between the mid-1740s and about 1780.[26] The largest dwellings typically consisted of three or four rooms to a floor and a street frontage of 10 or 12 yards, with a yard and garden and sometimes workshops in the rear ⟨*see* plate 9⟩. These are described occasionally in advertisements in *Aris's Birmingham Gazette*, mentioning the number of rooms though not their individual size. Thus on 8 April 1771, a house was advertised in the centre of Paradise Row, having bow windows, with three rooms on the first and second floors, a large hall, handsome staircase and spacious landing, and four rooms on the third floor, with a back kitchen and garden. Such houses fetched several hundred pounds when first placed on the market. In January 1738 a carpenter named Jonathan Johnson obtained £400 for a leasehold house he had erected the previous year. When this was offered for sale again in December 1743, it was described as 'containing 12 yards in the front, four rooms on a floor', and (as in the deed of

---

[25] P.R.O. B1/101, pp. 110–18; for a Birmingham case of subcontracting by a 'builder and mason' to a carpenter and joiner between 1766 and 1774, E112/2019/76.
[26] This study of housing in Birmingham built between about 1745 and 1780 illustrates the difficulty regarding the absence of sources on the structure and layout of houses. Most surviving photographs and drawings concern the bigger dwellings, and there is no large-scale map of Birmingham delineating individual dwellings before the 1880s, by which date the tenement property erected over 100 years earlier had been converted or rebuilt for commercial or industrial use. All the prices quoted below are derived from contemporary title deeds (*see* Appendix III and Note on Sources), except where noted.

1738), as including a brewhouse, stable and summerhouse in a large garden.[27]

More numerous were dwellings of approximately half the size, with two rooms per floor and two or three stories. Examples of these are common in the *Gazette*, such as the 'new, handsome well-built house' in Edmund Street on the Colmore Estate offered to let in January 1761, consisting of two rooms per floor, with a pump in the yard, a brewhouse and chamber over it, and a garden, with the offer to construct workshops 'for a good tenant on lease'.[28] These smaller dwellings sold when comparatively new for between £80 and £200. Two were erected under contract in 1740 by Jonathan Johnson for a cutler, William Caldwall, for £260: the agreement stated that they were each to have a frontage of 5 yards, and to be of three floors, with workshops and chambers over them, brewhouses and houses of office, and a pump each in the yards.[29]

Such property let for £7 or £8 a year upwards. If rented by a single family, it would have been beyond the resources of the majority of townsmen. Some of these houses were probably occupied by more than one family, since the ratio of persons to a house was 5·7 in 1751 and 6·0 in 1778, a proportion markedly higher than in the early nineteenth century.[30]

The majority of houses sold new for well under £100, and probably consisted of no more than two or three rooms. Some of these were tenements lying with workshops in the yards of bigger houses, of which Birmingham was full in the early and mid-eighteenth century ⟨*see* map 25⟩. There are many references to these in *Aris's Birmingham Gazette*. On 7 January 1751, for example, 'two new leasehold houses fronting Stafford Street, and three other little houses, not quite finished, behind and adjoining the said front houses' were advertised for sale. One court for which evidence survives, built about 1776 off Whittall Street on the Weaman Estate, was entered by a covered passage through the front range of buildings: it included dwellings on each side of the court, each comprising a storage cellar and three rooms one above the other.[31]

Further, by the 1770s back-to-backs were being constructed, consisting of one room per floor, in a row parallel to the street. At least

---

[27] B.R.L. MS. 329284.
[28] Again, a dwelling advertised on 2 July 1753: 'to be lett, and entered upon immediately, a new-built house, situated at the upper end of Snow Hill, Birmingham, with two rooms on a floor, a pump, garden and other good conveniences'. B.R.L. T.C.6292.
[29] B.R.L. T.C.6292.
[30] See below, p. 338
[31] *V.C.H. Warks.* VII, pp. 52-3.

twenty were erected from 1774 in Queen Street and Pinfold Street by John Lewis, bricklayer.[32] This type of tenement may have been constructed one or two decades earlier, but the evidence is not clear on this point. Other tenements probably consisting of no more than one room per floor lay in small rows in some of the side streets and passages scattered over the town. These smaller dwellings sold for between about £35 and £60 when new. Among the leasehold back-to-backs erected by John Lewis in the 1770s, eight sold for £484 15s. od. in 1777, four for £220 in 1782, and another eight in 1794 for £351.[33] Property of this small kind rented for between about £3 and £5. In one instance involving one of these small tenements, it is possible to link the cost of building to physical dimensions. In June 1778, John Strickland, carpenter and joiner, agreed to build a house for a victualler named Thomas Smith. The building was 14 feet square and of three stories, that is, probably of three rooms. According to Smith, the house was valued at £67. This was slightly higher than most dwellings with similar accommodation. The difference might be explained by the fact that this was a single house, not one of a block.[34]

There were no major changes in types of houses in Birmingham in the great boom between the middle of the 1780s and mid-1790s, when about 6,000 dwellings were erected, nor in the next boom, which reached a peak about 1812–14. Back-to-back dwellings parallel with the street became an accepted type of housing for the artisan and labouring classes ⟨*see* map 26 and plate 7⟩. Sometimes they were combined with one or two rows of tenements at right-angles to the street in the court behind them. Courtyard dwellings were still to be found everywhere ⟨*see* map 27 and plate 6⟩. Most of the bigger houses consisted, as earlier, of the normal terrace type, with a frontage of 14 or 15 feet and two rooms per floor, with two stories and garrets ⟨*see* map 28⟩. They were intermixed with a much smaller number of double-fronted houses with four rooms per floor, and sometimes a warehouse and workshops, for the well-to-do ironmonger or manufacturer.

House prices did not rise markedly in the 1780s, and dwellings offering apparently similar accommodation to those built before 1780 were sold new for much the same prices as earlier. Tenement property sold for between £40 and £60. For example, fifteen dwellings in Price Street, erected in 1786, consisting of three front houses and twelve

[32] British Rail deed room, Mornington Crescent: B.E. 123, 124.
[33] *Ibid.*; see also B.R.L. 372112, 372538, 441163–70, 491073.
[34] P.R.O. E112/2019/86; Strickland disputed this valuation, but the difference was not more than a few pounds.

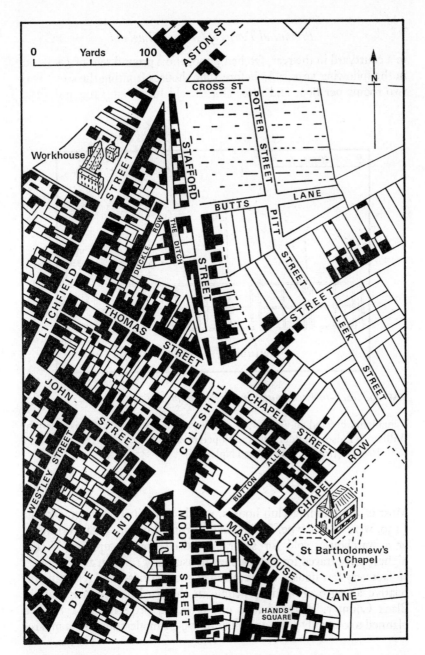

MAP. 25. *The developing townscape of Birmingham, c. 1720–50*

The extent of courtyard housing is clearly suggested by this section from Bradford's *Map*, 1750. These streets were mainly developed since about 1720. At the bottom Hands Square consisted of at least eight tenements built by John Hands, Bricklayer, on a site leased on 5 November 1743 and mortgaged to a toymaker in 1746.

199

in a courtyard in the rear, fetched £700, and a ground rent of £4 8s. 6d. in the following year.[35] As before 1780, houses fronting the street with two rooms per floor and three stories sold for about £100 and £150.

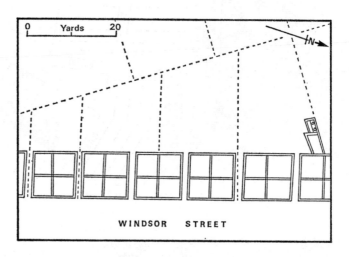

MAP 26. *Back-to-back houses in Birmingham, c. 1790*

Tenements erected in Ashted, *c.* 1788–93: the twenty-two houses left by William Windsor, builder, and developed on a site leased in 7 April 1788 from John Brooke (from B.R.L. West Hapley 60).

Most of the building-club houses, which cost between about £80 and £150, were of this type.[36] The double-fronted houses with workshops, or a warehouse, sold for several hundred pounds upwards.[37] The highest price traced for a single new house was £1,000 in about 1793.[38] In fact very few houses were erected at such a price level, reflecting the relative absence of wealthy people in the hardware industry of the Black Country. Birmingham's one crescent, projected in 1788, was planned to cost only £500 per house in 1795, a modest amount compared

[35] B.R.L. Lee, Crowder MS. 178b.
[36] B.R.L. MSS. 260742, 453531, Lee, Crowder MS. 18; Price, *Building Societies*, p. 61.
[37] E.g., B.R.L. MS. 407706; B.R. Manchester deed room: B.W.R. 85.
[38] P.R.O. B1/113, p. 16: in Bath St.

with the cost of crescent houses in Bath.[39] There is too little evidence to show the extent of the price rise during the Napoleonic boom.

In Nottingham in the 1760s and 1770s, the smallest new dwellings, probably of two or three rooms on top of each other, no more than 5 yards square, and without their own yards and gardens, sold new for £40 or

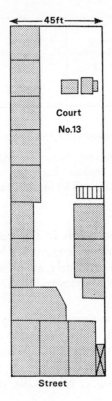

MAP 27. *A Birmingham Court, c. 1820*

Thirteen houses and malthouse built for Thomas Dealey, comb-maker, shortly after purchasing the site for £110 on 6 May 1820 (B.R.L.: T.C. 17915–18).

£50. This included the land, which cost between about 5 and 15 per cent of the sale price, depending on the location. They lay in short rows up back streets or alleys, or in courtyards ⟨*see* map 29⟩. In April 1760, a bricklayer named John Nixon bought a site in Gibraltar Place near Bellar Gate. He erected five dwellings in a row. In October he sold two houses for £80 on 48 square yards, and another for £43 10s. od. on 25 square yards. The other two, both on about 26 square

---

[39] Norton, *Proposals*, p. 5. Even the villas erected in the Hagley Road on the Calthorpe Estate after 1815 appear to have cost well under £1,000: B.R.L. Lee, Crowder 281a. Another crescent was planned as part of the Ashted development, but never built.

yards, were sold in November 1760 and July 1762 for £40 10s. 0d. and £51 respectively.[40] The land had cost Nixon between £3 and £4 per house. The first known houses erected in Nottingham as a row of back-to-backs were built in 1775, and four were sold the following year for £240.[41]

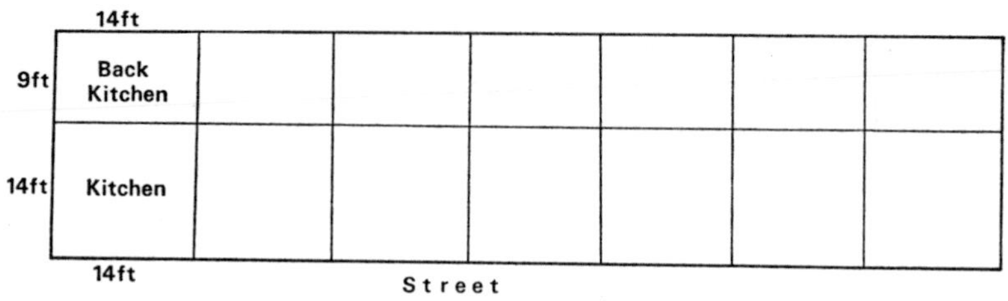

MAP 28. *Building Society houses built in Birmingham 1790–1794*

Seven houses in Tennant Street, costing *c.* £120 per house, erected for the Amicable Building Society by John Dickens, builder. Each had a cellar, kitchen and back kitchen, 2 chambers and a garret. The outside walls were 9 inches thick (B.R.L. Lee, Crowder MS. 18).

Tenements continued to be built in courtyards in the traditional way into the early nineteenth century. Numerous long rows of back-to-backs were being built from the mid-1780s. Fortunately, a contemporary description of the tenements built between the 1780s and the 1800s has survived:

'The houses of the working-class, at the present time, generally consist of a cellar, a room to dwell in, called the house-place, a chamber [i.e. bedroom], a shop over it to work in, a room in the roof, called a cock-loft, and a small pantry, though in the manner of building there are many exceptions...; brick walls, some 4½ and some 9 inches thick.'

In Dr. Chapman's words, 'they consisted of three 'boxes' placed on top of each other, used respectively for living, sleeping and working, with a cellar'.[42]

The back-to-backs were laid out at right-angles to the existing lanes which bounded the fields on the eastern edge of Nottingham, so that the unused land between the rows became courts or alleys or minor roads. On Sherwin's fields, the land was laid out in long rectangular strips, and

[40] Nottingham Archives TC2/87/31–2, and bdl. 5639.
[41] Debenham and Co: Victoria Station deeds G.189.
[42] Chapman, 'Working-Class Housing in Nottingham', p. 139.

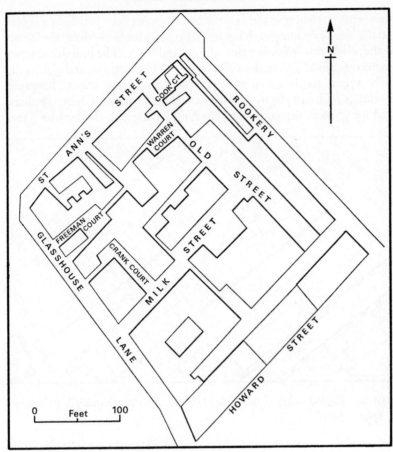

MAP 29. *Nottingham court houses*
Part of this district was built in the 1760s and 1770s. The earliest known
back-to-backs were erected here in 1775, though their precise location is
unknown (from Stretton's *Map, c.* 1800).

a row of houses was erected down the middle of each strip.[43] Most of
these dwellings were back-to-backs of one room per floor. A few were
through-houses of double the size, some having cellars in separate
occupation. The earliest row erected on the Sherwin Estate, Portland
Place, built between 1783 and 1785, consisted of through-houses,
placed down the middle of the land.[44] The existence of courtyard

[43] See above, p. 118.
[44] Nottingham Archives M.21922–5, 23183–5.

tenements elsewhere in the town of one room per floor may have suggested the idea of dividing each house to form two back-to-backs, the layout
of the whole row following that of Portland Place. The individual tenements cost about £50 in the 1780s, rising to between £60 and £70 in the
early 1790s, partly on account of increasing land prices. Fourteen
dwellings built in 1789 by a joiner named Smith on the Cherry Orchard
sold for £700 in the same year, the land having cost the builder £119.

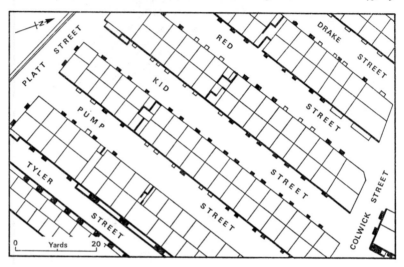

MAP 30. *Back-to-back houses built on the Sherwin Estate, Nottingham,
c. 1790–1800*

Sixteen of the houses between Kid Street and Red Street were erected by John
Nixon, builder, in 1790, and sold for £1,320 in 1797. Fifteen of the dwellings
between Pump Street and Tyler Street were built by John Hopewell, joiner,
about 1800, and sold by his heirs in 1813 for £860. When the purchaser
obtained a mortgage he insured them for £650 (from Jackson's *Map*, 1851–61).

He sold ten more in 1792 for £67 10s. 0d each.[45] The through-houses
sold for approximately twice the amount. In 1792, a builder named
Thomas Riste erected six such dwellings with cellars underneath in
another of Sherwin's closes, Tylers Close, and sold them in December
1793 for £685.[46] By the beginning of the 1790s, building land in these
fields was costing the builders between about 12 or 13 and 20 per cent of
the sale price of the new houses.

[45] Nottingham Archives TC2/163/1–5, M.23149, 23157.
[46] Nottingham Archives TC2/10/1–4.

Accompanying the rise in the cost of labour and materials, there was an increase in the average price of back-to-backs after 1800. Between 1807 and 1813, they were fetching between £50 or £60 (the level of the 1780s) and £80 or £90. This was true both of dwellings erected in the boom of the beginning of the 1790s, which were now fifteen to twenty years old, and of tenements built in the 1800s. For example, twenty-two dwellings erected by a brickmaker, William Walters, on Sherwin land in 1791 fetched £1,450, or an average of £66, in October 1808.[47] On Panier Close, sold by the Duke of Newcastle for building in 1807, a joiner named Thomas Sumner obtained £300 for four back-to-backs on the west side of Newcastle Street in August 1809, and £350 for four more the following April[48] ⟨*see* map 31⟩.

In Manchester, the cost of tenement property in the later part of the period was similar to that at Nottingham, when account is taken of the existence of rent charges for the land. This is shown by a study of house prices in the 1780s and 1790s. The layout of this housing had its special features. The siting of houses from the 1770s was often determined by the tendency of the big estates to lay out their streets on a gridiron pattern, the blocks of building land being oblong. The four sides of each block were lined with buildings. The land in the middle, usually forming a long strip, was sometimes left vacant. If it was large enough, it was partly covered by more small tenements.

In the great boom of the 1780s and early 1790s, smaller dwellings were thus laid out in several ways. Many fronted the streets in rows, having the advantage both of a street frontage and of direct access to the yard in the rear, in spite of their small size. Others were placed in small courts, and a few were built in short rows of back-to-backs. These became important at least two decades later than in Nottingham, at the beginning of the nineteenth century. Occupation of houses by more than one family, and particularly the use of cellars as separate dwellings, was widespread. If two or three rooms was the normal accommodation for a labouring or artisan family, then such a practice offered an alternative to habitation of a back-to-back. The description of the cellar dwellings of Manchester in 1796 is often quoted: 'each consists of two rooms under ground', that is, a kitchen and a back room with one small window near the roof.[49]

---

[47] Nottingham Archives TC2/51.
[48] Debenham and Co: Victoria Station deeds C.156, D.133; this conclusion on prices is also based on data in the following deeds: M.16388, 19952–6, 23431–40, bdls. 22, 5005.
[49] Quoted in E. P. Hennock, 'Urban Sanitary Reform a Generation before Chadwick?', *Econ. H.R.*, 2nd ser. X (1957), p. 116.

The layout and price of the tenements erected in these boom years is best shown by two or three examples. In 1788, the developer and builder Joshua Reyner erected a row of eleven dwellings in Hart Street on the east of the town ⟨*see* map 32⟩. On 18 October he sold them to a liquor merchant, named Robert Thompson, who completed the row by 1794 adding five more dwellings. They measured an average of 15 feet by about

MAP 31. *House building on Panier Close, Nottingham, c. 1807–1810*

The back-to-back dwellings between Clare Street and Union Place were erected by a building society which included a joiner, a baker, two framework knitters and 'divers others'; two of the larger houses between Newcastle Street and Newcastle Court sold for £180 in 1815 and 1816. The back-to-backs between Newcastle Street and Mount Earls Court were built by Thomas Sumner, joiner. Four were sold for £300 and another four for £350 (from Jackson's *Map*, 1851–61).

20 feet, accommodating one or two rooms per floor. Each fronted Hart Street, had its own yard or had access to the alley behind. Thompson paid £577 10s. od. for the eleven houses, and a ground rent of £8 15s. 5d. for the whole site of the sixteen dwellings, or about 11s. od. a house. If one capitalizes the ground rent, then the houses with the land were worth an average of about £60 to £65.[50]

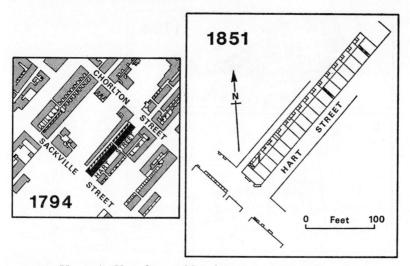

MAP 32. *Houses in Hart Street, Manchester*
This shows the sixteen dwellings erected between 1788 and 1794.

On the south of the town in Fleet Street, two carpenters, a timber merchant, and an architect were involved in the construction of at least forty-five houses in 1790. Eleven were sold on 25 March 1791 for £450 and a rent charge of £8 11s. 3d., involving an average total value (with the land) of about £55.[51] (Map 33.) Eight were back-to-back, adjoining the street, and three were 'blind-backs' in the rear courtyard. They were also smaller than the houses in Hart Street, the back-to-backs being 4 or 5 yards square, and had no private yards. In view of these disadvantages, the lower price is understandable. In contrast, on the opposite side of Fleet Street were two adjoining houses fronting the street, each measuring about 5 yards by 8 yards, probably with two rooms per floor, and their own back yards, and these fetched

---

[50] Manchester Town Hall deeds W.15: the block of dwellings are shown on Green, *Map of Manchester* (1794), and the individual tenements on Bancks and Co., *Plan of Manchester and Salford* (1832), and Ordnance Survey town plan of Manchester (1851).
[51] B.R. Manchester deed room: MC6(c), and maps.

£184 together, with a rent of £3 7s. 2d., after they were completed in November 1791.[52] Houses of this type were often occupied by more than one family. For example, four houses built near the London Road on the east side of the town after 1783 by a brickmaker named Nicholson were sold in 1787 for £330 and a rent of £1 6s. od., the householders being Nicholson and five others.[53]

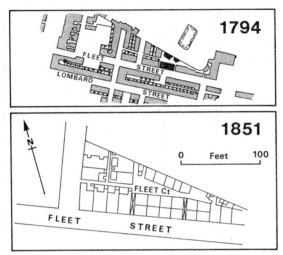

MAP 33. *Houses in Fleet Street, Manchester*

As in Birmingham, houses in Nottingham and Manchester occupied by the more substantial townsmen, manufacturers or merchants in the textile trades or professional men, often cost from £200 or £300 upwards. A few were sold for more than £1,000. In the fashionable Mosley Street in Manchester a merchant, Shakespeare Phillips, erected a house, stables and coachhouse on a site acquired in 1792, which he occupied and mortgaged for £3,000 in 1795.[54] In Nottingham, we have seen that the houses erected on Standard Hill near the Castle on land sold by the Duke of Newcastle in 1807 consisted of a select development of large dwellings erected under restrictive covements. In 1834 they were said to have been 'chosen as the residence of some of the most respectable inhabitants'. In 1810, William Stretton, architect, surveyor and builder, 'began to build on Standard Hill three houses which cost about £4,000 besides land'.[55]

[52] B.R. Manchester deed room: MC43, 86 and maps.
[53] Manchester Town Hall: deeds box 25 pcl. 10.
[54] Manchester Town Hall: deeds box R.17.
[55] See above, p. 121; *History, Topography and Directory of the Town of Nottingham* (Nottingham, 1834), p. 33; G. C. Robertson (ed.), *The Stretton MSS.* (Nottingham, 1910), p. 208.

3 NEW HOUSING IN THE SEAPORTS

In Liverpool by the 1760s and 1770s, tenements were of one, two or three rooms on top of each other, and were usually no more than 4 or 5 yards square. They were often erected in yards and passages in ones, twos and threes and sometimes more, behind front houses. Others were erected in rows in the smaller streets. It is usually difficult to identify them with certainty on nineteenth-century maps, but the following newspaper advertisements illustrate the layout of such dwellings:

> *24 January 1766:* 5 new, substantially built and well-finished small houses in an entry, court or passage out of Edmund Street, each four yards 'and upwards' fronting the entry, with the right to draw water from a large cistern adjoining the dwellings, occupied by a cabinetmaker, joiner, labourer, potter and brewer.

> *10 May 1776:* 3 houses 'on the north west side of a certain intended street, at the top of Cropper Street . . .; containing to the front of the said street 4 yards each, and running in depth backwards 4 yards and a half each . . ... There is a good yard and pump, which are enjoyed in common by the tenants of these houses . . .'.[56]

Such tenements cost between £40 and £60 when new. The high price of land already pushed up the price of houses (mainly leasehold), since the fines alone (in addition to the small rent of 1s. 0d. per yard frontage) cost between 10 and 20 per cent of the sale price of the house.[57] Four small dwellings built by a cabinetmaker called William Fairclough on a leasehold site measuring 13 by 20 yards acquired in 1766 in Cropper Street for a fine of £26 and a rent of 13s. 0d. fetched £150 in 1771; another four houses built by a bricklayer named James Oldham on land measuring 5 by 36 yards in Frederick Street bought in 1760 for a fine of £35 and rent of 5s. 0d. sold for £250 in 1768.[58] Again, dwellings with two rooms per floor and a frontage, usually in a street, of 4 or 6 yards were numerous. One such house was described in a sale advertisement in the *Advertiser* on 29 March 1776:

> 'Three houses in Preston Street . . . each 12 feet four inches in front, and the land runs 55 feet back, with two rooms per floor, 3 stories, and good cellars under, kitchen, good yard, very convenient for most kinds of mechanics, let for £6 6s. 0d. per annum each.'

[56] From *Williamson's Liverpool Advertiser*.
[57] Liverpool R.O. 534B, 693B, 785B, 802A and B, 885C, 886B and C, 887A.
[58] Liverpool R.O. deeds 531A, 680A; I have been unable to identify these properties on nineteenth-century maps.

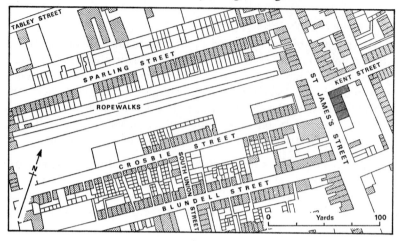

MAP 34. *Liverpool Building Development in the 1770s and 1780s*

Sparling Street was developed in the 1770s by the Virginian merchants Sparling and Bolden, on land leased from the Corporation. The houses, erected mainly by craftsmen-builders, sold new for between £150 and £250. The far larger terrace houses at the south-east corner of Kent Street and St. James Street marked with deeper shading were built by a mariner named Dickenson and sold for £1,620 in 1778. Some of the earliest back-to-back tenements erected in small courtyards were built between Crosbie Street and Blundell Street in the 1780s. (From Harwood's *Plan of Liverpool*, 1803).

Such dwellings sold for between about £80 and £200. The more substantial houses with a frontage of 7 or 8 yards or more and three or four stories often in the more commercial or fashionable streets fetched about £300 or £400 or more. Four dwellings erected by George Dickenson, master mariner, on a site acquired after 1766 in St. James Street, one of the main thoroughfares, sold for £1,620 in 1778 ⟨*see* map 34⟩, and a house erected by Robert Waln, bricklayer, in the fashionable St. Pauls Square on the northern edge of the town fetched £500 in 1768.[59] A house in this price range with commercial premises was advertised on 31 October 1766 in the *Advertiser:*

> 'A new house, warehouse and stable on the north side of Cable Street, on eight by 72½ yards . . . comprising a grocer's shop, parlour backwards, good kitchen, large lead cistern, cellared, two

[59] Liverpool R.O. deeds 853A; B.R. Manchester L. and Y. 3022R.

large rooms on the second floor, three on the third floor, with a warehouse over the whole premises on the fourth floor.'

A few of the houses and commercial premises such as warehouses and counting houses of the big merchants in the main streets might fetch over £1,000, such as that built by Richard Kent, merchant, on a site in Duke Street bought in 1771 with a frontage of 14 yards, and sold in 1786 for £1,500.[60]

From the 1780s, builders responded to rising land prices and growing demand for houses by increasing the number of houses built on back plots. Groups of six, eight or ten tenements became common, often lying back-to-back with the dwellings in the adjoining courts. In some cases the front houses were occupied by more than one family. Cellars in such houses tended to be in separate occupation. The *Liverpool Guide* of 1797 noted that 'inhabiting cellars, is extensively practised in some parts of the town', and mentioned 'the inhabited rooms of a house that all communicate by one common staircase; in which situation many families reside, who are unable to rent a whole house; and some entire streets are inhabited by tenants of that description.'[61] The size of the court tenements may be illustrated by two or three examples. Three dwellings erected after 1788 in a passage a few feet wide off Rigby Street on the north side of the town lay in a row with a combined ground space of 14½ feet by 40½ feet ⟨*see* map 35⟩:[62] they sold for £130 in 1793. Some of the tenements erected in Toxteth Park on the south side of the town after 1800 were even smaller. A house built in 1804 in a court named Harrington Court and sold for £73 10s. od. in the same year lay on a site of 13 by 11 feet.[63] ⟨*See* map 36.⟩

If Liverpool housing from the 1780s was characterized by innumerable cellar dwellings and tiny court tenements, there were at the other extreme streets and squares lined by substantial terrace houses. These were occupied by merchants or wealthy professional men. At the beginning of the nineteenth century, they sold for between £500 or £600 and £2,000 or £3,000 ⟨*see* plates 12, 13⟩. The price paid for the land varied between 18 and 30 per cent. Typically they had a ground space of between 6 and 8 yards by 12 or 15 yards, had three stories, cellar rooms, and possibly one or two tiny garrets. ⟨*See* maps 37, 38.⟩ One of the houses in Great George Square ⟨*see* map 38⟩ built by a bricklayer

[60] Liverpool R.O. deeds 546B.
[61] W. Moss, *The Liverpool Guide* (Liverpool, 1797), pp. 141–2.
[62] B.R. Manchester deed room L. and Y. 2917–19.
[63] B.R. Manchester deed room L.C.51.

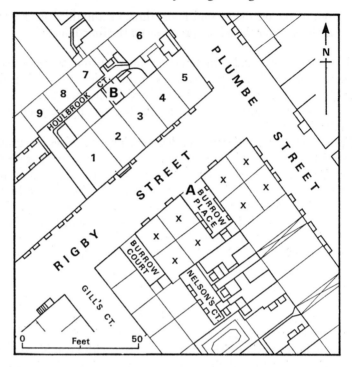

MAP 35. *Liverpool court tenements in the 1780s*

In the building project marked 'A' eight tenements (marked 'x') were erected by a joiner named James Sumner on a site bought for £95 in November 1786 and sold in December 1787 for £425. In the building project marked 'B' the nine dwellings were built by two joiners, Alex Midghall and Thomas Wignell on a site costing £170 acquired in December 1788. Nos. 306 were sold in 1789 for £450, nos 1–2 in 1793 for £265, and the tenements nos. 7–9 for £130 in 1793 (O.S. town plan, 1850, and B.R. Manchester L. and Y. 2916–19)

named John Worthington was sold for £1,150 in 1812, the land having cost £266.[64] One of the first houses erected as part of the Mosslake land project, a dwelling built after October 1816 in Chatham Street near Abercrombie Square, sold for £1,000 in 1820, the land having cost £180.[65]

[64] Liverpool R.O. 609B.
[65] Liverpool R.O. 525A.

In Hull, the housing pattern between the 1780s and 1820 resembled that of Liverpool. Multi-occupation of front houses and densely-packed courtyard tenements provided the main accommodation for the working classes. The back dwellings were as small as those in Liverpool, lying in

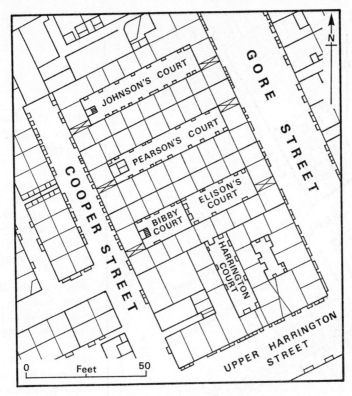

MAP 36. *Court tenements built in Toxteth Park, Liverpool, in the 1800s*

Five of the dwellings in Johnson's Court, built by Richard Gardner, joiner, were sold in 1805 for £375. Four in a row had a combined ground surface of 15 yds. x 13 ft. (O.S. town plan, 1850, and B.R. Manchester L.C. 12)

passages or yards tucked behind the front houses ⟨*see* plate 27⟩. For example, in 1801 the local newspaper advertised 'five new messuages or tenements, comprising 91 square yards and three feet, and passages leading thereto and fronting the same, comprising 56 square yards'; the dwellings thus had an average size of 4 by 4½ yards.[66] Among about

[66] *Hull Advertiser*, 11 April 1801.

213

ninety tenements erected by a bricklayer named Metcalfe in the following years, some measured as much as 5 by 6 yards and some as little as 12½ by 8 feet.[67] Tenement property of this kind sold new for between about £60 and £80, including the land, between 1800 and 1820. For example, two

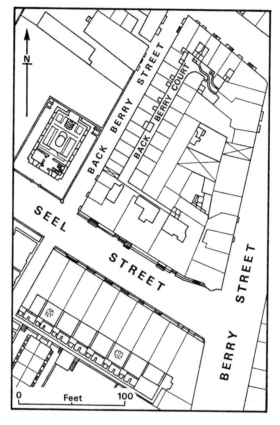

MAP 37. *Various houses erected in Liverpool in the 1790s*

The substantial terrace houses in Seel Street were erected by a bricklayer and builder, William Harvey on a site acquired in June 1791 (*see* plate 13); the Back Berry Street project was the work of John Walmsley, marble mason after 1796 (O.S. town plan 1850 Liverpool R.O. 870C and B.R. Manchester L.C. 13).

tenements that had been erected, having a combined floor space of 49 square yards, sold for £120 in 1810.[68] At the other extreme, substantial terrace property was less extensive than in Liverpool, because the population was much smaller. It was confined to a few streets, mainly on the north side of the town in the Sculcoates district. Nevertheless the structure of the houses, with three stories, cellars and sometimes garrets, strongly resembled the new dwellings of the well-to-do in Liverpool ⟨*see* plates 28, 29⟩.

[67] Hull R.O.: Manor of Tupcoates with Myton court book 2, pp. 110–13, etc.
[68] Hull R.O. S.B.H. 434.

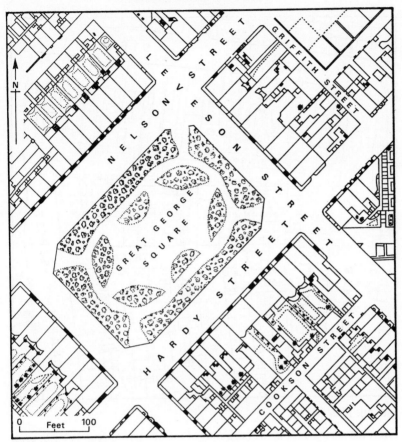

MAP 38. *Great George Square, Liverpool*

Some of the most expensive houses in Liverpool were erected in the Square in the years after 1806. They sold for various prices between about £1,000 and £3,000. Apart from the attraction of facing the Square they had deep garden plots at the rear (O.S. town plan, 1850; Liverpool R.O. 609A and B).

One of the principal features of the new housing in the three industrial towns and the two seaports was the differing extent of household occupation. By the beginning of the nineteenth century, one family to a house was the norm in Birmingham; in Liverpool and Manchester, cellar habitations were innumerable. By contrast Liverpool, and probably Manchester, had many more of the expensive terrace houses costing £1,000 or more.

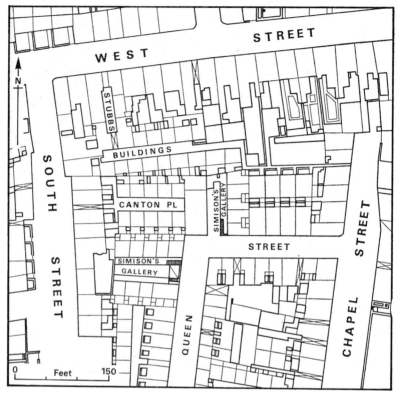

MAP 39. *Hull Courts*

Court tenements built in the beginning of the nineteenth century (O.S. town plan, 1853). (For the Stubbs Buildings *see* plate 27).

In all these towns there seems to have been a typical price for the smallest single tenements. In the 1780s it was between about £40 and £60. From the 1770s and particularly the 1780s, there was a tendency for this type of dwelling to be erected in larger groups. It was in these years that tenements built in groups of back-to-backs became common, lying either in rows parallel to the street (as in Birmingham and rather later in Manchester), or at right-angles to it. Several factors may have encouraged their building. The increase in the rate of urban population growth led some builders to erect more tenements in housing projects. Rising land costs and the desire to save on building expenditure en- couraged them to build dwellings in as tightly-packed groups as possible, and in so doing to keep the number of exterior walls per tenement to a minimum. In the latter respect, back-to-backs were ideal, because all except the end houses in the row had only one outside wall. Further. in Birmingham and possibly Nottingham, their occupation may have offered the artisan or labouring family a more attractive type of accommodation than sharing a larger house.

4 THE NEW HOUSES OF PORTSEA AND BATH

The following discussion of the housing of Portsea and Bath deals mainly with a different type and size of dwelling from the court or back-to-back tenement so prevalent in the major town of the industrial Midlands or the north. In Portsea there were of course some small dwellings in yards, but most houses had a street frontage. This was between about 12 and 15 feet. The houses were of two stories, or two stories with a garret floor, and sometimes with cellar rooms or a detached kitchen, comprising a total of between five and eight rooms, with a garden at the rear ⟨*see* plates 22–25⟩. These dwellings were often occupied by more than one family. Houses with a double frontage were rarely built in Portsea.

Because most dwellings were of a standard type, the price range was narrower than in the major towns of the Midlands and the north. Most houses sold freehold for between £60 and £160 between the 1740s and the 1770s. The land cost on an average about 10 per cent of the price of the house. A bricklayer named Osmund Martin bought a double site measuring 28 by 116 feet in King Street in March 1748 for £28, and sold the two houses he erected for £206 16s. od. in October.[69] In the same year and the same street, John Sellman, shipwright, bought 14 by 116 feet for £14, and twelve years later he sold the house for £140.[70]

A similar price range existed in the 1780s and 1790s, with a few houses selling for up to £200, or a little more. During the Napoleonic Wars, higher costs were reflected in prices varying between about £80 and £300, depending on the size of the house. A very few fetched £400 or £500. The majority sold for between £100 and £150. In 1812 two small dwellings consisting each of four rooms with a coal vault and yard and a frontage of 11 feet sold for £100 each. In a neighbouring street, a house with a frontage of 15 feet and comprising a kitchen and washhouse in the basement, three living rooms and three bedrooms (of which two were on the attic floor) sold for £280 in 1817.[71]

[69] Portsmouth R.O.: deeds re. King St.
[70] *Ibid.*
[71] Messrs. Brickwoods deeds re. site of Southsea Brewery; *Hampshire Telegraph and Sussex Chronicle*, 28 September 1812; Portsmouth R.O. D7496.

One factor in higher prices was the rising cost of building land. Between about 1800 and 1820, 15 to 25 per cent of the sale price of a new house represented the cost of the site. For example, on the Croxton development in a street called Diamond Street, a bricklayer named John Rees bought a site in May 1811 for £42. In October he sold the completed house to a marine for £220.[72]

Bath had its small courtyard tenements for the artisan and labouring classes, and small front houses costing £100 or £200 similar to those in Portsea and the industrial towns.[73] Yet its distinguishing characteristic was the large number of substantial terrace dwellings for its leisured residents, seasonal visitors, and its own well-to-do tradesmen and professional people ⟨*see* plates 2–5⟩. New, these cost between £800 and

[72] Portsmouth R.O.: deeds D4172/1.
[73] E.g. Somerset R.O.: DD/SAS C/120 and DD/GLC; Bath Guildhall: deeds re. Saville Row no. 5, and Hensley deeds.

MAP 40. (*above opposite*) *Terraced houses in Portsea, c. 1790–1810*

The alignment of the streets and building plots were typically determined by the layout of the open strips in Halfmilestone Furlong in East Dock Field. The houses on the east side of Hope Street, erected in the early 1800s, with a frontage of only 12 ft., were among the smallest terraced property built at the beginning of the nineteenth century. One sold for £75 in 1803, and another in 1808 (when prices were nearing their peak) for only £84. By contrast the bigger houses on the east side of Clarence Street (with frontages of over 15 ft.) were fetching £150 and £200 by 1800 (Portsea in O.S. *Hants*, 1870).

FIG. 41. (*below opposite*) *Terraced houses in Southsea, after 1807*

In this part of the town developers used closes, each of several acres, and the streets were laid out to supply the maximum number of building plots. Croxton's 'Town' was banded on the north side by Wish Street, on the west by King's Terrace, on the south by the south side of Copper Street, and on the east by a line halfway between Stone Street and Little Southsea Street. King's Terrace was one of the few rows in Portsea planned according to a fixed elevation; elsewhere in the field Croxton advertised that 'there is no compulsion for building, except in a straight line, in streets . . . .' The large houses on the south side of Wish Street fetched several hundred pounds; those on the north side of Copper Street between £100 and £120 (Southsea 25 in O.S. *Hants*, 1870)

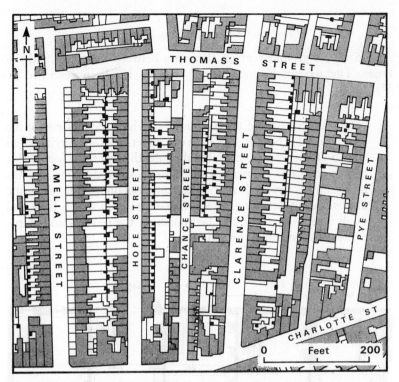

£1,500 with a ground rent, in the years between the 1740s and the 1790s. The accommodation of such property has been described by Mr. Ison:

'The standard type of terrace house, to which the majority of the Bath examples belong, usually has a street frontage varying from 20 to 25 feet in width, and a building depth of 35 to 50 feet, with a garden or yard in the rear according to the site conditions. Accommodation is arranged at a basement containing the domestic offices and kitchen, ground and first-floors each with a large and small reception room; and bedrooms on the second- and third-floors, this last usually an attic storey.'[74]

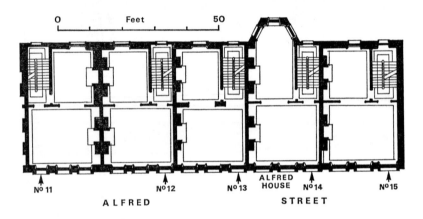

MAP 42. *Terraced houses in Bath, c. 1772*

Ground plan of houses in Alfred Street, similar to those in Bennett Street (from Ison, *Bath*, p. 112).

For example, among the houses erected on Corporation land in Bennett Street in the 1770s, one house with a frontage of 22 feet sold for £1,100 in 1778. Another fetched the same price in 1776, its width being 25 feet ⟨*see* plate 3⟩.[75] Among the industrial and port towns, it was only Liverpool that erected so many substantial and expensive houses, after 1800. By then Liverpool was three times the size of Bath.

---

[74] Ison, *Bath*, p. 109.
[75] Bath Guildhall: deeds re. nos. 3 and 22 Bennett St.

5 HOUSE PRICES DURING THE NAPOLEONIC WARS

There was no marked change in the cost of the various types of house before 1790. Prices rose sharply after 1800. This reflected in particular increasing wage and material costs, which had been rising since the beginning of the 1790s and continued to grow in the 1800s. Ashton drew attention to the great rise in building costs:

'In 1821 . . . wholesale prices in general stood about 20 per cent above the level of the year 1788. In the same period the price of building materials had risen far more: bricks and wainscot had doubled; deals had risen by 60 per cent and lead by 58 per cent. The wages of craftsmen and labourers had gone up by anything from 80 to 100 per cent. The costs of a large number of specific operations are given annually in the *Builders' Price Books* published in London. They show an increase in the cost of plain brickwork of 120 per cent. Oak for building purposes had gone up by 150 per cent, and fir by no less than 237 per cent. The cost of common painting had doubled, and that of glazing with crown glass had increased by 140 per cent.'[76]

It is difficult to generalize about the extent of the rise in building wages. In the south of England craftsmen's wages rose by about two-thirds between the 1780s and the 1810s, from 2s. 5d. to 4s. 0d. a day.[77] In the Midlands, building wages in the towns roughly doubled between the 1780s and the later years of the Napoleonic Wars. According to the unpublished figures of Mr. Eccleston, Nottingham building craftsmen were receiving 2s a day in the 1780s, and as much as 4s. 6d. between 1811 and 1814, the rate being 3s. 9d. in 1819 and 1820.[78] There is also a little evidence from the industrial north-west, showing considerable variations. Manchester carpenters and bricklayers were earning 18s. 0d. a week in 1793 and 25s. 0d. and 22s. 6d. respectively in the 1810s. Over the same period, their labourers' wages rose from only 13s. 6d. to 15s. 9d.[79] Macclesfield bricklayers and carpenters earned 18s. 0d. weekly in 1793 and 24s. 0d. in 1815; their labourers' earnings rose from 10s. 0d. to 16s. 0d.[80] But account must be taken of some rise in building

[76] Ashton, 'Treatment of Capitalism', p. 48.
[77] E. H. Phelps Brown and S. V. Hopkins, 'Seven Centuries of Building Wages', in E. M. Carus-Wilson (ed.), *Essays in Economic History*, II (1962), p. 178.
[78] I owe this information to Mr. B. Eccleston.
[79] A. L. Bowley, *Wages in the United Kingdom in the Nineteenth Century* (Cambridge, 1900), p. 60.
[80] A. L. Bowley, 'The Statistics of Wages in the United Kingdom during the Last 100 Years', Part VI, 'Wages in the Building Trades—English Towns', *Journal of the Royal Statistical Society*, LXIII (1900), p. 304.

wages in the boom of the beginning of the 1790s.[81] Clearly there were marked regional and local differences in the extent of the rise: increases may have varied from as little as about 40 per cent to as much as 100 per cent.

More important than wages in total building costs was the price of the materials.[82] In Tooke's words, referring to the years between 1800 and 1811:

> 'in the case of houses, the increased taxes upon building-materials, and the great rise in the price of timber, in consequence not only of the heavy duty, but of high freight and charges on importation, when combined with an increased population, operated as a premium on all existing buildings, and necessarily caused a great rise in that description of property.'[83]

It is safe to assume that the price of bricks at least doubled. In addition to the effect of the labour content in brickmaking, the tax was raised in 1794 and 1797. Apart from Ashton's conclusion, presumably based on London prices, there is evidence for provincial England. In south Lancashire at the end of the war, bricks cost 'from 30/- to 40/- the thousand'.[84] To illustrate building costs in areas distant from London, the author of *Plans for Cottages* chose a Stockport cottage as an hypothetical case: in 1792 he said that the bricks cost 11s. 0d. per thousand; in the edition of 1806 his figure was 35s. 0d.[85] A Staffordshire building society decided to pay 18s. 0d a thousand at the end of 1794.[86]

Timber also contributed substantially to the increase in the cost of materials, and it was foreign timber that showed the greatest price rise. Between 1787 and 1789, a load of Memel fir cost (including the duty) between about £1 10s. 0d. and £2. Its price rose in the beginning of the 1790s, and then remained fairly steady until 1798. In 1800 and 1801, it cost between £5 and £6 10s. 0d. It was lower for most of the period between 1802 and the first half of 1806. In this year timber for the Stockport cottage was estimated to cost 3s. 0d. per foot compared with 1s. 8d. in 1792.[87] The price rose sharply later in 1806 with the interruption of supplies caused by the French occupation of Prussia, and

---

[81] *Manchester Mercury*, 19 May 1792: reference to wage increases for journeymen plasterers.
[82] See above, p. 193.
[83] Tooke and Newmarch, *A History of Prices*, I (1928), p. 313.
[84] Dickson, *Lancashire*, p. 103; a tax of 1s. 6d. per thousand was placed on bricks in 1794, and a further 1s. in 1797: 34 Geo.3 c.15 and 37 Geo.3 c.14.
[85] See Appendix IV.
[86] Price, *Building Societies*, p. 29.
[87] See Appendix IV.

particularly in 1808 when the hostility of Russia and Denmark excluded British shipping from the Baltic. It then cost at least £17 a load. Between the later part of 1809 and early 1813, its price varied between £10 and £14. It fell sharply later in 1814, and could be purchased for £6 or £7 in 1816. Thereafter the price steadied. With the maintenance of timber duties at wartime levels, Baltic timber was still at least three times the price of the later 1780s, and more than twice that of the early 1790s.[88]

A permanent result of these higher prices was a switch by many builders to the use of North American timber, mostly yellow pine. This was despite the fact that it was regarded as inferior 'owing to its supposed greater liability to dry rot and comparative deficiency in strength and durability'. Its use began to spread between 1807 and 1810 with the scarcity of Baltic supplies; its import was greatly encouraged under the combined influence of the raising of duties on foreign (but not colonial) timber in 1812–13 and the end of the American War at the close of 1814, which reduced freights and allowed the import of United States wood through Canada. By 1820 the preference was about £2 1s. per load, allowing for different freight rates. In 1821 it was said that the use of Baltic timber was confined to the 'higher and more valuable description of buildings, and to purposes for which the increased strength and bearing was necessary or desirable'. Even so, if yellow pine cost about £4 a load it was still at least twice the price of Memel fir in the later 1780s.[89]

A contributory factor to rising building costs, though less important than the rise in the price of materials, was the growth in land values. It is almost impossible to generalise about them. In many cases site prices in comparable situations rose between the 1780s and 1810s by about 50 per cent; but the increase was sometimes less (as in Birmingham) or more (as in Liverpool). On some working-class property, savings were made in land costs by building tenements more closely together. Further, except on certain favoured locations and more generally in one or two of the major provincial towns, land costs tended to be less than 20 or 25 per cent of the price of the finished dwellings.[90]

House prices rose more slowly during the French Wars than the cost of materials, particularly timber. According to a contemporary, writing

---

[88] See Appendix IV: the duty has been included in the prices quoted in the text.

[89] J. H. Clapham *The Economic History of Modern Britain: The Early Railway Age* (Cambridge, 1964), p. 238; W. Smart, *Economic Annals of the Nineteenth Century 1821–1830* (1917), pp. 24–8; H. A. Shannon, 'Bricks—A Trade Index, 1785–1849', in Carus-Wilson (ed.), *Essays in Economic History*, III (1962), pp. 198–9; T. Tooke, *Thoughts and Details of the High and Low Prices of the Thirty Years from 1793 to 1822* (1824), pp. 367–8; the preference was reduced in 1821.

[90] See above, p. 191.

in 1823 about the increase in prices of real property since the year before the outbreak of war:

> '*Land*. The farm which, in 1792, let for 170*l.*; and which, in 1803 . . . afforded a rental of 240*l.*, let in 1813, for 320*l.*

> *Houses*. The house which, in 1791, let for 50*l.*, and in 1806, for 65*l.*, might be considered in the latter years of the war as worth 70*l.*, the rise being less great in houses than in land. Its value, as a purchase, originally 1000*l.*, was raised towards the middle of our long contest to 1300*l.*, and eventually to 1400*l.* or 1500*l.*'[91]

This case suggests that the writer was thinking chiefly of the more expensive housing. His starting-point was 1792; rising timber and labour prices and the general prosperity had presumably raised house prices already above the level of the later 1780s. Thus the rise in prices of the bigger houses between about 1788 and 1811–12 may have been as much as 60 or 70 per cent. According to Tooke, prices fell after about 1814 'in consequence of the reduction of the cost of building materials'. Presumably he had cheaper Baltic and American timber chiefly in mind. The widespread business depression of 1815–16 may also have been a contributory factor.[92]

To what extent was the price rise reflected in the cost of smaller dwellings? In the industrial villages and new towns, cottages were worth £40 or £45 in the 1770s and £60 during the French Wars.[93] It has been shown that prices of new tenements in some of the major provincial towns do not appear to have risen faster. In Nottingham, back-to-backs fetched about £50 or £60 in the 1780s and an average of £70 or a little more about 1806–15.[94] In Portsea, prices varied in the 1780s between £60 and £160–£200, compared with about £80–£300 about 1810.[95] Thus the price of new smaller dwellings rose more slowly than that of the larger housing.

Any explanation of the difference between the rise in building costs and that of house prices, particularly of tenements, must be tentative. In the mid-1790s, there is evidence in several towns of an over-supply of houses: in such a situation, prices presumably did not rise, and in one town, Bath, they are known to have fallen.[96] Speculative builders who

[91] Lowe, *Present State of England*, pp. 59–60.
[92] Tooke and Newmarch, *Prices*, II, p. 12; see below, p. 287.
[93] S. Pollard, 'The Factory Village in the Industrial Revolution', *English Historical Review*, LXXIX (1964), p. 519.
[94] See above, p. 205.
[95] See above, p. 217.
[96] See below, p. 282.

continued to undertake new projects were faced with rising labour and material costs which they were unable to pass on either by selling at a higher price or letting for higher rents. The choice lay between squeezing profit margins or skimping on the use of materials, or both. The extent to which either occurred cannot be known, but evidence of both has been found. In London, the Foundling Hospital Estate complained in March 1796 that the builders were not using 'sufficient bond timbers in the buildings to hold them together, therefore the walls will be apt in settling to give way and separate, which must prove very injurious'.[97] In Birmingham in 1795, Charles Norton explained the cheapness of the houses he proposed to build in the Crescent on the grounds that 'I purpose to give my time and profits in this business, to content myself with the ground rent alone, which enables me to build the houses for so small a sum (notwithstanding the great advance of labour and all kinds of building materials)'.[98] The recovery of demand from the later 1790s and its continuation through most of the 1800s enabled building owners to raise house prices and rents. Even so, house prices seem to have risen more slowly than those of materials, particularly timber, and builders must have been under constant pressure to contain costs. As we have seen some switched after 1807 at least in part from European to North American timber, which was regarded as inferior. In Nottingham in August 1809, the Corporation ordered that, following the report of its Annual Committee, only English oak or foreign timber were to be used in buildings erected on its Estate, presumably to prevent the use of Canadian timber.[99] But the main saving in costs only came as a result of the addition to the duties on foreign timber in 1812 and 1813 and the ending of the American War at the close of 1814, by which time Baltic timber was also falling in price. Between 1816 and 1820 the use of American instead of Baltic timber may have reduced timber costs by about one third.

Other savings could have been made by reducing the depth and soundness of foundations, by sparser use of timber in joists and roofing, and possibly by the use of inferior bricks. Commenting on the rising cost of materials, and particularly of timber, Cockerell, the surveyor on the Foundling Hospital Estate, wrote in 1807 (even before the Napoleonic Blockade had its full effect): 'if I had pressed the builders to the

---

[97] Olsen, *Town Planning*, p. 81.
[98] Norton, *Proposals*, p. 3.
[99] *Nottingham Records* VIII, p. 89; on 5 August 1809 the *Nottingham Journal* advertised 'four new houses built with foreign timber', while on 30 March 1812 the *Birmingham Gazette* offered nine houses in the town 'particularly well built, the timber is of the best quality'; such references to the quality of house timber are frequent in this later stage of the Napoleonic War.

extent of the power I possessed under their contracts [regarding the use of materials], most of them must have failed.'[100] In the case of tenement property another possibility is that builders sometimes erected dwellings of slightly smaller dimensions than in the 1780s and 1790s. For example

A = total of ordinary deals and fir timber   B = ordinary deals only
N.B. Small quantities of spruce deals omitted.
Figures missing for 1705 and 1712.

FIG. 41. *Official values of timber imports into England and Wales, 1700–1760* ⟨*see* p. 257⟩.

some of the back-to-backs erected on Panier Close, Nottingham after 1807 appear to have been several square yards smaller than most of those built in the 1780s and 1790s. But there is no clear pattern.[101] In some instances builders may have allowed their profits to decline,

[100] Olsen, *Town Planning*, p. 88.
[101] See Figs. 30 and 31; but many of the houses in Panier Close were similar in size of ground plan to those on Sherwin's land.

but there was a limit to the extent to which they were able, still less willing, to do this. In all probability the soaring costs over the period were met in a variety of ways.[102]

[102] Even so, the amount of saving on materials and workmanship must have been considerable to explain the divergence between the rate of increase in costs and house prices. Thus, if house prices rose 50 per cent and potential costs by a 100 per cent, the builders would have spent only about three-quarters of the amount spent before 1790, in real terms, on providing houses of a similar type, if the equivalent profit margins were preserved. As always, there is an absence of contemporary comment on this phenomenon. As far as the provincial towns are concerned, there is no evidence of savings in costs from economies of scale as output increased (through changes in the organization of house construction) or of technical improvements in construction leading to a rise in labour productivity.

Ashton believed that high interest rates contributed to jerry-building during the French Wars, through their influence on rents. 'At least two-thirds of the rent of a dwelling consists of interest charges: rates of interest were rising, and for more than a generation they remained high. This meant that if dwellings were to be let at rents which the workers could afford to pay they had to be smaller and less durable than those of the 'eighties': T. S. Ashton, *The Industrial Revolution 1760–1830* (1948), p. 160. But it needs to be remembered that interest rates remained officially at 5 per cent in provincial towns during the Wars, at the level they had been generally in the 1780s; at least a few provincial builders paid more through selling annuities or paying premiums; on the other hand many building owners did not rely on loan capital: see below, pp. 240, 294–5. To the extent that jerry-building was accentuated during these Wars, the cost of materials (which Ashton also emphasised) must bear the main responsibility.

9
Capital in Building: Outlay and Credit

I THE SIZE OF BUILDING PROJECTS

The last two chapters concentrated on describing certain aspects of building investment in the major provincial towns between the 1740s and 1820. We saw that in each centre hundreds of the more substantial townsmen were drawn into speculative building. For most of them it was a part-time occupation. Many of the dwellings were erected for long-term letting. They were each worth anything from £40 or £50 to £1,000 or more. This chapter deals with the building undertakings themselves, both in terms of the number and value of houses erected, the extent to which they were based on loan capital, and by implication their individual size. In addition, who financed the builders who depended on credit?

In the industrial towns and in Liverpool between the 1740s and the 1770s, the intermittent or once-for-all outlay of sums of a few hundred pounds was the typical investment for building owners. In the case of Birmingham, evidence has been found from the surviving contemporary title deeds for 150 enterprises between 1746 and 1780: sixty-nine consisted of one or two dwellings, and all except twelve involved the erection of ten houses or fewer; none built more than twenty-seven.[1] The median number in the 150 undertakings was three. Although blocks of eight, ten to twelve tenements were often erected as part of a single enterprise, these usually consisted in part of courtyard dwellings which fetched about £50 or a little less; houses which cost more than £100 to build were more often erected singly or in pairs, or occasionally in

---

[1] Out of the 150 projects for which evidence of the number of houses constructed has been found, eighty-five involved between one and three houses each, twenty-five concerned four or five dwellings each, and only twelve involved more than ten.

threes and fours. In most cases the total outlay on a project was consequently no more than few hundred pounds. The majority of undertakings probably involved the construction of house property which, if sold, fetched between about £150 and £800 or £900.[2] In 1760, Isaac Newton, ironmonger, got £540 for the large house he had erected on Snow Hill on a site 8½ by 67½ yards, which he had acquired in 1750.[3] Henry Gough, bricklayer, erected sixteen tenements on a large leasehold site in Edmund Street 35 by 51 yards leased on 2 May 1763; eight sold in March 1765 for £440 and the rest for £400 in September 1769.[4]

For most building owners in Birmingham in the second and third quarters of the eighteenth-century investment was small, not only with regard to individual sites but also to the number of undertakings handled over the course of their careers as builders. Since the names of many of the builders are known, some approximate indication may be given of the scale of their activity. Most building owners' names appear in the surviving records in relation to just one known project. Thus in the years 1746–80, when about 5,000 dwellings were erected, it has been possible to trace the names of 337 people who are either known to have built or may be presumed to have done so as lessees of building plots, involving a total of over 1500 houses. 285 of these people appeared only once in the evidence: only fifty-two are known to have handled two or more undertakings of whom the name of the builder is known, and none were traced as taking more than seven sites. Thus about two-thirds of the projects for which there is evidence were undertaken by men whose names are known only in connection with one of them. If we knew the builders of all the sites developed in this period the number of undertakers responsible for more than two or three sites would naturally be multiplied. It is still likely that most builders would be found to have handled just one or two sites each. On one large estate for which the information is complete, that of the Gooch family between 1766 and 1780, 139 building leases were granted to 129 people.[5]

Those in the building trade predominated among the takers of more

---

[2] In the case of seventy-six projects involving the construction of dwellings sold within twenty years of the conveyance of the site, it was possible to find the exact or approximate total price received on sale; only twelve undertakings involved the receipt of over £750, and only five of more than £1,000.
[3] B.R. Mornington Crescent Deed Room: O.B.R. 825.
[4] B.R.L. MSS. 329089–91. The biggest known project in financial terms was that of John Lewis on 3,448 square yards leased from the Inge family in Queen Street: he received at least £2,900 for twenty houses sold in four lots between January 1777 and June 1786, but these were erected over a number of years, and Lewis was still building on the site in 1789: B.R. Mornington Crescent Deed Room: B.E. 80, 123, 124.
[5] Based on all the surviving deed evidence in B.R.L., and in the B.R. deed Rooms; for the Gooch Estate, see above p. 85, note 24.

than one site; even so, their enterprises were spread over a number of years, so that construction in a single year would have involved just a few houses. Among the builders who are known to have obtained sites in 1764, William Stevens, bricklayer, erected two houses which sold in 1777 for £140; John Horton, cabinetmaker, was responsible for four dwellings sold in 1767 for £250; Isaac Sargent, toymaker, built two houses sold in 1803; and Rebecca Pritchit seven houses still owned by her family in 1818; none of these people is known in connection with another undertaking. On the other hand, Edward Sawyer, toymaker, acquired sites in 1760 and 1763 as well as 1764, and Thomas Saul, builder, possibly the biggest undertaker of the 1760s, also obtained plots in 1760, 1763, 1767, 1769 and 1773.[6] Not only did most building owners spend no more than a few hundred pounds, but their speculations were only occasionally repeated.

The investment pattern in Manchester and Nottingham was similar in the second and third quarters of the eighteenth century. One reason for the small size and number of undertakings of the average builder was the fact that much new property was held for many years after construction. Even though part of the cost of building was covered by a mortgage, the tying up of capital in property already owned placed some limit on further projects. Again, many of the building owners were investing occasional legacies or savings, and similar sums were seldom or never available to them again.

In Portsea, the typical undertaking involved the construction of just one or two front houses. Probably over half the projects concerned the erection of one dwelling, and over two-thirds the building of one or two. Most undertakings involved the expenditure of less than £300 or £400. Further, construction on more than one site was confined to a few people, mostly in the building trade.

By contrast, the building of the more expensive housing at Bath typically involved undertakers in at least twice this amount, even though most undertakers were content with one house per project. For the minority who handled several houses at a time, an outlay of £2,000 or £3,000 was sometimes involved. As elsewhere, some of the builders were probably concerned with just one or two undertakings in their career as undertakers. On the other hand, the names of a few occur again and again in one enterprise after another. For example, William Selden, mason, built four houses worth several hundred pounds on a site leased in 1754, at least one large house in the Circus about the same time, five dwellings in Milsom Street on land obtained in December

[6] B.R.L. MSS. 372084-5, 410005, 444643, 329099, T.C. 15101-10, etc.

1763, worth several thousand pounds, two or more in Westgate Buildings on a site acquired in 1765 ⟨*see* plate 2⟩, and a house in St. James Parade in 1767.[7] Further evidence would probably reveal more undertakings.

It has been seen that the types of people involved in housing projects and the predominant purpose for which they built did not change markedly from the 1780s. There was also relatively little alteration in the size of most building enterprises. Houses with a street frontage continued often to be built in ones and twos, and tenements in groups of four or six. However, in most of the largest provincial towns, a few enterprises now involved more than a score of dwellings, most of which were tenements. For example, in Nottingham as early as 1785 the stonemasons Thomas and Charles Osborne erected fifty-eight back-to-back houses on the east of the town, and in 1790 another builder, the younger John Nixon, erected at least forty-eight tenements in the same area.[8] In Hull between 1801 and 1805, eighty-nine little tenements built by the bricklayer Metcalfe were worth about £5,000 or £6,000.[9]

These larger undertakings are particularly noticeable in the later 1780s and beginning of the 1790s. Instances have been found in these years both at Birmingham and Manchester, but none has been traced after 1800. In the case of Hull, most of the several hundred building owners working in the early 1800s have been traced, and Metcalfe's work appears exceptional.[10] At Nottingham after 1800, the largest undertaking to be traced for any single person was that of John Roberts, silk-dyer, who was responsible for twenty houses in 1808. They were sold in June 1810 for £1,850.[11] Big projects involving the expenditure of several thousand pounds were helped between about 1785 and 1792 (and particularly in the beginning of the 1790s) by easy credit. More generally, over the whole period from the 1780s the expansion of demand which accompanied the unprecedented urban population growth encouraged some builders to work on a bigger scale.

Nevertheless, small projects involving the expenditure of under £1,000 remained typical in most towns. In Portsea, the construction of

[7] Bath Guildhall: collection of Corporation leases; deeds re. Union Passage no. 20; deeds re. Westgate Buildings no. 11; Bath Library: Walcot Estate Papers: memo. 28 Mar. 1755.
[8] Nottingham Archives: M.16433–40, 19137–50, 23234–50, TC.2/51.
[9] Hull R.O.: Manor of Tupcoates with Myton court book, vol. 2; S.B.H. 434; see above, p. 214.
[10] Myton court book, vol. 2; East Riding Deeds Registry: registers CC–CK; between 1801 and 1804 inclusive, these sources show that 109 people were certainly active as builders and about 100 further people acquired sites, some of which were built on in these years.
[11] Nottingham Archives: TC.2/155/5–8.

houses in ones and twos remained the norm, even during the unprecedented building expansion late in the Napoleonic Wars. Only a handful
of builders erected more than a dozen houses per project, and the majority
built only one. This was in spite of the fact that between about 1806 and
1816, the number of houses rose from about 5,000 to nearly 8,000. For
example, among the builders in the short Lower Southsea Street
developed after about 1808, a bricklayer named Thomas Hartley contributed at least four houses, a butcher and coal merchant called
William Payne was responsible for three dwellings, a bricklayer and
carpenter two each, and a tailor, shipwright, mariner, two carpenters
and a painter appear to have contributed another one each.[12] In Bath,
construction of the big terrace houses in the 1780s and 1790s continued
to involve sums of at least £1,000 or £2,000. The same was true of the
numerous terrace houses erected after 1800 in Liverpool in streets such
as Rodney Street ⟨*see* plate 12⟩, or in Great George Square, when
outlays were naturally raised by inflation. Elsewhere the expenditure
of such sums was exceptional.

In most towns there was little growth in the number of projects handled
by most building owners during their careers. In Liverpool alone
among the towns studied here, did this happen. As the joiners became
increasingly predominant as building owners, with the help of credit
from attorneys, many of them concentrated more on their own speculations. More and more they tended to move from one project to another,
spending anything between £500 and £2,000 at a time. They remained in
business as jobbing craftsmen or timber dealers, but spent more of their
time on their own undertakings than their counterparts would have done
a generation or two earlier. The positoin was different in the manufacturing centres. As the number of new houses in the manufacturing towns
grew in the 1780s and 1800s, so did the number of building owners.
In Nottingham, the builders of about half the 1,886 houses erected
between 1779 and 1801 are known: out of a total of ninety-four builders
whose names have been discovered, eighty handled only one project (in
the available evidence), and none was responsible for more than three.[13]

2 CAPITAL OUTLAY IN PROVINCIAL BUILDING AND OTHER BUSINESS UNDERTAKINGS

In comparison with undertakings in some sectors of industry at the
end of the eighteenth century, most building projects were small in
financial terms. It is true that in size of outlay building undertakings

[12] Portsmouth R.O. D4780, 7448, 7495, 7605, 8679, 8696, 8709, 8879.
[13] Based on all the surviving deed evidence in Nottingham Archives.

were often larger than units in outwork or small workshop manufacture. Expenditure on housing probably rivalled the outlay on materials and storage space of the smaller capitalist employer of outworkers in nail-making or woollen cloth making, or often exceeded that on tools and premises as well as on materials of the Birmingham buttonmaker or the Sheffield cutler, though on the precise capital needs of such entrepreneurs evidence is sparse. In the case of the Birmingham manufacturers, according to Hamilton,

> 'since nothing more than very ordinary machinery was required in the button and buckle trades and in the various branches of the brassfoundry business, these could be carried on by men of small property, so that the greater part of the manufacturers of Birmingham did not require large capitals, and many worked with less than £100'.[14]

But expenditure in housing so far as single projects were concerned was dwarfed by many enterprises in mining and metal smelting. The copper and brass manufacturing firms had tended to employ several thousand pounds each as a minimum from at least the early eighteenth century.[15] While the smallest English coalmines, those in Staffordshire, were probably much nearer to house-building projects in terms of capital outlay, at least in the north-east coalmining enterprises by the end of the eighteenth century involved sums far in excess of those employed by all but a handful of provincial builders. The purchase of a steam engine alone cost more than most builders spent on a single project:

> 'In 1787 Lord Ravensworth's Friar's Goose pit was reported to have cost £20,000 to sink. The cost of a steam engine was then put at £700–£3,000, tramways at about £450 a mile, and a complete colliery sunk to the depth of 100 fathoms might cost anything from £15,000 to £40,000.'[16]

Only the smallest type of cotton factory in the Pennine region in the last three decades of the eighteenth century, which employed horse capstans for driving carding machines, cost under £1,000. The larger mills relying on water power cost between about £3,000 and £5,000, and the taller steam-powered mill that began to be built at the end of the

---

[14] Hamilton, *Brass and Copper Industries*, p. 271.
[15] *Ibid.*, pp. 244–8.
[16] S. Pollard, *The Genesis of Modern Management* (1964), p. 63.

century cost a minimum of £10,000.[17] Numerous commercial under-takings involved capitals of several thousand pounds by the beginning of the nineteenth century, as advertisements for partners in local news-papers suggest. Thus on 8 January 1803 the *Hull Advertiser* included an entry for 'a partner in a commercial business to manage an accomp-ting house, and advance £1,000 to £1,500', and on the 29th for a partner by a 'gentleman with £3,000 upwards'. Thus by 1800, provincial house-builders were being left far behind in terms of outlay by many branches of business.

It is also worth noting by comparison that, at least in the last three decades, a few builders had emerged in the West End of London who worked on a scale far bigger than any provincial builder, with the pos-sible exception of one or two builders in Bath and Bristol in the begin-ning of the 1790s. The two developers of Bedford Square and the ad-joining streets after 1776 themselves built the whole of the south side of the square and many of the houses on the other sides. One of the principal subdevelopers, Thomas Leverton, wrote in 1797 that he had 'actually laid out for my friends and myself above forty thousand pounds in new buildings and improvements on it', and 'had a major concern in promot-ing the finishing of Bedford Square, and built among other houses in it that of the Lord Chancellor besides several on my own account, in one of which I now reside'.[18] The chief builder and developer on the Camden Estate after 1790, Alexander Hendy, builder, was found to owe £33,912 after his bankruptcy early in 1793.[19] No house-builder in England at the end of the eighteenth and beginning of the nineteenth centuries is likely to have rivalled in scale the outlay of James Burton, who estimated in 1823 that he had between 1798 and 1803 built houses on the Bedford Estate worth £299,400.[20]

It has been shown that a few enterprises appeared in the industrial towns after 1780 involving the construction of fifty or more tenements. Such undertakings involved at the most the outlay of several thousand pounds; in any case, they do not appear to have been typical. The expansion of demand that accompanied the Industrial Revolution and the growth of urban population in general did not alter radically the size of most building undertakings. A few larger projects emerged, but at least in the major industrial towns nearly all continued to invest sums ranging from £100 or £200 to £800 or £1,000.

[17] S. Chapman, 'Fixed Capital Formation in the British Cotton Industry, 1770–1815', *Econ. H.R.* XXIII (1970), pp. 238–41.
[18] Olsen, *Town Planning*, p. 48.
[19] P.R.O. B1/87, pp. 268–70.
[20] J. M. Baines, *Burton's St. Leonards* (Hastings, 1956), p. 17.

3 TEMPORARY CREDIT

Investment in house-building has never been limited to the capital which the building undertakers provide themselves. Some have always relied to a greater or lesser extent on short- or long-term credit. We have seen that many hundreds of people invested directly in housing projects in the biggest provincial towns in the later eighteenth century. Many more were involved indirectly through the loans which they made to builders. It greatly increased the number of men and women who contributed to capital formation in house-building. In particular, it drew into building the funds of more people in the general trades and crafts, and of more leisured men and women.

There is a little material about the sources of short-term credit in proceedings of lawsuits in the Exchequer and Chancery Courts, almost all at the end of the eighteenth and beginning of the nineteenth centuries. Most of the evidence on loan capital comes from credit secured by mortgages. They were granted on half-finished or completed houses to secure debts incurred in building which the undertaker was unable to discharge, or to pay off a supplier of temporary credit by means of a longer loan from another source, or to provide the money to build further dwellings on the site. Some, but by no means all, mortgages will thus provide a guide to the sources of short-term finance.

An important source of temporary credit for the craftsmen-builders was the builders' merchants. For concrete evidence, one has to rely on occasional legal proceedings. When Charles Frime of Bath ran into debt over a house he erected in 1766, he owed £70 to a local timber merchant, Charles Brett.[21] In the case of the bankruptcy of John Hughes, a Manchester joiner, in 1793, one creditor was a timber merchant, and one of the assignees of his estate (who were normally creditors) was another timber dealer.[22] Since the granting of credit by vendors was so widespread in all kinds of business in the eighteenth century, documentary evidence is almost certainly insufficient to emphasize the importance of this form of lending. Mortgages by timber merchants were rare everywhere, suggesting that they were reasonably successful in preventing temporary accommodation being converted into a permanent loan. Such reluctance is understandable. The success of their business depended on the ability to supply credit for a constantly-changing range of builders and projects.

[21] P.R.O. C12/1632/4.
[22] P.R.O. B1/84, pp. 254-5; see also B1/136, p. 75, relating to the bankruptcy of a Liverpool joiner in 1809 whose estate was assigned to two timber merchants.

One cannot estimate the extent of accommodation among craftsmen. In view of their ceaseless business links in the subcontracting of both jobbing and speculative work, it is certain that temporary assistance amongst themselves was considerable. In every town the occasional mortgage was made between building craftsmen. For example, during the building boom in Portsea at the end of the 1740s, one of the leading craftsmen-builders, a bricklayer named Osmund Martin, borrowed £100 from a house carpenter on mortgage a few days after the acquisition of a site, and repaid it when he sold the houses built on it later in the year; another bricklayer named John Rice mortgaged four houses he was building to a joiner for £300 in February 1751.[23] In Liverpool in the early nineteenth century, when craftsmen dominated speculative building, a few mortgages were made between men in the various trades. Presumably these indefinite loans reflect a far greater volume of temporary credit: most craftsmen would have been reluctant to reduce the personal capital available to their own business.

The growth of country banking in the later eighteenth century opened up a potential new source of credit to the building undertaker. According to the author of the standard work on provincial banking during the Industrial Revolution:

'there is nothing to suggest that the building of small houses—a subject upon which economic history has woefully little to say at present—received much encouragement from banks .... The thinness of the record suggests that bankers were disinclined to finance building. Mortgages, short-term financing by the craftsmen employed, and building clubs for artisans' houses: these were the more likely methods.[24]

The number of banks outside London grew from 119 in 1784 to 291 in the 1790s, and again to about 650 or 750 between 1810 and 1815.[25] Hence one would be most likely to find evidence of links between banks and house construction from the mid-1780s to the end of the period.

One possible approach is by a study of the lenders in the innumerable surviving mortgages obtained by the builders. They have revealed that in the case of each of the seven towns which are the principal subject of this book, and also at Brighton and Plymouth, the occasional mortgage was granted by a bank, but that in most instances their number was trifling. However, Professor Pressnell has shown that 'bankers generally

[23] Portsmouth R.O. D12605/12, 22.
[24] L. S. Pressnell, *Country Banking in the Industrial Revolution* (1956), p. 339.
[25] *Ibid.*, pp. 10–11.

disliked mortgages', that they rarely secured an initial loan by this means, and that most were 'taken as collateral or to secure existing advances'.[26] Banks did not generally wish to lend on long term, preferring to provide credit which, at least initially, was intended to be temporary.

Thus one might expect short-term advances to builders to have greatly exceeded the number of mortgages. To estimate the possible extent of this practice, a study was made of several surviving ledgers of banks existing in three of the major provincial towns. These give only the names of bank clients: neither occupations nor the purpose of the credit are stated. Contemporary directories supply some of the occupations, but in the case of undertakers from outside the building trades it is of course impossible to decide whether the money was used for housing speculation or some other business activity. Hence the use of the ledgers was restricted to the identification of craftsmen.

The first two ledgers of Taylor and Lloyds Bank in Birmingham provided ten names of people known to have been craftsmen-builders or possibly just craftsmen between 1775 and 1782 out of a total of several hundred clients; others were identified in the 1790s.[27] Again, the first ledger of Heywoods Bank in Liverpool covering the years 1787 to 1790 revealed much the same pattern, with the names of four or five builders identifiable among several hundred borrowers.[28] Finally, among the seventy-four borrowers from Raikes, Currie and Co. in Hull between 1808 and 1813, only one man was identified as a craftsman, compared with at least nine merchants and insurance brokers and nine-or ten other tradesmen.[29] While other building undertakers might doubtless be traced if further evidence were available, it seems clear that builders as a group were usually not important clients of the banks. Although some craftsmen-builders borrowed periodically from banks, the merchants, manufacturers and tradespeople dominate the ledgers, in terms both of numbers and of amounts of money borrowed.

Nevertheless, there were exceptions to this general pattern. In Nottingham, John Nixon, bricklayer, perhaps the largest speculative builder in the 1760s, was partly financed by the Wrights. Surviving

---

[26] *Ibid.*, p. 309.
[27] Lloyds Bank MSS.: records of Taylors and Lloyds, Birmingham, 'private ledger A 1775–1780' and 'ledger B 1780–1798'.
[28] Barclays Bank Ltd, Liverpool: records of Heywoods Bank (later Martins Bank), ledger 1787–90. The balance sheets of Leyland and Bullins of Liverpool, 1807–19, were also examined: Midland Bank Ltd., Ajax House, Colindale: records AE15, 16.
[29] Williams and Glyn's Bank Ltd, 3 Bishopsgate: records of Raikes, Currie and Co.: East Riding balance books 1808–13.

mortgages reveal that they lent him £300 in 1765 secured on one property, £480 in 1766 on another group of houses, and a total of £2,400 on a third property between 1769 and 1772. They also lent £500 in 1774 to another bricklayer, James Batty, to build a public house and at least one other dwelling.[30]

The great period of credit expansion in the provinces at the beginning of the 1790s, which coincided with a general building boom, saw considerable lending to builders in several of the big provincial towns by some banks. In Manchester after the bankruptcy of the builder James Boardman in November 1792, his bankers, the Heywoods of Manchester, found that they were owed £4,269 13s. 8d.[31] At Bath, at least five banks were involved in the building expansion; three were Bath banks, one was at Salisbury and the other at Chippenham.[32] It is also likely that banks provided additional money during the credit expansion between about 1807 and 1810 for building in the non-industrial south.[33]

These are all special instances. Despite the unusual policy of the Wrights in the 1760s and 1770s, and lending to builders in Nottingham by several banks at the beginning of the 1790s, no evidence of a bank mortgage has been traced in the town after 1800. In the case of Manchester, no evidence has been found of bank lending at any time apart from the case just quoted and an instance in 1791. The impression remains that in general direct bank help for builders was small: they only became important clients when the banks were flush with funds or over-confident in creating credit. Perhaps bankers gave preference to local notables, such as merchants, manufacturers, tradesmen and professional people, where sizeable sums were concerned. They may have regarded craftsmen-builders as a less good risk. Where small sums were concerned, bank credit may often have been unnecessary because other and more traditional sources, such as builders' merchants, or even perhaps friends or relations, provided credit until building was well enough advanced for a mortgage to be obtained.

Attorneys were also supplying an increasing amount of building credit. They provided both temporary accommodation and mortgage

---

[30] Nottingham Archives M.17540, 17553-5, TC.2/178; Debenham and Co. G.189.
[31] Manchester Town Hall: deeds H.18, P.26.
[32] The Bath City Bank helped to finance the builders of Bathwick such as Baldwin, Hewlett and Eveleigh, and its collapse in April 1793 helped to bring about their bankruptcy; another banker lent £14,000 to the developer of Lansdowne Crescent, etc.: Ison, *Bath*, p. 40; Bath R.L.: deeds re. John Eveleigh; P.R.O. C12/649/6-7, 202/30, which I owe to Dr. Ward.
[33] Brighton examples: Pressnell, *Banking*, p. 339; P.R.O. B1/109, p. 330, etc.; a Plymouth case in E112/1423/496; Southampton R.O.: bankruptcy papers of John Griffiths of Milbrooke, slater and builder, 1810 (D/PM 14/4/2, 7), who was indebted to three Hampshire banks.

loans with their own money and cash placed on deposit by local clients. Again, it is likely that many lawyers were reluctant to lend indefinitely and that on the available evidence, mostly derived from mortgages, a considerably greater amount of short-term credit was being tapped. Attorneys were active in this field at least by the 1760s and 1770s in some of the big provincial towns. A few mortgage loans were made to builders by attorneys in Birmingham, Liverpool and Bath in these decades.[34] If there had been more trades directories (which list attorneys) published in these years, other instances would doubtless have been traceable.

The financial role of attorneys became more important in some towns in the 1780s and 1790s, with the emergence of some bigger enterprises. At the end of the eighteenth century and in the first two decades of the nineteenth century, their significance seems to have varied from town to town. In a recent unpublished study Dr. Ward has drawn attention to their activities in financing the craftsmen builders of upper-class housing in Bristol at the beginning of the 1790s.[35] At least three attorneys lent to builders in Bath at this time, but here at least banks were the more important source of credit.[36] On the other hand, in Liverpool the role of the attorneys seems to have grown as more and more of the new houses were erected by joiners speculating on their own account. Out of 115 mortgages traced between 1801 and 1820, thirty came from attorneys.[37] Almost certainly the proportion of short-term credit which they supplied was even greater. Here they may have made the use of banks unnecessary. By contrast, in another seaport, Hull, the contribution of the attorneys, though traceable, was much smaller in these years.[38] In Manchester it was also small.[39] Clearly local custom and the inclination of individual attorneys affected the local pattern. Attorneys tended to be prominent where the craftsman builder, more in need of credit than the undertaker from outside the trade, was most in evidence.

[34] B.R.L. MS. 372538; B.R. Mornington Crescent Deed Room, B.E. 313; Liverpool R.O.: deeds 886A and C; B.R. Manchester Deed Room: L. and Y. 2914–15; P.R.O. E112/1933/441.
[35] Dr. J. R. Ward, unpublished paper.
[36] P.R.O. E112/1949/1032, and C12/1413/34; Bath Guildhall: deeds re. 3 Cross Bath St.
[37] Liverpool R.O. and B.R. Manchester: deeds.
[38] East Riding Deeds Registry, Beverley: registers CC–CK; Hull R.O.: Myton court book, vol. 2.
[39] In Birmingham, only the attorney-developer and builder John Brooke was prominent in the supply of capital, to builders on his own estate, at the beginning of the 1790s: see above, p. 88. In Nottingham, the attorneys Francis Evans and W. R. Middlemore supplied loans to builders both in the early 1790s and again in the early 1800s: Nottingham Archives M.18342–57, 19197–207, bdl. 5007, TC.2/44, 2/48, 2/111, 2/126, 2/167/27, 2/169/1–8, 2/178.

4 MORTGAGE FINANCE

In the industrial towns and in Portsea, between about a quarter and one-third of the undertakings of which the history has been traced were found to have been subject to a mortgage loan within two years of the conveyance of the site. This understates to some extent the proportion of undertakings which were helped by mortgages. Further, some builders may have obtained indefinite credit, secured only by bond or a promise to pay, for which no evidence survives in the deeds. Even so, the great importance of building undertakers' own capital is certain ⟨*See* Appendix V.⟩

Generally, undertakers who were not craftsmen borrowed on mortgage less often than men in the trades. The victuallers, grocers and more substantial tailors who existed in great number in every town, the small metal manufacturers in Birmingham, or the dockyard shipwrights in Portsmouth tended to build on a small scale for longterm letting as a means of investing a few hundred pounds, and often did not need loan capital. On the other hand, it was the important role played by craftsmen in the supply of new houses in Nottingham in the 1780s and 1790s that explains the high proportion of projects which were helped by mortgage finance. Their continuous involvement in repair work or some aspect of new construction must have made the temptation for some craftsmen to begin their own projects on credit, when it could be obtained, overwhelming.

The general contrast between the proportion of projects which needed loan finance in the industrial towns and the percentage in Liverpool is marked. Here, from the middle of the century nearly half the building projects for which evidence has been found needed outside help. Although many houses were sold within one or two years of the conveyance of the site, the craftsmen who were responsible for a majority of them still needed a mortgage to secure debts in the interval between building and finding a purchaser. In Bath the number of building projects for which evidence has been found is much smaller than for Liverpool, yet here a majority of undertakings appear to have relied on secured loans throughout the period. This is again linked to the predominance of craftsmen among the undertakers.

The amounts lent ranged from under one-quarter of the sums received from the sale of the houses to almost the full amount (and in a few instances more than the full amount). The majority were for between about one-half and five-sixths of the sums obtained on sale. As one would expect from the financial size of most undertakings, sums lent were nearly all small. At Birmingham, over one-third of the loans were under £150 throughout the century, and well over half were under £300. Loans of over £750 were few. In Manchester similarly, over half the mortgages were for under £300, the principal difference from Birmingham being the bigger number of loans for more than £750, which reflected the existence of some larger undertakings than in Birmingham, particularly in the 1780s and early 1790s. In Nottingham, the big mortgages are marked in these decades, mostly to finance the large undertakings of a few building craftsmen. Larger loans were far fewer both in Manchester and in Nottingham after 1800, accompanying the practical disappearance of the big undertakings. In Portsea, the smaller size of most enterprises was matched by smaller loans: over half the mortgages throughout the period were under £150, and none has been found before 1800 which involved the loan of more than £750. Because of the bigger financial outlay involved in the large houses for the well-to-do in Bath, mortgages were often correspondingly big: most mortgages were over £300 in the 1760s and the 1770s, and mortgages involving more than £1,000 were common from the 1780s.

With a few rare exceptions, these loans were made by local people. The growing development of a national capital market had made no noticeable difference by the 1790s. Mortgagees lived in the town or within a radius of 10 or 15 miles. For example, throughout the period, the majority of building mortgages in Liverpool were supplied by townsmen. The rest were granted by inhabitants of the neighbouring country parishes or of Cheshire across the Mersey. For example, the developer James Gill sold two adjoining plots on the land he leased from the Corporation in 1799 to a planemaker named Thomas Moore in 1800 and 1801 respectively. Moore borrowed £200 from a Liverpool widow on the security of the six houses he was erecting on the first plot, and £300 from a cordwainer in Prescot, 8 miles from Liverpool, on the three houses on the other plot.[40]

In Manchester and Nottingham, those who made a livelihood from the manufacture and marketing of textiles supplied only a small proportion of the loan capital. At Birmingham, metalworkers made a more substantial contribution to mortgage capital. Presumably in Manchester and Nottingham the industries themselves absorbed most of the potential loan funds. On the other hand, in Portsmouth, where there was no comparable investment for the shipyard workers, they made an important contribution to builders' loan capital, particularly before 1800.

Everywhere the biggest contributions were made by the numerous

[40] Liverpool R.O.: deeds 878C.

general tradesmen, that is, all tradesmen and artisans not in the local basic industry, and by the professions and leisured people, male and female. In Bath, where there was no manufacturing industry, the brewers, victuallers and wealthy tradesmen were a particularly important source of loan capital to the craftsmen-builders before 1780. In the other towns, at least one-quarter of the lenders were in this category in every period. Further, while the professional and leisured classes supplied relatively few builders, they were numerous among the financiers of building. In Manchester and Nottingham, women provided between 10 and 20 per cent of the loan capital among the mortgages which have been traced, while in Birmingham between 1745 and 1800 it was over 20 per cent. Again, while their number remained small, professional men (clergy, schoolmasters and doctors) appear more often as mortgagees than as entrepreneurs. Further, those described as 'gentlemen' were numerous as lenders to builders, and some of these were retired tradesmen. Thus mortgages appear to have attracted those who were interested in security rather than speculation.

Finally, a minor source of building finance from the 1770s was various types of club. The earliest known lending by these associations was secured on houses built on the Norfolk Estate in Sheffield. In his lease book the agent recorded twenty-two mortgages by building tenants between 1778 and 1786 (mainly in the first four years) to societies for sums of between £20 and £120. Most, if not all, were not specifically building clubs, and are referred to just as clubs or societies, with an address. Some of them made more than one building loan.[41] Since no systematic study has been made of the sources of mortgage capital in Sheffield, one cannot assess the importance of these loans as a contribution to the building mortgage market in general in these years. The number of such loans in about 1780 suggests that at that time the role of these clubs was important. Like Birmingham, Sheffield was a community of small manufacturers in the metal trades, particularly cutlery, for whom clubs for raising money by subscription would have been attractive, and the large number of loans from this source probably reflects the popularity of such societies in the town.

Elsewhere these loan societies were less prominent in providing capital for building, although some of them had been specifically formed for that purpose. In Birmingham in the later 1780s and early 1790s, there were a few 'building' and other clubs which lent money to housebuilders (their own members) on mortgage; but this type of society was not so common as the club which itself built, and its contribution to the

[41] Sheffield Archives: Arundel Castle MS. S.382.

total volume of loanable funds was tiny.[42] The only other place and occasion where the available evidence suggests that this source of finance was important was Manchester in the post-war burst of activity beginning about 1818 and continuing into the early 1820s, in which the contribution of *lending* building societies supplying money to their members begins about 1820.[43] In Liverpool and Portsmouth, charitable or capital societies also made a trifling contribution to building funds in the early nineteenth century.[44] Since the growth of clubs was a universal feature of urban life in these years, some lending by those with funds to invest was natural. What is more significant is the emergence of associations *lending* specifically for building, which collected subscriptions and lent the proceeds to members to erect their own houses, again, like the *building* societies, mainly in the industrial towns.

Like house-building, trade and industry depended to a considerable extent on temporary accommodation, part of which was provided by the suppliers of goods or of the raw materials to be processed. The main sources of mortgage capital in house-building were similar to those of the indefinite loans on which merchants and manufacturers depended. According to A. P. Wadsworth, one important Manchester firm, 'Titus Hibbert and Son, yarn importers and merchants, had in 1773 deposits of from £10 to over £1,000 from single women, professional men, country gentlemen and small tradesmen. These deposits might be untouched for years.'[45] Again, a firm of Blackburn cotton weavers, spinners and merchants borrowed small sums from widows and spinsters, clergy, friendly societies and some others between the 1780s and 1815.[46] Such firms differed from most house-builders only in respect to the total amounts they usually needed to borrow, not in the people who lent to them or the size of these loans. Thus house-building was one of several important business activities which drew small sums from countless local people who wanted above all a steady income without administrative worries.

5 CONCLUSION

The history of land development and building in these seven towns had common features deriving from the economic and social structure

---

[42] B.R.L. MS. 371953; B.R. Manchester deed room B.W.R. 12; B.R.L. Lee, Crowder 1100.
[43] Manchester Town Hall: Box 28B, F, P1/138.
[44] Liverpool R.O. 537A, 951A; Dr. Chapman also notes the contribution of money clubs in Nottingham, though no evidence of this was traced in the title deeds seen by me: 'Working-Class Housing', p. 143.
[45] Wadsworth and Mann, *Cotton Trade*, pp. 249–50.
[46] Edwards, *British Cotton Trade*, pp. 255–7.

of eighteenth-century England, and the nature of house-building as a financial activity.

Land-developers and house-builders tended to be different people, as they were to remain until the present century. Some land-developers built houses and lent money to other builders, but even in these cases the majority of dwellings were constructed in projects undertaken by other people. Further, original landlords, who often passed individual sites direct to builders, almost never built. The layout of building plots and streets, the provision of basic amenities such as roadmaking, the possible provision of drainage and open spaces was largely in different hands from those who organized house construction. Land-development was often a highly profitable, though speculative, undertaking. It often required larger amounts of capital or credit than was needed in the typical small-scale house-building projects. Thus, where the land-developer was not the original owner of the land, he tended to be a wealthy townsman or a man of sufficient business standing to draw on the necessary credit. Because of the further capital needed and the smaller profit levels obtainable in building, he passed most or all the building sites to other townsmen.

Everywhere construction involved the capital of innumerable people. The building undertakers fell naturally into two groups. There were the craftsmen who speculated on their own account, using their own labour and subcontracting work in skills outside their own. These often hoped for a quick sale, but were sometimes prepared to hold dwellings as an indefinite investment. There were also many speculative builders from outside the trade who had houses erected on contract with one or more craftsmen, mainly with the intention of retaining them for letting. Others introduced further capital into building as well. Many houses were mortgaged during or after construction to repay short-term creditors, the money being provided by numerous local people who wished above all for a regular, reasonably secure income without the administrative problems involved in direct property ownership. Capital was also supplied indirectly by the large number of local people who bought new houses from craftsmen who sought an early sale.

In one or two towns, craftsmen were more active in speculating on their own account than in building new houses by contract, and thus tended to predominate among the builders. But building or lending to builders, or at least the purchase of new houses, was generally an activity which involved hundreds of people, nearly all on a small scale and based on capital of between £100 and £2,000. The growth of demand from the 1780s encouraged the emergence in most towns of a few undertakers prepared to spend bigger amounts; yet the overall investment characteristics did not change at the end of the eighteenth and beginning of the nineteenth centuries. The large number of investors reflects important aspects of the nature of eighteenth-century economy, such as the tendency for savings to seek predominantly local investments and the size of the urban middle class. Apart from the few wealthy people in the large urban communities, there were many people, male and female, with moderate capital. Almost all of them preferred a local investment to purchases on the London stockmarket, at least before the 1790s. The wealthiest people preferred trade, manufacture and banking, and in some centres land-development. Thus the field of house-building or ownership or lending on mortgage was left open to those with more limited sums to invest. To them it was sufficiently attractive: house-ownership of artisan tenements yielded a respectable if unspectacular gross return between 8 and 10 per cent, and lending on mortgages usually a net yield of between 4 and 5 per cent.

These common features must not obscure the fact that building in each of the seven towns had a history peculiarly its own. Bath, the only town in which the physical structure still largely survives, is in many ways a special case. Between the later 1720s and the 1790s, building was linked predominantly to the demands of its well-to-do residents and visitors, for whom the substantial stone terraced houses cost between £400 or £500 and £1,500 or £2,000. The spacious layout of many developments, with their wide streets, squares and open spaces, the careful attention to building design to provide blocks of architecturally harmonious houses, all reflects the taste of the educated classes. The building undertakers were mainly craftsmen, and, more unusually, the majority of land-developers were drawn from the same people, as well as architects and surveyors. The general tradespeople also built, but they and some professional men and women were perhaps more important as suppliers of mortgage loans. Without them, the activity of the craftsmen builders would have been limited.

Despite its special features, at least in the last quarter of the eighteenth century, Bath conformed to some extent with the pattern of national fluctuations in house-building over time. As in the country as a whole, there were building slumps during the American War of Independence and the French Revolutionary War, and a boom at the end of the 1780s and beginning of the 1790s. Portsmouth, or more specifically its greater dockyard suburb of Portsea, was distinctive in that its house-building took place mainly in war, when demand for immigrant dockyard labour was at its height. Both the rate of growth and the absolute

245

increase in the number of houses reached a peak between 1806 and 1816, when the unprecendented demand for accommodation sparked off a boom in land-development that provided sites for builders for several decades in the slower expansion during the long period of ensuing peace. Throughout the period, the developing townscape was formed by the use of numerous open-field strips just wide enough for a narrow lane lined by a single row or building plots; the two-or three-storey houses, frequently occupied by more than one artisan household, usually fronted the street and had gardens in the rear. The strips were developed individually, no large sums being needed to purchase and prepare one for building. The houses were built by speculative crafts-men, strongly supported by tradesmen and dockyard workers, both as building undertakers and as mortgagees; the developers were frequently responsible for a few houses in their strips and sometimes came from the same occupational groups as the builders.

In the way its inhabitants earned their living, Hull was a smaller version of Liverpool, though in many respects its land-development and building investment pattern was very different. The town began to expand beyond the medieval walls in the 1770s with the opening of the first dock. Its new building land lay in separately-owned closes of several acres each: sometimes it was sold direct by the original landlord to the builders in small plots, sometimes developers were involved. Its developers were often merchants or shipowners. The builders of its terrace houses and court tenements were bricklayers and joiners, mari-ners, shipwrights, victuallers, brewers, tailors and many other categories of tradesmen and craftsmen.

In Liverpool, land-development tended to be dominated by the big merchants during the middle of the eighteenth century. By 1800 it was passing increasingly into the hands of local attorneys who supplied joiners—undertakers of most of the speculative building—with the necessary credit. Mortgages and early sales by the craftsmen builders helped to diversify the capital in new housing. Much of the land was owned by the Corporation, and following the normal practice of cor-porate bodies it was let on building lease. The single ownership offered the possibility for large-scale town planning, but the opportunity was only partly taken. The Corporation's committees approved the street plans of individual developers, and began to impose strict building covenants where housing was intended for the well-to-do from the 1780s, but there appears to have been no single scheme for consistent building over the Corporation's lands. The big Mosslake project did not begin to provide houses until after 1816. There were numerous substantial terraces erected for occupation by the wealthier townsmen from the 1780s, but most of the inhabitants lived in multi-occupied front houses or in tightly-packed courtyard tenements.

Land was particularly dear in Liverpool because the Mersey prevented expansion to the west, and builders were faced with the payment of a heavy initial fine. By contrast, Birmingham builders and owners benefited from the payment of ground rents which, if capitalized, would appear small in comparison with the Liverpool fines. Most of the land and basic amenities were supplied to builders without the aid of developers by the original landlords, several of whom held large blocks of land which they laid out on a gridiron pattern. With its numerous small manufacturers in the metal trades, wealth in Birmingham was more evenly spread than in the other major towns of the Midlands and the north, with the exception of Sheffield. This is reflected in the numerous buttonmakers and gunmakers and many other skilled artisans who participated in both building and supplying mortgage capital; from this too derives the fact that Birmingham's builders, with one or two small exceptions, did not provide terraces of the length and quality of Rodney Street or St. Anne Street, or squares on the scale of Great George or Abercrombie Squares, all in Liverpool. Its houses were more modest, two- or three-story front houses backed by courts containing tenements and workshops. Further, at least from the 1770s, rows of back-to-back dwellings parallel to the street provided further working-class accommodation. In many respects, in the passing of relatively cheap land direct from landlords to undertakers on building lease, in the types and detailed layout of its dwellings, and probably too in the occupational background of its builders, Birmingham was probably closely paralleled on a smaller scale by Sheffield, where industry was again based on innumerable metal manufacturers using their own workshops.[47]

As in Birmingham and Sheffield, no physical impediment hindered the expansion of Manchester and Salford. On the other hand, the practice of conveying land for an annual rent on long leases or in perpetuity, instead of on short building leases, raised the costs of builders and owners, and thus ultimately house rents. On account of the growth of the cotton industry, the town expanded at least three times between the 1770s and 1800: immigration was particularly marked in the 1770s and between about 1785 and 1792, encouraging two successive land booms. The second and by far the greater of these speculative bursts in land-development supplied sites not only for contemporary builders but for many

[47] Sheffield Archives: Arundel Castle MSS. S.382,383 etc,; information from Miss K. Youel.

projects in the first two or three decades of the nineteenth century. As in Birmingham, the big estates, particularly those of the Mosley, Aytoun and Lever families, have left their mark in the street patterns of much of the south and east side of the town developed in these years.

The peculiar character of Nottingham's building history has been emphasized by many scholars. The town was almost surrounded by fields with common rights which could not be extinguished, and builders used a shrinking number of small closes and back gardens within the old physical limits of the town, and a few small fields on the immediate edge of the built-up area. Because of this, land promotions, mostly by the original owners, were on a small scale, each involving the independent layout for building of parcels of land between about half an acre and 4 or 5 acres. The building owners comprised a mixture of craftsmen-builders, general trades people, and men in hosiery manufacture. Perhaps the most striking feature of its housing were the long rows of back-to-backs erected in large numbers from the 1780s, though as usual a varied range of larger terrace housing was also erected.

In many ways it is land-development that helps to give building expansion a special character in each town. The pattern of land-ownership, the presence or absence of developers and the various legal means of conveying building land all contribute to this end. Thus building in each of these towns deserves in due course to be the subject of a book. Yet even in the case of land-development, there are enough common features to make possible a general survey. For example, in all the centres the price of land rose as the town expanded in the later eighteenth century. In all of them, some landowners and developers began to try to impose some basic covenants on builders by the 1780s and 1790s. In all of them, the type of landowner had some discernible influence on the development of land. This general discussion has tried to define the common characteristics of urban building expansion, as well as trying to isolate some of the features peculiar to each town.

Part IV
The Course of Urban Building

10

1740-1800

The building activities which we have been considering in this book did not take place steadily over the years. They proceeded by fits and starts, and it is easy to see why. Investment in any sector of an economy has an inherent tendency to fluctuate, and in house-building more widely than most. The experience of the last century shows that the volume of this investment has tended to fluctuate according to a cycle about twenty years long.

The pattern of the building cycle in the later nineteenth and early twentieth centuries is reasonably well known.[1] The model is a comparatively simple one. There are years of depression in which the available supply of houses is ahead of demand. This produces many unoccupied dwellings, amounting at times to 5 or 10 per cent or more of the housing stock. It often brings prices down. To the extent that the housing market is glutted and prospects look poor, some builders go out of business or fail to take on new apprentices, and construction falls off. Towards the end of a depression, demand begins to recover, and vacancies diminish, but owing to little activity in the immediate past, builders do not recognize that times are changing and remain nervous of making new starts. The industry may also be unable to step up supply immediately because of the relative lack of recruitment in the preceding years. Recovery begins after demand increases further, uninhabited dwellings become occupied, prices become more buoyant as shortages develop, and construction thus becomes attractive to builders. The profitability of these ventures in a time of rising prices, and possibly also of rising rents, activates more and more builders, and the recovery becomes a boom. Supply then expands rapidly, demand is eventually surpassed,

[1] The following paragraphs are based on R. C. O. Matthews, *The Trade Cycle* (Cambridge, 1959), ch. vi; J. Parry Lewis, *Building Cycles and Britain's Growth* (1965); C. D. Long *Building Cycles and the Theory of Investment* (Princeton, 1940); C. E. V. Leser 'Building Activity and Housing Demand', in *Yorkshire Bulletin of Economic and Social Research*, III, no. 2; (1951), pp. 131–49, W. Isard, 'Transport Development and Building Cycles', in *Quarterly Journal of Economics*, LVII (1942).

and vacancies begin to reappear. But it is not until the number of empties becomes considerable—perhaps 5 or 10 per cent of the housing stock—that builders begin to see that the market is in danger of being glutted once more. Rents tend to stay firm because most landlords prefer a few empty houses rather than lowering rents. Gradually, building starts to tail off as confidence drops—the more so as some builders over-reached themselves in the height of the boom and are hit financially by the tighter conditions—and eventually the industry becomes completely depressed. Even so, some building usually goes on.

Such fluctuations occur in house-building on a regular pattern. Some explanation is needed for this regularity, particularly as it tends to occur on a longer time-base than the trade cycle, which commonly has a duration of eight to ten years. A partial answer may be that it reflects basic changes in society and the economy, which affect the *demand* for housing, or so it is suggested by the experience of the nineteenth and early twentieth centuries. Thus, following the evidence relating to Britain from the 1830s, Professor Parry Lewis has linked the level of building to the degree of population growth, which is particularly important in the number of new families which it creates: 'faster growth in population in the 1830s, the 1850s, and 1860s and 1870s, the 1890s and the inter-war period', he writes, 'was accompanied by higher levels of building activity and greater net increases in housing stock'.[2] For the United States in the same period, it has been argued that develop-ments in transport, by redistributing the population, directly affected the construction cycle. In the nineteenth century the agent was the rail-roads, after 1900 streetcars and electric railways, and in the 1920s automobiles. 'The last two innovations', it has been argued, 'exerted their influence on building through making possible suburban develop-ment and decentralization of population.'[3]

The trade cycle itself also affects the demand for housing. In years of prosperity greater employment and higher wages tend to encourage more marriages, and the creation of new households puts pressure on accommodation. Families in shared dwellings will have an incentive to seek houses of their own, and those already occupying whole houses may be encouraged to move into larger ones. Given the fact that economic expansion tends to be an urban phenomenon, it is the towns which suffer this pressure most acutely. Immigration from the countryside may be considerable.

[2] Parry Lewis, *Building Cycles*, pp. 164–5.
[3] A. Achinstein 'Economic Fluctuations' in S. E. Harris (ed.), *American Economic History* (New York, 1961), p. 174.

In order to explain fully why the building cycle does not follow the trade cycle more completely, one needs to look also at the nature of houses and at house-building as an investment. An important element in the situation is that houses are more durable than most forms of capital: machinery wears out and has to be replaced even if production is stagnant, but houses last for generations. In a depression, 'if the number of houses in existence is excessive in relation to the demand for house-room, the passage of time as such will do little to eliminate the surplus in the absence of a rise in demand'.[4] No replacement of obsolescent stock can stimulate recovery, and demand has to rise sufficiently to mop up existing empties before confidence begins to return. Again, a pronounced shortage may need several years of building to make good. This is 'because houses are so durable: an average year's building adds only a few per cent to the total number of houses in existence'.[5] It helps to lengthen the period of building recovery. The structure of the building industry also helps to lengthen the construction cycle. When recovery is possible, building may be delayed by a lack of labour, or simply by the existence of large numbers of small builders—a situation which, R. C. O. Matthews points out, does not make for well-informed reactions.[6] For the same reason, after some years of high activity builders become over-confident and react slowly to the rising number of empties at the end of a boom.

The level of building activity may also be affected by the availability of capital or the rate of interest. Easy credit may help a building recovery; its absence will tend to delay it. Plentiful credit may help to extend a boom despite the rising number of empties; a sudden financial crisis will hasten its end. Building may also suffer occasional shocks from outside the system, such as war or bad harvests.

Several attempts have been made to explain the building fluctuations of the eighteenth and early nineteenth centuries. H. A. Shannon did so in financial terms, suggesting that brick output between 1785 and 1850 moved up and down in sympathy with changes in the rate of interest, because many builders work on credit.[7] This view was developed by Ashton for the eighteenth century. A rise of a half or 1 per cent in the price of loans is important in industries 'concerned with building and means of communication (where a long time must elapse between the beginning of an enterprise and the return of profits) . . . A rise in the rate of interest might not merely check new enterprise but bring projects

[4] Matthews, *Trade Cycle*, p. 101.
[5] *Ibid.*, p. 101.
[6] *Ibid.*, pp. 102–3.
[7] Shannon, 'Bricks', p. 197.

already begun to a halt'. Further, when the rise reached a critical point more borrowing might be impossible. This was because the Usury Laws prohibited private borrowing or lending at more than 5 per cent. People were unable to compete for loans by offering higher rates. Potential lenders he thought, unable to obtain higher interest, might prefer to invest in government stock if the yield was sufficiently attractive. He believed this happened in some war years. He also implies that the financial panics of the eighteenth century were important in cutting off credit and bankrupting builders.[8] Although we have seen that small changes in rates below 5 per cent did not happen often on provincial mortgages after about 1780, and may not have been crucial when they occurred,[9] Ashton's argument about the effect of the Usury Laws and the financial crises must be considered carefully in their effect on building.

Our understanding of building fluctuations in this period has recently been extended by Parry Lewis. In an important book, *Building Cycles and Britain's Growth*, he suggests that the building cycle of some seventeen to nineteen years operated in this period, and argues that this stemmed partly from alterations in demand based on demographic changes. His belief is that several years of high marriage and birth rates (the result perhaps of a rise in real wages created by good harvests and high employment) tended to produce an echoing demand for housing some fifteen to eighteen years later, as the younger generation grew up This produced several family bread-winners whose earnings might require or make possible a move into larger accommodation. A few years later, their marriage created a further potential demand for new housing. These pressures became effective if they coincided with prosperous employment conditions.

Before this happened, the demand for living room was likely to have been low. This is because couples married in the previous peak period had to spend almost all they had on food for themselves and their children, who were not old enough to add to the family budget: 'when the bulge-children are perhaps about seven or eight', Parry Lewis writes, 'the ratio of food-requirements to earning power is probably greatest, and the ability to translate demands for housing into actual building most likely to be frustrated.' He believes this pattern is traceable fairly certainly from the 1760s, and possibly from the 1720s. Particularly when upswings in marriages and births were accompanied by general prosperity, itself the reflex very often of good harvests and cheap credit, the demand for houses would have been increased by the migration of

[8] T. S. Ashton, *Economic Fluctuations in England 1700–1800* (Oxford, 1959), chs. 4 and 5.
[9] See above, pp. 162, 227, 240.

young marriageable or married adults to the towns, as also by the desire of both the wealthy and lower classes to move into better accommodation.

Supply, he suggests, also fluctuated because building was largely a speculative activity. After a housing depression, confidence returned only slowly, but 'as each house is built and occupied, so the attractions of solid investment become apparent', and 'in the large towns a vast number of people . . . become responsible for launching a flood of projects'. Credit was 'widely demanded and easily obtained' as a result of the general optimism, and this encouraged large-scale building to continue beyond the point at which demand had been satisfied. When the boom finally broke, widespread financial difficulties, caused not so much by the excessive number of unrewarding empties as by building debts, discouraged any revival for several years.

He also emphasizes that bad harvests and war also had a depressing effect on building. Dear foodstuffs reduced the purchasing power of the lower classes and consequently delayed marriages, and both in turn reduced the demand for housing. War made the supply of houses tighter because it involved 'the removal of men, a shortage of various provisions including timber, high Government borrowing and an export of specie to pay out troops abroad'. He also emphasized that financial factors needed to be favourable to help satisfy the demand for housing: 'some activities require more credit than others, and probably none requires so much as building, in which the long period of production compels the builder to pay his wage-bill before he himself gets paid, while when the building is finished a great deal of capital is tied up irretrievably'. He followed Ashton in believing that the Usury Laws sometimes terminated supplies of credit.[10]

Lewis's demographic thesis has not gone uncriticized. According to Sir Alec Cairncross in a review of the book, 'he develops [the] . . . theory of an echo effect in the births of successive generations (without carrying conviction this had much influence on the housing cycle) . . . household formation is analysed too much in terms of marriages and too little in terms of the secular tendency for different generations to live apart instead of under the same roof'.[11]

It is the aim of this and the next chapter to augment Ashton's and Lewis's general study of fluctuations in the national level of house building by studying the course of building in the leading provincial towns

[10] Parry Lewis, *Building Cycles*, chs. 2 and 3, and pp. 174, 186–94.
[11] A. K. Cairncross, Review of Parry Lewis's *Building Cycles*, in *The Economic Journal*, LXXVII (1967), p. 363.

between about 1740 and 1820. One must remember that much building took place in the countryside between the 1740s and 1820, for which at present no evidence is available. A full breakdown of national activity into its regional and urban/rural components is not possible. These two chapters try to show the extent to which the timing of the fluctuations coincided or varied from town to town. How do local urban building levels compare with national trends? How may the local building patterns be explained?

Although Lewis's echo argument is dubious, attention is given to the possible link between local fluctuations in the number of marriages and births and the volume of building. Many newly-wedded couples among the artisan and labouring classes may not have set up a household immediately, but the pressure to do so once children began to be born was great.[12] A bulge in marriages and births together may have been important in affecting housing demand. A growth in marriages may also indicate local trade prosperity, which usually brought migrants into the town. In the general absence of population estimates a sharp rise in weddings and baptisms which was sustained probably indicates population growth.

I THE COURSE OF BUILDING, 1740–1760

The pattern of changes in the level of building and construction in England in the eighteenth century has already been studied by Ashton and Parry Lewis on the basis of the imports or output of certain building materials.[13] Before the 1780s, the most important are the annual official values of imported deals and firs: in Ashton's words, 'the first have relevance to building, and the second to both building and construction. For the early decades they are almost the only guide.'[14] In normal times the level of building activity pushed up imports, and they declined if building was depressed; occasionally in wartime the high cost or interruption of supplies from the Baltic might help to cause the depression. There are also figures for the output of 'stained' paper, that is, wallpaper, but this was a luxury for the wealthy and needed frequent replacement. Hence the volume produced has only a slight link with total new building.

Because of the link between capital and building, it has been argued that the yield on government stock (of which the yield on Consols was taken as an example) could be used as a possible indicator of national

[12] This pattern has been revealed in a case study of family structure in mid-nineteenth century Preston: M. Anderson, *Family Structure in Nineteenth Century Lancashire*, (Cambridge, 1971), pp. 48–53.
[13] Ashton, *Economic Fluctuations*, ch. 4; Parry Lewis, *Building Cycles*, ch. 2.
[14] Ashton, *Economic Fluctuations*, p. 90.

building activity.[15] A low yield revealed the existence in general of cheap money conditions, a high yield reflected a high rate of interest. It also may have meant, Ashton and Lewis argued, a drying up of the availability of funds for private borrowers. This was because the Usury Laws, as we have seen, are supposed to have prevented private borrowing at more than 5 per cent. When government borrowing was heavy, there was nothing to prevent the yield on Consols rising to a point when its return was more attractive than private loans at 5 per cent: consequently they thought that investors preferred the Funds and the private sector, including house construction, was unable to get the money it needed.

This argument depends on the assumption that there was a national capital market: in Ashton's words, 'it is reasonable to assume that, since the provinces were closely linked by trade with London, rates would move up and down freely with those at the centre.'[16] In fact although there were financial connexions between London and the provinces, they were not close enough to bring about much correspondence in interest rates, at least before the 1770s and 1780s. A recent study of turnpike trust finances has revealed that the rates paid by provincial trustees showed little response to changes in the London market, at least before the American War of Independence. Thereafter the link was closer.[17] As we have seen, the habit of investment in the Funds by provincial townsmen was not very common in the middle of the eighteenth century; it probably grew between the 1760s and the 1780s, especially in the American War, though the extent is uncertain until the French Wars after 1793.[18] For much of our period the yield on funds may be an indicator of the price (and, at times, of the availability) of credit to London builders, but not necessarily to those in the provincial towns which are the main subject of this study.

Using the deal and fir timber imports, Parry Lewis traced an alternating pattern of peaks and troughs in building in the eighteenth century, which strongly indicated recurring building cycles ⟨*see* table 6⟩. Nevertheless, it should be remembered that timber imports are not a sure indicator of the level of house-building alone: public buildings, ships, docks and harbours were also consumers of timber. Parry Lewis believed, without having conclusive evidence of it, that 'probably housing moved in much the same way as the timber index', both because of

[15] Parry Lewis, *Building Cycles*, p. 13.
[16] Ashton, *Economic Fluctuations*, p. 88.
[17] W. Albert, *The Turnpike Road System in England 1663–1840* (Cambridge, 1972), pp. 128–30.
[18] See above, pp. 159.

TABLE 6. *Peaks and troughs in building in the eighteenth century*

Trough	Peak	Trough	Duration (years) between Peaks	Troughs
c. 1698	1705?	1711?		
c. 1711	1724	[1729][19]	19	[18]
[1729][19]	1736	1744	12	[15]
1744	1753	1762	17	18
1762	1776	1781	23	19
1781	1792	1798	16	17

the qualitative evidence for the chronology of building presented by Ashton and because house-building tends to move in cycles of roughly the length revealed by the timber index.[20]

The combined imports of deals and fir timber, and of deals alone, suggests that building was at a higher level for part of the 1720s than it was to be again until the 1760s. It was lower in the 1740s not only than it had been in the 1720s, but also compared with the level in the 1730s. The volume of construction rose from about 1749–50, but for the 1750s as a whole it was still less than that of the early 1720s. Throughout the period 1700–1760, the level fluctuates about a roughly horizontal trend.[21]

In the 1740s and 1750s, the pattern made by the course of building differed in London and two or three of the largest provincial towns. Between the 1730s and the early 1760s, construction in London never reached the high level which it had attained in the 1720s. In fact the pattern of building in the capital reflected, and because of its size did much to create, the changing levels of construction for England as a whole. According to Sir John Summerson, 'the war period of 1743–8 seems to have witnessed building activity at its lowest ebb' in London. There were signs of revival in the 1750s, at least in the West End. The

[19] In Lewis's book the figure is '1727?'. In his words: 'the year 1727 is queried because the imports in 1729 were but barely higher than those in 1727. If the discrepancy is due to statistical error, then 1729 must be classed as the trough.' (*Building Cycles*, p. 14) Lewis relied on Ashton's approximate figures of deal and fir timber imports (Ashton, *Fluctuations*, p. 188) which contain several discrepancies from the detailed figures of Mrs. Schumpeter (see note 21 below) on which they were presumably based, and in fact the latter show that imports were lower in 1729 than in 1727 (*see* Fig. 1).

[20] Lewis, *Building Cycles*, pp. 14, 187.

[21] See Fig. 3: this is based on the annual official values of (a) ordinary deals and (b) ordinary deals and fir timber imported into England and Wales. The figures are from E. B. Schumpeter, *English Overseas Trade Statistics 1687–1808* (1960), Table XV. Ashton combined the deal and fir timber figures because he was studying building and construction: I have also presented the deal figures alone before 1760 to show that, although they may be a purer indicator of building alone, no major difference in the pattern is apparent.

contrast in trend during and after the 1720s reflected demographic and commercial influences. Population grew until the 1720s, and then stagnated or declined. Foreign trade passing through London may have followed a roughly similar course, the decline or stagnation in the 1740s being partly caused by the war.[22] Because of the relative absence of demand, London builders only intermittently took advantage of the low interest rates existing in the capital between the early 1730s and the Seven Years' War.

If building was restricted in London in the later 1740s, it was active in two of the largest provincial towns, Birmingham and Liverpool. In Birmingham, builders had been active in the mid-1720s and again in the later 1730s. There was a sharp fall in construction in the beginning of the 1740s, possibly associated with low marriages in 1740–41, and high mortality in 1741–2. But the interruption was brief. Building revived about 1743, and reached its height about 1746–50. Two landlords, Colmore and Jennens, put sites on the market for the first time, and in large quantities; activity also continued in the properties being promoted before 1746, such as that of the Weaman family. Marriages reached a record number in 1742–3 and remained high throughout the decade ⟨*see* figure 2⟩. Baptisms rose almost continuously between 1742 and 1751. Almost certainly population grew greatly. Domestic demand for industrial goods is likely to have risen with the exceptionally low corn prices of 1742–4, and these did not rise very much during the rest of the decade. More certainly, wartime needs increased the prosperity of the Birmingham gunmakers.

Building in the town was back to a low level between 1750 and 1753, and dropped further until 1758. Marriages declined sharply in 1752 and 1753, (to be followed by a fall in baptisms between 1754 and 1758) perhaps reflecting a depression consequent on a fall of gunmakers' orders in peacetime. But building on an unprecedented scale in the later 1740s may have caused an excess of supply over demand in the housing market. A record low level of interest on local mortgages (4 per cent) did not tempt builders at all.[23] There was a brief, sharp

[22] Summerson, *Georgian London*, pp. 98–112; M. D. George, *London Life in the Eighteenth Century* (1966 edn), pp. 38, 320–21; Swann, 'London Estates', pp. 43–5, 99. On building in the 1750s, F. H. W. Sheppard, *Local Government in St Marylebone, 1688–1835* (1958), p. 81, and maps of London show extensive development on the north side of Oxford St. in this decade: J. Rocque, *Plan of the Cities of London and Westminster* (1746), *A New Map of the Cities of London and Westminster* (1749) and *Plan of London* (1761).

[23] These paragraphs on the level of building and the rate of interest on mortgages in Birmingham are based on the outstanding number of surviving deeds: B.R.L. Chubb, ff. 318–51, Colmore MSS., T.C. 924, 993–5, 1908, 2395–8, 4748–9, 6222–5, 6248–54, Lee, Crowder 11A, 148, 344a, 1159, MSS. 329287, 329437, 372083, 372120, 372230, 372553–4, 409149, 452134, 491101, 575327–35; B.R. Mornington Crescent deed room O.B.R. 825, 832, 840.

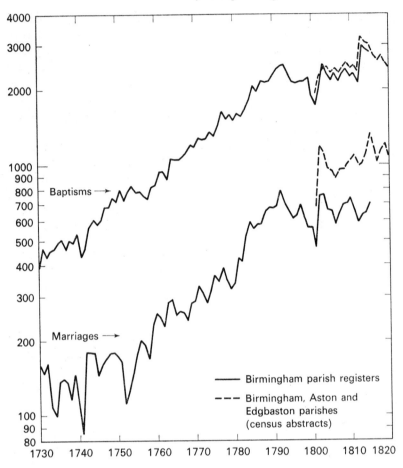

FIG. 2. *Birmingham marriages and baptisms, 1730–1820.*

recovery in 1759–61, which led *Aris's Gazette* to declare in 1759 that 'there are now more new buildings carrying on in this town than have been for many years past and more contracted for, that only want for hands to execute, which at this time are very much wanted'.[24] Marriages were low in 1758, but rose sharply in 1759–61 at the same time as building. Further, the whole of the years 1753–61 showed a rising trend in the

[24] Dent, *Old and New Birmingham*, p. 121; for evidence of building 1759–61, B.R.L. Colmore MSS., Lee, Crowder 344g, S.H.B. 59, MSS. 372203, 372538.

number of marriages. Again, wartime gunmaking as well as the general domestic prosperity may have provided the basis for the recovery.

In Liverpool, builders were also very active in the later 1740s, and again there was a sudden slackening of demand in the beginning of the 1750s. After a relative lull in construction in the early 1740s, building was on an unprecedented scale. On the great Corporation Estate, important developments included the neighbourhood of Cleveland Square; both Williamson and Clayton Squares were begun in these years. Smaller landowners such as the Earl of Derby and Plumbe were busy disposing of plots.[25] Building seems to have been a response to demographic growth and outstanding commercial prosperity. Marriage reached 200 a year for the first time in 1745 and 300 in 1749, the average for the five years 1745–9 being 256 compared with 177 between 1740 and 1744. Baptisms rose continuously between 1741 and 1750 ⟨*see* figure 3⟩. As in Birmingham the population probably grew rapidly. On account of the comparative security of the route through the Irish Sea, Liverpool benefited in particular from the War of the Austrian Succession: it was said in 1753 that war had led to such prosperity that if it had lasted 'seven years longer it would have enlarged the size and riches of the town to a prodigious degree'.[26]

The early 1750s may have brought a pause for several years in the rapid growth of the prosperity of Liverpool, as trade returned to London and other ports on the resumption of peace. However, except in 1751 and 1754, marriages did not fall much below the high level of 1748–50. Thus it is likely that the fall in rents and house prices by the end of 1752 reflected a glutted market which was the consequence not so much of a sudden fall from the previous level of demand but of over-construction at the end of the 1740s. Two houses mortgaged in June 1750 for £200 were assigned outright to the mortgagee in November 1752, when they were valued at only £141, 'the rents of houses in Liverpool . . . being then much fallen in value'.[27]

The evidence is insufficient to trace the course of building in Manchester, Nottingham and Hull in these years. Construction in Bath and Portsea reflected special circumstances. At Bath there was a boom in the mid-1750s in the building of substantial houses for the well-to-do

---

[25] P.R.O. PL.6/80, 82; B.R. Manchester deed room: L. and Y. 2905 etc.; Liverpool R.O. Council minutes X and deeds 431C, 502A, 554C, 555A, 762C, 879B, 907E etc.: Picton, *Architectural History*, pp. 28–9.
[26] *V.C.H. Lancs.*, IV (1911), p. 30.
[27] Liverpool R.O. deeds 431 C.

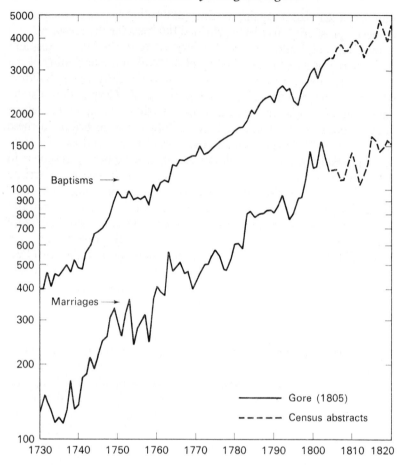

FIG. 3. *Liverpool marriages and baptisms, 1730–1820.*

visitors and leisured residents.[28] Naturally, building was heavy in both the dockyard towns of Portsmouth and Plymouth in the 1740s and the later 1750s, with a depression in the intervening years of peace.[29]

[28] Bath Guildhall: deeds re. King's Circus, 11 October 1771 (containing schedule of earlier leases), deeds re. Gay St. no. 2, Union Passage no. 20; Somerset R.O.: Bath deeds; information from Professor R. S. Neale.

[29] Portsmouth R.O. deeds re. Cumberland, King, North, Orange and Kent Sts. etc.; Treasury Solicitor's Deeds 2348–50/62 etc.; Plymouth Library: Manor of Stoke Damerel survey books 1–4.

The differences in the pattern of building among some of the major towns in the 1740s and 1750s are reasonably clear. In particular, in the later 1740s builders were active in Birmingham, Liverpool and the dockyard towns, while they were quiescent in London. In the early 1750s, construction revived in the capital while it was restricted in these provincial towns. In theory it might be possible to explain regional differences in the course of building in terms of the absence of a national capital market and a contrasting availability (or even price) of credit. In fact there is no evidence of this. For example, money was cheap both in London in the early 1750s (where building was reviving) and in Birmingham, where it was depressed. The contrasting pattern between London and several provincial towns is better explained in terms of varying demand. The differing effects of war and the resumption of peace on the economy of London on the one hand, and on that of several of the provincial towns on the other, was the basic influence.

2 PROLONGED EXPANSION, 1764–78

Building was at a low ebb in several major towns, such as Birmingham, Hull and Bath, in the final war years at the beginning of the 1760s. In Hull it was associated with commercial difficulties. In 1764 it was said that 'the great number of failures we had among our townsmen three or four years ago had greatly lowered the rents of houses and occasioned many to stand empty'.[30] Even in Birmingham, building declined for about two years after the sharp burst about 1759–61.

The timber figures suggest that construction in England in general was restricted in these years. In contrast, building at the national level was almost uninterrupted between about 1764 and 1778. ⟨*see* figure 4.⟩ This is indicated by the figures of deal and fir imports. They suggest that building rose sharply from 1763 to about 1766, then levelled off or declined slightly for several years. It climbed again during the early and mid-1770s, the peak being at about 1776. House-building was not the only sort of construction reflected in the timber figures, nor was it confined to the towns, for about half or more of the houses erected lay in the countryside. Yet qualitative evidence suggests that urban house-building followed roughly the same course as construction in general. About 1776–7, house-building reached a new height, not only in London but also in several industrial towns.

Building was not the only major type of investment to take place in

[30] Jackson, *Hull*, p. 200.

these years. This long phase of urban expansion overlapped, but did not quite coincide, with a major wave of transport development. Canal construction was at its height in the later 1760s, though it continued at a high level until the mid-1770s. Turnpike road improvements were important throughout the 1750s and 1760s, but fell off after 1772.[31] Investment in transport was thus declining before building reached its final peak.

In London occurred the second of the three great waves of building activity which characterized the construction of the Georgian capital.[32] Probably in the building depression of the early 1760s, a backlog in supply was created, because the London craftsmen-builders reacted immediately to the additional demand that came with the return of trading prosperity, being helped by easy money conditions. The next four or five years saw pressure on materials and labour natural in a sharp recovery: bricks often came to the site (in the words of a contemporary) 'before they are cold enough to be handled', and construction 'drained the country of all sorts of labourers and mechanics and raised wages'.[33] Building continued for all or most of the years until 1773 at a high level. The four or five years beginning about 1774 saw one of the biggest surges of building in London of the century. The basis of the prosperity which stimulated this expansion was not so much foreign trade, which fell off after 1775, but rather a wave of domestic commercial growth based on rising population and low food prices. It is possible that in 1776 and 1777 capital was diverted out of stagnating foreign trade into building. In view of the number of ambitious development projects in the West End, it is likely that by 1776 and 1777 supply was over-shooting demand, possibly based (as in the beginning of the 1790s) on ample credit for the craftsmen builders.[34]

In the provincial ports such as Liverpool, Bristol and Newcastle, there was considerable construction for most of these years. The level of building was highest at Liverpool. It was encouraged by large-scale migration into the town, the result of a rapidly-expanding commercial prosperity. Population increased by over one-third between 1760 and

[31] Albert, *Turnpike Road System*, p. 125.
[32] Summerson, *Georgian London*, p. 24.
[33] Ashton, *Fluctuations*, p. 98.
[34] *Ibid.*, p. 100; Summerson, *Georgian London*, pp. 164–6; Dorothy Stroud, *Henry Holland His Life and Architecture* (1966), pp. 43–5; Marylebone R.L. MS. D/Wh.

FIG. 4. *Building materials, marriages, baptisms, and the price of 3 per cent Consols, 1755–1820.*

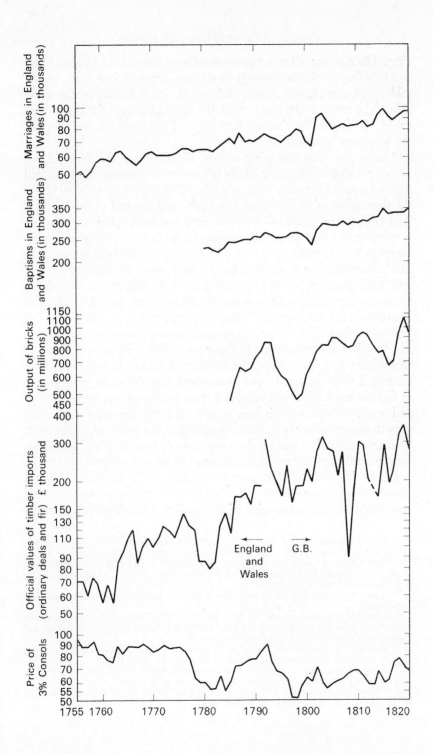

1773. The number of houses grew even faster, from about 4,200 to 6,340 and building continued strongly in the next three or four years. In the mid-1760s, the Plumbe family laid out St. Pauls Square in the north side of the town; in the early 1770s, the ill-fated scheme for a new town called Harrington in Toxteth Park beyond the southern boundary of the town was launched.[35]

Among the manufacturing towns, Birmingham and Nottingham alone provided evidence for all the fifteen years. Birmingham expanded without a pause between 1764, when building picked up suddenly after the depression of the previous two years, and the end of the 1770s.[36] The commercial crisis of 1772 hit the town hard, Matthew Boulton remarking that the trade of Birmingham is 'so dead . . . that the London waggons have to make up their loading with coals for want of merchandize'. Its effect was intensified by the high price of corn in the town, and marriages were low in 1772–3.[37] Yet the depression was too brief to affect the prevailing optimism among the builders, and the leasing of sites continued uninterrupted. Between 1774 and 1779, the disposal of plots was at its height. According to one exaggerated newspaper reference in 1776, it was 'further proof of our present flourishing situation . . . that within these two years, the number of houses in this town have encreased four thousand; and money and inhabitants in proportion', in fact the stock of houses increased from 6,025 to 8,042 between 1770 and 1778.[38] Even so, this was slower than the dramatic population growth of over 50 per cent, from about 31,000 in 1770 to 48,253 in 1778. The great surge in building does not seem to have strained the capital supply until 1777, for mortgages were available at 4, 4½ or 5 per cent.[39]

In Nottingham, builders were particularly active between 1763 and about 1768, all over the town.[40] There is some reason to think that this was based on the prosperity of the hosiery manufacturers: Strutt's

---

[35] For Bristol: Ison, *Bristol*, pp. 204–10; W. Barrett, *The History and Antiquities of the, City of Bristol* (Bristol, 1789), p. 98. For Newcastle: Newcastle R.O. S.C. 1884 and 3244 DD20/45; Common Council minutes 1743–65, 1766–85 (see particularly 1766, 1769 and 1776). For Liverpool: Enfield, *Liverpool*, pp. 24–5; see above, p. 110; Liverpool R.O. deeds; B.R. Manchester deed room: L. and Y.

[36] A record of about half the total number of building leases granted in these years has been traced.

[37] Ashton, *Fluctuations*, p. 157; D. E. C. Eversley, 'The Home Market and Economic Growth in England, 1750–80', in E. L. Jones and G. E. Mingay (eds.), *Land, Labour and Population in the Industrial Revolution* (1967), p. 243.

[38] *Williamson's Liverpool Advertiser*, 11 October 1776; Price, *Reversionary Payments*, p. 311; *An Historical and Descriptive Sketch of Birmingham* (1830), p. 71.

[39] B.R.L. MS. 372542, 410046; B.R. Manchester deed room: B.W.R. 24; *Aris's Birmingham Gazette*, 1777, *passim* (for advertisements concerning mortgages).

[40] Nottingham Archives TC2/85, 154, 178, 179, M.17540, 17553–5; Debenham and Co. B.329, 340, 378, C.243, 249, D.151, W.300, 320.

266

'Derby rib' patent (1759) started an era of experiment in knitting new meshes and garments on the stocking frame, and a 'large factory' was built in the town in 1763.[41] Marriages fell off sharply in 1766–8 ⟨*see* figure 5⟩, and building a year or two later. Construction continued at a relatively low level in the early 1770s, despite a recovery in marriages,

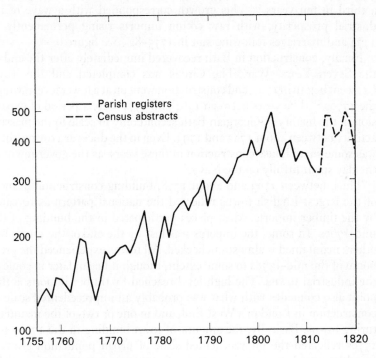

FIG. 5. *Nottingham marriages, 1755–1820.*

and did not reach a new peak until 1777–8, when new sites were again being bought in large numbers.[42] This is best seen as a building spurt following on from the local prosperity felt in the mid-1770s. Marriages were at a record level in 1776–7.

In Manchester, there was again a boom between about 1775 and

[41] S. D. Chapman, 'The Transition to the Factory System in the Midlands Cotton-Spinning Industry', *Econ. H.R.*, 2nd ser., XVIII (1965), p. 528.
[42] Nottingham Archives TC2/82, M.19177–80, 19395–438; Debenham and Co; M.395, J. 70, B.333, Box 18 etc.

1778. According to Henry, 'the town extended on every side, and such was the influx of inhabitants, that though a great number of houses were built, they were occupied even before they were finished'.[43] A visitor in June 1777 found that 'great additions of buildings and streets are daily making.'[44] The number of houses in Manchester township increased from 3,446 at the end of 1773 to 4,606 in 1782—an addition of nearly a third in ten years.[45] This growth corresponded with a wave of industrial prosperity, with raw cotton imports rising permanently in 1774 and marriages following suit in 1775–8. ⟨*See* figure 6.⟩

Finally, construction in Bath recovered immediately after the end of the Seven Years' War. The Circus was completed and the Royal Crescent begun in 1767, and construction went on at a lower level through the 1770s.[46] The years between 1764 and 1771 were a period of expansion in the history of Georgian Bath second only in scale to the massive activity between about 1785 and 1793. Even in the dockyard towns, there was some small house construction in these years, as the government of the day spent fitfully on the Navy.[47]

Thus, between 1763 and about 1778, building construction in most of the largest English towns reflected the national pattern as revealed by the timber imports. Most places participated in the building of the mid-1760s. In some, the impetus was lost by the end of the 1760s, but others maintained it almost unchecked. All towns experienced the great boom of the mid-1770s to some extent, though it began later in some of the industrial towns. The high level reached by timber imports at this point also coincides with what was probably an unprecedented scale of construction in London's West End, and in one or two of the manufacturing towns. Basically, the amount of town building in the 1760s and 1770s reflected the unprecedented scale of urban population growth. London's numbers were rising again after the apparent stagnation of the middle of the century: Birmingham, Liverpool and Manchester were

[43] Chaloner, 'Manchester', p. 41.
[44] Quoted in *Manchester Guardian*, 16 August 1904, from S. Curwen, *Journals and Letters* (New York, 1842).
[45] Price, *Reversionary Payments*, p. 314.
[46] Ison, *Bath*: 'Plan of the City of Bath shewing the principal buildings erected during 1700–1830, with the dates and architects . . .', p. 212; information from Professor R. S. Neale.
[47] Portsmouth R.O. deeds; Plymouth Library: St. Aubyn Estate survey books.

FIG. 6. *Raw cotton imports in Great Britain, and Manchester marriages, 1760–1820.*

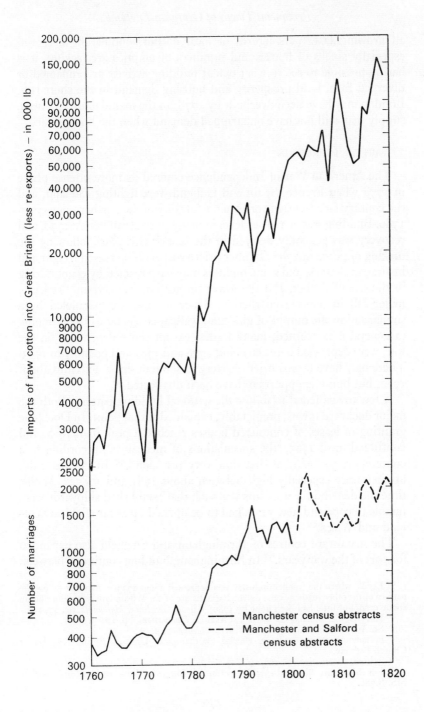

all growing fast.[48] As figures of local output, population size, and especially stocks of houses and numbers of empties are lacking, it is hardly possible to see to what extent building activity accompanied or diverged from local prosperity and housing demand in the short run. London may have been overbuilt by 1778: in the manufacturing towns, supply may still not have outstripped demand when the boom ended.

3 WARTIME DEPRESSION

The American War of Independence entered its more intense phase in 1778 when France, Spain and Holland were fighting England, and the country faced a league of armed neutrality of the northern powers in 1780. Building was at a lower level in many towns than before 1778, and recovery was generally delayed in the one or two years following the making of peace in 1783. Timber prices rose with increased freight and insurance charges, and some builders may have reacted by economizing in the use of timber. But the lower timber imports certainly reflect a major fall in house construction. Their decline was paralleled by a similar fall in the output of glass and wallpaper. As far as the economy in general is concerned, many trades, except those dependent on the war, were depressed between about 1778 and 1781 and possibly in 1783. There may have been a brief recovery in some business activities about 1782, but building appears to have been unaffected.[49]

A few towns failed to follow the national building pattern. Both the major dockyard towns, predictably, expanded at that point. In Dock, the granting of leases of completed houses reached a peak in 1779–81 and continued until 1785, 'the speculations of mechanics', according to a contemporary, 'being at that time very prevalent'.[50] In Portsea, sales of sites were especially high between about 1781 and 1785.[51] At this time the demand for warships was such that established shipyards were unable to cope and new yards had to be opened up as far afield as Scotland and Wales.[52]

The metalware centres of Birmingham and Sheffield also expanded for part of the war years.[53] In Birmingham, building continued between

---

[48] Leeds, where the woollen industry was depressed about 1773–7, may not follow the pattern of the other textile towns: on the Parks Estate of the Wilson family building began about 1768, but little had been done by 1780: Wilson, *Gentlemen Merchants*, pp. 47, 198.
[49] Parry Lewis, *Building Cycles*, p. 12; Ashton, *Fluctuations*, pp. 162–5.
[50] St. Aubyn Estate survey books; Worth, *Devonport*, p. 21.
[51] Portsmouth R.O.: deeds re. Hawke, Southampton, Unicorn, Spring Sts., Lower Church Path etc.
[52] Ashton, *Fluctuations*, p. 163.
[53] For Sheffield: Sheffield Archives: Capital Burgesses lease register and Norfolk MS. S.382.

1778 and 1781, but not so fast as in the mid-1770s: 340 dwellings were erected in these years, according to Hutton's figures.[54] But the leasing of sites rose all over the town in 1781 and may have been at a record level in 1782.[55] The stimulation of the wartime demand for small arms presumably boosted local trade, thus encouraging the continuation of building.

But the expansion in these towns was exceptional. Construction was restricted in both the textile towns of Manchester and Nottingham until after the war.[56] Building also declined in Liverpool and possibly in Newcastle.[57] At Bath, except for a block of five houses, no buildings of architectural importance were erected in these years.[58] In London, building fell sharply in the West End by 1779, and for the next three years comprised only a quarter that of the previous four years; it continued at a low ebb immediately after the War.[59]

There were several reasons for the building depression in the towns. There was a financial crisis at the end of 1777 and during 1778, marked by a rise in the number of bankruptcies and 'an uncommon great and general scarcity of money'. It was caused as much by overtrading in the previous years as by the declaration of war early in 1778.[60] Rising yields on government securities were also causing problems for those needing money by 1779, when Pulteney wrote:

> 'Our manufacturers, our traders, our farmers and even our landed gentlemen know to what a degree this expectation of Government premiums has affected them. Money cannot now be borrowed on mortgages, on the former terms. The price of land has fallen, the quantity of circulating cash in the hands of our merchants, manufacturers, builders, improvers, is remarkably diminished.'[61]

These difficulties were probably important in bringing to an end the construction boom in London, where builders were mainly craftsmen working on credit. At least some of the provincial towns were affected by

---

[54] *Historical and Descriptive Sketch*, p. 71.

[55] B.R.L. Gooch and Colmore deeds, etc.

[56] For Manchester, see the comment of Henry below, and deed evidence; the numerous surviving deeds for the 1770s and 1780s for Nottingham suggest that there was little building in these years.

[57] For Newcastle there is only one reference to a building lease in the Common Council minutes between 1780 and 1784: Newcastle R.O.: Common Council minutes 1766–85.

[59] Ison, *Bath*, p. 161, for Somersetshire Buildings (1782): no other major building scheme has been traced.

[59] Swann, 'London Estates', pp. 81–3.

[60] Ashton, *Fluctuations*, pp. 108–10, 130, 162.

[61] Quoted by D. M. Joslin 'London Bankers in Wartime 1739–84', in *Studies in the Industrial Revolution*, ed. Pressnell, p. 175.

the crisis of 1777–8. Bankruptcies were high in Birmingham in 1777, in Liverpool in 1778 and Manchester in 1779.[62] Yet with many building owners in the manufacturing centres relying on their own funds, their importance is uncertain. Again, one cannot say certainly how important at this stage was the purchase of government stock on local capital markets. It is possible, as Pulteney seems to imply, that the effect was becoming more widespread than earlier in the century.

Financial factors remained important in curtailing building in London during the early 1780s. High government borrowing led to a shortage of capital until 1785. According to one of the principal developers on the Bedford Estate in Bloomsbury in February 1784 'the great scarcity of money, occasioned by the unhappy American War, so severely affected many of the persons concerned under us [that is, the builders], that some were compelled to stop, and we found ourselves under the unfortunate necessity of taking back the ground, and completing the houses thereon . . . .'[63] This situation continued through 1784: 'every one must remember how impossible it was for individuals to borrow money on any security for any premium towards the end of 1784', wrote George Chalmers.[64] Whether capital was short for building elsewhere is uncertain. There was certainly an upward pressure on provincial interest rates by the beginning of the 1780s. Turnpike trusts raised their rates in the early 1780s if they had not done so earlier.[65] Liverpool Corporation advanced the interest it paid on certain loans to 4½ per cent in August 1778 and 5 per cent two years later; it paid 5 per cent for some

---

[62] W. Bailey *A List of Bankrupts*, 1772–93 (1794), from which the following figures were derived:

Date	No. of bankruptcies in:	Liverpool	Birmingham	Manchester and Salford
1773		6	3	8
1774		7	5	2
1775		7	3	6
1776		9	3	5
1777		11	15	5
1778		18	8	6
1779		11	8	12
1780		4	9	7
1781		6	4	4
1782		4	6	10

[63] Olsen, *Town Planning*, pp. 47–8.
[64] Ashton, *Fluctuations*, pp. 100–01.
[65] Albert, *Turnpike Road System*, p. 129.

new money in 1782.[66] Provincial urban rates for new mortgages seem to have been invariably 5 per cent by the beginning of the 1780s. Whether some provincial builders were unable to borrow at all or had to pay premiums in addition to 5 per cent interest to secure loans is unknown.

A comment on Manchester suggested that the high cost of materials was a deterrent to builders. According to Henry,

> 'several causes have contributed to restrain the spirit of building. During the war, the high price of timber was a considerable obstacle; and since the peace, the frosts, which were, for two years together, very intense, and continued until the spring was far advanced, have prevented the making of bricks, and together with the tax, greatly enhanced their price.'[67]

Yet possible supply difficulties were unable to prevent a boom where housing demand was outstanding, in the dockyard towns.

As far as most of the provincial towns are concerned, the early part of the building depression may also be seen in terms of a slump in demand. According to one contemporary, there was a fall in the demand for lodgings at Bath, which may account for the restricted building: 'from the year 1778 to the year 1783 by reason of our dispute with America, our army and navy being then on service, the seasons at Bath were so little frequented that houses in Bath were greatly reduced in value.'[68] At Liverpool, trade was hit at least during the first two or three years of war. One local observer noted in 1810 that 'during the war, the improvements of the town of Liverpool were mostly suspended, commerce languished, and except for the occasional bustle of numerous sales by auction of the cargoes of prizes taken from the enemy, there was very little business transacted in the port'.[69] In the case of the textile towns Ashton noticed signs of depression between 1778 and 1780, and possibly in 1781. 'In June 1779', he said, 'riots broke out at Nottingham as a result of a refusal of Parliament to regulate wages and framerents. In Lancashire, disorders, which included the burning of Arkwright's factory in October, were attributed to unemployment resulting from the loss of the Irish market. In the following year anti-machinery riots occurred at Leeds . . . .'[70] Even so, in the case of the cotton industry

[66] Liverpool R.O.: Common Council minutes, Vol. XII, 1776–90, 5 Aug. 78, 2 Aug. 80, 2 Jan. 82, 3 Apl. 82.
[67] Chaloner, 'Manchester', p. 42.
[68] P.R.O. E134/34 G.3 Mich. 14.
[69] [J. Corry?], *The History of Liverpool* (Liverpool, 1810), pp. 161, 168.
[70] Ashton, *Fluctuations*, p. 163.

import figures of raw cotton suggest a halt to further growth rather than a real recession. Supply factors may have delayed the building recovery fairly generally in the early 1780s. In the case of Manchester, marriages rose strongly throughout 1782–4, corresponding with a jump in imports of raw cotton. They suggest a resumption of business prosperity. The high cost of materials, lack of confidence among builders and a shortage of available labour after several years' depression may all have contributed to restrain builders for two or three years. At least in London, continued capital shortage was important. In the mid-1780s, speaking of Manchester, Henry wrote of 'the want of houses to accommodate' the poorer classes, as a result of the restrictions on building.[71] A shortage of housing may have become fairly general in urban England by the time building recovered in the mid-1780s.

4 RECOVERY AND BOOM

The recovery of building which began in the mid-1780s led to the biggest boom of the century. It was one in which all towns participated, with the exception of those whose economies were directly dependent on war. The great expansion in industrial output, and of the internal and overseas trade which accompanied it, led to massive migration to industrial towns and major ports, creating an unprecedented demand for housing. The prosperity of the landed and commercial classes increased the popularity of the pleasure towns, particularly Bath, and also of a host of tiny seaside towns. In the final stages of high activity, particularly after 1790, vast credit expansion encouraged builders in some towns to undertake ever more grandiose building projects. Nor was building the only major form of investment in these years. A peak in building in the early 1790s coincided with a boom in transport development, in the shape of canals. Industrial investment also rose to new heights.

In these years the tax on bricks gives us another and more important indicator of national building activity, the volume of brick output. Brick-making rose steeply to 1787, paused briefly during 1788 and 1789, before rising to a peak in 1792 and 1793.[72] ⟨*See* figure 4.⟩ The pattern of the timber import figures corresponds, though in the later 1780s the rising trend is more gradual. Whether the peak in 1792 is much sharper than in the figures of brick output is not clear, because at this precise point the timber figures relate to Great Britain, and no

[71] Chaloner, 'Manchester', p. 42.
[72] The brick figures are given in Shannon, 'Bricks', p. 200.

longer to England and Wales.[73] Except for a slight recession about 1789 (which both sets of figures reflect), the two suggest a rising trend reaching a peak about 1792. It still needs to be remembered that urban housing took less than half of all the bricks produced. They were also used in rural housing, factories and canal construction. In particular canal building was also booming in the beginning of the 1790s.

All the industrial towns, whether their manufacture was affected directly by fundamental technological change or not, saw a great housing expansion based on local prosperity. In Birmingham, although population rose sharply from 1781–2, it is probable that, unlike in Manchester the period of recovery was not marked by housing shortage, since production had kept up well during the later war years. But the number of sites leased rose strongly in 1785 and stayed high into the early 1790s. Building reached its peak between 1790 and 1792. This long burst of building resulted in an increase in the housing stock between 1781 and 1791 from 8,382 to 12,681 or 51 per cent, compared with a population growth of about 46 per cent.[74] Here the building undertakers more than kept up with a remarkable expansion of population. Hutton was told by another Birmingham man in November 1790 that 'the town was over built . . . and there were a vast number of empty houses', a view with which he does not appear to have disagreed.[75] In this period the town greatly extended itself south-eastwards as far as, and beyond, the River Rea; nearly all the remaining land on the main block of the Colmore Estate on the north-west of the town was covered with houses, and two outlying estates of the Rector at Islington and Brooke at Ashted were created.[76] Building also continued strongly in the other principal hardware-producing centre, Sheffield.[77]

Among the textile towns Nottingham had recovered from its building depression by the mid-1780s. It was in these and the following years that several of the remaining small orchards and other closes on the east of the town between the built-up areas and the open field provided the sites for the long rows of back-to-backs which now became typical in Nottingham. House-building probably reached its height at the beginning of the 1790s. Prosperity lasted to 1792, two new spinning mills being opened in that year.[78] Manchester underwent one of the most outstanding

[73] The official values of fir and deal imports are stated in Schumpeter, *Overseas Trade Statistics*, Table XVII.
[74] *An Historical and Descriptive Sketch*, p. 30.
[75] Langford, *Birmingham Life*, I, p. 456.
[76] B.R.L. deeds, and see above, pp. 87–8.
[77] Sheffield Archives: Norfolk MS. S.383, 384 and Capital Burgesses Register; information from Miss K. Youel.
[78] See above, pp. 118, 202–4; Chapman, 'Factory System', p. 537.

periods of building in its history, accompanying the great expansion of the cotton industry. Sites probably began to be conveyed on a large scale in 1784, conveyances rose further in 1788, and reached a peak in 1790–92. This closely follows the marriage figures, with the annual number of weddings jumping from 567 in 1782 to 682 in 1783 and 848 in 1784: by 1790 they were 1,122, in 1791 1,301, and in 1792, the peak year, 1657. A huge new area was now developed on the south and south-west of the town, prinicpally on the Mosley, Aytoun and Lever estates. By May 1789 it was being reported that 'the buildings have encreased so rapidly in Manchester within the last four years, that Ardwick-green, which was once a mile and a half from the town, now joins it.'[79] Even at the very end of the boom, it was said that, 'population appears to have increased more rapidly than buildings'. The result was that rents rose 'to a degree scarcely known in other places'.[80] Thus, the normal situation at the end of a boom, when supply catches up and runs ahead of demand, never appears to have been reached in these years of unprecedented activity in Manchester. The inflow of capital from London and the Home Counties (and the failure of supply to outpace demand) may indeed have reflected a shortage of local capital at the beginning of the 1790s, when the remarkable growth of industry took much of what there was.

Among the ports, Newcastle builders were busy from 1785.[81] At Hull, this was the period in which the first big expansion occurred beyond the line of the old town walls, especially into Sculcoates on the north and on the west of the new dock.[82] At Bristol, there took place the biggest speculative boom of the century: building began on a large scale about 1786 and reached a peak about 1791.[83] But the biggest expansion was in Liverpool, supported by the great growth in its trade between the end of the American War and the outbreak of the French Revolutionary War. The building recovery may have started earlier here than in the other ports. As early as 1783, several big land-developers were at work, suggesting considerable optimism about the course of building in the town.[84] Construction took place all over the town in the next ten years. When the King's Dock was opened in 1788, several streets were laid out on the north-east, and 'so great was the

---

[79] *Nottingham Journal*, 16 May 1789.

[80] Barfoot and Wilkes, *Directory*, III, p. 766, written 1792 or the beginning of 1793.

[81] Newcastle R.O.: MS. 30/1–24/53, S.C. 1884, Common Council minutes, 1766–85, 1785–99.

[82] Hull R.O.: deeds re. Dock, West, Mill, Middle, George, Albion Sts. etc.; GC deeds.

[83] Ison, *Bristol*, pp. 26, 214, 230.

[84] Liverpool R.O. Council minutes XII.

influx of strangers, that the new houses were occupied as soon as they were habitable'.[85] Other developments included the laying-out of Kent Square and neighbouring streets, and building along important thoroughfares such as Bold Street, St. James Street, Great George Street, and Mount Pleasant. In 1785 the area between Byrom Street and Soho Street was practically unbuilt on; by 1795 there were houses in more than twenty streets. Beyond the built-up area, Everton developed as a wealthy suburb.[86]

Bath likewise underwent its largest phase of building expansion of the century. The biggest project was the Bathwick project of the Pulteney family intended as a 'New Town'.[87] Again, construction reached its height in the beginning of the 1790s. Finally in London construction in the West End did not reach anything like its pre-war level until about 1787. This may have been because financial conditions did not become easier until 1787. It may also have been a response to the possible existence of a large number of empties, or simply because craftsmen-builders were slow to regain confidence after the chilling experience of the depression. By 1788–91 construction was at as high a level as the mid-1770s, and Walpole could talk of 'the rage for building' as being 'impetuous', and go so far as to say that 'there will soon be one street from London to Brentford'.[88]

In some towns supply was overshooting demand by the beginning of the 1790s. This was the result of a great nationwide expansion of credit and the outflow of funds from London into the provinces. Mortgages were made for unprecedented sums, and attorneys and banks were conspicuously free with credit for builders in some towns.[89] Although trade, industry and agriculture remained buoyant throughout the country, thus maintaining demand at a high level, it was loanable funds which enabled builders to embark on more ambitious schemes, and it was these, rather than the pressure of demand, that pushed the output of bricks and imports of timber to a peak level about 1792. In Bristol, the growth of foreign trade had given a solid base for building expansion, and it was attracting large numbers of visitors and residents to its Clifton Spa on the outskirts of the town. Yet the expansion was in danger of getting out of hand, and there were references to the taking of ground for more than 3,000 houses in 1791. In Bath, 2,000 were planned. We have also

---

[85] [Corry], *Liverpool*, p. 176.
[86] C. Eyes, *A Plan of the Town and Township of Liverpool* (1785); R. Phillips, *Plan of the Town of Liverpool* (1795); Aikin, *Description*, p. 376.
[87] See above, p. 80.
[88] Swann, 'London Estates', pp. 82–3; Ashton, *Fluctuations*, p. 102.
[89] See above, pp. 238–9.

seen that Birmingham was also probably becoming overbuilt by the beginning of the 1790s. On the other hand, in Manchester, though the land which was acquired for building by the end of 1792 was still being used by undertakers twenty or thirty years later, supply was still hardly meeting demand. In south Lancashire, the unprecedented rate of expansion of the cotton industry may have created a demand that local builders were unable every to meet fully.[90]

By 1792, there were signs of pressure in two respects, those of labour and capital. Craftsmen were pressing for more wages, and in May 1792 the plasterers of Manchester advertised in the *Manchester Herald* that they were obliged to raise the price of their work on account of their journeymen frequently raising their wages.[91] There were signs, too, of financial strain by 1792. An external drain of bullion began in the later months of 1791, at a time when high employment and rising wages increased the demand for cash, credit having been over-extended for some months.[92] In Manchester, one of the biggest land-developers and house-builders, Joshua Reyner, who had had a banking account with a firm of London tea-dealers and had borrowed money on mortgage in various parts of the country, was bankrupt by the beginning of 1792, and in November another local builder. James Boardman, followed suit.[93] When war broke out on 1 February 1793, general financial panic ensued, heralding the end of the boom.

Apart from the speculative frenzy which had been fed by easy credit during the final phase, some of the substantial housing being put up gave the period a special character. In several towns small suburbs emerged as almost physically separate entities beyond the built-up area, and included much better-class housing for wealthy townsmen whose place of business remained in the centre of the town. This phenomenon reflects the growing wealth of the upper ranks of the urban community, as well as the pressure on space in the town centre for purely commercial uses. There were also small developments of substantial housing on the edge of the main built-up area. Even Birmingham had one crescent which was begun before the outbreak of war led to its abandonment, and in Leeds the Wilson Estate underwent considerable building for merchants and other well-to-do townsmen.[94] In the resorts of Bath and Bristol, the

[90] See above, p. 276; cf. also Aikin's comment on Stockport that 'the population has of late years been amazingly on the increase, so that before the war, houses could not be built fast enough for the demand', *Description*, p. 446.
[91] *Manchester Herald*, 19 May 1792; this also happened in Bristol: information from Dr. Ward, who drew my attention to this point about labour pressures.
[92] Ashton, *Fluctuations*, p. 168.
[93] Manchester Town Hall: deeds H.18 and Current bundles 8673.
[94] Hutton, *Birmingham*, p. 468; Leeds Archives deeds re. Wilson Estate.

crescents and squares had a splendour never to be matched again. Two factors probably explain this surge of house construction for the well-to-do townsmen at this particular time. On the one hand, the exceptional prosperity in trade and industry encouraged merchants and manufacturers to move into larger and more fashionable accommodation; while on the supply side ample credit encouraged speculative builders, particularly craftsmen builders, to launch into more expensive projects than they would normally have contemplated.

5 THE EFFECT OF THE FINANCIAL CRISIS OF 1793 AND THE DEPRESSION OF THE LATER 1790S

Evidence that the year 1793 was the end of the national building boom is given by the brick and timber figures. The output of bricks fell in the tax year running from July 1793 to July 1794 (though remaining at a relatively high level) and dropped very sharply the following year, falling continuously, to a trough in 1798–9. Timber imports in 1793 were well below the level of 1792, and fell successively in 1794 and 1795. Although recovering in 1796, they reached their lowest point in 1797. The course of the brick and timber figures is reflected in urban housing. In the mid-1790s house building declined faster in some major towns than in others, but it was depressed in almost all of them between 1795 and 1800. But while building activity fell in 1793–5 and remained depressed in the later 1790s, the course of trade and industrial activity was rather different.

Prosperity in general was interrupted by the 1793 financial crisis, of which the basic factor was the over-extension of credit during the previous boom years on account of the growth of the country banks and the creation of bank notes and finance bills. Contributory causes were the external drain in 1792, the fear of war by the end of the year, and the outbreak of war in February, which was followed by a run on the banks for coin, and a high rate of bankruptcies.[95] The effect of the war was to produce a sharp fall in exports in 1793, but foreign trade recovered in 1794 and, apart from the year 1797, which was marked by another financial crisis, remained generally buoyant.[96] Exceptionally high corn prices in 1795, 1799 and 1800 may have depressed domestic demand, but because of buoyant industrial output and trade, migration into most of the major towns continued in some of these years. The major

[95] Ashton, *Fluctuations*, p. 133.
[96] *Ibid.*, pp. 169–72, 183–4.

279

problem is thus to try to explain the contrast between the often prosperous business conditions and the course of building, which did uot
recover until after 1800.

In at least three of the industrial towns, the downturn was not immediate, despite the commercial depression of 1793. In Birmingham,
the outbreak of war caused a trade slump on account of the growing
dependence on the French market, particularly as a result of the Commercial Treaty of 1786. Europe probably took about a quarter of
Birmingham's output by 1790, France being a preferred market.
Exaggerated claims were being made in Birmingham in March 1793
that there were 10,000 out of work in the town as a result of the interruption of foreign trade.[97] Hutton wrote in 1795 that the war brought about
'the destruction of commerce, caused about 500 of our tradesmen to
fail, stagnated the currency, [and] thinned the inhabitants'.[98] From 1793,
population was falling, the decline continuing through the rest of the
1790s. In 1791 there were said to be 73,653 inhabitants in the town, and
there were probably more at the beginning of 1793; by 1801 the number
was 69,384.[99]

But there was a lag of about two years after the outbreak of war
before building stopped. According to Hutton in 1795, depression had
'left the town about twelve hundred empty houses, which has laid the
spirit of building'. Yet despite the bankruptcy of the leading developer
of the Ashted project, John Brooke, building in general continued in
1793–4. Leases of sites may have been as high in 1793 as they had been
the year before, and were still numerous in 1794. In January 1795, the
speculative mania was reported to be certainly continuing, with the
building societies active in the adjoining parish of Handsworth, despite
the fact that 'there is now supposed to be a thousand houses untenanted
in the parish of Birmingham'.[100] This was two years after the outbreak
of war. In fact, the leasing of sites in 1795 was only tiny compared with
previous years, but the level of activity in 1793–4 suggests how slowly
building speculation ebbed, despite the probability that the new houses
were merely adding to the stock of empties.

In Nottingham the conveyance of building sites appears to have continued unchecked in 1793–4.[101] In Sheffield, where there was a business
depression in 1793, the leasing of completed houses on the Norfolk

---

[97] *V.C.H. Warks*, VII, pp. 116–17, 282.
[98] Hutton, *Birmingham*, p. 469.
[99] *An Historical and Descriptive Sketch*, p. 30; the trend of marriages, baptisms and
burials was downward for the whole period 1793–1800.
[100] Langford, *Birmingham Life*, II, p. 6.
[101] For example, Nottingham Archives TC.2/52, 53, 59, 103, 104, 111, 126, 127, 155.

Estate, one of the main sources of building land, was at its pre-war level in 1793, 1794 and 1796; only in the following years were the numbers much smaller.[102] The ratio of persons per house in 1788 and 1796 suggests that there were a large number of empties by 1796, since even at a rate of one family per house (which was characteristic of Sheffield) the 1796 ratio was very low:

Year	No. of houses	No. of persons	Ratio of persons per house[103]
1788	6,161	25,141	1 :4 :1
1796	7,657	29,013	1 :3·8

In Manchester demand for housing may have been hit by the unemployment consequent upon the contraction of European trade on the outbreak of war, and supply was hindered in the first half of 1793 by a shortage of cash for builders following the financial crisis. In May 1793, there were said to be about 7,000 'destitute of employment' in the town, and it was noted that 'the present very great scarcity of money, etc. . . . (has) . . . hindered many house builders, and others, from carrying on their several intended works, which otherwise might have been done to advantage, during this temporary stop of the course of business' etc.[104] In fact at least some building continued through 1793. But activity died away as business prosperity revived in 1794–5.

In London, Bath and Bristol, the collapse was immediate. Building in the West End was hit by the crisis of early 1793, and remained restricted.[105] Despite the fact that financial confidence was soon restored and 'until the close of 1795 money was as plentiful as in time of peace', building did not respond.[106] One reason may have been the collapse of several leading builders in 1793; another possible cause may have been over-building during the boom and the consequent absence of demand. In Bath and Bristol, the onset of the slump was dramatic. With the sudden cutting-off of supplies of credit for builders in early 1793, carcasses of houses were left unfinished, and sales of unused materials took place.[107] At Bath, the failure of the Bath City Bank brought ruin to the principal developers of Bathwick and other builders, and little

[102] Sheffield Archives: Norfolk MS. S.383.
[103] J. Holland *The Picture of Sheffield* (Sheffield, 1824), p. 77.
[104] Edwards, *Cotton Trade*, p. 12; Ashton, *Fluctuations*, p. 168; *Manchester Mercury*, 7 May 1793; Manchester Town Hall: deeds B.136, H.18, P.27 and 3/465.
[105] Swann, 'London Estates', pp. 82–3.
[106] Quoted in A. D. Gayer, W. W. Rostow and A. Schwarz, *The Growth and Fluctuation of the British Economy, 1790–1850* (Oxford, 1953), I, p. 44.
[107] For Bristol: Ison, *Bristol*, p. 27.

more construction was done. In 1795, property in the town was said to have fallen in value, and there was little encouragement for builders to start work again.[108]

One can contrast the dramatic collapse of activity in London, Bath and Bristol, and the more gradual decline over two or three years in Birmingham and Sheffield. In the former case, most houses were constructed by craftsmen builders who relied to a great extent on credit. Because of easy money at the beginning of the 1790s, their schemes had tended to be particularly ambitious, but in 1792 there were already signs that their halcyon days were coming to an end, and many became insolvent in the early part of 1793. With their credit cut off, many builders abandoned their schemes half complete, and those who remained solvent and finished their projects would have been unable to borrow further, even if they had not been deterred by the general malaise among their fellow tradesmen. In Bath at least, a fall in house prices helped to deter a recovery a year or two later. On the other hand, in Birmingham and probably Sheffield, construction was mainly financed by undertakers outside the trade.[109] Many of them supplied their own funds. Moreover, in Birmingham the building societies were strongly rooted and their subscriptions provided ready cash for new projects. Here, and probably also at Sheffield, the decline was the result of a collapse not of credit but of demand. It was largely because a multitude of small builders failed to realize soon enough that commercial depression aggravated the tendency of speculative housing to overreach itself. Investment only gradually petered out as more and more houses were left on the market, untenanted.

In most of the largest manufacturing towns, trade and industry were brisk for much of the later 1790s, but not building. In Manchester, things remained prosperous until the autumn of 1796; and after the financial difficulties of 1797 there was another period of commercial expansion from 1798, which included investment in cotton factories.[110] Yet house construction failed to rise to its former level at any time after 1793. About 600 houses were erected in Manchester township between 1796 and 1801, compared with over 3,600 between 1788 and 1796. In the later 1790s, the cotton industry was pressed by difficulties in raising money, and cotton may have taken much of the capital available for local investment.[111] In Leeds it has been estimated that 200 new houses

---

[108] Ison, *Bath*, p. 40; P.R.O. C12/1413/34.
[109] For Sheffield, see the occupations of the building lessees on the Norfolk Estate: Sheffield Archives: Norfolk MSS.
[110] Edwards, *Cotton Trade*, p. 13.
[111] See below, p. 289 and Aikin, *Description*, p. 157; Edwards, *Cotton Trade*, pp. 221–2.

were built in each year between 1790 and 1795, but in the next quinquennium the number fell to a quarter of that amount.[112] This was in
spite of local business prosperity suggested by a rise in the output of
woollen cloth in the West Riding in the later 1790s, and a particularly
high marriage rate in 1796–9.[113] In Nottingham some building occurred
between 1797 and 1799, but not on the scale that the record number of
marriages between 1796 and 1799 might have warranted. Even in
London there was little building between 1797 and 1799 in the West
End.[114] An important influence here may have been the attraction of
capital into Funds, which yielded between 5 and 6 per cent in 1797–9.[115]

There were probably several causes for the building depression of the
later 1790s. The financial crisis of 1793 was important in some towns in
bankrupting some builders and destroying the confidence of others. In
many centres the boom of the beginning of the 1790s created an over-
supply of houses, the effect of which was sooner or later felt by builders.
In the mid-1790s rising wage and material costs may have been a dis-
couragement, particularly where a plentiful supply of houses kept down
or even lowered house prices and rents. As far as the availability of
capital is concerned, it may have restricted builders in some towns, such
as Manchester and London, from 1796. One would have expected demand to have been rising almost everywhere by 1797–8, but building
recovery was probably further delayed by the bad harvests of 1799–1800,
which put pressure on the incomes of the lower classes in most of the
big towns, and encouraged the sharing of accommodation. In fact it is
likely that the tendency of wages to lag behind the rising cost of living
during the mid- and later 1790s may have reduced effective housing
demand among the artisan and labouring classes in the period in general.
Tooke wrote of a rise in wages of artisan and industrial labour; between
1792 and 1801; but in a small proportion only to the rise in the price of
necessaries'.[116] A rise in the price of Baltic timber between the later
months of 1799 and 1801 may also have made a marginal contribution
at the end of the period.[117]

The effect of the delay in the recovery is visible in the first census

[112] Rimmer, 'Working Men's Cottages', p. 187.
[113] Ashton, *Fluctuations*, p. 191; F. Beckwith, 'The Population of Leeds during the
Industrial Revolution', *Publications of the Thoresby Society*, XLI, part 2, Miscellany 12,
part 2 (1948), pp. 184–5.
[114] Swann, 'London Estates', pp. 82–3; Olsen, *Town Planning*, pp. 82–3.
[115] Ashton, *Fluctuations*, p. 187.
[116] Tooke and Newmarch, *Prices*, p. 226 (footnote); Gayer, Rostow and Schwarz,
British Economy, I, pp. 54–6.
[117] See Appendix IV.

taken in March 1801: in the leading industrial towns (except Birmingham and Sheffield) and in the ports of Hull and Liverpool, the number of uninhabited houses was negligible and a higher proportion of families were sharing accommodation than at the time of the following decennial censuses ⟨*see* Appendix VI⟩. In many of the towns which are the subject of this book, the eighteenth century ended with a shortage of housing.

II

1800–1820

I WARTIME BUILDING

Building between 1799 and 1820 consisted of one cycle of activity covering seventeen years from trough to trough, 1799–1816, and a recovery period between about 1818 and 1820, preceding the boom of the mid-1820s. These are predominantly years of high *national* activity, whatever their regional variations. Between 1800 and 1813, the rise in building construction halted only once, from 1807 to 1809, but there was no real recession. When depression eventually came, in 1816–17, it was brief and relatively mild.

In the first part of the 1800s, brick figures are a less sure guide to the level of house construction than at any other time between 1800 and 1820, because this was a time of heavy investment in the docks and cotton factories.[1] Yet the fact that, in most major provincial towns in which

[1] Gayer, Rostow and Schwartz, *British Economy*, pp. 35–7; Edwards, *Cotton Trade*, pp. 14–15; D. Swann, 'The Pace and Progress of Port Investment in England 1660–1830', *Yorkshire Bulletin of Economic and Social Research*, 12 (1960), pp. 38–9. The effect of non-housing construction on brick output is seen in the following table by Cairncross and Weber (England and Wales):

	1801–11	*1811–21*	*1821–31*
Average brick output (mills.)	811·6	859·0	1,230·9
Percentage increase		+5·8%	+43·4%
Net increase in houses (000)	215·1	309·3	443·5
Percentage increase		+43·8%	+43·4%

It suggests that houses absorbed a lower proportion of bricks between 1801 and 1811 than in 1811–21; A. K. Cairncross and B. Weber, 'Fluctuations in Building in Great Britain 1785–1849', *Essays in Economic History*, III, p. 322. Theoretically it is possible to explain the smaller proportion of additions to the housing stock between 1801 and 1811 in relation to the total brick output either (a) by more rebuilding or extention than after 1811; (b) by the construction of a higher percentage of larger houses than in the second and third decades; (c) by a high use of central sites for commercial purposes or public utilities which led to the wholesale demolition of existing dwellings, as in the later railway booms. (a) is just a possibility, though no evidence for it appears to be available; (b) is unlikely because war and trade oscillations tended to discourage some purchasers of new larger houses; (c) available evidence suggests that this did not occur on any but the smallest scale.

construction had been depressed in the later 1790s, house-building increased sharply some time between about 1800 and 1804 implies that the rise was widespread. Building probably rose almost continuously between 1800 and 1806. After a slight reduction in brick output between 1807 and 1809 (which may to some extent reflect a decline in construction other than in housing), it rose to a new high level between 1810 and 1812. While construction was low in the textile towns it was active in London and some of the major provincial centres. The amount of rural building is a major unknown factor. Nevertheless, house building in the towns and perhaps in the country was the basis of the high brick output, since other investment was low by 1811–12. Brick output began to fall from 1813.

No prolonged burst of general prosperity supported this building activity, as had happened between 1785 and 1792. The period between 1800 and 1816 was one of frequent economic fluctuations. The various sectors of the economy were affected in different ways at the same time. War distorted foreign trade. Generally speaking the years around 1801–2, 1806, 1809 and 1813 were in some degree commercially prosperous, and those about 1804, 1808, 1811 and 1815–16 saw widespread depression. Rises in grain prices in 1804 and 1809 lowered real incomes, at least temporarily. Marriages were particularly high in 1802–3, then declined in 1804–5, remaining roughly at the same level until they jumped again in 1814–15, just as building was declining. In fact there is little correlation between the annual number of weddings and the course of building between 1802 and 1816.

In the absence of knowledge about the course of rural building an explanation of the long surge in national house building activity must remain tentative. Population was growing fast, creating a continuously rising potential demand. In the towns there was presumably particular pressure on housing accommodation, each time there was a burst of prosperity, especially among the artisan and labouring classes. Brick output rose from 1800, probably helped by the investment in docks, factories and canals. But it seems likely that the business revival which reached a peak in 1801 and 1802, higher real incomes between 1801 and 1803 and possibly easier credit conditions than existed for part of the later 1790s all contributed to establish a recovery in house building. The depressions around 1804, 1808 and 1811 may have been partly or wholly 'bridged' by building through the usual slowness of builders to react to changed conditions. At least in one or two towns, builders reacted to the effect of commercial difficulties on housing demand about 1808. But more generally the halt to the rise in brick output about 1807 to 1809 was the result of the rising cost of imported timber in 1806 and 1807 and its unprecedented price in 1808 with the interruption of Baltic supplies. Brick output was particularly high between 1810 and 1812 despite prolonged commercial difficulties. In this case some builders were encouraged to keep going by the flow of capital out of trade into construction.

The situation between 1814 and 1816 seems to have been particularly discouraging for builders, both from the side of demand and in the availability of credit; falling timber prices were not important enough on their own to offset these problems. In Tooke's words:

'there was, from 1814 to 1816, a very general depression in the price of nearly all productions, and in the value of fixed property, entailing a convergence of losses and failures among the agricultural, and commercial, and manufacturing, and mining, and shipping, and building interests, which marked that period as one of most extensive suffering and distress'.[2]

Unlike the 1780s and 1790s, the period between 1800 and 1815 witnessed considerable regional variations in the course of urban building activity, particularly in the manufacturing towns. Among the industrial centres, recovery came very late in Birmingham. This was largely because of the severity of the depression of the mid-1790s and the failure of population to grow towards the end of the decade.[3] Unusually, there was a large proportion of empties in 1801—some 12 per cent of the total stock of 15,650 houses. Population grew by 12,000 between 1801 and 1811, but these vacancies almost met their need. Throughout 1801–11, only 446 houses were added to the stock, compared with nearly ten times as many in both the two previous decades. The housing slack was finally taken up about 1807–10, and by 1811 empties were as low as 1½ per cent of the housing stock. ⟨*See* Appendix VI for this and the following references to population and housing stock in 1801, 1811 and 1821⟩. The final recovery from about 1810 may have been slow in coming simply because builders needed a lot of convincing that the demand for housing was picking up and took time to recruit a labour force after such barren years. What may have finally nudged them was the rising prosperity of the small metal trades in 1809, which reached a peak the following year.[4] From 1811 the dislocation of the American

---

[2] Tooke, *Prices*, II, p. 12. Pressnell, *Country Banking*, pp. 470–2, for the financial and business difficulties.

[3] See above, p. 280.

[4] P. Crouzet, *L'Economie Britannique et le Blocus Continental (1806–13)* (Paris, 1958), II, pp. 515–18.

trade (which was said to take half the output of the town) and the depression and unemployment which followed[5] failed to deter builders once they had begun to work again, and capital may have been diverted from trade to building during the slump. Construction was at a high level until 1815 or 1816. In 1811–16, the number of houses increased by 3,700 in the parish of Birmingham alone.[6]

In the textile towns, the main burst of building activity came earlier, because population had continued to grow through the 1790s and was pressing on the available housing by 1801. In Leeds, building revived in the early 1800s. It has been estimated that about 900 houses were erected between 1800 and 1805 on the edge of the town. Then between 1805 and 1811 the number declined to about half.[7] Between 1801 and 1811, the percentage of vacant houses rose and the excess of families over occupied houses declined; by 1811 there were more houses than families, suggesting that the shortage in 1801 had been removed.[8] Depression in the local woollen industry in 1808 and 1810–12 probably helped to worsen the slump in building.[9]

At Nottingham, too, construction was high between about 1802 and 1809, with a peak around 1807. The early 1800s were prosperous times for hosiery, as they were for cottons. The low number of uninhabited houses in 1801 compared with 1811, and the high proportion of families sharing dwellings in 1801, suggests a shortage, which had partly disappeared by 1811. It was probably worsened by the jump in marriages in 1802–3, though the number fell in the following years, well before the peak in building ⟨*see* figure 5⟩. The end of the boom may have been hastened by the interruptions to foreign trade from 1807, since Nottingham sold 40 or 50 per cent of its industrial output overseas. In the depression of 1808 over 16,000 were dependent on poor relief, and in 1812, at the time of the Luddite outbreaks, the number was 22,000.[10]

Manchester's house-building revived in the early 1800s. It was based on a new surge of prosperity in the cotton industry beginning about 1798. In 1801 there were few uninhabited houses and there were signs of overcrowding. Again it was presumably worsened by the record number of weddings in 1802–3, though these figures were not sustained. That supply was seriously in arrears in the early 1800s is suggested by a

[5] *V.C.H. Warks.*, VII, p. 286.
[6] R. Jabet *et al.*, *A Concise History of Birmingham* (1817), p. 32.
[7] Rimmer, 'Working Mens' Cottages', pp. 187–8.
[8] *Ibid.*, pp. 175–6.
[9] R. G. Wilson, 'Transport Dues as Indices of Economic Growth 1775–1820', *Econ. H.R.* 2nd ser., XIX (1966), p. 117.
[10] R. A. Church, *Economic and Social Change in a Midland Town: Victorian Nottingham 1815–1900* (1966), p. 13.

comment in the *Manchester Guide* for 1804: 'the number of houses, which are now building, is thought by many very intelligent persons to be larger than was ever known in any preceding year; and yet at this time, the notification of "houses to let" is almost a singularity.' The major phase of industrial investment came to an end about 1803, just before house building gathered momentum, but the figures of raw cotton imports suggest that the industry remained generally prosperous until 1807.[11] Construction continued at a high level as late as about 1808, when it declined sharply to a relatively small amount for eight or nine years. Consequently the amount of new housing noted in the rate books for the quinquennium 1811–16 was low, in relation both to the preceding and the following five years:

TABLE 7. *House-building in Manchester, 1796–1820*

Period	No. of houses added in Manchester township	Percentage increase
1796–1801	599	6·1
1801–6	1,231	12·2
1806–11	1,766	15·1
1811–16	770	5·8
18 16–20 (four years)	1,811	13·0[12]

A serious depression in the cotton trade about 1808 probably hastened the downturn; in January 1809 the *Manchester Mercury* reported that 'perhaps never before has the distress of the poorer classes in Manchester been greater . . ..'[13] Construction failed to respond to the trade revival of 1809–10 and that beginning after 1813, and building did not recover until well after the close of the war.[14]

Presumably in response to massive additional employment in the dockyards, both Portsmouth and Plymouth expanded their stock of houses most rapidly between about 1806 and 1817 ⟨*see* plate 29⟩. Portsea's houses almost doubled between 1801 and 1821. Marriages rose nearly continuously between 1805 and 1811, reflected in a rising number of site purchases from 1806, sales reaching their peak between 1810 and 1813. The early part of the period showed the familiar pattern

[11] *The Manchester Guide* (Manchester, 1804), p. 49; Edwards, *Cotton Trade*, pp. 14–15; see also Fig. 48.
[12] Manchester Archives: rate books; there are no Salford rate books surviving for these years, and none for Manchester in 1821.
[13] Parry Lewis, *Building Cycles*, p. 27.
[14] Edwards, *Cotton Trade*, pp. 17–22.

of supply lagging behind demand. On 26 September 1808, the *Hampshire Telegraph* commented on the large number of houses erected in the past eighteen months: 'and they are constantly increasing . . . for such is the demand for houses that they are generally taken as soon as the foundations are laid.'[15]

Construction revived early in Liverpool and Hull. At Liverpool, the population was growing rapidly in the later 1790s, especially about 1798 when many Irish came in. New houses filled up immediately and rents rose.[16] Building was in full swing by 1801 and continued at a high level until 1807. There may have been a temporary downturn in 1808 and 1809 as demand slackened on account of the interruption to the American trade, and as the price of Baltic timber rose sharply. We have noticed the local comment in September 1808 that house prices 'are lower than they generally are and should trade revive . . . they will be as high as ever'.[17] Building recovered until the end of the war. Contemporary comments on the level of construction for any town are so rare that it is ironic that the two or three references to the state of building in Liverpool during the business depression of 1811–12, caused principally by the interruption to the American trade, should conflict to some degree. On balance, the evidence points to active house construction for most of these two years. Building appears to have reacted more to the trade depression of about 1808 than to that of 1811–12, and in the second depression men with capital were prepared to build in order to find an outlet for their money without any immediate prospect of finding tenants. According to the editorial of the *Liverpool Mercury* of 3 April 1812, commenting on the increase in poverty:

'there are indeed many buildings which are still continued by the capital of men who cannot trade and are mistrustful of the public funds, and who, although they cannot derive any immediate rents from the houses they are rearing, are not unwilling to look forward to a revival of commercial activity. This affords relief to many of the labouring poor . . ..'[18]

This building activity at a time when demand may have been slack led to a large number of empties by the end of 1813. Their number

---

[15] Portsmouth R.O.: deeds; Plymouth Library: St. Aubyn survey books.
[16] Picton, *Architectural History*, p. 48; [Corry], *History of Liverpool*, p. 198.
[17] Liverpool R.O.: deeds 468B.
[18] Professor Crouzet traced one reference for the beginning of 1812 that house-building slowed down, and another relating to September 1811 that 'les constructions publiques et privées continuent activement'; Crouzet, *L'Economie Britannique*, II, p. 765; when the census was taken in May 1811, 228 houses were being built, more than twice the number in Manchester; deed evidence has been traced for building in at least fifteen streets on the Corporation Estate alone in this period.

subsequently declined, perhaps as a result of a recovery in the number of weddings in 1814 and their record level in 1815.[19]

Though construction in Hull had continued through the later 1790s, there was a renewed burst of building from about 1800. In the Sculcoates suburb north of the dock, four small freehold estates began selling building land within about two years; and in 1804–6 there was much building in a new area to the far west of the town near the River Humber.[20] In the census of 1801 the number of empties was small and the ratio of families to houses high, suggesting that supply was lagging behind demand, as in other provincial towns. By May 1811, there were four times as many empties and a lower ratio of families to dwellings. At this date only sixteen houses were being built, and construction was presumably very low about this time. In this respect Hull's building history was different from that of Liverpool, where we have seen that construction soon recovered from the minor building depression around 1808.

In London, building recovered soon after 1800, and was at a high level through 1802–6.[21] Builders were particularly active between 1811 and 1815. In Mrs. George's words, 'the latter part of the great war reversed the tradition as to building in war-time, and was a period of great building activity.' Better-class housing construction was prominent.[22] This coincided with a period when government pressure for capital was still heavy, but builders benefited from commercial depression in 1811 and 1812. Capital rendered inactive on this account flowed into building.[23] It may have been encouraged by a high demand for housing to buy or to rent.[24]

In Bristol, the depression of the later 1790s had been particularly severe, and it is not surprising that it lasted into the early 1800s. There were signs of revival by about 1805, but many unfinished houses were still standing in Clifton: builders were relatively active between about 1809 and 1814.[25] In Bath also recovery came late, and twice as many

[19] *Liverpool Mercury*, 3 December 1813: 'as there are so many uninhabited houses at present in Liverpool . . .'; *ibid.*, 15 December 1815: a survey showed that the number of empty front houses was 731 compared with 1,422 in 1813.

[20] A. G. Chamberlain, 'The Northern Suburb of Hull: Historical and Architectural Notes for the V.C.H.', (1966) pp. 13–16; B.R. Eastern Region Estate Surveyor, York: deeds 260, 263, 266, 269, 302, vol. 11; manor of Tupcoates with Myton court books 2, 3; East Riding Deeds Registry: registers CC–CK.

[21] Information kindly supplied by Professor Dyos; Olsen, *Town Planning*, pp. 52–5, 83–4; George, *London Life*, p. 89.

[22] George, *London Life*, p. 89; Summerson, *Georgian London*, pp. 173–4, plates 31–32.

[23] Crouzet, *L'Economie Britannique*, II, p. 868.

[24] Shannon, 'Bricks', p. 198.

[25] Ison, *Bristol*, pp. 27, 226–36.

houses were built between 1811 and 1821 as in the previous decade. Again there was much activity between about 1808–9 and 1813–14.[26]

2 THE POST-WAR BOOM

The revived activity beginning about 1818 (after the mild trough of 1816 and 1817) has been referred to as a 'post-war housing boom'.[27] There was little dock construction in these years, and brick output, which reached new records, was used mainly for housing. Thus, in 1818–19, the national stock of houses was almost certainly growing faster than ever before. On the side of demand, nationally the population continued to grow, and potential pressure on accommodation would have been increased by the high number of marriages of 1814 and 1815. There was a business revival in 1817–18, which would have helped to make this demand effective. It is unlikely that the previous housing boom had created a major over-supply of houses, as had happened in towns in the early 1790s. On the side of supply, credit was becoming more abundant by 1817, and timber was much cheaper.

Even in this period, not all towns enjoyed the boom. The dockyard towns were bound to feel the return of peace adversely. In Portsea, there was some lag between the growth of unemployment following the end of the War and the cessation of the development of new building sites. In March 1816, 300 artificers were discharged from the dockyard, and by August there was great distress in Portsea, with upwards of 600 people in the Poor House and 3,276 paupers outside it.[28] Yet both 1816 and 1817 were relatively good years for the sale of building sites, and it is clear that, once again, builders were slow to respond to the change of climate after the nine or ten years' uninterrupted activity. But the sale of sites died away to a trickle in 1818–19.[29] In 1821 there were only seventeen houses being built in Portsea, compared with 148 in 1811. In Dock, leases of completed houses did not fall sharply until 1820, although marriages had declined from 1816, suggesting that here, as at Portsmouth, prosperity ended with the war.[30]

In Birmingham alone among the other major provincial towns can we be sure that the national pattern had no answering echo. The great burst of activity that had characterized the last years of the war had spent itself by 1815–16 and, except for an uncertain recovery about 1819,

---

[26] Ison, *Bath*, p. 212; Bath Guildhall: deeds; British Museum: Eg. MS. 3650.
[27] Gayer, Rostow and Schwartz, *British Economy, II*, p. 704.
[28] H. and J. Slight, *Chronicles of Portsmouth* (1828), p. 230.
[29] A conclusion based on the numerous title deeds surviving from these years.
[30] Plymouth Library: St. Aubyn survey books.

construction remained small. By 1821, fewer than 800 houses had been added in Birmingham parish in five years, compared with 3700 in the previous quinquennium. No doubt the decline was hastened by the post-war slump. The gun trade felt the return of peace keenly, and hardware and cutlery exports also failed to revive before 1821.[31]

Elsewhere, urban building seems to have been fairly general. Among the ports, the joiners of Liverpool were particularly active, especially from 1817.[32] It was now that the most ambitious land development project so far in the whole history of the town, that of Moss Lake Fields, was slowly getting under way, and in the last year of this period the construction of houses in Abercrombie Square was going ahead fast.[33] There was also considerable building taking place towards Everton, as there was on many streets within the physical limits of the town.[34] In London, construction followed the national pattern by rising sharply in 1818 and 1819; this was helped by the return of easy credit from 1816.[35] From about 1816, building began to revive at last in Manchester, reflecting the usual lagged response to a jump in marriage numbers in 1814 and 1815, and by the year of Peterloo construction was at a high level. In the four years 1816–20 the stock of houses in the township of Manchester increased by 13 per cent, compared with less than 6 per cent in the five years prior to 1816.[36] There was even a burst of activity in the coastal resorts, the population of Brighton, for example, doubling between 1811 and 1821, and construction boomed near the end of the decade, 400 houses being built in 1818 alone.[37]

The building cycle of 1800 to 1816 differed from the cycle which lasted from about 1781 to 1799 in that there was no outstanding peak such as occured in the beginning of the 1790s, and it ended with no catastrophic depression. In this the Napoleonic cycle also differed from the boom and ensuing slump of the 1820s. Some reasons for the absence of a long depression in the later 1810s have been suggested. Some explanation for the absence of a previous peak may be given so far as urban building is concerned. The course of activity in this period was fundamentally determined by the war. One effect of it was to halt the rise of construction nationally in 1807–9 by the interruption of foreign trade and the sudden jump in the price of timber as a result of the Continental

---

[31] *V.C.H. Warks.*, VII, p. 118; Gayer, Rostow and Schwarz, *British Economy*, I, p. 151.
[32] Evidence of deeds for over twenty streets; also J. Gore, *A Plan of Liverpool* (1814) and *A Plan of the Town and Township of Liverpool* (1821).
[33] Liverpool R.O.: 357A, 524A, 525C, 862D.
[34] *Plans* (1814, 1821).
[35] Gairncross and Weber, 'Fluctuations', p. 326; Summerson, *Georgian London*, p. 188.
[36] See above, p. 289.
[37] E. W. Gilbert, *Brighton: Old Ocean's Bauble* (1954), p. 93.

Blockade. This may have checked somewhat the natural course of the cycle before supply overtook demand. Regional variations help to explain the absence of a sharp peak about 1811–13. While building was at a high level in London, Birmingham, Liverpool, Bath, and the dockyard towns, there was little in Nottingham and Manchester, and the amount in Leeds and Hull may also have been small.[38]

Another reason for the protracted nature of the cycle and the absence of a sharp peak was the absence of easy credit, especially for large sums. There is no reason to doubt that heavy wartime government borrowing was now drawing capital from all over England. The peak at the beginning of the 1790s had been largely the result of plentiful funds, which had encouraged undertakers, especially small men, to attempt more than they could really handle, as was also the case in the mid-1820s. According to the *Annual Register* for 1825, 'on all sides new buildings were in the progress of erection; and money was so abundant that men of enterprise, though without capital, found no difficulty in commanding funds for any plausible undertaking'.[39] At no time during the Napoleonic War were financial conditions so easy. The Bank of England and the country banks expanded credit between 1807 and 1810, but thereafter the *general* supply was tighter. The failure of building to reach an outstanding peak between about 1811 and 1815 may owe much to the fact that the money situation was never favourable enough to builders. Referring to the years between about 1810 and 1816 (when the situation eased), it was remarked in 1818 before the Select Committee on the Usury Laws that 'for the period of, I think, six or seven years, mortgages were not to be obtained', and 'I should think, that in many cases people have been obliged to borrow at the rate of from 9 to 12 per cent, by granting annuities'. Although the evidence related largely to landed estates, builders were also said to have been affected: 'scarcely any man entered into a building speculation, with a small capital, who did not raise money by annuities, upon the security of his buildings, and very frequently before they were covered in.'[40] Presumably the witness had London chiefly in mind. In some provincial towns, the sale of annuities was used to raise building capital, but mortgages remained the normal method. This is detectable in four of the largest provincial towns, Birmingham, Portsmouth, Liverpool and Bath, in all of which builders were active. Annuities were used most in Bath, and even here mortgages

[38] In Leeds there was no building on the important Wilson Estate until 1816: Rimmer, 'Working Mens' Cottages', p. 188.
[39] Shannon, 'Bricks', p. 190.
[40] *B.P.P.*, 1845, xii: Report from Select Committee on the Usury Laws (1818), QQ. 61, 68, 96, 134, 197, 540.

were more common for loans secured on houses. In the other three towns, annuities were seldom used.[41] In Birmingham some people may have been prepared to pay a premium to secure a mortgage.[42] Newspaper advertisements for these years included many offers of money as well as numerous requests for loans, though they indicate that it was much easier to borrow £200 or £300 than, say, £2,000 or £3,000. In at least one or two towns the pressure was eased by the fact that business depression diverted capital into building. Probably in most towns the demand for building capital was just met. Yet builders were nowhere encouraged to construct at the unrealistic level of that of the beginning of the 1790s in such towns as Bath and Bristol, by a superfluity of capital.

CONCLUSION

One possible approach to an explanation of the national building fluctuations is to place the emphasis on influences on the side of supply. Between about the middle of the eighteenth century and 1820 the growth of population, and thus of the potential demand for housing, seems to have been almost uninterrupted. Thus the uneven response of builders over time to accommodation needs may have been caused by occasional material shortages, the differing availability of capital, or the nature of house building as an industry.

Among them, the supply of materials was probably least important. Bricks were either made on the spot or in brickfields on the edge of the town. Temporary local shortages may have arisen occasionally during a sudden upturn in building activity, because of the need to open up more brickfields or recruit more labour, or as production was curtailed in a severe winter. There were also difficulties over the supply of foreign softwoods during the American War of Independence and at the height of the Napoleonic Blockade. In the latter case the shortage and high cost seems to have temporarily halted the rise in building output. But in most years the supply of timber did not have a significant influence on building fluctuations.

---

[41] For Liverpool, forty-five mortgages were traced among the deeds seen for 1810–16, but no annuities; for Portsea, mortgages traced totalled eighty-six, and one annuity. Only one annuity was traced for Bath: advertisements in the *Bath Chronicle* suggest that they were used, but less often than mortgages. Advertisements in the *Birmingham Gazette* (1811–13) suggest their occasional use, but that mortgages were the normal means of obtaining a long loan.

[42] On 30 March 1812 an advertiser in the *Birmingham Gazette* offered 'a very handsome premium to any gentleman who will advance £1,200 or £1,300 on freehold houses'. But such an advertisement was a rarity in the *Gazette* between 1811 and 1813.

It is impossible to deny the close connexion between the course of building and the supply of capital. At least in London, easy credit seems to have helped building in the mid-1760s and the mid-1770s. Capital difficulties may have been fairly general in the years after about 1778, corresponding with a sharp decline in timber imports and other evidence that urban building was at a low level. The availability of credit became easier after about 1785, when construction revived, and was generally abundant in the beginning of the 1790s, when building reached its peak. The low level of activity in the later 1790s again corresponded with a shortage of capital which may have been widespread. Capital difficulties helped to prevent building reaching a sharp peak about 1811–12, though they did not stop a high level of activity. Easier credit encouraged the revival of 1818–19.

It would be wrong to assume that building rose and fell just with a change in the cost of borrowing, that is, with the rate of interest. This study suggests that in fact the pattern was more complicated. Many building owners, particularly in the industrial towns, drew on their own capital and did not borrow. In the case of building owners relying on credit, changes in the rate of interest are unlikely to have been the crucial factor in decisions to build, particularly for working-class housing. It has been shown that before 1780 mortgage rates fluctuated within a very narrow margin between $4\frac{1}{2}$ and 5 per cent, or at the most between 4 and 5 per cent. From the 1780s rates never dropped below 5 per cent in the provincial towns, except for some mortgages about 1790. A gross return of 8 or 10 per cent on tenement property usually made undertakings based on mortgage loans paying 5 per cent profitable.[43] Before 1780, there is no local evidence to suggest a close correspondence between the cost of credit and the volume of building.

It remains true that for some war years—1778–84, 1796–9 and *c.*1810–16—builders may have been deterred by the need to borrow through the sale of an annuity or the payment of a premium. This in fact involved the payment of a rate substantially higher than 5 per cent. Annuities were rarely used by builders in most provincial towns. Premiums were paid for mortgages. Written evidence of them is rare, but one would not expect to find references to them in title deeds, and the extent to which the Usury Laws were evaded in this way is unlikely ever to be known. It may be tentatively suggested that small sums of £100 or £200 were much more easily obtained at legal rates than large amounts of £1,000 or more, and that the extent to which the law was evaded (if at all) varied from town to town.

[43] See above, pp. 163–5.

The extent to which local credit dried up altogether in a few years is also unknown. Contemporary comment attests to this having occurred in London during, and just after, the American War of Independence, presumably because of the attraction of government stock. No firm evidence has come to light to show that demand from manufacturing industry stopped house-builders raising capital in the industrial towns, though such difficulties may have happened occasionally, as in south Lancashire in the later 1790s. In some years small sums of £100 or £200 may have been available, but larger sums may have been difficult to borrow.

Sometimes a local financial crisis brought the work of a few builders relying on credit to an abrupt end. In such a case loanable funds might exist, but in an atmosphere of financial panic few potential lenders were willing to part with them, or to resist recalling loans already made. In particular, the desire to hoard coins made it difficult for builders to get cash to pay wages. Such crises did not last long, though they were generally long enough for the ranks of the leading builders to be reduced by bankruptcy. Conversely, during a boom, plentiful capital encouraged builders to speculate too much, and to continue to build while the number of empties rose. Sometimes it helped a building recovery. But at least in the provincial towns it was the availability more than the cost of capital that was crucial.

As far as the towns were concerned the effect of the investment characteristics of building and the organization of the industry as suggested by building cycle models were also important. To some extent this view must be tentative, because information is usually absent on such points as the percentage of empties or the short-term course of rents and house prices. Nevertheless, while one would like more evidence, the occasional references to labour shortage in a recovery, speculative fervour in a boom, and signs of building continuing after it had outstripped demand, particularly when credit was available, all point to this conclusion.

However, to explain the building fluctuations in term of supply only is almost certainly too simple. To what extent did changes in the level of demand over time affect building? How valid is Lewis' demographic analysis? On general grounds, his view that building might be affected fifteen to eighteen years after a marriage and birth bulge by the great number of teenagers going out to work is most debateable. How great the pressure for *larger* accommodation among families with one or two new breadwinners among the artisan or labouring classes would have been in practice we do not know. Even if such a demand is accepted, it did not create *more* households. Possibly more important was the more distant demographic echo occurring after say twenty-five or twenty-eight years or even more which resulted from the marrying of children born to parents whose weddings formed the initial bulge. Thus the high number of marriages in the early and mid-1760s probably reflected the increase in births in the 1730s. These marriages may have been echoed in turn in the great number of marriages and births between the mid-1780s and the early 1790s ⟨*see* figure 4⟩. This may have contributed to the unprecedented housing demand of these years. But these marriages also reflected exceptional prosperity based on such influences as rising export demand and the application of new industrial techniques. In fact, fluctuations in marriages throughout the period also suggest a strong immediate link with grain prices and trade conditions (which were often connected): prosperous years and good harvest produced a jump and the opposite a fall in weddings. This is particularly evident between about 1795 and 1805. Again, if one accepts the existence of a twenty-five, to thirty but not a fifteen to twenty year echo, it weakens a demographic explanation of the building cycle. One can no longer try to link one bulge or trough in construction to its immediate predecessor by this means, since they repeated themselves roughly every fifteen or twenty years.

How far were fluctuations in marriages and births reflected in the volume of house building? One would not expect a close correlation if only because the marriage series reveals in part a succession of peaks and troughs every six or seven years, generally linked to the quality of the harvests or the trade cycle. On the other hand we have seen that it is possible also to detect some longer fluctuations. Both marriages and baptisms were much higher between about 1784 and 1793 than they had been about 1780; marriages were low on average by comparison between 1793 and 1801 when account is taken of the continued growth of the population. Before 1800 it is possible to detect some correlation between vital statistics and building though it is far from uniform. The high level of marriages in the mid-1760s, round 1770 and in the mid-1770s, and in marriages and baptisms between about 1784 and, 1793 all coincided with a large volume of building; only the bulge in marriages and baptisms about 1798 found no reflection in building. The troughs in marriages about 1767 and 1772-3, and the halt to the rise in marriages about 1788-90 found little reflection in building; on the other hand the decline about 1780 and the troughs about 1795 and 1800 coincided with a low level of construction. From about 1804 building and demographic fluctuations appear to follow different paths. Marriages were not particularly high between about 1805 and 1812, and one cannot see the high volume of building in these years as coinciding with a high marriage rate for most of the period. Even baptisms showed no pronounced rise between 1803 and 1813. Marriages and baptisms jumped about 1814–15 just as building was declining. The bulge in marriages and baptisms about 1798, 1803 and 1815 ultimately swelled the demand for housing, but seem to have had little immediate influence.

It is likely that demographic fluctuations had some influence on building between the 1760s and the 1790s, but their precise effect must remain in doubt. A further question is the importance of changes in the economic climate over time, which altered the amount of employment and level of incomes. Apart from the effect on the number of weddings and hence on accommodation, business prosperity increased migration into the towns, and perhaps encouraged those previously sharing accommodation to occupy separate dwellings. A depression reduced migration and encouraged the sharing of houses by the poorer classes. A difficulty is that the trade cycle tends to last less than ten years, while building fluctuations were of fifteen or eighteen years' duration. Many instances have been noted in which building does not seem to respond to changes in the commercial climate. Building did not respond to the trade revivals of the mid- and later 1790s; in some important towns construction continued through the commercial difficulties between 1810 and 1812, and nationally brick output was at its height. Whether or not builders reacted to a change in business conditions depended on a range of factors such as the size of the existing housing stock in relation to demand, the speed with which building owners and the building trades reacted to changed conditions, and the availability of capital. Sometimes funds moved into building because they could not be used in trade; if a financial crisis accompanied a trade slump the effect on building might be worsened for as long as the monetary panic lasted. It also naturally depended on the length and scale of the commercial prosperity or slump. At least for part of the period it is possible to detect changes in the level of prosperity longer than the normal trade cycle, despite the existence of short-term fluctuations, which probably affected building. The years between 1785 and 1792 were a time of almost uninterrupted commercial and industrial expansion. There was a sharp and long depression between about 1778 and 1781, which was more intense than, for example, the previous slump of 1772–3. Again, despite trade revivals, the period of the mid-1790s and later 1790s seem to have been a time of declining real wages. Each of these phases is likely to have involved a change in the effective demand for housing long and intense enough to have contributed to the level of building. Such a possible link is less obvious in the next building cycle, with no very long period of prosperity accompanying the high level of building, as between 1785 and 1792, but the feature was to occur again in the early 1820s.

Turning to consider the pattern at the local level, for at least part of the period, we can see that some of the more rapidly growing centres underwent building fluctuations at intervals of between about twelve and eighteen years. This is noticeable in the course of house construction in the textile towns. In Manchester house-building reached a high point around the years 1776–7, 1790–92 and 1804–7; construction was at a low level about 1780, the later 1790s, and in the last years of the Napoleonic Wars; recovery was in full swing by the end of the 1810s, the four years between 1816 and 1820 contributing more than two and a half times the number of houses added to the town's stock in the five years between 1811 and 1816. In the case of Nottingham, it is just possible to trace a pattern as far back as 1760. Builders appear to have been particularly active in the early 1760s, around 1777, at the beginning of the 1790s, and about 1806–7, and there were troughs in the years about 1770, the early 1780s, the later 1790s, and after about 1810.

Again, in Birmingham, it is possible to detect peaks in activity around 1775–6 and at the beginning of the 1790s, with a brief, mild trough about 1780 and a long and severe one after about 1795; on the other hand, building did not reach a peak again until about 1812–13, at least twenty years after the previous high point, as a result of the prolonged depression of the mid- and later 1790s, which was the consequence of the war. In the middle of the eighteenth century, building had boomed in the later 1740s, and there was a trough in the mid-1750s: building is known to have been active about 1759–60, but the pattern for the early 1760s is not clear enough to enable one to detect a high point.

In the case of the provincial ports, the evidence is not clear enough for similar conclusions to be drawn. Liverpool builders seem, to have been active in the later 1740s, for much of the 1760s and 1770s, in the mid- and later 1780s and early 1790s, and between about 1800 or 1801 and 1807 and at the end of the 1810s. Probably they were less busy in the years about 1780, in the mid-1790s, and about 1808–9. But some of these suggestions are tentative. London appears to have followed (and because of its size done much to create) the national pattern, with peaks about 1776–7, 1790–92, and after a prolonged period of activity, about 1811–12.

Enough has already been said to suggest the importance of supply factors, such as the availability of capital and the lag in the reaction of builders to changes in the housing market, in helping to shape these local fluctuations. But the importance of changes in the level of demand for housing is much clearer at the local than at the national level. Although all the major provincial towns in this study grew rapidly between the 1740s and 1820, their development over time was uneven. Marked spurts of population growth and local prosperity, often covering five or ten years, were interspersed with periods of slow growth and occasional stagnation. Normally the volume of building tended to move in sympathy with prolonged changes in the local economic climate. This is not to deny that there was sometimes a time lag of several years and that building therefore often failed to move in sympathy with short term fluctuations in local prosperity over, say, one, two or three years.

A difficulty in revealing this fully is that we do not know enough about the detailed economic history of all these provincial towns to be able always to specify with certainty which were the periods of prosperity and depression, though some evidence is available. Nor do we know enough about the course of population growth. One possible indication that may be used cautiously if other evidence is lacking is the number of marriages and baptisms. In a small way they may be an echo of the number of marriages and births twenty-five or thirty years earlier in the town, but because urban population growth depended as much if not more on migration than on natural increase the effect would have been limited. Apart from this, an outstanding jump in marriages which was largely or wholly sustained probably reflects local prosperity and population growth.

The degree of the possible link between the local economic climate, the number of marriages and the volume of building may be illustrated in the case of Manchester. For this town both the figures of British raw cotton imports (of which south-east Lancashire was a main consumer) and other evidence provides some indication of changes in the level of local prosperity ⟨*see* figure 6⟩. Raw cotton imports and local prosperity grew sharply in the mid-1770s, both imports and investment in the local cotton industry jumped in the mid- and later 1780s and beginning of the 1790s, and there was a similar growth at the end of the 1790s and in the early 1800s. Imports were at a brief peak about 1810, and were high again in the later 1810s. Except between 1800 and 1810 marriages moved in sympathy. They also tended to decline when the rise in imports was halted or fell. Building in Manchester was clearly linked to local prosperity, of which marriages were usually one indicator, though sometimes with a time lag at least two or three years long.

The evidence is rather less clear for Birmingham, since we have no possible indicators of local output. But a pattern still seems to emerge when we combine the evidence of marriages and baptisms, the ebb and flow of local prosperity, and population growth ⟨*see* figure 2⟩. The sharp rise in marriages and baptisms (which seems to have at least a partial basis in population growth) in the later 1740s, and the temporary drop in weddings in the early 1750s and the smaller decline in baptisms two or three years later, was echoed in the volume of house building. The recovery in construction at the end of the 1750s accompanied a rise both in marriages and baptisms. Prosperity, population growth and building all seem to have reached a peak in the mid-1770s. The great jump in population between 1781 and 1791 was echoed in an addition to the housing stock of roughly the same proportion. In the mid-1790s the local economy was heavily depressed, and until 1801 there was a decline in weddings and baptisms, which reflects a fall in population. New building virtually ceased. Only after 1800 is the correlation absent between marriages and baptisms on the one hand, and building on the other. The surge in the vital statistics in the early 1800s had no immediate echo in building and the later peak about 1815 came at the end of the Napoleonic building boom in the town.[44]

Less can be said about either the course of building or of local prosperity in Liverpool. What evidence there is, as that for the later 1740s and early 1750s, seems to suggest that building again moved in sympathy with the more prolonged or outstanding changes in the economic climate. One exception is around 1811–12, when building remained active during the commercial slump. The tendency of building and commercial prosperity to be sometimes out of step between about 1800 and about 1814 noticeable in Manchester, Birmingham and Liverpool in part reflects the violent and frequent fluctuations in the state of trade and industry which was the result of war conditions; the innate slowness of building to react to changes in demand led it to 'jump' some of the commercial changes of these years. In Birmingham the huge number of empties available in the early 1800s was a special factor in the absence of

---

[44] Again, in Nottingham the peaks in marriages about 1762–5, 1776 and 1802–4 all found an echo in a high volume of construction, though with some lag in the last case. Building slumps appear to have accompanied the fall in the number of weddings in the late 1760s, about 1779, and about 1811–13. On the other hand there is no clear peak in marriages between 1785 and 1800, yet we know that builders were much more active in the first half of the period than in the second part. I have not graphed Nottingham baptisms in figure 5, because figures derived from the MS. parish registers were not available to me, and Professor Chambers drew attention to the weakness of the figures in the *Census Abstracts* (Chambers, 'Population Change in Nottingham', p. 124).

building in these years. On the other hand there is little doubt that between the 1740s and 1800 the volume of building in most of the provincial towns tended to correspond with the longer or more intense bursts of prosperity or depression. The most extreme case of this phenomenon is that of the dockyard towns, where the amount of building appears to have been almost always a function of wartime prosperity and peacetime stagnation.[45]

[45] The link between regional building fluctuations and local economic conditions is also visible later in the nineteenth century: D. H. Aldcroft and P. Fearon 'Introduction' in Aldcroft and Fearon (eds.), *British Economic Fluctuations 1790–1939* (1972), p. 72.

303

12

House-Building and Urban Growth

This book has been concerned with builders and land-promoters, the houses they erected and the money they spent. It has tried to show that innumerable people in each provincial town supplied building land, speculated in construction, bought new houses, or lent to builders. Their work has been treated particularly from the point of view of the individual estate promotion or building project, and has been seen to fluctuate over time. It remains to try to assess the contribution which builders made to the growth of the urban community at large.

First, how should one rate their performance in their prime function— the supply of accommodation in towns which were growing at an unprecedented speed? Did the addition to the housing stock keep up with the growth of population? Secondly, what role did they play in the local urban economy? What was the approximate magnitude of capital formation in housing, and how did builders' expenditure contribute to local prosperity? Lastly, what contribution did the builders make to the process of urbanization in the nineteenth century, and to the much greater expansion of provincial towns from the 1820s onwards?

I BUILDING AND WORKING–CLASS LIVING STANDARDS

We have seen that in some ways the living conditions for the town artisan and labourer worsened in the period covered by this book. In some of the towns, housing densities increased as more and more tenements were crammed into ground behind the dwellings fronting the street. Jerry-building was particularly rife during the Napoleonic Wars. The builders themselves were hardly to blame. Packing the houses in was a reaction to rising land prices, and skimping on materials a response to their soaring costs. Gross returns on working-class property, about 8 or 10 per cent, were not high when compared with profits in commerce or larger enterprises in manufacturing industry. There is no evidence that they *rose* perceptibly as a result of these practices.

Above all, the social contribution of builders should be looked at in terms of the number of houses erected in relation to local population growth, and the size of the accommodation in the new dwellings. There is no way of comparing the rate of population growth with the increase in the housing stock in England as a whole before 1800.

Between the census years of 1801 and 1821, which includes the post-war building boom of 1818–19, the average number of inhabitants to a census house in England remained approximately the same, being 5·67 in 1801, 5·68 in 1811, and 5·76 in 1821.[1] In London, which contributed 8 or 9 per cent of new houses, the ratio increased marginally.[2] Among the bigger regional centres, whose growth-rate was mostly slower than that of the major provincial towns which are the main subject of this study, the pattern varied. In Maidstone, Yarmouth and York there were more houses in relation to the population in 1821 than in 1801; in Exeter, Worcester and Chester, on the other hand, the position was perceptibly worse. In the counties in which the population mainly consisted of country people and inhabitants of market towns, the ratio remained fairly steady in 1801, 1811 and 1821. In the major textile-manufacturing towns and northern seaports of Hull, Liverpool and Newcastle, the outstanding characteristic of these two decades was the fact that the addition to the housing stock was greater than the growth of population between 1801 and 1811. For example, the population of Nottingham grew by 19 per cent and its housing stock by 34 per cent. This of course reflects the housing shortage around 1800, which was the result of the general building depression of the later 1790s in the face of the continued population growth in these towns. To a more limited extent it also reflects the depressed commercial conditions of 1811 in many areas, and the consequent temporary halting of the demand for houses. However, it reveals that where secular growth of demand was sufficient, builders were more than able to keep pace with the growing population in this war decade, despite sharply rising timber costs.

In the case of most of the manufacturing towns, the available material suggests that the ratio of persons per house did not deteriorate over a period in which the population grew several times. In Birmingham, there was some deterioration in the situation during the period of demographic growth in the 1770s, but in the 1780s building appears at least to have kept up with a further population explosion. The average number of

---

[1] G. R. Porter, *The Progress of the Nation*, (1851), p. 525.
[2] For the following estimates, see Appendix VI.

persons per dwelling from 1801 appears to have been much lower than it was earlier, and shows the relative rarity of multi-family occupation by the beginning of the nineteenth century. It is possible that the apparently changing pattern merely reflects a different local definition of a dwelling before and after 1800. On the other hand, it may show that the back-to-backs being erected in increasing numbers were replacing multi-occupied front houses, or the change may be linked to the slowing down in the growth of the town after the early 1790s. At the least, Birmingham's builders had faced a population growth of about five times between 1750 and 1820, and at the end the pattern of one family to a dwelling was the norm. There is also the real possibility of considerable improvement over the whole period. Sheffield at least trebled its population between the 1750s and 1820, without disturbing the established pattern of one family per house. This pattern was also true of Leeds and Leicester at the end of the period. In both cases, in terms of number of dwellings, builders had coped successfully with a population growth of about three times in the previous fifty years.

In the case of Nottingham, Manchester and Liverpool, a conclusion is more difficult to reach. Taken at face value, the available figures for the later eighteenth and early nineteenth centuries suggest that over the period as a whole the ratio of persons to a house did not deteriorate, except possibly at Liverpool. At Nottingham and Manchester they show some improvement. However, it is theoretically possible that the figures conceal a change in the definition of a house before and after 1800. All had numerous cellars in separate occupation, Liverpool and Manchester more than Nottingham. If the definition of a house in some or all the censuses in the later eighteenth century included cellars as part of houses (as was the case in the Liverpool census of 1790), though in the official censuses of 1801–21 they were included as separate dwellings, then the ratio of persons to a house almost certainly declined. In fact this is unlikely: in the 1831 census, in contrast to 1841 (when instructions were more specific), 'the buildings and not its subdivisions were returned' in the case of towns 'where it is custom to let off as separate tenements the flats and floors under the same roof',[3] and it is reasonable to assume that 1831 reflected earlier practice in 1801–21; that is, cellars in 1801–21 were not treated as separate dwellings.[4]

---

[3] M. W. Flinn (ed.), *Report on the Sanitary Conditions of the Labouring Population of Great Britain, by Edwin Chadwick, 1842* (Edinburgh, 1965), pp. 5, 188–9.
[4] There are also a few figures available for the more slowly growing regional centres before 1800. Although the material is scanty and there is the possibility that the single year quoted for Gloucester or Maidstone or Worcester may be exceptional, a contrast with the rapidly developing towns of the Midlands and the north is noticeable. In some of the older

A lower ratio of persons per dwelling may be an indication of greater privacy, but not *necessarily* of more living space per family. Recent research has provided some evidence about the accommodation of working-class dwellings both before 1780 and between 1780 and 1820. For Liverpool Mr. Taylor has shown that eighteenth-century tenements sited in gardens or yards began as small one-storied thatched or lean-to buildings.[5] Presumably they had no more than one or two rooms. By the 1780s builders were erecting cellared, three, storied-brick back-to-backs of one room per floor.[6] We have seen that this became the normal type of back tenement in Liverpool. In Nottingham, the back-to-backs built from the 1780s with three rooms represented an advance on the one- and two-roomed cottages which had previously been a typical dwelling of of the lower classes.[7] In the case of Leeds, Professor Rimmer has shown that cottages in the older central districts in 1790 'occupied by working class families with four or five people usually had two rooms, a living-room with a sleeping-chamber above'.[8] According to the recent work of Professor Beresford, the new rows of back-to-backs being erected from the mid-1780s 'initially had only one ground-floor room and one bedroom above, the "one-up, one-down"'.[9] Presumably some also had cellars, though some of the cellars of these houses may have been in separate tenancy. The size of the rooms of these back-to-back tenements was roughly the same as that of the older cottages, about 14 feet square.

On balance, it is likely that the secular pressure on living accommodation did not worsen in the industrial towns, and that in some it improved slightly. This is not to deny that there were severe temporary shortages. Although there were occasional short-term difficulties in the supply of capital for building, on the whole it was adequate, coming from the resources of a multitude of more substantial townsmen. Inhabitants of working-class districts of the centres of the Industrial Revolution probably suffered deterioration in living conditions in many ways as towns expanded: worsening sanitation, increasing isolation from the countryside and open spaces, and in some cases increasing housing density and poorer house construction. Yet the accommodation of the houses

---

regional centres housing does not appear to have kept pace with population growth after the middle of the eighteenth century, despite the relatively modest demands placed on builders.

[5] Taylor, 'Court and Cellar Dwelling', p. 76.
[6] *Ibid.*, pp. 79–82.
[7] Chapman, 'Working-class Housing in Nottingham', pp. 137–9.
[8] Rimmer, 'Working Mens' Cottages', p. 179.
[9] Beresford, 'The Back-to-Back House in Leeds', p. 97.

themselves did not worsen. In some instances they may have improved by the beginning of the nineteenth century.

2 BUILDING AND THE URBAN ECONOMY

This study has also considered the amounts of money spent on individual building speculations, and the fluctuations that have occurred over time in the total volume of building. We also need to discuss what urban construction meant in terms of capital outlay. How did its size compare with other forms of regional investment, and what was its effect on prosperity within the town?

Between 40 and 50 per cent of the houses erected in England and Wales between 1750 and 1800, and again between 1801 and 1821, were in towns. On an average, urban building was rather more expensive than rural construction. Land was dearer and labour was more expensive in the biggest towns, while the average house may have been larger. Thus one may assume that about half, or perhaps a little more, of total national house-building investment was urban.

There is no way of estimating at all exactly total national expenditure on new housing. Miss Deane has suggested that by the beginning of the nineteenth century net capital formation 'may have reached about 7 per cent [of the national income]. . . . Whether this level was maintained during the period of war and its aftermath is doubtful. Certainly there is no reason to suppose that it was increased.'[10] With regard to the proportion of a nation's capital formation that is spent on housing, a growth economist has remarked that it 'varies according to the rate of growth of population. It is probably also particularly high in countries where a transfer of population from agriculture to industry is still taking place, since this requires a rapid expansion of the towns . . .. Probably the less developed countries need more than 25 per cent of their investment to be in housing if the towns into which their people will move as development gets under way are not to repeat one of the worst features of most industrial revolutions.'[11] Britain had some of the characteristics of a 'less developed' country at this time. Its rate of population growth was high, and the move from country to town was gaining speed. House-building was keeping up with national population growth. Thus one might assume that house construction absorbed about 25 or 30 per cent of capital formation. If Miss Deane's total estimate is approximately correct, then one might expect house-building

[10] Deane and Cole, *British Economic Growth*, pp. 262–3.
[11] W. A. Lewis, *The Theory of Economic Growth* (1955), pp. 210–11; this relates to residential building only, since Lewis groups public buildings, streets etc. in a different category.

to have absorbed between about 1½ and 2 per cent of the national income and urban housing alone about 1 per cent.

Capital formation in building during part of our period has been estimated by Professor Pollard.[12] He works back from house rentals in the 1820s and 1830s, and the result must be treated as approximate. He has suggested that by about 1815 residential building in Great Britain absorbed about seven-and-a-half million pounds annually, to which public buildings and amenities added about another million. Thus all building, including public construction and roads, etc., took between 2½ and 3 per cent of the national income. According to this estimate, all urban building comprised about 1½ per cent of the G.N.P. This compares with the other figure of about 1 per cent for housing alone.[13]

It is perhaps unwise to pursue further the question of macro-economic estimates, since they cannot be very exact. One needs also to consider the problem of capital formation in housing within the towns which have been the major subject of this book. In Nottingham 1,886 dwellings were added to the housing stock between 1779 and 1801. The average price in the case of 286 new houses for which evidence has been traced in these years was about £90 (including land); if these prices were representative the total capital formed would be just under £170,000. In fact this must be taken as a *minimum* figure, as the material is probably over-representative of artisan (and especially back-to-back) housing.[14] Nor does it take into account the unknown number of new houses which replaced demolished dwellings, or extensions to older property. Since building fluctuated violently in these twenty-two years, an average

[12] S. Pollard, 'The Growth and Distribution of Capital in Great Britain, c. 1770–1870', *3rd International Conference of Economic History, 1965* (Paris, 1968), p. 353.

[13] Miss Deane has also made an interesting attempt to suggest the proportion of the G.N.P. devoted to housing in the country as a whole, for the early nineteenth century. 'Between 1801 and 1811 the number of inhabited houses increased by an annual average of about 23,000 a year, between 1811 and 1821 by about 33,000 and between 1821 and 1831 by about 42,000. If we value the new houses at £100 each this represents an annual new investment rising form about 1 per cent of national income in the first decade to nearly 1·5 per cent in the 1820s' (P. Deane 'Capital Formation in Britain before the Railway Age', in F. Crouzet (ed.) *Capital Formation in the Industrial Revolution* (1972), p. 106. She admits that 'this is a token figure only'. It is based on an adaptation of a valuation by Colquhoun *circa* 1812 of *all* houses existing in Britain at £133 each, on the basis of an annual rental of £6.65 capitalized at twenty years purchase. While an average of £133 is admittedly too high for *all* houses, for which £100 seems a more reasonable figure, £100 is almost certainly too low for *new* dwellings. My own evidence, concerning provincial urban figures alone, cannot of course be used to estimate a national average, but I believe that such an average may have been at least as high as £150. Although the smallest new tenements in provincial towns cost only about £60–£80 after 1800, and country cottages as little as £40–£60, the *average* would have been pushed up strongly by the (relatively few) houses in the £500–£1,500 price range, which included some farmhouses as well as town houses, and, of course, the dwellings of intermediate value.

[14] Based on all the contemporary title deeds available to me: see a Note on Sources.

figure (about £7,700) is meaningless. Certainly the amount spent per annum at the beginning of the 1790s may have been two or three times this figure.

Secondly, in Portsea between 1801 and 1811, the stock of houses increased by 1,444 dwellings. Evidence has been traced for 113 new houses in these years with an average sale price of £148.[15] If these houses are roughly representative (and the range of house types was narrower here than elsewhere), the total annual average amount of capital formation in housing was about £21,000. The figure would have been higher around 1807–10, when more (and more expensive) houses were being built, and extensions and replacements would have added to it.

In aggregate, as one might expect, house-building investment compares well with capital formation in early factory industry. Dr. Chapman has estimated that between 1770 and 1795 £386,000 had been invested in cotton and worsted mills in the Midlands, especially in Nottinghamshire and Derbyshire; housing in Nottingham alone between 1779 and 1801 probably cost at a minimum nearly half this amount.[16] Transport investment was more sizeable than that in industry, and the amounts look more imposing, but even this does not overwhelm the capital investment in housing in the largest towns. Over 9,000 houses were added to Birmingham's stock between 1770 and 1800. If the average price of the new houses was only £100, then capital formation in housing in the town was nearly a million pounds. By comparison about fifteen-and-a-half million was invested in *all* canals between 1760 and 1820.[17]

If brickmaking is included, labour was a crucial cost element in house-building, and an important effect of a surge of house-building activity was the additional purchasing power it placed in the hands of building craftsmen and their labourers. This money would largely be spent in the local community, in shops, markets and public houses, and in the form of rent to local house-owners. In other words, the multiplier effects of investment in housing would be felt mainly in the town itself. Bricks were generally made from local clay, so that no payments for carriage would be made outside the town in this case. Only the purchase of timber represented a major loss to the wealth of the community, partly to the importing merchants and through them to the Scandinavian suppliers, and partly to the land or water carriers within the country.

It is true that no major industry was stimulated by house-building, as coalmining was by the growth of the domestic iron industry after the

---

[15] For the title deed evidence on which this was based, see Appendix VII.
[16] Chapman, 'Fixed Capital Formation', p. 247.
[17] See above, p. 159, for canal investment.

mid-1780s, or as the iron industry was to be in the mid-nineteenth century by railway-building. Like the cotton industry of the late eighteenth century, house-building lacked any major 'backward-linkage' effect of this kind. On the other hand, house-building brought in its train a demand for a whole range of products. Apart from bricks, building created a demand for several minor materials. Iron was used for railings, fanlights, in rings, locks and bolts, nails and, at the end of the period, in balconies and verandahs. The output of glass (excluding bottles) charged with duty nearly trebled between about 1750 and the early 1800s. The output of 'stained' paper (i.e. wallpaper) which paid duty at least doubled between the early 1750s and the mid-1780s. More houses meant an increased demand for certain consumer durables, especially all types of house furniture, which brought more work to the joiners and cabinetmakers. Housing also creates a need for a range of urban amenities. While they were much fewer than today, some were basic even in the eighteenth century. The costs of roadmaking and drainage have been discussed. Among public construction, the building of docks, quays and corn exchanges were more a response to the growth of local business prosperity than to additional housing, and in the present connection churches were most important. In Birmingham between the 1740s and the 1790s, three Anglican churches were built, each costing several thousand pounds, the parish church was altered, and another church was converted from a house: at least half-a-dozen new Dissenting church buildings were erected.[18] There was also occasional expenditure on additions to the workhouse, market building, the theatre, dispensary, hospital and school buildings. But altogether such expenditure on amenities cannot have been more than about 10 or 20 per cent (at the most) of expenditure on housing. Taking one year with another, one would expect the wages paid out in house-building, and brick, glass and ironmaking, related consumer durables, periodic public buildings and road construction to make a useful if not outstanding contribution to the demand for urban goods and services. It was not a 'leading sector' in Rostow's terms, but then no industry or sector of the economy was.[19]

It is of course still possible that house-building expenditure was particularly significant when local industry or trade was at a relatively low ebb. Thus the wages earned by craftsmen and labourers helped to create local purchasing power in Birmingham in 1773, when Boulton referred to the trade of the town as 'dead', or during 1811–12, when the American trade was interrupted. We have seen that contemporaries

18 *V.C.H. Warks.*, VII, pp. 361–417.
19 I am grateful to Professor R. S. Neale for his suggestions on the discussion in this paragraph.

noted that building investment kept some men employed in Liverpool in the distress of 1811–12. At least in some industrial towns, such as Birmingham, Sheffield and Nottingham, the commercial crisis of 1793 must have been cushioned slightly by the building investment lag, since construction took two or three years to die away.

Building sometimes provided a useful outlet for capital when trade was depressed, as in the case of London in the mid-1770s and 1811–12. More generally, the absence of large investment in transport, enclosure or industry about 1817–19 may have helped the flow of funds into building.

But much more often than not, house construction coincided with business prosperity. It sometimes contributed to the 'overheating' of the economy by reaching its peak at the same time as other investment. The over-extension of credit in building in 1791 and 1792, simultaneously with heavy financial outlays in industry and canal development, contributed to the breakdown of the credit mechanism, and hence general business collapse in 1793. Building in the mid-1770s may also have overstrained some urban economies, thus contributing to depression at the end of the 1770s, though evidence is not clear on this point. Similarly, some building slumps coincided with commercial stagnation. Depression in some years about 1780, or about 1815–16 added to poverty when trade was also weak.

It is difficult to point to any time in which building may be said to have 'led' general economic revival, either nationally or locally. In view of its narrow effect on purchasing power and its minimal direct influence on other industries by its demand for materials, this is understandable. In 1764 the immediate post-war building boom in London may be said to have accompanied the general prosperity, but not to have preceded it, and still less to have caused it. The high rate of building activity in the later 1780s in London followed the general commercial revival of the mid-1780s, since exports had recovered as early as 1783 and imports in 1783–4. In Manchester building growth followed the surges in imports of raw cotton from 1782 and again from 1798. In fact, it was often usual for construction to follow a revival of trade, because commercial depression encouraged the sharing of existing accommodation and reduced the effect of two of the most important immediate causes of housebuilding, immigration and the marriage rate. A revival of construction was more likely to follow the recovery of trade or industry, which naturally put pressure on existing house room.

No systematic study has been made of the work of land-promoters, building owners or the craftsmen who actually erected the houses in

English provincial towns later in the nineteenth century. It is likely that the characteristics of investment in building remained much the same. The combination of land-promotion with construction by the same firm of builders is a comparatively recent phenomenon. Typically, building on a suburban estate involved numerous builders, each supplying a small block or row of courtyard tenements or back-to-backs, or two or three more substantial dwellings.

By 1820, the colossal growth of the largest English provincial towns was only just beginning. By twentieth-century standards they were tiny. The circumference of Manchester and Salford, with Liverpool the biggest of the provincial towns, was between 4 and 6 miles. Its bounds could have been walked briskly in an hour or an hour and a half. Yet one must not for this reason belittle the achievement of the Georgian builders in the provincial towns. Both in financial and physical terms it was impressive.

The achievement in terms of capital formation has already been stressed. In the other aspect, the physical core of what were to be the major cities of Victorian and twentieth-century England had been created. The largely residential streets of the Georgian town became the central business districts of the later cities, five or ten times their size. A few of the dwellings were demolished later in the century to make way for railway termini, others for shops, warehouses or factories, but the majority of houses erected in our period provided homes for at least a hundred years. Some of the smallest were condemned as jerry-built as early as the 1840s. Some tenements erected in Nottingham in the later eighteenth century were described as weakly founded and very slightly timbered, mostly built without bond timber; the roofs were 'very slight' and the floor joists so far apart that the plaster floors laid on them often broke.[20] Others were more substantially built. In Birmingham, a sizeable development of about ninety houses built on land belonging to the Lench Charity Trust after 1752 was described in the 1920s as mostly still standing 'in a state of good repair and occupied by respectable tenants, and likely to stand for another thirty or forty years'.[21] Nearly all the small dwellings, and except in Bath the majority of the big houses, have disappeared in the twentieth century. The street plans of the centres of our principal provincial cities survive as the chief memorial to the work of the Georgian land-promoters and builders.

[20] *B.P.P.*, 1844, xvii, *First Report of the Commissioners for Inquiring into the State of Large Towns*, p. 67.
[21] Chalklin, 'Housing Estates', p. 83.

Appendices

APPENDIX I: THE URBAN POPULATION IN 1801

Clearly the proportion of the total population living in towns was higher in 1800 than it had been in 1700, but a reasonably accurate percentage would be impossible to establish, even approximately, without exhaustive research. The reason is that the basic population unit in the 1801 census is the parish (or, in the case of some northern counties, the township), and that most smaller towns and some bigger centres lay in parishes of varying size, and the rural inhabitants are not distinguished from those living in the town. A knowledge of the local history of the individual towns and parishes enables one to make a rough estimate in some cases, but to attempt to collect this information town by town for the whole country would be a monumental task. An attempt was once made by T. A. Welton to estimate the percentage of town-dwellers in 1801, but as it ignored the boundary problem, it cannot be accepted in its existing form even as a rough guide to the proportion of urban inhabitants in England as a whole.[1] However, it provides some useful indications of regional differences, particularly when some modifications are made. Welton's conclusions, worked out on a regional and county basis, were as follows:

Region	Percentage of urban inhabitants
Cumberland and Westmorland	33
Durham and Northumberland	37
North and East Ridings	31
West Riding	32
Lancashire and Cheshire	45
Lincs., Notts., Rutland, Leics, Derbyshire	23
Staffs., Warks., Worcs.	43
Wales, Salop. Herefordshire, Mon.	17
Gloucs., Somerset, Dorset, Devon, Cornwall	29
Wilts., Hants., west Berks., part Sussex	27
Metropolitan circle (London, Middlesex, Surrey, Kent, Essex, Herts., part Beds., part Bucks., part Oxon., east Berks., part Sussex)	57
Northants., Hunts., part Beds., part Bucks., part Oxon.	19
Norfolk, Suffolk, Cambs.	23
All England and Wales	36

[1] T. A. Welton, 'On the Distribution of Population in England and Wales, and its Progress ... from 1801 to 1891', *J. Royal Statist. Soc.*, LXIII (1900), pp. 527–89.

Very simply, though recognizing that there were towns with less than 1,000 inhabitants, and that census units with more than 1,000 people often had a rural element even though they might be described as towns, Welton included as towns the units in the census described as 'towns' or 'townships' with more than 1,000 people. But this excluded units described as 'parishes', some of which had a partly urban content, and both 'parishes' and 'townships' or 'towns' with an urban sector in units with *under* 1,000 people. On the other hand, in the north and part of the Midlands the 'township' was the standard census unit, and townships of over 1,000 people were occasionally purely rural areas. More important in its bearing on the final regional percentages is the rural element, often considerable, in only partly urban 'towns' and 'townships' with a population of over 1,000. In the north, the net effect was to exaggerate the proportion of town-dwellers, and the urban percentage in Welton's first three regions is probably at least 5 or 6 per cent higher than it should be. Thus an analysis of the 1801 census for Cumberland and Westmorland which takes account of some rural inhabitants of a township such as Kirby Stephen (3,522 acres) or a 'town' such as Kirby Lonsdale or Kendal, would reduce the total percentage for the two counties to under 30 per cent, despite the presence of two large towns, Carlisle (10,221), and Whitehaven (10,628) in a total population of 158,847. In the densely populated West Riding and southern Lancashire, there were numerous densely inhabited rural townships with more than a thousand people, and in these regions again the urban content is over-estimated by a few per cent; the same applies to a lesser extent to the three counties making up the Black Country. In central England, Welton's percentages are probably nearer the correct figure, since the rural population in 'towns' was to some extent balanced by the description of some partly urban geographical units as 'parishes', which Welton ignored: thus in Buckinghamshire, Amersham and Marlow, and in Northamptonshire, Kettering and Oundle, are 'parishes'. But in the south-west, in counties such as Dorset and Cornwall, some of the 'towns' again had a strongly rural element which exaggerated the total urban percentage slightly. Altogether it would be safe to say that Welton's figure for the whole country (36 per cent) over-estimates the national proportion by several per cent, and that the correct figure was between about 28 and 33 per cent. This implies an increase of between 6 and 10 per cent since 1700.

Despite my comments on Welton's figures, this final suggestion may seem low, but it should be remembered that the growth of London had been no faster than the national increase since about 1700 (and London provided about one-tenth of the total figure), and that in the agricultural areas there had been little change in the ratio between town and country: thus the increase was almost all supplied by the industrial regions.

If it is difficult to arrive at an approximate figure for the percentage of town-dwellers among the total population in 1801, even more acute boundary problems and the absence of a similar study by Welton make a calculation almost impossible in 1821, even allowing for a broad margin of error. But if account is taken of the fact that the population of London (*c.* 900,000 in 1801, *c.* 1,274,000 in 1821) grew only slightly faster than the total population of England and Wales, and that in the agricultural areas urban growth remained roughly in proportion to the total increase, it is unlikely that the urban percentage grew by more than 4 or 5 per cent.

Welton's figures are valuable for regional comparisons, if used cautiously. Particularly interesting is the high urban proportion among the inhabitants of the northern regions, even when allowance is made for his over-estimates. This owes much to the presence of relatively few large towns which were either industrial centres or ports based principally on the service of an industrial hinterland; most of them had grown rapidly during the previous half-century. In Cumberland, the coal ports of Whitehaven, Workington and Maryport contributed at least 10 per cent of the total population of Cumberland and Westmorland.[2] In Northumberland and Durham, Newcastle, and its suburb of Gateshead, and Sunderland contributed almost one-sixth of the inhabitants. Hull accommodated almost one-tenth of the population of the North and East Ridings. Liverpool and Manchester comprised about 20 per cent of the combined population of Lancashire and Cheshire. In comparison with that for Lancashire and Cheshire, or even with that for the other Ridings, the figure for the West Riding is rather less than one might expect, because apart from Leeds and Sheffield, which accommodated together about $12\frac{1}{2}$ per cent of the population of 563,953, there was no other town with more than 10,000 inhabitants; this was the result partly of the fact that the West Riding 'was still for the most part a county of industrialized villages',[3] since woollen manufacture remained based largely on the outwork system, and partly of the geographical accident that the ports which handled the trade of the Riding, notably Hull and Liverpool, lay outside its borders. In the Midlands, the figure for the counties of the Black Country reflects in particular the size of Birmingham; the relatively low figure for the east Midlands that agricultural Lincolnshire is combined with Nottinghamshire, Leicestershire and

---

[2] The population of Maryport ('Cannonby township') was 2,932, and that of Workington 5,716, but the latter may have contained a rural element.
[3] Deane and Cole, *British Economic Growth*, p. 120.

Appendix I

Derbyshire; in industrial Nottinghamshire in particular, where Nottingham alone comprised 20 per cent of the population, the percentage was markedly higher than the average of the five counties. On the rest of the country there is less to say. In the south-west, although Dorset and Cornwall lacked a town of more than 5,000 people, the average for the five counties was raised by the inclusion of Bristol, Bath and Plymouth. The relatively low figures for East Anglia reflects the failure of the towns to grow faster than the rural population in the later eighteenth century, either in the worsted or the agricultural area. Finally, the south-east Midlands lacked any large town in what was basically an agricultural area, and the same applies to the border counties and to Wales, where Shrewsbury, with 14,739 inhabitants, was by far the largest centre. The major provincial towns remained small in comparison with London and even with the rural populations of their regions, but their size was beginning to have a perceptible effect on the proportion of town-dwellers within their counties. Comparable figures are not available for 1821, but the first two decades of the nineteenth century strengthened the tendencies visible in 1801, with an increasing urban element in the population of parts of the Midlands and the north, and with the town: country ratio much the same as in the early eighteenth century in most of the rest of the country.

APPENDIX II: POPULATION GROWTH OF MARKET TOWNS AND SEAPORTS IN PREDOMINANTLY AGRICULTURAL AREAS[1]

Lincolnshire: number of families:[2]

	1705	1801	Increase greater or less than that of county (+ or −) 1705–1801	1821	Increase greater or less than that of county (+ or −) 1801–21
Boston	650	1,334	+	2,404	+
Bourn	300	334	−	460	−
Market Deeping	140	183	−	204	−
Grantham	450	617	+	881	+
Holbech	400	574	+	715	−
Horncastle	c.220	406	+	665	+
Lincoln	735	1,619	+	2,166	−
Louth	400	934	+	1,287	−
Market Rasen	120	182	+	266	+
Sleaford	250	332	−	463	+
Spalding	500	779	+	1,125	+
Stamford	470	1,075	+	1,038	−
County total	31,900	42,629		58,760	

[1] Based on *parishes*, and excludes towns with probably less than 400 people c. 1670.

[2] R. E. G. Cole (ed.), *Speculum Dioeceseos Lincolniensis*, Lincoln Record Society IV (Lincoln, 1913): Gainsborough is omitted because the figure for 1705 (2,000 families) is clearly inaccurate; as the 1705 census is a return of families I have used the number of families in 1801 and 1821 for comparison.

Bedfordshire: number of persons:[3]

	1670[4]	1801	Increase greater or less than that of county (+ or —) 1670–1801	1821	Increase greater or less than that of county (+ or —) 1801–21
Bedford	2,204	3,948	+	5,466	+
Dunstable	704	1,296	+	1,831	+
Leighton Buzzard	1,153	1,963	+	2,749	+
Luton	2,055	3,095	—	4,529	+
Potton	906	1,103	—	1,498	+
County total	38,166	63,393		83,716	

[3] Using King's ratios, I have multiplied urban households by 4·4 and rural households by 4 (D. V. Glass, 'Two Papers on Gregory King' in D.V. Glass and D. E. C. Eversley (eds.), *Population in History* (1965). pp. 198–9); there is a case for using a higher multiplier for households in large towns, but as these towns were mostly small, and there is a strong case for being consistent in a single table in whatever multiplier is chosen, I have used these ratios throughout.

[4] L. M. Marshall (ed.), 'The Rural Population of Bedfordshire', *Publications of the Bedfordshire Historical Record Society*, XVI (1934)

Dorset: number of persons:[3]

	1662–64[5]	1801	Increase greater or less than that of county (+ or —) 1670–1801	1821	Increase greater or less than that of county (+ or —) 1801–21
Beaminster	977	2,140	+	2,806	+
Blandford	805	2,326	+	2,643	—
Bridport	1,610	3,117	—	3,742	—
Cerne Abbas	735	847	—	1,060	—
Dorchester	2,323	2,402	—	2,743	—
Lyme Regis	1,637	1,451	—	2,269	+
Melcombe Regis	887	2,350	+	4,252	+
Poole	1,650	4,761	+	6,390	+
Shaftesbury	1,346	2,433	+	2,903	—
Sherborne	1,866	3,159	+	3,622	—
Sturminster	1,143	1,406	—	1,612	—
Wareham	1,025	1,627	+	1,931	—
Weymouth	791	1,267	+	2,370	+
County total	70,053	114,452		144,499	

[5] C. A. F. Meekings (ed.), *Dorset Hearth Tax Assessments, 1662–1664*, Dorset Natural Historical and Archaeological Society (Dorchester, 1951).

Pembrokeshire: number of persons:[3]

	1670[6]	1801	Increase greater or less than that of county (+ or —) 1670–1801	1821	Increase greater or less than that of county (+ or —) 1801–21
Haverfordwest	1,980	2,954	—	4,145	+
Tenby	766	984	—	1,554	+
Pembroke	1,113	1,832	—	3,904[7]	+
Fishguard	—	1,503	+	1,837	—
County total	6,691	56,280		74,009	

[6] 'Pembrokeshire Hearths in 1670', *West Wales Historical Records*, XI (1926).
[7] The great increase was attributed to the presence of the dockyard.

APPENDIX III: SOME EIGHTEENTH-CENTURY TITLE DEEDS

The following calendars of title deeds from three typical deed bundles have been chosen to illustrate the information which may be derived from this source.

I HOUSE IN CUMBERLAND STREET, PORTSEA, BUILT 1747–8

29 and 30 October 1747:

sale by Richard Davies of Portsea, scavelman to William Sprake, late of Gosport, now of Portsea, mariner, for £7 17s. 6d.

> plot measuring 15 feet from east to west and 83½ feet from north to south, leaving 15 feet vacant at the north end for a road; bounding west to land sold by Davies to James Gudge, east to other land of Davies, south to the land of Henry Friend and north to the land of Sanuel White; being part of the land bought by Davies from Richard Ridge of Kilmiston, Esq., son of Thomas Ridge of Portsmouth, Esq., late occupied by Nicholas Bettesworth, on 1 and 2 June 1747.

12 July 1748:

mortgage from Sprake to John Robinson of Portsea, gentleman, for £130

> messuage erected by Sprake on the plot; bounding east to land sold by Davies to George Horwood on which he has erected a house, west to land of Gudge on which he has built a house, south to the land of Friend and north to the land of White.

22 March 1749:

assignment of mortgage from John Robinson to William Robinson of Portsea, apothecary, in trust for John Robinson.

23 and 24 March 1749:

sale by Sprake to John Robinson for £150 (deducting the money owing on mortgage).

Portsmouth R.O. D1806

2 HOUSES IN SPARLING STREET, LIVERPOOL, BUILT *c.*1775

30 March 1776:

sale of leasehold interest by Edward Mason and Cornelius Bourne, timber merchants, to John Webster, slater and plasterer, all of Liverpool, for £63

> plot measuring 10 yards fronting Sparling Street by 20 yards 16 inches; bounding east to land of John Sparling and William Bolden, west to other land of Mason and Bourne, north-west to Sparling Street and south-east to a ropeway; with four houses built by Webster;

(reciting 1 February 1773:

lease for three lives and 21 years from the Corporation of Liverpool to Mason and Bourne

> parcel of unbuilt land measuring 51½ yards fronting Sparling Street by 20 yards; bounding on both sides to land of Sparling and Bolden and back on a ropery of Mason and Bourne (lot no.1 in plan on original lease;
> parcel of do. measuring 51½ yards fronting do. by 17 yards; bounding on one side to Sparling's land and on the other to a street called Wapping, and backing on the ropery (lot no.2)
> parcel of do. measuring 51 yards fronting do. by 24 yards 1 foot; adjoining other land of Sparling and Bolden and backing on the close of Mary Pownall, widow (lot no.3)
> parcel of do. measuring 51 yards fronting do. by 23 yards; adjoining the land of Sparling and Bolden and backing on Mary Pownall's close (lot no.4))

10 April 1776:

mortgage for £100 from Webster to William Mather of Liverpool, yeoman

28 September 1776:

sale of leasehold interest by Webster to David Whitby of Liverpool, bread baker, for £300 (deducting £100 to discharge the mortgage)

> the four houses on the plot

Liverpool R.O.: deeds 886C

3 HOUSES NEAR DEANSGATE, MANCHESTER, BUILT 1788–89

7 and 8 May 1788:

conveyance in perpetuity from Benjamin Sothern of Worsley, Lancs. yeoman to John Horrocks of Manchester, blackball maker and his trustee, James Wild of Manchester, gentleman, for £7 a year

> plot on the east side of Alport Lane [Deansgate], measuring 37 yards from north to south, 10 yards on the east and 12 yards 29 inches on the west, of which 3 yards on the north side is to be added to the street; comprising 421 square yards; bounded on the north by a way to a garden etc., of John Ratchford intended for a 12 yards street, south to lands and buildings of Nathaniel Street, west to a 6 yards street, and east to Alport Lane; and messuages lately built by Horrocks, with use of a well and pump of Sothern

covenants: to build one or more dwelling houses of brick, stone and lime mortar, to cover with slate or tiles and keep in repair, of the clear yearly value of £14, and of the height and description specified to leave a 4 foot passage through the land to Street's land to flag 1 yard wide along the north side of the plot and pave 2 yards into the street from the flagging, to pave half of the 6 yard street and half of Alport Lane

(reciting 28 and 29 September 1786:

conveyance in perpetuiry from John Dickenson of Taxall, Cheshire and Charles White of Manchester, Esqs., trustees for Sir John Parker Mosley of Ancoats Lane and his first son Oswald, Esq., to Thomas Richardson of Manchester, joiner, Sothern, and Richard Tonge of Worsley, carpenter

> parcel of Mosley's land on the west side of Alport Lane, measuring 33 yards 16 inches on the north side, 33 yards on the south side, and 68 yards on the east and west; bounding north on the way to Ratchford's land, east and west to 6 yard streets, and south by a 12 yard street; parcel of do. measuring 37 yards from east to west by 71 yards; bounded north to the way, south to the 12 yard street, west to the 6 yard street on the east of the first parcel, and east to Alport Lane

and reciting 21 and 22 March 1788:
conveyance from Richardson and Tonge to Sothern of their third shares, with other property)

24 July 1789:
mortgage from Horrocks to William Royle of Barlow, Lancs., yeoman, for £400 at 5 per cent

> 421 yard plot as in 7 and 8 May 1788, and five messuages lately built, occupied by Chell, Alderson, Doughty, Pixton, and Wright

10 February 1804:
assignment of mortgage for £400 from Charles Poole of Altrincham, surgeon, and Thomas Royle of Broughton, Lancs., yeoman, executors of William Royle, and John Priestner of Manchester, blackball maker, devisee of Horrocks, to Thomas Twiss of Manchester, shopkeeper

> the same plot and five houses

3 July 1817:
assignment of mortgage for £400 at 5 per cent from John Booth of Manchester, grocer and his wife Elizabeth, daughter and administratrix of Twiss, and John Priestner, to John Brown of Salford, innkeeper

22 February 1827:
additional mortgage for £100 at 5 per cent
John Horrocks Priestner, first son and heir of John Priestner to Brown

> the same plot and five houses

Manchester Town Hall: deeds L2

APPENDIX IV: ASPECTS OF BUILDING COSTS, c. 1780–1820

1 BUILDING COSTS IN STOCKPORT IN 1792 AND 1806 (hypothetical cases)

(a) *Price of a rod of brickwork in which a rod equals 272 square feet of wall 1½ bricks thick:*

Input	Cost in 1792	Cost in 1806
4,500 bricks	11s. per M. = £2 9s. 6d.	35s. per M. = £7 17s. 6d.
30 bushels lime	6d. a bushel = 15s.	6d. a bushel = 15s.
2 cartloads sand	6d. a load = 1s.	1s. a load = 2s.
1 man to mix mortar	for a day = 1s. 2d.	for ¾ day at 2s. = 1s. 6d.
5 days bricklaying	1s. 8d. a day = 8s. 4d.	3s. a day = 15s.
5 days labouring	1s. 2d. a day = 5s. 10d.	2s. a day = 10s.
	£4 0s. 10d.	£10 1s. 0d.

(b) *Price of a square of roofing*

Input	Cost in 1792		Cost in 1806	
13 feet of timber	1s. 8d. per foot = £1	1s. 8d.	3s. per foot = £1	19s. 4d.
8 feet of board	2¼d. per foot =	1s. 6d.	5d. per foot =	3s. 6d.
100 feet of sawing	at 2s. 6d. =	2s. 6d.	at 3s. 6d. =	3s. 6d.
24 holdfasts	½d. each =	1s. 0d.		
nails	=	1s. 7d.	=	1s. 6d.
labour	=	3s. 0d.	=	6s. 0d.
		£1 10s. 3d.		£2 13s. 4d.

(c) *Price of a square of flooring:*

in 1792	in 1806
£2 12s. 2¾d.	£4 4s. 4d.

Sources: J. Wood, *A Series of Plans for Cottages or Habitations of Labourers* (1792), pp. 11–15, and *Ibid.*, (1806), pp. 11–13. These were hypothetical cases, chosen to illustrate the pattern of costs in areas distant from London, where they were cheaper than in the capital.

2 PRICES OF MEMEL FIR, PER LOAD

Note The prices quoted in the left hand column are for various months in the year, arranged chronologically; where the price varied in a month the left hand column is the lowest price, and the right hand the highest.

Year	Price excluding Duty £ s.	£ s.	Duty £ s. d.
1782	3 5 3 10		4 1
1783	3 10 1 12		4 1
1784	1 15 2 10		4 1
1785	1 15 2 5 1 13		4 1
1786	1 17 2 0 1 15		4 1
1787	1 12 1 5	1 10	6 8
1788	1 15 1 11	1 14 1 8	6 8
1789	1 7 1 11	1 8	6 8
1790	1 10 2 0	1 15 2 5	6 8

Year	Price excluding duty £ s.	£ s.	Duty £ s. d.
1802	3 12 3 4	3 14 3 3	16 4
1803	3 10 5 5 3 15	3 15 6 5 4 5	16 4
1804	3 15 3 0	4 0 3 5	1 0 0 1 5 0
1805	3 0 3 15 3 10	3 5 4 0 3 15	1 5 0 1 5 6
1806	3 10 6 8	3 15 6 13	1 5 6 1 7 4
1807	8 0 4 0 6 10	8 10 5 0 6 15	1 7 4
1808	6 10 15 10	7 0 17 0	1 7 4
1809	14 0 11 0	14 10 11 10	1 7 4
1810	10 10 8 10 11 10	11 0 9 10	1 7 4

Year	Prices		Year	Prices		Avg.
1791	2 2 / 3 0 / 2 11	3 2 / 2	6 8	1811	11 0 / 10 0 / 11 0	12 10 / 11 10 / 12 10	0	1 7 4
1792	2 8 / 2 13 / 2 0		6 8	1812	9 10 / 8 10	10 0 / 10 9	0	2 14 8
1793	2 8 / 2 3	2 9	6 8	1813	7 10 / 5 10 / 8 0	8 0 / 7 0 / 9 0	0	3 4 11
1794	2 16 / 2 5 / 2 18		6 8	1814	7 5 / 4 10	7 15 / 5 10	0	3 4 11
1795	2 15 / 4 0	3 0	6 8	1815	5 0 / 3 5	5 10 / 3 15	0	3 4 11
1796	3 2 / 2 10	2 15	6 8	1816	3 5 / 2 5	3 15 / 3 5	0	3 4 11
1797	2 15 / 3 5	3 10	10 0	1817	3 5 / 2 10 / 3 5	3 15 / 2 15	0	3 4 11
1798	2 10 / 3 3	3 0 / 3 5	10 0	1818	3 5 / 3 10	3 10 / 3 15	0	3 4 11
1799	3 8 / 4 18	3 10 / 5 0	10 0	1819	3 10 / 2 5	3 15 / 2 15	0	3 5 0
1800	5 10 / 5 15	5 15 / 6 0	10 0	1820	2 15 / 2 10 / 2 15	3 0 / 2 15	0	3 5 0
1801	5 15 / 4 5	6 0 / 4 10	10 0					

Source: T. Tooke *Thoughts and Details of the High and Low Prices of the Thirty Years, from 1793 to 1822* (1824), Appendix to Part IV, pp. 66–8

APPENDIX V: MORTGAGE CAPITAL

1 AMOUNTS OF THE MORTGAGES: (see notes on *Sources*, p. 335)

Period	Number of mortgages worth:					Percentage of undertakings mortgaged within 2 years of site conveyance
	under £150	£151–300	£301–500	£501–1,000	over £1,000	
(a) *Birmingham*						
1746–80	32	30	17	12	1	35
1781–1800	34	28	14	3	1	32
1801–20	5	6	5	1	0	29
(b) *Nottingham*						
1751–80	7	8	12	3	1	29
1781–1800	8	22	17	15	7	52
1801–20	6	17	15	9	0	36
(c) *Liverpool*						
1746–80	27	10	3	2	0	46
1781–1800	17	18	11	9	5	48
1801–1820	2	41	40	19	7	53
(d) *Bath*						
1736–80	6	6	12	8	2	61
1781–1820	0	2	6	14	7	60
(e) *Manchester*						
1781–1800	21	20	11	11	4	27
1801–20	4	19	10	2	2	27
(f) *Portsea*						
1736–70	25	13	1	1	0	26
1771–1800	46	19	3	9	0	26
1801–20	60	52	10	6	2	23

2 THE OCCUPATIONS OF THE MORTGAGEES:

(a) *Birmingham—number of mortgagees from:*

Period	Building trades	Metal industries	Other crafts & trades	Professions & leisured class (male)	Women	Building or loan society	Total
1701–45	1	9	8	3	8	0	29
1746–80	2	17	26	26	25	0	96
1780–1800	1	13	24	20	17	5	80
1801	1	7	5	5	1	0	19

(b) *Nottingham—number of mortgagees from:*

Period	Building trades	Textile industries	Other crafts & trades	Professions & leisured class (male)	Women	Loan society	Total
1751–80	1	2	11	17	3	0	33
1781–1800	0	7	19	35	13	0	74
1801–20	4	5	21	15	13	0	53

(c) *Liverpool—number of mortgagees from:*

Period	Building trades	Maritime & shipbuilding occupations	Other crafts & trades	Professions & leisured class (male)	Women	Loan society	Total
1746–80	1	3	8	18	10	1	41
1781–1800	0	7	15	25	15	0	62
1801–20	10	4	35	58	13	1	121

(d) *Bath—number of mortgagees from:*

Period	Building trades	Other crafts & trades	Professions & leisured class (male)	Women	Total
1736–80	1	16	12	6	35
1781–1820	1	7	16	7	31

(e) *Manchester—number of mortgagees from:*

Period	Building trades	Textile industries	Other crafts & trades	Professions & leisured class (male)	Women (widows & spinsters)	Loan society	Total
1781–1800	0	7	20	25	11	1	64
1801–20	0	5	16	11	5	4	41

(f) *Portsea—number of mortgagees from:*

Period	Building trades	Dockyard and naval occupations	Other trades & crafts	Professions & leisured class (male)	Women (widows & spinsters)	Loan society	Total
1736–70	5	15	13	9	4	0	46
1770–1800	4	20	24	25	3	0	76
1801–20	9	21	39	27	14	2	112

Sources for Appendix V:

1 These tables are based on the deed evidence examined by me, which does not necessarily represent a random sample and should be taken as a rough guide only to the sizes of mortgages and the types of people who supplied them. In particular the percentages of undertakings found to have relied on a mortgage are merely intended to show that many more builders relied on their own capital in the industrial towns than in Liverpool and Bath.

2 The mortgages are derived from the typical bundles of deeds or abstracts of title which begin with the sale or lease of the site and then record each conveyance of the houses, including mortgages, where made (see Appendix III). They comprise those granted to builders within two years of the conveyance of the site, and mortgages replacing them which were made within 10 years of such conveyance. Since most of the first mortgages granted on a property were made within the first or second year after the conveyance of the site, it suggests that nearly all those granted within the first two years were building mortgages, being either (a) to provide money to complete the project (which is stated as the reason in some mortgages), or (b) to pay off short-term loans from suppliers of materials or other persons, or (c) to provide money for a new speculation. The periods are those of the site conveyances, not of the mortgages. For the following reasons the percentages probably understate the proportion of geared undertakings: (a) while bundles of title deeds normally keep all mortgages, despite later cancellation, a few may be missing; (b) not all sites were built on within the first two years. On the other hand, a few of the mortgages raised within two years of the site conveyance may have been for a purpose unconnected with building.

3 One does not know to what extent (if at all) builders borrowed indefinitely just on the security of a bond or promise to pay: cotton manu-facturers did so (Edwards, *Cotton Trade*, p. 256); among the debts of a Southampton slater and builder in 1810 was £126 10s. lent in 1805 on a promissory note: Southampton R.O. D/PM 14/4/47; in what was probably an unusual case a Bath widow lent increasingly large sums to a local builder between 1805 and 1819, apparently without mortgage security for at least part of the time: P.R.O. E112/1954/1176.

APPENDIX VI: HOUSES, FAMILIES AND POPULATION IN THE LATE EIGHTEENTH AND EARLY NINETEENTH CENTURIES

I POPULATION, FAMILIES AND HOUSES IN 1801, 1811 AND 1821

Manchester

1801

	Inhabited houses	Families	Uninhabited houses	House building	Persons
Manchester	10,343	15,617	251	(not given)	70,409
Salford	2,204	2,943	28	,,	13,611
Ardwick	318	348	4	,,	1,762
Chorlton Row	111	123	2	,,	675
Hulme	285	381	2	,,	1,677
	13,261	19,412	287		88,134

1811

	Inhabited houses	Families	Uninhabited houses	House building	Persons
Manchester	12,929	16,913	615	57	79,459
Salford	3,424	4,107	277	17	19,114
Ardwick	467	555	27	17	2,763
Chorlton Row	495	534	20	8	2,581
Hulme	555	665	41	1	3,081
	17,870	22,774	980	100	106,998

1821

	Inhabited houses	Families	Uninhabited houses	House building	Persons
Manchester	16,653	22,869	604	116	108,016
Salford	4,503	5,449	267	48	25,772
Ardwick	617	735	32	7	3,545
Chorlton Row	1,630	1,683	106	110	8,209
Hulme	749	890	53	21	4,234
	24,152	31,626	1,062	302	149,776

Nottingham

	Inhabited houses	Families	Uninhabited houses	House building	Persons
1801	4,977	6,707	100	(not given)	28,861
1811	6,514	7,230	287	41	34,253
1821	7,375	8,752	270	68	40,415

Appendix VI

Liverpool
1801

Liverpool	11,446	16,989	338	(not given)	77,653
do.: seamen in port					6,000
Toxteth Park	323	413	29	,,	2,069
West Derby	445	485	18	,,	2,636
Everton	87	91	2	,,	499
Kirkdale	73	78	6	,,	393
	12,374	18,056	393		89,250

1811

Liverpool	15,589	20,552	418	155	94,376
do.: seamen in port					7,000
Toxteth Park	1,192	1,192	48	40	5,864
West Derby	690	728	20	14	3,696
Everton	140	140	8	19	913
Kirkdale	120	129	3	0	665
	17,731	22,741	497	228	112,514

1821

Liverpool	19,007	25,309	1,140	192	118,972
do.: seamen in port					9,000
Toxteth Park	2,224	2,580	121	46	12,828
West Derby	1,100	1,148	69	36	6,304
Everton	320	332	11	21	2,109
Kirkdale	149	163	7	1	1,273
	22,800	29,532	1,348	296	150,486

Hull (with Sculcoates)

1801	4,285	7,027	97	(not given)	27,609
1811	5,914	8,087	398	16	32,944
1821	7,005	9,562	417	76	39,040

Portsmouth
1801

Portsmouth	1,130	1,640	4	(not given)	7,839
Portsea	4,393	5,524	26	,,	25,387
	5,523	7,164	30	,,	33,226

1811

Porstmouth	1,084	1,711	13	6	7,103
Portsea	5,768	7,823	95	148	33,464
	6,852	9,534	108	154	40,567

1821

Portsmouth	1,100	1,784	96	0	7,269
Portsea	7,527	8,676	532	17	38,379
	8,627	10,460	628	17	45,648

2 AVERAGE NUMBER OF PERSONS PER HOUSE

(a) *The manufacturing towns*

Date	Population	Total no. of houses	Persons per house	No. of occupied houses	Persons per occupied house
Birmingham					
1751	23,688	4,170	5·7	4,058	5·8
1770	30,804	6,025[1]	5·1		
1778	48,252	8,042[1]	6·0		
1781	50,295	8,382[1]	6·0		
1791	73,653	12,681	5·8		
1801	69,384	15,650	4·4	13,800	5·0
1811	81,253	16,096	5·0	15,837	5·1
1821	85,416[2]	18,483	4·6	17,323	5·0
Leeds					
1771	16,380	3,345	4·9	3,237	5·1
1801	30,669	6,882	4·5	6,694	4·6
1811	35,951	8,191	4·4	7,861	4·6
1821	48,603	11,191	4·3	10,338	4·7
Manchester (excluding Salford)					
1773	22,481	3,446	6·5	3,402	6·6
1788	42,821	5,916[1]	7·3		
1801	70,409	10,594	6·6	10,343	6·8
1811	79,459	13,544	5·9	12,929	6·1
1821	108,016	17,257	6·3	16,653	6·5
Nottingham					
1739	10,010	1,806[1]	5·6		
1779	17,711	3,191[1]	5·6		
1801	28,861	5,077	5·7	4,977	5·8
1811	34,253	6,801	5·0	6,514	5·3
1821	40,415	7,645	5·3	7,375	5·5
Sheffield					
1755	12,001	2,667	4·5		
1788	25,141	6,161	4·1		
1801	31,314	7,159	4·4	6,518	4·8
1811	35,840	7,870	4·5	7,672	4·7
1821	42,157	10,036	4·2	8,726	4·8
Leicester					
1801	16,953	3,290	5·2	3,205	5·3
1811	23,146	4,683	4·9	4,609	5·0
1821	30,125	6,538	4·6	6,085	4·9

[1] In these instances it is not clear whether the figure relates to all houses or just the occupied ones.
[2] Population of Birmingham parish *only*.

338

Appendix VI

(b) *The seaports*

Date	Population	Total no. of houses	Persons per house	No. of occupied houses	Persons per occupied house
Liverpool					
1773	34,407	6,340	5·4	5,928	5·8
1790	53,853	8,865	6·1	8,148	6·5
1801	77,653[1]	11,784	6·6	11,446	6·8
1811	94,376[1]	16,007	5·9	15,589	6·1
1821	118,972[1]	20,147	6·0	19,007	6·3
Hull					
1801	27,609	4,382	6·3	4,285	6·5
1811	32,944	6,312	5·2	5,914	5·6
1821	39,040	7,422	5·3	7,005	5·6
Newcastle					
1801	28,366	3,296	8·6	3.162	9·0
1811	34,026	4,234	8·0	4,082	8·3
1821	43,177	5,408	8·0	5.144	8·4
Sunderland					
1801	24,444	2,928	8·4	2,862	8·5
1811	25,180	3,502	7·2	3,452	7·3
1821	30,887	3,966	7·8	3,856	8·0

(c) *Regional centres*

Date	Population	Total no. of houses	Persons per house	No. of occupied houses	Persons per occupied house
Exeter					
1801	16,827	2,728	6·2	2,590	6·5
1811	18,896	2,971	6·4	2,879	6·6
1821	23,479	3,374	7·0	3,256	7·2
Chester					
1801	15,052	3,194	4·7	3,109	4·8
1811	16,140	3,457	4·7	3,296	4·9
1821	19,949	4,047	4·9	3,861	5·2
York					
1801	16,145	2,479	6·5	2,407	6·7
1811	18,217	2,732	6·8	2,661	6·9
1821	20,787	3,299	6·3	3,206	6·5
Yarmouth					
1801	14,845	3,159	4·7	3,081	4·9
1811	17,977	3,576	5·1	3,486	5·2
1821	18,040	4,138	4·4	3,981	4·5
Worcester					
1782	11,001	2,060	5·3		
1801	11,352	2,370	4·8	2,237	4·8
1811	13,814	2,489	5·5	2,425	5·6
1821	17,023	3,109	5·5	3,037	5·6

[1] Parish of Liverpool only: figures do not include sailors in port.

Date	Population	Total no. of houses	Persons per house	No. of occupied houses	Persons per occupied house
Maidstone					
1782	5,755	1,115	5·2		
1801	8,027	1,346	6·0	1,330	6·0
1811	9,443	1,745	5·4	1,706	5·5
1821	12,508	2,234	5·6	2,131	5·9
Chichester					
1740	3,712	783	4·7		
1762	3,610	767	4·7		
1769	3,970	859	4·6		
1774	4,203	844	5·0		
1801	4,744	831	5·7	821	5·8
1811	6,425	1,115	5·8	1,083	5·9
1821	7,362	1,319	5·6	1,245	5·9
(d) *London and Middlesex*					
1801	818,129	118,483	6·9	112,912	7·2
1811	953,276	134,939	7·1	130,613	7·4
1821	1,144,531	160,396	7·1	152,969	7·5
(e) *Agricultural counties*					
Berkshire					
1801	109,215	21,195	5·1	20,573	5·3
1811	118,277	22,667	5·2	22,104	5·4
1821	131,977	25,327	5·2	24,705	5·3
Buckinghamshire					
1801	107,444	20,986	5·1	20,443	5·3
1811	117,650	22,486	5·3	21,929	5·4
1821	134,068	25,425	5·2	24,876	5·4
Cambridgeshire					
1801	89,346	16,451	5·4	16,139	5·5
1811	101,109	17,489	5·8	17,232	5·9
1821	121,909	21,316	5·7	20,869	5·8
Dorset					
1801	115,319	22,262	5·2	21,437	5·4
1811	124,693	24,051	5·2	23,210	5·4
1821	144,499	26,692	5·4	25,926	5·6
Lincolnshire					
1801	208,557	42,489	4·9	42,395	5·0
1811	237,891	47,467	4·9	46,368	5·1
1821	283,058	54,792	5·2	53,813	5·4
Oxfordshire					
1801	109,620	21,193	5·2	20,599	5·3
1811	119,191	23,201	5·1	22,702	5·3
1821	136,971	26,025	5·2	25,594	5·4
East Riding (excluding Hull)					
1801	111,824	22,080	5·1	21,496	5·2
1811	134,409	24,976	5·4	24,427	5·5
1821	151,409	28,245	5·4	27,385	5·5

Appendix VI

Sources:

1 Manufacturing towns: S. Bradford, *Plan of Birmingham* (1750); *An Historical and Descriptive Sketch of Birmingham* (1830); p. 71; F. Beckwith 'The Population of Leeds during the Industrial Revolution', *Publications of the Thoresby Society*, XLI, part 2, Miscellany 12, part 2 (1948), p. 127; T. Percival 'Observations on the State of Population in Manchester, and other adjacent places', in Percival *Essays Medical, Philosophical and Experimental*, II, (1789), p. 2; Aikin, *Description*, p. 157; F. C. Laird *Topographical Description of the County of Nottingham* (1820), pp. 140–41; J. Holland, *The Picture of Sheffield* (Sheffield, 1824), p. 77.

2 Liverpool: [J. Corry], *The History of Liverpool*, (Liverpool, 1810), p. 149; [J. Wallace], *A General and Descriptive History of the Ancient and Present State of the Town of Liverpool*, (Liverpool, 1795), p. 69

3 Regional Centres: *Collections for the History of Worcestershire*, II, (1782), p. cxvii; J. Howlett *Observations on the Increased Population, Healthiness, etc. of the Town of Maidstone*, (1782), pp. 20–21; A. Hay, *The History of Chichester*, (Chichester, 1804), p. 573

Figures for 1801, 1811 and 1821 from the *Census Abstracts*

APPENDIX VII: SOURCES FOR FIGURES 1–6

The graphs were based on the following sources:

FIGURE 1: E. B. Schumpeter, *English Overseas Trade Statistics 1687–1808* (1960), Table XV.

FIGURE 2: MS. parish registers of St Martin, St Philip, St Mary and St Paul, Birmingham, 1730–1815; *Census parish register abstracts*, 1801–20.

FIGURE 3: *Gore's Liverpool Directory* (Liverpool, 1805); *Census parish register abstracts*, 1801–20.

FIGURE 4: B. R. Mitchell and P. Deane *Abstract of British Historical Statistics*, (Cambridge, 1962), p.28 (for marriages and baptisms); H. A. Shannon 'Bricks—A Trade Index, 1785–1849', in E. M. Carus-Wilson (ed.), *Essays in Economic History*, III, (1962), p.200 (for bricks and the price of consols from 1784); Schumpeter *Overseas Trade Statistics*, Tables XV and XVII (for values of timber imports up to 1808); *B.P.P. Finance Accounts*, published annually (for values of timber imports, 1809–20, the figure for 1813 being missing); J. Sinclair *History of the Public Revenue of the British Empire* (1803), Vol. II, Appendix II, pp.34–41 (for the the price of consols, 1755–84). In the case of the price of consols before 1784 I have followed Shannon's method in averaging the monthly price of consols given by Sinclair; between 1785 and 1815 the tax year for brick output ran from July and I have used Shannon's estimated figures of output for the calendar years. There are no annual figures of baptisms before 1780 or of brick output before the tax year 1784–5.

FIGURE 5: W. P. W. Phillimore and J. Ward (eds.), *Nottingham Parish Registers. Marriages*, Vols. I–IV (1900–1902); I have not graphed Nottingham baptisms, because figures derived from the MS. parish registers were not available to me, and Professor Chambers drew attention to the weakness of the figures contained in the *Census parish register abstracts* (Chambers, 'Population Change in Nottingham', p.124).

FIGURE 6: *Census parish register abstracts* (for marriages); Mitchell and Deane, *Historical Statistics*, pp.177–8 (for raw cotton).

341

A Note on Sources

I PRINTED SOURCES

On most aspects of the history of the financial aspects of house-building in the English provincial towns of the eighteenth and early nineteenth centuries, secondary sources have little to contribute. The best town histories published in the last twenty years ignore the town builders and their activities, and urban land-development gets merely a passing reference. The latter subject is briefly handled in two or three recent *V.C.H.* volumes, particularly that for Birmingham (*Warks.*, VII) and Hull (*East Riding*, I). However, only three special topics have received more than casual attention. One topic which has been studied is the course of national building activity. T. S. Ashton devoted a chapter of his last book, *Economic Fluctuations in England, 1700–1800* (1959), to the subject of building and construction, and building at the national level is also briefly considered, with the other sectors of the economy, in A. D. Gayer, W. W. Rostow and A. Schwartz, *The Growth and Fluctuations of the British Economy, 1790–1850* (1953). Building from 1785 is also discussed briefly in H. A. Shannon, 'Bricks—A Trade Index, 1785–1849' (*Economica*, n.s. 3 (1934), pp. 300–318) and A. K. Cairncross and B. Weber, 'Fluctuations in Building in Great Britain, 1785–1849' (*Economic History Review*, 2nd ser., ix (1956), pp. 283–97). More recently, J. Parry Lewis, in *Building Cycles and Britain's Growth* (1965), has made an important analysis of building fluctuations over the whole period, which he believes can be shown to follow the typical building cycle pattern. These studies have been made possible by the availability of figures relating to building materials, especially for annual brick output (from 1785) and for timber imports (throughout the period). But these indicate aggregate national activity, and one has to look elsewhere for evidence of regional fluctuations. A little evidence on the course of housing output in Leeds from the 1780s is presented by W. G. Rimmer, 'Working men's Cottages in Leeds, 1770–1840', (*Thoresby Society*,

xlvi (1961), pp. 165–99), and a little may be gleaned from two books by
W. Ison, *The Georgian Buildings of Bath, from 1700 to 1830* (1948) and
The Georgian Buildings of Bristol (1952). Apart from these works, one
must rely on primary sources.

Building societies of the period have been studied by S. J. Price,
Building Societies their Origin and History (1958), and E. J. Cleary,
The Building Society Movement (1965), though both authors are more
concerned with later trends. It has been possible to add considerably to
their evidence of the distribution of early societies by the detailed local
studies on which this book is principally based. Tenement accommodation and layout from the 1780s have been considered in S. D. Chapman,
'Working-class Housing in Nottingham during the Industrial Revolution' and M. W. Beresford, 'The Back-to-Back House in Leeds, 1787–
1937', both in S. D. Chapman (ed.), *The History of Working-Class
Housing* (1971), and by I. C. Taylor, 'The Court and Cellar Dwelling:
the Eighteenth-Century Origin of the Liverpool Slum', in *Transactions
of the Historic Society of Lancashire and Cheshire*, CXXII (1971). Cottage
property and their rents have also been discussed by Rimmer for Leeds
in the paper just quoted. There is also C. A. Forster *Court Housing in
Kingston upon Hull*, University of Hull Occasional Papers in Geography
no.19 (1972). The building development of Leeds has also been discussed by Beresford in 'Prosperity Street and others: an essay in visible
urban history', in M. W. Beresford and G. R. J. Jones (eds.), *Leeds and
its Region* (Leeds, 1967), pp. 186–97.

Primary printed sources are useful on a wide range of topics. The
census returns of 1801, 1811 and 1821 give the number of houses
existing in each town, thus enabling one to calculate the number of
houses added to the existing stock in the first two decades of the nineteenth century. Advertisements in local newspapers concerning building
land and new houses are useful. Those relating to larger dwellings for
sale or to let sometimes included a description of the accommodation
available. Cottage tenements were rarely described in this way, but
their rents were occasionally stated if for sale. Unfortunately no house
prices are normally stated. The following provincial newspapers were
consulted in the local library or the British Museum Newspaper
Library:

Aris's Birmingham Gazette (and excerpts in J. A. Langford, *A Century
of Birmingham Life* (1870))
Manchester Herald; Manchester Mercury
Hull Advertiser

Liverpool Advertiser; Liverpool Mercury
Nottingham Journal
Hampshire Chronicle or Portsmouth, Winchester and Southampton
Gazette; Portsmouth Gazette and Weekly Advertiser; Hampshire
Telegraph and Portsmouth Gazette
Bath Chronicle

Contemporary town maps are available in the local library or British Museum Map Room for each of the towns which form the major object of this study at different dates from the beginning of the period, with the exception of Portsmouth. All reveal the streets of the town concerned and a few the size and shape of the buildings. Those used were as follows:

Birmingham: Westley, 1731; Bradford, 1751; Hanson, 1778, 1785; Kempson, 1810; Copley, 1820

Liverpool: J. Eyes, 1765; C. Eyes, 1785; Phillips, 1795; Horwood, 1803; Troughton, 1807; Gore, 1814; Sherwood, 1821

Manchester: Casson and Berry, 1751; Tinker, 1772; Green, 1794; Pigot, 1819; Bancks, 1830

Nottingham: Badder and Peat, 1743; Wild and Smith, 1820

Hull: Thew, 1784; Anderson, 1814

Bath: see maps in Ison

The following O.S. maps were used: town plans of Liverpool, Hull and Manchester, *c.* 1850; 1st edn. 25-inch of Hants, 1870 (for Portsea).

Further, a wide range of contemporary (or near-contemporary) directories, guide books and histories relating to individual towns were used, although these provided normally just the occasional brief reference of value. More important than most are W. Hutton, *A History of Birmingham* (1781) and later editions; Hoxland, *Guide to Plymouth Dock* (Plymouth, 1792); *The Picture of Plymouth* (1812); [J. Corry], *The History of Liverpool* (Liverpool, 1810); of particular use on account of the number of towns covered by its survey is J. Aikin, *A Description of the Country within Forty Miles of Manchester* (1795).

   Finally, printed collections of documents, containing a few useful references, are rare. The most important are *The Records of King Edward's School Birmingham*, II–V (1928–63) and *Records of the Borough of Nottingham*, VIII, VIII (1947, 1952).

2 MANUSCRIPT SOURCES

Because of the relative lack of material in print, this study was based fundamentally on manuscript sources. The following were the main classes of records used:

Records of the Law Courts, in the Public Record Office:

Court of Bankruptcy: order books, 1786–1816 (B1/77–145)

Court of Exchequer: bills and answers, arranged by county: Devon, 1760–1820 (E112/1408–1426); Durham, 1760–1820 (E112/1433–41); Kent, 1760–1820 (E112/1503–22); Lancashire, 1727–1820 (E112/1147–53, 1523–50); Northumberland, 1760–1820 (E112/1895–1901); Nottinghamshire, 1760–1820 (E112/1902–5); Somerset, 1727–1820 (E112/1269–75, 1921–54); Warwickshire, 1760–1820 (E112/2017–24); Yorkshire, 1760–1820 (E112/2057–89); these are more useful for the years *c*. 1790–1820, but there are a few interesting earlier lawsuits.

Court of Exchequer: depositions by commission, 1714–1820 (E134): of little use in this study;
Palatinate Court of Lancaster chancery court, 1725–1820 (PL.6/60–112): most useful after 1800;
Court of Chancery: Chancery proceedings: certain bundles, 1758–1800 (C12), 1800– (C13); Chancery masters' exhibits (C104, 105, 107, 108, 110, 113).

The least useful of these series, E134, and the masters' exhibits, are the only ones provided with a calendar; the others only have an index of names; to trace the few lawsuits of use for this study, all documents had to be consulted, except in the vast Chancery series, where a few relevant suits in C13 were located by the index of names. A variety of topics are illuminated by the proceedings of these courts, including the expenditure of developers and their use of building covenants, disputed contracts between builders and craftsmen about fhe method of payment for house construction, and sources of finance tor builders. The Chancery masters' exhibits include accounts, deeds and correspondence. The other legal series are in the form of statements by plaintiffs, and sometimes answers by defendants, in lawsuits. Thus the statements are not always reliable. Further, since they involve land-promoters, builders or craftsmen in financial or legal difficulties, there is the problem of how representative were the transactions in which they were involved. Nevertheless, they supply a fascinating range of material unobtainable from other sources.

House of Lords Records, in the House of Lords Records Office:

Main papers: petitions, judges' reports and draft bills relating to estate acts sought by landowners, individual and corporate, concerned in urban land-development in provincial towns, 1728–1820. Committee minute books, 1760–1820: minutes relating to these estate bills.

These two series throw light on several aspects of the supply of building land, particularly the estimated gross rent per acre on the conversion of land to building use, or the price of building land.

Local Records

Most of the manuscripts consulted were in local archives, particularly city record offices.

(a) *Correspondence:* little estate correspondence relating to land-development in the leading provincial towns has survived. This was in spite of the fact that collections of urban estate records are numerous, twenty-five having been used in this study. The Walcot Estate papers in the Bath Reference Library contain a few letters about the younger Wood's Circus project in the later 1750s, and the Sefton/Molyneux MSS in the Lancashire Record Office a few letters about the Harrington scheme. The Norfolk MSS and the Fitzwilliam MSS in the Sheffield Archives Dept. of the Library include a little correspondence of use, for the years *c*. 1790–1820. The rarity of readily accessible material of this type was disappointing, though more will doubtless come to light in archives still in private hands.

(b) *Minutes and order books of corporate bodies:* those for Liverpool, Newcastle, Bath, Hull, Coventry, Swansea and Exeter Corporations were consulted in the respective City Record Office; the eighteenth-century vote books of Hull Trinity House were seen at the House, and the minutes of the Hull Dock Commissioners and Dock Company of Hull in the custody of the British Railways Board, York (HDC 1/1–2); the minute book of Lench Trust, Birmingham, 1771–1805 (B.R.L. ZZ329) was seen; also Herculaneum Potteries minute book, 1806–22, in the Liverpool Record Office. Generally a rather disappointing source, since the orders or minutes are very formal; the most common references are bare records of leasing building land.

(c) *Accounts and other financial records:* corporation accounts for Liverpool, Bath and Exeter, in the respective City Record Offices; Lench Trust account books, 1694–1874 in the Birmingham Reference Library (Lee, Crowder 345 and ZZ329); rent books and ledgers of the Gooch Estate, Birmingham; estate accounts for the Sheffield estate of the Duke of Norfolk, 1777–97 (Sheffield Archives Dept.: Arundel MSS S.185); these all concerned urban landlords involved in building-land development, but references to expenditure on amenities were found only in the Norfolk accounts and those of the Liverpool treasurers, and were few even in these; most accounts consist of brief items of payment to individuals without specifying the work. On the whole, the accounts of corporate bodies survive less often than their minutes or order books. Other relevant accounts seen included those of William Fairbank of Sheffield, surveyor, 1760–1820 (Sheffield Archives AB.1–12); the accounts of J. R. Pease relating to houses in Manchester, *c.* 1780–1800 (Hull Wilberforce House Museum: Pease MS 133); house-building estimates in the Boulton and Watt MSS (B.R.L.); the ledger of John Eveleigh of Bath, architect and builder, *c.* 1790 (Bath Reference Library); account of debts of John Griffiths of Milbrooke, Southampton, slater and builder, 1810 (Southampton Record Office).

None of these items was of outstanding help. Several accounts and ledgers of building craftsmen in provincial towns were traced in the lists of business records compiled by the National Register of Archives, but these mostly related to minor contract work (e.g. repairing walls or stables) and were of little use.

The following bank records were consulted to trace evidence of credit given to craftsmen: ledgers of Heywoods Bank, Liverpool, 1787–90 (Martins Bank Ltd., now Barclays Bank Ltd., Liverpool); balance sheets of Leyland and Bullins, Liverpool, 1807–19 (Midland Bank Ltd., Stationery Dept., Ajax House, Colindale); ledgers of Taylor and Lloyds, Birmingham, 1775–80, 1780–98 (Lloyds Bank Ltd., Head Office, 71 Lombard St); ledgers of Raikes, Currie and Co., Hull *inter alia*, 1808–13 (Glyn, Mills and Co.).

(d) *Rate books:* (poor-rate assessments): the series for Birmingham parish, 1735–1820 (B.R.L.) were consulted, those for Manchester, 1796–1820 (Manchester Reference Library), for Portsea, 1785–1820 (Portsmouth Record Office). None was traced for Nottingham, none survived for Portsea between 1726 and 1784, and only a few rates exist for Liverpool; the rates for Manchester are frequently missing before the 1790s (and none was traced for Salford); although there is an uninterrupted series for Birmingham parish, few have survived for Aston, which provided part of the built-up area of the town of Birmingham. The excellent series for Leeds was used by Rimmer to give an approximate indication of additions to the stock of houses in each quinquennium from the 1790s, and I used the Manchester rate books, 1796–1820, for this purpose. In my experience, not all rate books assess every property, as in the case of Portsea, and of Birmingham for certain years (especially the 1770s); on the other hand, those for Manchester appeared complete (by comparison with the number of houses in the census returns).

(e) *Title deeds, registers of deeds, and related MSS:* collections of deeds were far more numerous than any other relevant type of MS material consulted, and were used extensively in this study. They were available in the following forms:

(1) bundles of deeds each relating to a specific property including ideally the conveyance of the land plot, followed sometimes by one or more mortgages and then the sale by the builder. These are sometimes all copied into a single document known as the 'abstract of title'. They were available in City Record Offices as deposits by solicitors or private individuals, or by transfer from the town clerk's department in the case of property owned by the authority (particularly relating to properties purchased in the last two decades for redevelopment). Other bundles were consulted in the deed rooms of town halls (relating to city property), in the muniment rooms of British Rail (relating to house property purchased by the various railway companies in the nineteenth century for station sites), and in the deed collections of a few breweries, co-operative societies, insurance and property companies. The consultation of these records would appear at first sight to be time-consuming. This did not prove to be the case where a large collection of relevant deed bundles were available together and could be studied at one time, and especially if the bundles had been well listed, so that those without relevant material did not have to be opened and inspected.

(2) *deeds forming part of the estate MSS of urban landowners:* naturally most numerous were the building leases or freehold sales conveying the land, either before or after the construction by the builder; however, in the case of leasehold property a few estates kept the later documents

(in the form of assignments of the lease) which were surrendered with the property by the lessee at the expiration of the term, and these form part of the estate MSS.

In addition to title deeds themselves, the conveyances were sometimes recorded in a number of ways which provide at least part of the information supplied in title deeds:

(i) *the Yorkshire deeds registers:* those for the East Riding at Beverley cover Hull and for the West Riding at Wakefield relate to Leeds and Sheffield. The East Riding registers were used for Hull entries, but no systematic use was made of those of the West Riding, on account of the current studies of the building history of Leeds by Professor Beresford, and of the Norfolk Estate at Sheffield by Professor Olsen.

(ii) *manorial court books:* recording surrenders and admissions by holders of land within the bounds of the manor, in the case of copyhold property.

(iii) *registers of leases or sales of land*, or of agreements to convey, kept by estates.

Title deeds provide evidence on a wide range of topics: among them are the names and occupations of builders and their mortgagees, sometimes the names of the first occupiers, the size of the sites and the number of houses constructed in a project, the dates of land conveyance and sale of the completed property by the builder, land and new house prices and amounts of mortgages (and sometimes the rate of interest). Owing to the frequent destruction of older title deeds, registers or court books when in existence will give a more comprehensive coverage of property transactions within their respective areas. Generally they do not record all the detail given in deeds. The manorial court books may not record house prices or freehold land prices. The East Riding registers omitted all prices and it is sometimes difficult to distinguish between trustees and the real buyers and sellers. Estate registers of conveyances were not numerous and are sometimes just bare notes of the names of the parties (without their occupations), dates, and the street and rent involved.

Altogether, title deeds or the various deed registers offer a wealth of material for the student of the people and capital involved in building-land promotion and house construction which is unobtainable in the period from other sources. Among their limitations are their failure to record the names of the craftsmen who contracted with the building owner to erect the houses, and that they rarely contain house plans, thus giving no evidence by themselves about the physical character of the houses.

The following collections of deeds and related documents were consulted:

Birmingham: all relevant deeds in the Birmingham Reference Library, especially the Colmore and Gooch Estate MSS (building leases and the various assignments), the Lee, Crowder collection (solicitors), and the Town Clerk's collection (deeds of City property deposited by the Town Clerk); deeds in the custody of British Rail: Birmingham Extension (B.E.) and Oxford and Birmingham Railway (O.B.R.), Mornington Crescent deed room; Birmingham and Wolverhampton Railway (B.W.R.), Manchester Hunts Bank deed room.

Bath: all relevant deeds in the Bath Record Office at the Guildhall, especially the Corporation lease collection, deeds to property owned by the Corporation, and collection of deeds relating to the site of the Circus and neighbouring streets; deeds in the custody of the Bath Reference Library.

Nottingham: all relevant deeds in the Archives Dept. of the City Library, mainly transferred from the Town Clerk's Office; deeds relating to the site of Victoria Station in the custody of Debenham and Co., solicitors; deeds in the custody of Nottingham University Archives Dept. and of the University Hospital Management Committee.

Portsmouth: about four-fifths of the huge collection of deeds to City property at the Guildhall, Portsmouth, involving the use of 550 deed bundles; deeds in the custody of Messrs Brickwoods, brewers (55 bundles); some deeds in the custody of the Treasury Solicitor, London (50 bundles).

Hull (for the period 1781–1820): deeds registers, Beverley Deeds Registry; all available deeds in the Hull Record Office; court books for the manor of Tupcoates with Myton, Hull Record Office.

Manchester: deeds to City property in the Town Hall (208 bundles); deeds in the Manchester Reference Library (24 bundles); deeds in the custody of British Rail: Manchester Central Station (M.C.), Manchester Hunts Bank deed room (79 bundles) and Manchester Piccadilly Station (M.B.R.), Mornington Crescent deed room (49 bundles); a few deeds in the custody of the John Rylands Library, Manchester, Manchester Cathedral and the Lancashire Record Office; deeds in the possession of the Co-operative Wholesale Society, Manchester (14 bundles), by courtesy of Mr. N. C. Wright; deeds belonging to the Hulme Trust in the keeping of Messrs. Taylor, Kirkman and Mainprice; deeds in the possession of the Co-operative Insurance Society; deeds belonging to Wilson's Brewery, Manchester (6 bundles).

Liverpool: about half the bundles of leases and assignments relating to Corporation property (totalling *c.* 1,000 bundles) deposited by the Town Clerk in the Liverpool Record Office; deeds in the custody of British Rail: Lancs. and Yorks. Railway (L. and Y.) (88 bundles) and Liverpool Central Station (L.C.) (43 bundles), Hunts Bank deed room, Manchester: both collections concerned house property developed freehold, in contrast to the Corporation Estate. Another later unlisted Corporation collection of deeds of large but uncertain size, mainly relating to nineteenth-century development, deposited in the Record Office was not consulted: unlike the deeds for Nottingham and Manchester (which sometimes involved blocks of six, eight or more dwellings), those for Liverpool were nearly all concerned with one or two houses at a time, which made the potential deed material to be consulted too enormous for *all* of it to be seen in a comparative study of this kind: it would offer excellent scope for a specialized study of urban land-development and house-building for Liverpool alone after about the 1770s.

A smaller number of deeds and related MSS were consulted for the following towns:

Newcastle: deeds in the custody of the Newcastle Record Office: a thorough study was impossible because many of the older deeds for property bought by the Corporation appear to have been destroyed.

Plymouth: a few bundles of deeds relating to the building development of Plymouth town were seen in the Plymouth Guildhall, and many more may survive relating to the centre of the town; very few building leases have survived for the Dock estate of the St. Aubyn family (in the Plymouth Archives Dept., Central Library), but the survey books of the estate appear to provide a comprehensive list of all leases granted by the estate in Dock between about 1740 and the early nineteenth century (in the Archives Dept. and the St. Aubyn Manor Estate Office, Devonport); no surviving records for Stonehouse were traced, either in the Guildhall, or the Archives Dept., or in the Mount Edgecumbe Estate MSS in the Cornwall Record Office, Truro.

Sheffield: two volumes of agreements to lease, 1772–1816, in the Norfolk MSS (S.382, 383); and a small collection of leases, 1776–98, in the same (SD 868/175–203, SD 870/50–107) were seen in the Sheffield Archives Dept. A difficulty with these MSS is that they do not specify whether the houses were erected by the lessee, though in most instances they doubtless were; deeds in the Wheat MSS and the Collection of Miscellaneous Documents and typescript catalogue of Sheffield deeds; Fitzwilliam MSS: correspondence; Capital Burgesses register of leases; all in the Archives Dept.

Sunderland: the court book of the rectory of Bishopwearmouth manor, 1783–1820, and the manor of Houghton court books, 1783–1801, were seen in the Manuscripts Dept. of the University of Durham; although prices are not stated (though ground rents are) and only the Bishopwearmouth part of Sunderland town is covered, these would repay a careful study.

Brighton: the calendar of deeds in the Sussex Archaeological Society Collection, a few deeds, and the court books of the manors of Brighton and Atlingworth were seen in the East Sussex Record Office.

Leeds: deeds in the Wilson MSS, calendared by Professor Beresford, were seen in the Archives Dept. of the Leeds City Library.

Index

353

Index

Haverfordwest, 323
Hawkins, Stephen, Dock, contract dispute, 194
Hearth-tax assessments, 5
Hendy, Alexander, London, bankruptcy of, 234
Hensley, John, Bath landlord, 183
Herculaneum Pottery cottages, Liverpool, income, 166
Hereford, growth, 30
Herefordshire, population, 316
Hertford, population, 18
Hetherley, Thomas, Nottingham developer, 116
Heywoods Bank, Liverpool, building clients of, 237
Hill, Sir Francis, quoted 30
Hinckley textiles 41
Holbeach 320
Holland,
    war with 23, 270
Holte Estate, Birmingham 88
Holywell 47
Hope, Samuel, Manchester architect 148
Hope Street, Portsea 218
Horncastle 320
Horton, John, cabinet maker
    houses of, 230
Hosiery industry, 20-1, 40-1, 46, 50, 160n; 174, 266-7, 288
    see also Nottingham, Leicester
House/Houses, 188-227, 336-41; wartime, 285-92
    census, definition of, 306
    ownership as an investment, 157-67, 245
    prices, 166-8, 191-2, 198, 205, 218, 221-7, 261
    rents, 166-7
    sharing in depression, 299
    vacant, 287
    see also Bricks, Timber, Capital, Mortgages, Builders, Building activity
Housing
    capital formation, 309, 310
    stock (1818-19), 292, 305
    and urban amenities, 311
Huddersfield, 4, 38
    population, 39
Hughes, John, Manchester, bankruptcy of, 235
Hull, ix, 4, 17, 48, 66, 67, 113, 114, 180, 188, 237, 261, 283, 291, 318
    builders' occupations, 169, 182, 231, 246
    building, finance, 239; revival, 290; in wartime, 263
    Corporation, 129, 131, 136
    cost of street paving, 150
    court tenements, 216
    economy of, 13, 40, 50
    estate development, 128-34
    growth of, 68-9, 276

housing, 68, 213-14, 305
    industries, 50-1
    land promotion, 58, 60, 128-34, 153n, 246
    persons per house, 339
    population, 13, 51, 54
    post-war building, 294
    statistics, 337
    trade, 13, 50
    whaling industry, 51
Hull, river, 129
Hull Trinity House, 195
Hulme, Manchester development, 36, 89, 336
Humber, river, 13, 129, 291
Hunt, C. H., Stratford-upon-Avon, banker, 88
Huntingdonshire, population, 316
Hutton, Thomas, Nottingham, developer, 117

Imports, 20, 27, see also Timber
Improvement Commissioners and paving, 150n
Industrial centres, 3, 7, 11-12, 20-3, 42-7
Industrial Revolution, 157, 234, 236, 307
Industrial towns
    building owners in, 167-74
    new housing, 196-208
    see also Birmingham, Manchester, Nottingham, Leeds, Leicester
Industrialists
    houses of, 186, 198
    supply building capital, 247
Industries and building finance, 241
    income in, 19
Inge Estate, Birmingham, prices, 142
Inge family, Birmingham landowners, 84, 87, 185
Inhabitants per census house, 305
Interest rates
    effect on builders, 253-4
    and jerry-building, 227n
Investment, see Capital
Ipswich, 9, 16
Ireland
    trade with, 20
Irish market
    effect of riots on, 273
Irwell, river, 89, 90, 91
Islington Building Society, 176-7
Islington, Birmingham, 275
Italy
    exports to, 50

Jarratt, John, Hull, 131
Jennens family, Birmingham, landowner, 84 site and estate of, 85, 259
Jerry-building, 227n, 304
Johnson, Jonathan, Birmingham, craftsman-builder, 169, 196-7
Johnson Court, Liverpool, dwellings, 213

359

Margate, 4, 25
  population, 53
  trade of, 53
Market Deeping, 320
Market gardening land, cost of, 140–1, 145
Market Place, Hull, 129
Market Place, Nottingham, 121, 122, 141
Market Street Lane, Manchester development, 89
Market Rasen, 320
Market towns, 4–7, 11, 17, 26–7, 29–30
  population growth, 320–3
Marlborough Buildings, Bath, promoters, 77
Marlow, 317
Marriages and building fluctuations, 254 ff
Martin, Osmund, bricklayer, houses of, 217
  mortgage of, 236
Marylebone Street, Portsea, 127
Maryport, 318
Materials, housing, 273, 274, 295, 311
Meadley, John, Hull, contracts of, 195
Medway towns, probate assessments, 158
Melcombe Regis, 322
Mellor, cotton spinning in, 47
Memel fir costs, 222, 223, 330–31
Merchants, as land promoters, 59, 60, 91, 92, 93, 95, 96, 97, 100, 110, 111, 129, 131, 187
  as building owners, 151, 181, 182, 206, 208, 211, 232
Mersey, river, 70, 98–100
Merthyr Tydfil
  building in, 186
  industry, 44
  population, 44
Metalware industry, 42, 46, 270, 287
  and building, 171, 270, 287
Metcalfe, bricklayer, Hull
  tenement of, 214, 231
Middle classes, increased wealth of, 19
Middlemore, W. R., Nottingham attorney, 239n
Middlesex, population, 316
Midghall, Alex, Liverpool, building of, 212
Midlands, 13
  population, 318, 319
  industries, 50
  towns and land prices, 122
  see also Birmingham, Nottingham, Leicester
Migration, 299, 274
  effect on building, 264
Milsom Street, Bath, dwellings, 230
Mines, 12
Molyneux, Lord, Earl of Sefton, 100
Monkwearmouth, 48
Monmouthshire, population, 316
Montagu Row, Portsea, 127
Moore, Thomas, Liverpool, building loans, 241

Morley Close, Nottingham, 118
Morriston, population, 45
Mortgagees, occupations of, 333–4
Mortgages, 161–2, 183–5, 235–7, 238–43, 246, 266, 277, 294; interest rates, 162, 254, 296; premiums on, 296
Mosley Estate, Manchester, 276
  covenants, 138n
  development, 95, 97, 208
Mosley family, building land of, 58, 95, 248
Mosslake Fields, Liverpool, 109, 152
  development, 102, 212, 246, 293
  scheme, 105
Mount East Court, back-to-backs, 206
Mount Pleasant, Liverpool, development, 107, 277
Multi-occupied houses, 306
Municipal authorities as landowners, 58
Mynshull family of Manchester, 91

Nance, hatter of Portsea, 126, 128
Napoleonic Wars
  effect of, 44, 124, 128, 134, 143, 152, 159, 162, 176, 178, 191, 201, 217, 232, 293, 294, 295, 300, 304
Narrow Marsh, Nottingham, 114
Neath, 12
Nelson Place, Bath, 80
Newark industry, 40
Newcastle, ix, 4, 17, 13n, 180, 318
  building activity, 264, 276
  Common Council viewing committee, 136
  Corporation, 136
  housing, 68, 72, 305
  land ownership, 58
  population, 14, 48
Newcastle, Duke of, 113, 118, 120, 121, 135, 205, 208
Newcastle Street, Nottingham, house prices, 120, 205, 206
New Manchester Guide, quoted, 37
New Street, Birmingham, 137
Newton, Isaac, Birmingham, ironmonger
  house of, 229
Nicholson, Manchester, brickmaker
  house of, 208
Nile Street, Bath, development, 80
Nixon, John, Nottingham builder, 118, 201–2, 204, 231, 237–8
Norfolk, 32
  population, 316
  worsted industry, 12
Norfolk Crescent, Bath development, 79, 80
Norfolk, Duke of, building land, 58, 72
North American commerce, 15, 223
  see also American trade
Northampton, population, 18
Northamptonshire, population, 316, 317
North and East Riding, population, 316, 318

Index

Seaside resorts, 25, 52–4, 293, *see also* Brighton
Seely, John, Plymouth, 139
Selden, William, Bath
  building of, 230
Seal Street, Liverpool, houses, 214
Sellman, John, Portsea, shipwright
  house of, 217
Select Committee on the Usury Laws, 294
Select Improvement Committee, Liverpool, 105–6
Sefton, Earl, Liverpool land promoter, 58, 100, 110, 136, 138
Services, urban
  demand for, 28–9
  see also Market towns, Regional centres
Seven Years' War, 143, 259, 268
Severn, river
  transport on, 15, 190
Sewers, 57, 58, 62, 64, 97, 101, 104, 105, 106, 112, 130, 148, 149
Shaftesbury, 322
Sheffield, ix, x, 4, 25, 247, 282, 283, 312, 318
  building activity, 270, 275, 280–1
  land, 58, 61, 71, 72
  society, 178, 180
  business depression (1793), 280
  housing, location of, 68
  industries, 22, 23, 43, 46, 50
  mortgages, 151, 242
  persons per house, 281, 338
  population, 23, 281, 306
  roadmaking, 150n
  Vicar of, 71n
Shepley, Edward, Manchester
  development of, 95, 96
Sheppard, shoemaker, Portsea, 126
Sherborne, 322
Sherlock, Bishop, Thomas, 82
Sherwin, John, Nottingham land promoter, 118, 120, 171, 173, 185, 202
Sherwin Estate, Nottingham, 203, 204
Sherwood Forest, 190
Shipbuilding, 6, 23, 48, 50
  service trades, 43
Shipyard prosperity, 270
Shopkeepers, in towns, 8, 11, 17, 27
Shoreham, 6
Short-term credit, *see* Temporary credit
Shrewsbury, 9, 34, 319
Shropshire, population, 316
Simnor, Robert, Liverpool
  mortgages of, 101
Sleaford, 320
Sleaford Navigation Co., 159
Smith, joiner, Nottingham
  houses of, 204
Smith, Thomas, Birmingham, houses, 198
Snow Hill, Birmingham
  house at, 229

Soho Street, Liverpool, 277
Somerset, population, 316
Southampton
  distribution centre, 8, 47
  population, 18, 48
  trade of, 8
Southsea, 128, 218–19
  see also Portsea
South Field, Leicester, common land, 72
South Wales, personal wealth in, 158
Spicer, Anthony, Birmingham, 173
Spitalfields, 3n
Spain, 270
Spalding, 30, 320
Sparling and Bolden, Liverpool, developers, 187, 210
Sparling Street, Liverpool, development, 325
Spas, 4, 24, 51, 52, *see also* Bath
Staffordshire, 43
  Building Society, and brick prices, 222
  coalmines, 233
  industry, 8
  population, 316
Stafford Street, Birmingham, 197
Stamford, 30, 320
Standard Hill, Nottingham, 121, 208
Statham and Hughes, Liverpool developers, 101
Steam engines, cost of, 37, 233
Stevens, William, houses, 230
Stevenson, William, and Manchester development, 93, 94, 95
Stockport, 35
  building costs, 222, 328–9
  factories at, 46
Stocks, builder, Nottingham, 138
Stratford-upon-Avon, 18
Stretton, William, Nottingham Corporation Surveyor, 147, 208
Strickland, John, builder, Birmingham, 198
Strutt's "Derby rig" patent, effect of, 266–7
Sturminster, 322
Styal, cotton-spinning in, 47
Suffolk, population, 316
Sugar imports, 49, 50
Sumner, James, Liverpool, building of, 212
Sumner, Thomas, Nottingham
  buildings of, 205, 206
Sunderland, ix, 4, 48, 318
  housing, location of, 68, 72n
  persons per house, 339
  population, 13, 48
Surrey, population, 316
Surveyors, 65, 101–2, 104, 106, 109, 136, 147, 148, 152
  and land promotion, 59, 60, 107, 110–11
Sussex, 53
  population, 316
Swann, family, property, Portsea, 125

365

Index

Water supply, 149
Waterways and trade, 30
Wavertree, 49*n*
Weaman, Dorothy, Birmingham landowner, 85
Weaman, Mary, Birmingham landowner, 87
Weaman Estate, Birmingham, 197
Weaman family, promotion of, 84, 85, 259
Wear, river, 13*n*
West Derby, 49, 337
West Dock Field, Portsea, 123, 124, 125, 126
  land cost, 191
West Ella, 129
West End, London, development, 264, 268, 277, 283
Westgate Buildings, Bath, 78, 231
West Indian commerce, 15, 49
West Riding, 4, 7, 12, 40, 283
  Building Society, 178
  industrial area, 13
  population, 39, 316, 318
  textile region, 32, 38
  woollen industry, 50
  worsted manufacture, 32, 33
Westminster, 3*n*
Westmorland, population, 316, 317, 318
Weymouth, 4, 322
  Corporation lease bathing house sites, 52
  population, 53
Whaling industry, 51
White, Samuel, Portsea, sells plots, 125
Whitehaven
  distribution centre, 8
  coal industry, 19, 48
  population, 19, 48, 317, 318
Widcombe Crescent, Bath, 186
Wignell, Thomas, Liverpool dwellings of, 212
William Hulme Trust, 98
Williamson Square, Liverpool, development, 261

Wilson, Samuel, Portsea promoter, 126
Wiltshire, 9
  population, 316
Winchester, 11*n*
Winchester College landowners, 124
Windsor, William, builder, 88, 200
Wolverhampton, 42
  early building society, 175, 176
  land prices, 121
  market, 43
  population, 22
Women and building finance, 242
Wood, foreign, for house building, 190
  see also Timber
Wood, John, developer, 74, 76, 80, 139
Wood, John, Junior, architect, 74, 78, 80
Woollen industry depression, 288
Woolridge, Thomas, bricklayer, 173
Worcester, 9, 306*n*
  houses, 305
  industry, 30
  persons per house, 339
  population, 34, 316
Working classes, living standards, 304–8,
Workington, 318
Worsted industry, 21, 32
Worthing, 53
Worthington, John, Liverpool, house builder, 212
Wright, Mary, Nottingham promoter, 121, 139
Wrights, bankers, Nottingham, 237–8

Yardley, 186
Yarmouth, *see* Great Yarmouth
York, 13, 16, 25
  building, 305
  persons per house, 339
  population, 13, 18
Yorkshire, *see* West Riding

367